Nonverbal Communication in Political Debates

Lexington Studies in Political Communication

Series Editor: Robert E. Denton Jr., Virginia Tech University

This series encourages focused work examining the role and function of communication in the realm of politics including campaigns and elections, media, and political institutions.

Recent titles in the series

President Trump and the News Media: Moral Foundations, Framing, and the Nature of Press Bias in America, by Jim A. Kuypers
Media Relations and the Modern First Lady: From Jacqueline Kennedy to Melania Trump, edited by Lisa M. Burns
Alternative Media Meets Mainstream Politics: Activist Nation Rising, edited by Joshua D. Atkinson and Linda Kenix
Political Humor in a Changing Media Landscape: A New Generation of Research, edited by Jody C. Baumgartner and Amy Becker
The Influence of Polls on Television News Coverage of Presidential Campaigns, by Vincent M. Fitzgerald
Political Conversion: Personal Transformation as Strategic Public Communication, by Don Waisanen
The 2016 American Presidential Campaign and the News: Implications for the American Republic and Democracy, by edited by Jim A. Kuypers
A Rhetoric of Divisive Partisanship: The 2016 American Presidential Campaign Discourse of Bernie Sanders and Donald Trump, by Colleen Elizabeth Kelley
Studies of Communication in the 2016 Presidential Campaign, edited by Robert E. Denton Jr.
The Monstrous Discourse in the Donald Trump Campaign: Implications for National Discourse, by Debbie Jay Williams and Kalyn L. Prince
The Political Blame Game in American Democracy, edited by Larry Powell and Mark Hickson
Nonverbal Communication in Political Debates, by John S. Seiter and Harry Weger Jr.

Nonverbal Communication in Political Debates

John S. Seiter
Harry Weger Jr.

LEXINGTON BOOKS
Lanham • Boulder • New York • London

Published by Lexington Books
An imprint of The Rowman & Littlefield Publishing Group, Inc.
4501 Forbes Boulevard, Suite 200, Lanham, Maryland 20706
www.rowman.com

6 Tinworth Street, London SE11 5AL, United Kingdom

Copyright © 2020 by The Rowman & Littlefield Publishing Group, Inc.

All rights reserved. No part of this book may be reproduced in any form or by any electronic or mechanical means, including information storage and retrieval systems, without written permission from the publisher, except by a reviewer who may quote passages in a review.

British Library Cataloguing in Publication Information Available

Library of Congress Control Number: 2020945885
ISBN 978-1-4985-8522-4 (cloth)
ISBN 978-1-4985-8524-8 (pbk)
ISBN 978-1-4985-8523-1 (electronic)

To my son, Christian. For taking long naps when I was writing my dissertation; for being fond of nerds, including your parents; for your "day as a trout" and loving me to "infinity pieces"; for your grit, goodwill, and social glueyness; and even for your horrible taste in socks—I love you.
—John S. Seiter

To my mom for teaching me to love ideas.
—Harry Weger Jr.

Contents

Preface		ix
Acknowledgments		xi
1	A Rationale and Framework for Exploring Nonverbal Communication in Political Debates	1
2	A Primer on Nonverbal Communication	23
3	Nonverbal Behavior of the Speaking Candidate	41
4	Background Nonverbal Behavior in Political Debates: The Role of Nonspeaking Candidates	63
5	Mediated Nonverbal Communication and Political Debates	83
6	Applying Principles of Persuasion to the Social Scientific Study of Nonverbal Behavior in Political Debates	105
7	Humanistic Theories for Analyzing Nonverbal Behavior in Televised Debates	125
8	Nonverbal Behavior in the 2016 Presidential Debates: Applying Communication Theory to the Debates	153
Appendix: History of Televised General Election U.S. Presidential and Vice Presidential Debates, 1960–2016		181
Bibliography		185
Index		221
About the Authors		231

Preface

Over three decades ago, one of the authors, a newly minted college student, sat in the audience of a live academic debate, utterly baffled. He'd tried following arguments. In fact, part of his grade in an argumentation course depended on it. But as anyone who's attended a college forensics tournament knows, policy debaters are known for rattling off reasons at breakneck tempos. To the untrained ear, they merely babble. Yet, sometimes, the author noticed, their nonverbal behavior betrays an air of confidence, so why not use demeanors and appearances to judge who wins? That logic, he discovered, eventually earned him a "D" on the assignment.

Even so, years later, in 1992, when Bill Clinton, George H. W. Bush, and Ross Perot competed in televised debates for the U.S. Presidency, they simultaneously competed for the author's attention with a newborn baby, who was plenty fussy. Once again, the author, now a father, was largely reduced to observing debaters' nonverbal behavior. It led to a research project, and chats with a friend and colleague, who, as luck would have it, joined him for other research projects and eventually this book. Along the way, the authors learned that the role played by nonverbal behavior in political debates is far more complex than they'd first imagined. Indeed, such behaviors not only serve as mental shortcuts for evaluating debate performances, they function in ways far too complex to articulate and summarize in a handful of studies. Hence, this book. In the pages that follow, we present a framework for understanding the multiple ways that nonverbal behavior functions in political debates. In addition to considering both the intended and strategic objectives of such behaviors, we examine their nonstrategic and unintended consequences alongside historical examples of moments in political debates where nonverbal behavior played an essential role. Our examination not only includes a discussion of humanistic and social scientific approaches to understanding nonverbal persuasion and argumentation, but also a consideration of an immense range of factors (e.g., speaking and nonspeaking debaters' behavior, debate moderators' and audiences' reactions, predebate negotiators, and so forth) that influence how nonverbal behavior is enacted and portrayed. We hope this book serves not only as a useful resource, but as an invitation to integrate an array of perspectives and principles for understanding nonverbal behavior in political contexts.

Acknowledgments

We are extremely grateful to the folks at Lexington Books for their assistance with this project. In particular, we appreciate Bob Denton for sharing our vision for the book. We also thank our editor, Nicolette Amstutz, for her always efficient, competent, helpful, and gracious responses to our frequent and pesky questions. We also appreciate Sierra Apaliski and Jessica Tepper for helping us with materials, feedback, and ideas, and Megan DeLancey and Rae-Ann Goodwin, who helped with editing and proofreading.

John Seiter: I am grateful to my students, past and present, for being a continued source of inspiration, convincing me there is no better career, and engaging me as a fellow learner in conversations that matter. Because of you, I hurry to class. For those same reasons and more, I am grateful to my teachers and mentors, particularly Betty Gordon, Miss McIntosh, Kent Baird, Jim Skvarla, Pat Ganer, Joyce Flocken, Rich Wiseman, Michael Cody, Lynn Miller, Tom Hollihan, and, especially, Bob Gass, despite his meager jump shot. In addition, I thank my friends and colleagues from Utah State University—Harold Kinzer, Nancy Tobler, Charlie Huenemann, Gordon Steinhoff, Kent Robson, Diane Michelfelder, Felix Tweraser, Jennifer Peeples, Brad Hall, Matt Sanders, Jason Gilmore, and "The New Kids on the Block"—for being a joy to work with. Most importantly, I am grateful to my wife, Debora. When taking her wedding vows, she had no way of knowing that "for worse" included long nights of televised debates in the company of a remote controlling windbag. She represents the "for better" part of our lively marriage.

Harry Weger: I want to first express my deepest appreciation to my wife who managed to stay awake through almost all of my blathering on about classical Greek rhetoric, Obama's precision grip gesture, and the elocutionary movement. Jennifer makes my life magical. I also wish to express appreciation to my debate coaches, Bob Gass and Ed Hinck, whose enthusiasm for argumentation inspired me to dedicate my life to this field. I am also grateful to my dissertation advisor, Scott Jacobs, for his friendship and mentorship. I want to thank my long-time friend, mentor, and colleague Dan Canary, without whom, I would not be in this profession. I also want to acknowledge my brothers, sisters, and parents who held an evening debate club each night at dinner time. And finally, I cannot understate my appreciation for my friends, old and new—they are largely responsible for my sanity, or what I have left of it.

Chapter One

A Rationale and Framework for Exploring Nonverbal Communication in Political Debates

In a political world where appealing images often overshadow the substance of messages, it is ironic, perhaps, that the face of one of our least attractive, yet most sagacious, politicians is so ubiquitous, gazing back from the likes of statues and stamps, memorials and monuments, portraits and pennies. Indeed, by most accounts, the 16th president of the United States had an unpleasant appearance. Nathaniel Hawthorne described Abraham Lincoln as "the homeliest man I ever saw" (Holzer, 2009, para. 5), and, after first meeting his eventual boss, Edwin Stanton, Lincoln's future secretary of war, said, "I will not associate with such a damned, gawky, long-armed ape" (Edmonds, 1904, p. 18). An even more unflattering description appeared in *The Houston Telegraph*: "Lincoln is the leanest, lankest, most ungainly mass of legs, arms and hatchet-face ever strung upon a single frame. He has most unwarrantably abused the privilege which all politicians have of being ugly" (Goodwin, 2005, p. 258).

Not to be outdone, the greatest critic of Abraham Lincoln's physical appearance might very well have been Abraham Lincoln, whose sense of humor included a willingness to poke fun at himself, even in the midst of being attacked. During the Illinois Senate campaign of 1858, for example, Lincoln clashed with Stephen Douglas, the incumbent senator, in what may be the most famous political debates in American history. In one encounter, after Douglas accused his opponent of being two-faced, Lincoln replied calmly, "I leave it to my audience: If I had two faces, would I be wearing this one?" (Lederer, 2013, para. 7).

Flash forward nearly 160 years. In a 2016 Fox News debate, the physical appearance of Republican presidential candidates is once again a topic. This time, however, the nature of the conversation is described as jaw-dropping (see Costello, 2016). In the days leading up to the debate, Donald J. Trump, fond of comparing himself to Lincoln, had ridiculed his rival, Senator Marco Rubio, for being short ("Little Marco") and sweaty ("It looked like he'd just jumped into a swimming pool with his clothes on"), while Rubio taunted Trump's tan ("Donald is not going to make America great, he's going to make America Orange"), hairdo ("He's flying around on Hair Force One"), and whatnot ("Have you seen his hands? They're like this. And you know what they say about men with small hands?") (Berenson, 2016). When the two men ultimately took the stage on March 3, it was the latter of these insults that apparently prompted Trump's utterance. Specifically, the GOP front-runner for America's highest office reassured millions of American viewers: "Look at those hands, are they small hands? And, he referred to my hands—'if they're small, something else must be small.' I guarantee you there's no problem. I guarantee" (Krieg, 2016, para. 2).

AT FACE VALUE: PURPOSE AND OVERVIEW

It should come as no surprise that chatter focusing on political candidates' physical appearance—though distasteful and irrelevant to the task of leading a country—has wormed its way into presidential debates. Indeed, in a political environment that unfolds before cameras, that brands candidates in the manner of Madison Avenue, should we be at all surprised to find such feuding over appearances, or perhaps more expectedly, candidates and their campaigns manipulating images to appear more credible, likeable, and electable? As Sanghvi and Hodges (2015) noted:

> Today, elections are largely marketing driven in many parts of the world, with political campaigns carefully crafted at every level, from local to national candidates . . . Every aspect of appearance, including hairstyle, tie colour, and even footwear, is carefully selected to express a specific image designed to elicit a specific emotional response among voters. . . . As a result, appearance has become a critical aspect of political marketing to the extent that it can easily affect election outcomes. (p. 1676)

As evidence of the weight that politicians place on their physical appearances, consider Sarah Palin's $150,000 wardrobe makeover, John Edward's $400 haircut, and John McCain's $520 Ferragamo shoes, which all became news stories during the 2008 election cycle. Or consider the fuss made in pre-debate negotiations over podiums designed to make candidates—including Michael Dukakis in 1988 and Hillary Clinton in 2016—appear taller.

Regardless of how preposterous, prudent, or crafty such actions might be perceived, once observed, a question that naturally follows is *do such actions matter*, and, if so, *how*? These issues form the basis of this book. Specifically, our purpose is to examine the ways in which politicians are presented, and present themselves, in debate broadcasts. In the process of reviewing scholarship on what is known about this topic, we take stock of an expansive cast of characters—including political candidates, their campaigns, debate moderators, audiences, negotiators, production crews, and others—each playing a vital role in the enactment, presentation, and/or perception of nonverbal behavior. In addition, we present a framework for understanding and analyzing nonverbal behavior in political debates that not only addresses the strategic objectives of such behaviors, but also nonstrategic and unintended side effects as well. Moreover, we consider theory and research from both rhetorical and social scientific approaches to understanding persuasion and argumentation, and, along the way, visit key moments in the history of political debates where nonverbal behavior played an important role. Lest we get ahead of ourselves in discussing the importance of nonverbal behavior in political debates, however, we first address why we might spend our scholarly capital on studying these debates at all.

THE IMPORTANCE OF POLITICAL DEBATES

"If it hadn't been for the debates, I would have lost" said Jimmy Carter following his 1976 victory over then President Gerald Ford (Geer, 1988, p. 486). And, as it turns out, Carter was not alone in suggesting that debates play a significant role in political campaigns. To be sure, since that historical moment on September 26, 1960, when Richard M. Nixon and John F. Kennedy competed in the first-ever, televised general election debate, only a handful of candidates have participated in what has become a momentous, and highly anticipated, institutionalized event. To illustrate, consider the sheer number of viewers who watch U.S. presidential debates. In 1980, when Carter once again took the stage, this time facing Ronald Reagan, over 80 million viewers tuned in, the most in U.S. history—until 2016, that is, when Hillary Clinton and Donald Trump's first contest drew 84 million viewers (McKinney, 2018; Voth, 2017; Weprin, 2016)—only the Super Bowl attracted more American viewers in 2016. Considering a viewership as large as a country the size of Germany, it is clear that presidential debates present candidates an unparalleled opportunity to reach a vast number of voters.

As such, perhaps the most significant feature of political debates is their capacity to be influential. As the Racine Group (2002) concluded, "while journalists and scholars display varying degrees of cynicism about the debates, few deny that viewers find them useful and almost no one doubts that they play an important role in national campaigns" (p. 201). In fact, previous literature suggests that political debates are most important in close elections when converting a small number of voters at the margins might make a difference (McKinney & Carlin, 2004; McKinney & Warner, 2013). In addition, research indicates that televised debates can influence viewers' voting choices as well as their impressions of candidates' personalities and policy positions (e.g., Benoit, Hansen, & Verser, 2003; Benoit, McKinney, & Holbert, 2001; Benoit, Webber, & Bermann, 1998; Warner, Carlin, Winfrey, Schnoebelen, & Trosanovski, 2011). This is particularly true in the context of presidential primary debates and for floating and undecided voters (McKinney & Carlin, 2004; McKinney & Warner, 2013).

Alongside their ability to influence, a notable benefit of political debates is that they promote the value of democracy. As Weger, Hinck, and Seiter (2019) wrote, "The larger institutional purpose of televised political debates involves advancing democratic decision making through deliberation of issues by candidates for office" (p. 146). To the extent that such deliberation reaches a larger number of citizens, democracy is served. Similarly, extant literature suggests that political debates serve an educational function. Rowland (2019), for example, noted that debates provide candidates a forum for advocating positions they support. As such, the public not only learns about potentially substantive issues and where candidates stand on those issues, it receives information about characteristics of the candidates (e.g., leadership abilities, composure under stress, and so forth) that can help make decisions about who to support (see Benoit, et al., 2003; Winneg & Jamieson, 2017).

SCHOLARLY FOCUS ON VERBAL COMMUNICATION IN DEBATES

Considering these educational and democratizing features, alongside a rich tradition of debate scholarship rooted in the study of argumentation and rhetoric, it is easy to understand why the lion's share of academic attention has been devoted to studying verbal rather than nonverbal messages in debates. As Hoffman (2011) noted, "The deliberative element of democracy is believed to occur when arguments are articulated and debated through the use of language" (p. 323). This emphasis on verbal communication is reflected in a vast body of literature examining topics that include critical analyses of arguments employed in political debates (e.g., see Bitzer & Rueter, 1980) and candidates' use of verbal attacks, defenses, and acclaims (e.g., see Benoit & Brazeal, 2002; Benoit & Harthcock, 1999).

Even more so, perhaps, this prioritization is reflected in critics' frequently expressed dismay over the quality of presidential debates, lamenting the superficial deliberation of issues and lack of verbal clash. Such critics assert that, as a consequence of flawed formats, presidential debates are not *real* debates at all, but are akin to "joint press conferences" (Lanoue & Schrott, 1981). Auer (1962), for instance, referred to the Kennedy-Nixon television appearances as "counterfeit-" or "pseudo-debates," in which candidates neither talked to each other nor had time enough to develop arguments.

If that is not bad enough, critics have accused the media of presenting a biased account of political debates, a topic we cover in more detail in Chapter 6. For now, however, let it suffice to say that, through the use of various production techniques (e.g., lighting and camera angles), television presents the opportunity to shade reality, exaggerate the confrontational nature of debates, and, potentially, provide preferential treatment of one candidate over another.

For these and other reasons, scholars assert that the mediated nature of such events diminishes the impact of verbal messages. Specifically, because television highlights nonverbal appearances and behaviors, it privileges images over arguments (e.g., see Jamieson & Birdsell, 1988). As Alan Schroeder (2016) wrote, "presidential debates are best apprehended as *television shows*, governed not by the rules of rhetoric or politics but by the demands of their host medium. The values of debates are the values of television: celebrity, visuals, conflict, and hype" (p. 9). Presidential candidates seem to understand this notion as well. Indeed, after the 1960 election, Richard Nixon (1962, p. 340) confessed, "I had concentrated too much on substance and not enough on appearance, while John F. Kennedy noted, "It was TV more than anything else that turned the tide" (White, cited in Windt, 1994, p. 1).

THE IMPORTANCE OF MULTIMODAL CUES IN DEBATES

Of course, the notion that television accentuates images might also be seen as one of the strongest arguments for research devoted to understanding the role of nonverbal communication in political debates. Indeed, while, from a prescriptive standpoint, the call for more deliberation and clash in debates is worthwhile and welcome, from a descriptive and explanatory perspective, if a goal of communication scholarship is to observe and understand communication's functions and effects, it stands to reason that the prevalence and salience of communication behaviors, particularly those with potentially high-stakes consequences, provide a compelling rationale for investigation. That said, the lack of and need for attention to the nonlinguistic aspects of political communication is a frequent theme in previous literature (e.g., see Bucy & Grabe, 2007; Dumitrescu, 2016; Grabe & Bucy, 2009; Pfau & Kang, 1991; Seiter, 1999; Verser, 2007). With that in mind, the following paragraphs discuss a number of reasons why investigating nonverbal communication is important to the study of political debates. Our treatment here is brief as we return to many of these themes later in the book. In addition, these reasons are not necessarily mutually exclusive.

Audiences Attend to Nonverbal Communication

Classic persuasion theory suggests that effective social influence depends, in part, on the degree to which a target audience attends to persuasive stimuli (see McGuire 1989, 2001). Regarding political debates, research indicates that television audiences pay attention to candidates' nonverbal communication (Bucy & Stewart, 2018). In one study, for example, Gong and Bucy (2016a) used eye-tracking software to measure viewers' visual attention to segments of the 2012 presidential debates. Results indicated that viewers gazed longer and more often at Obama and Romney's inappropriate facial displays than at their appropriate displays. Another study (Shah, Hanna, Bucy, Lassen, Van Thomme, Bialik, Yang, & Pevehouse, 2016) examined which elements of the 2012 presidential debates sparked the most attention on social media. Results indicated that the public responded as strongly to the visual elements of candidates' behavior, including gestures and facial expressions, as they did to candidates' verbal communication.

Nonverbal Communication Affects the Perception and Memory of Verbal Communication

Although *Saturday Night Live* frequently lampooned presidential candidate Senator Bob Dole as a "snarling misanthrope," Richard N. Bond, former Republican Party chairman claimed, "Bob Dole is crusty, but he's not mean" (Nagourney, 1996, para. 1, 12). Either way, Dole's aides tried to counter his stern reputation by advising him to smile more. Relatedly, as we'll see later in this book, Dole's humor in debates was often perceived as mean-spirited without the accompaniment of amiable facial expressions to temper it. The point, of course, is that candidates' nonverbal communication affects perceptions of their verbal communication. As the old saying goes, "It's not what you say, it's *how* you say it that's important."

In addition, nonverbal communication can affect the durability of verbal messages. By way of example, in the eye-tracking study mentioned above, Gong and Bucy (2016) asked research participants to recall major themes and topics that were mentioned by Obama and Romney in their debates. Results indicated that the nature of candidates' facial displays affected viewers' memories. Specifically, recall was significantly greater when candidates' displays were appropriate rather than inappropriate.

Visual Cues are Influential, Even in the Absence of Verbal Communication

As with political debates in general, nonverbal behavior in such debates seems to matter most in close elections, when strong or weak performances can change the momentum of a campaign (see Bucy, 2016b). In addition, based on a review of research published over the course of a decade, Dumitrescu (2016) concluded that nonverbal cues make a difference, particularly when citizens have little information about issues or candidates or after quick exposure to visuals cues. Several studies, for instance, have found that poorly informed voters are influenced by the facial attractiveness of political candidates (e.g., see Ahler, Citrin, Dougal, & Lenz, 2007; Stockemer & Praino, 2015).

Moreover, research suggests that nonverbal communication can influences viewers' perceptions regardless of whether debaters are speaking or not. Consider, for example, behaviors that silent debaters display in the background while their opponents are speaking. We have conducted a number of studies—which Chapter 4 covers in detail—showing that such behaviors not only influence perceptions of debaters' traits, but also decisions regarding who won a debate. Additionally, research indicates that photographs have the ability to influence perceptions of candidates and voter preferences (e.g., Rosenberg, Bohan, Mccafferty, & Harris, 1986; Rosenberg & McCafferty, 1987).

Nonverbal Communication Is Often Given Precedence over Verbal Communication

Bucy and Grabe (2007, p. 668) refer to images as the *"lingua franca* of politics" for good reason. Indeed, research in the area of neuroscience and elsewhere indicates that visual communication channels are the dominant mode of learning and information processing. When visual and verbal stimuli occur simultaneously, the brain gives perceptual preference to visual information, processing it more quickly and retrieving and remembering it more readily (see Bauer & Carpinella, 2017; Bucy & Grabe, 2007). In addition, nonverbal communication has the potential to convey important, often reliable, social information about politicians' emotions and intentions, which can be accurate indicators of electoral suitability (Bucy & Grabe, 2007).

Richard Petty and John Cacioppo's (1986) elaboration likelihood model argues that when people lack the ability or motivation to scrutinize persuasive messages, they tend to rely on simple rules or heuristics, which serve as mental shortcuts, instead. In political contexts, where information is bountiful and verbal messages can become quite complex, nonverbal expressions and appearances can act as such heuristic cues, guiding audience's perceptions of candidates. Research, for example, suggests that viewers rely on nonverbal behavior to make inferences about candidates and that such inferences are often made quickly, automatically, and affectively rather than via any systematic process (see Stewart, Eubanks, Dye, Eidelman, & Wicks, 2017). What's more, research indicates that such snap-judgments are not only based on observations of political candidates' facial characteristics, they can predict the outcomes of political elections (see Olivola & Todorov, 2010). The use of heuristics also tends to inflate the importance of emotional cues, which have also been found to influence political behavior (Bucy, 2000).

Furthermore, when verbal and nonverbal behaviors contradict one another, viewers tend to believe nonverbal behaviors more (Burgoon, 1994). This may be due, in part, to the recognition that nonverbal behavior is more automatically linked to emotion than is verbal communication. As such, DePaulo (1992) noted that information that is conveyed nonverbally is sometimes more intense and personal than information that is conveyed verbally.

Nonverbal Behavior Enables Attributions about Qualities That Viewers Value and/or That Predict Candidates' Success

Because political debates are less scripted than other types of campaign messages (e.g., speeches or advertisements), and because nonverbal behaviors tend to be less controllable than verbal communication, nonverbal behavior displayed in debates provides viewers a unique opportunity to compare candidates' qualities in a relatively spontaneous exchange. Because the list of possible trait attributions is extensive, we mention only a few here, reserving others for later chapters.

Charisma and Debate Performance

In his published memoirs, Richard Nixon (1990) said of televised debates: "Because of the nature of the medium, there will inevitably be a greater premium on showmanship than on statesmanship" (p. 221). This, according to Schroeder (2016), was what often tripped up Barack Obama in the debate arena: "a reluctance to put on a show" (p. 91). Similarly, consider Michael Dukakis, whose lack of passion in political debates led his opponent, then President H. W. Bush, to characterize the Democratic governor as an "iceman." As noted above, because television accentuates images, the ability to shine in the spotlight, as evidenced by former actor Ronald Reagan, becomes a priority. In short, for some viewers, charismatic delivery is a sign of an electable candidate.

Relational and Emotional Messages and Responses

Compared to verbal messages, nonverbal behaviors, particularly those that are amplified on a television or computer screen, are particularly suited for conveying relational and affective information. To be sure, the close-up nature of television not only "gives us a more detailed look at our leaders than we have of most of our friends" (Jamieson, 1988, p. 62), it invites "candidates into an intimate space, a relationship with viewers" (Scholten & McNabb, 2019, p. 98). As such, when sizing up political candidates, viewers tend to rely on nonverbal cues, particularly those that communicate appropriate emotions or relational themes. By way of example, research indicates that when nonverbal messages communicate positive relational themes (e.g., similarity, affection, equality), they contribute significantly to candidates' persuasiveness in televised political debates (Pfau 2002; Pfau & Kang, 1991). In addition, a politician's emotional expressiveness is crucial in signaling his or her political viability (Bucy, 2016a; Bucy & Gong, 2018). Research indicates that leaders' televised nonverbal behavior evokes emotional responses (Bucy, 2000), more so, in fact, than do written or spoken messages (Patterson, Churchill, Burger, & Powell, 1992).

Credibility and Leadership Abilities

Although not conducted in the context of political debates, a study by Bucy (2000) found that political leaders' emotional displays influenced perceptions of their honesty, credibility, trustworthiness, and appropriateness. In addition, Senior's (2018, p. 2) review of relevant literature indicated that people are "very good" at using facial expressions to make accurate inferences about leadership effectiveness. Finally, perceptions of candidates' facial competence seems to be an especially potent influence on predicting election outcomes (Hall, Goren, Chaiken, & Todorov, 2009; Olivola & Todorov, 2010).

Nonverbal Communication and "Defining Moments" in Political Debates

On September 23, 1976, as millions of viewers watched the first televised presidential debate in sixteen years, Jimmy Carter stopped talking and, along with his opponent, Gerald Ford, stood speechless for almost half an hour. Moments before, the candidates had learned of an audio malfunction. The ensuing delay was not only long, it was chaotic. According to Wooten (1976, para. 2), "The audience buzzed, stagehands shouted, technicians screamed, and disembodied voices crackled frantically over intercom systems" (Wooten, 1976, para. 2). Meanwhile, Ford and Carter stood "frozen in comic parody" (Zelizer, 2016), "helplessly like two Hollywood stand-ins" (Witcover, cited in Zelizer, 2016, para. 10), and, as recounted by Carter himself, "almost like robots. We didn't walk over and shake hands with each other. We just stood there" (Winship, 2015, para. 9). To that, Ford added, "I think both of us were hesitant to make any gesture that might look like we weren't physically or mentally able to handle a problem like this" (Winship, 2015, para. 9).

In light of what we know about the high-stakes consequences of political debates, Carter and Ford's concern over potential blunders seems reasonable. Indeed, in his analysis of debates, Clayman (1995) described a "defining moment" as a singularly dramatic episode or exchange that comes to dominate news coverage, epitomize the debate, and survive over time. According to Grabe and Bucy (2009), such events can be categorized as "iconic moments," which are characterized by remarkable expressions of perceived greatness, or as "gaffes," which are represented by embarrassing slips that destroy candidates. As examples of the latter, Admiral James Stockdale began the 1992 vice presidential debate by asking, "Who am I? Why am I here?" (Holmes, 2005, para. 6), and, in a 2011 Republican primary debate, Texas governor Rick Perry pledged to eliminate three government agencies, yet couldn't remember the name of all three. "I would do away with, the education," he said, "uh, the . . . uh commerce . . . and, let's see. I can't. The third one, I can't. Sorry. Oops" (Rick Perry downplays, 2011, para. 10). Both blunders went viral, turning the candidates into punchlines.

Importantly, although examples like these illustrate the verbal nature of remarkable debate moments, Grabe and Bucy (2009) assert that such events can be nonverbal in nature too, including displays of signature expressions as well as inappropriate nonverbal behaviors. Focus groups, for instance, thought that James Stockdale's confused and nervous appearance served to increase his humiliation (Toon, 1994). Other examples of such behavior will be featured throughout this book. For now, however, we note, once again, that the close-up nature of television, coupled with interminable on-air and online rebroadcasting, only serves to magnify such moments, which can be important to understanding candidates' ability to demonstrate competence, composure under pressure, and other characteristics that make them viable and successful candidates. Alternatively, as Gentry and Duke (2009) argued,

> Since 1960, with the advent of televised debates, ineptitude in nonverbal communication has been part of many debates and may have played a part of the eventual electoral outcome. . . . Time after time, such mistakes in nonverbal communication have led many to believe that whereas nonverbal communication may not help a candidate win an election, it may hurt a candidate's chances of winning and play a role in a candidate losing the election. (p. 36)

Processing Nonverbal Communication Systematically

Up to this point, we have noted that visual images, including nonverbal communication and physical appearance, are a source of heuristics cues and emotional reactions. This, however, is not to suggest that politicians' verbal messages are solely processed systematically. To be sure, what politicians say can also serve as heuristic cues. By way of example, Nagel, Maurer, and Reinemann (2012) noted that the issues candidates talk about can be viewed as shortcuts used by viewers for evaluating those candidates. Relatedly, just because visual images can be processed heuristically does not mean that they are only processed in such a manner. Grabe and Bucy (2009), for example, point out that visual cues are processed in both non-rational and thinking parts of the brain. As such, visual cues are capable of evoking basic emotional responses, but are also subject to conscious appraisals and propositional evaluations.

TOWARD A FRAMEWORK FOR UNDERSTANDING NONVERBAL BEHAVIOR IN POLITICAL DEBATES

Up to this point, we have discussed a number of reasons for studying nonverbal communication in political debates, many of which point to the aims, functions, and effects of such communication. We have seen, for example, that nonverbal communication influences attributions that citizens make about politicians. In the sections that follow, we extend this discussion by introducing a framework for understanding and analyzing nonverbal behavior in political debates, which, in turn, provides further justification for its study and, more importantly, a foundation for future chapters. In so doing, we argue that such a framework must not only address a source's intended and strategic objectives for displaying certain nonverbal behaviors, but also the nonstrategic and unintended side effects of nonverbal stimuli as well. Given our conceptual framework, such nonverbal stimuli can be conceptualized as proactive (i.e., goal-oriented nonverbal behaviors), reactive (e.g., nervous behaviors that are unintentionally "leaked"), or nonactive (e.g., static facial features, including structure and color).

In addition, we argue that the framework must acknowledge the interactive aspects of political debates, alongside their uniquely complex and multi-faceted nature. Debaters, for example, not only occupy speaking and non-speaking roles, their messages may simultaneously affect perceptions of themselves and their opponents. Moreover, considering the complicated mosaic of possible message targets—including television viewers, live audiences, and, sometimes, the debaters themselves—we suggest that it is not enough to consider debates from a message source's point of view alone. Instead, a complete framework should take into account the perspectives of multiple audiences, including cognitive processes in receivers that may be affected by a source's nonverbal communication. Not only that, the framework should include a consideration of additional parties—including pre-debate negotiators, producers, directors, the press, and others—who potentially affect whether and how debaters' nonverbal behaviors are shown, portrayed, and talked about.

We acknowledge that our thinking about this topic was influenced by and benefited immensely from a diverse literature. Our framework incorporates, integrates, and expands on elements of impression management theory (Goffman, 1959), dual process models of persuasion (Guyer, Brinol, Petty, & Horcajo, 2019; Petty & Cacioppo, 1986; Chaiken, 1987; Chaiken & Trope, 1999), perspectives on nonverbal cue "leakage" (Burgoon & Buller, 2004, 2008; DePaulo, Zuckerman, & Rosenthal, 1980; Grebelsky-Lichtman, 2016; Zuckerman, DePaulo & Rosenthal, 1981), literature on the role of nonverbal behavior in perceptions of leaders (e.g., Bucy, 2016a; Bucy & Gong, 2018; Grabe & Bucy, 2009), and Benoit's (2007) work on the functions of verbal messages in political debates.

We also acknowledge that our framework leaves many stones unturned. Indeed, the following sections provide an overview of what we consider to be among the most important and prevalent aims, functions, and effects of nonverbal communication in political debates, but this framework is not intended to be exhaustive. Instead, the categories and subcategories provide what we hope to be a productive step toward understanding the intricate and expansive role that is played by nonverbal communication in debates. Similarly, the functions, aims and effects outlined next are not necessarily mutually exclusive.

Nonverbal Communication Shapes Images

Enhancing Images of the Self

In his landmark book, *The Presentation of the Self in Everyday Life*, Erving Goffman (1959) proposed a theory of impression management and self-presentation, suggesting that people in everyday life can be likened to actors on a stage, playing a variety of roles and, in the process, creating impressions that are consistent with the goals of the actor. This theatrical metaphor applies perfectly to political contexts, as illustrated by an exchange between former star of the silver screen, Ronald Reagan, and a cheeky reporter. When the reporter asked what it felt like to be an actor living in the White House, Reagan replied, "How could you be president and not be an actor?" (Roberts, 1993, cited in Erickson, 2009, p. 138).

To be sure, as noted above, political debates are as much, if not more, about projecting favorable images as they are about arguing positions on policy. According to Exline (1985), audiences closely monitor contestants "not so much to obtain information concerning candidates' beliefs or positions in regard to national issues, but rather to size up the candidates with respect to their competence, poise, and potential trustworthiness in handling themselves under stressful conditions" (p. 183). In this respect, then, theories of impression management and self-presentation (see Goffman 1959; Schlenker, 1980; Tedeschi & Norman, 1985; Tedeschi & Reiss, 1981) provide a useful foundation for discussing nonverbal communication in political debates. In fact, nonverbal cues are particularly important in fostering voters' perceptions of candidates' competence, trustworthiness, likeability, status, and power, as we'll see throughout this book.

Defending Images of the Self

According to impression management theory (Goffman, 1959), individuals as actors do not simply enhance their social images, they defend them as well. Likewise, Tedeschi and Norman (1985) argued that image management techniques can be either assertive or defensive in nature. Assertive techniques are used to promote positive, credible, and likeable images, while defensive techniques aim to avoid negative attributions. With regard to political debates, it is clear that nonverbal behaviors can function to defend a communicator's image. This is particularly true in debates that are telecast in split screen or other formats, which allow viewers to see both speaking and nonspeaking candidates simultaneously. Opponents who are being verbally attacked, for example, might smile and shake their heads in disagreement, as Hillary Clinton often did during the 2016 primary debates. Eventually, however, after repeated accusations of being a corrupt political insider from her opponent, Senator Bernie Sanders, Clinton let loose with a verbal defense, which one report described as "full-throated" (Frizell & Elliott, 2016, para. 17). That, combined with an earlier comment from the moderator—"If you're both screaming at each other, the viewers won't be able to hear either of you"—illustrates that, even if accompanied by verbal utterances, nonverbal communication can serve to emphasize (Frizell & Elliott, 2016, para. 5).

Undermining Images of Self

During the fifth Democratic primary debate of the 2020 election cycle, former Vice President Joe Biden was asked how he would address sexual violence and harassment against women. "So we have to change the culture, period," Biden said as part of his response, but then added, "And keep punching at it and punching at it and punching at it." For nonverbal emphasis, he made striking motions with his fist, making the gaffe all the more awkward. Laughter could be heard from the audience, and, not surprisingly, Biden's behavior provoked disparagement online, illustrating yet another function of nonverbal behavior in political debates. Specifically, whether alone or accompanied by verbal utterances, debaters' nonverbal actions have the potential to undermine their own image (Seiter, 1999). On this point we suggest that such behaviors can be categorized in one of two ways. First, they might be strategic and intentional behaviors gone wrong. In other words, candidates enacting such behaviors know what they are doing, but for whatever reason, cannot or do not perceive the negative consequences of their actions. Second, such behaviors might be nonstrategic and unintentional. In other words, candidates may try to project certain images, yet inadvertently "leak" nonverbal behaviors that undermine them. To be sure, although candidates may try to appear composed, their background nonverbal behavior might contradict them, and, in turn, affect audience perceptions. As Exline (1985) asserted:

> I incline to the view that the audience would be equally if not more concerned with assessing the candidates in terms of the effectiveness of their tension management under stress and thus would be particularly attuned to note relative differences in tension "leakage," developing more faith in the competence of the candidate who emitted fewer cues relevant to nervousness or a lack of poise under pressure. (p. 185)

Interestingly, in debates that they lost, both Richard Nixon and Barack Obama blinked at significantly higher rates than did their respective opponents. Nixon, for example, blinked 1,655 times in about 26 minutes on screen, while John F. Kennedy blinked 849 times in about 25 minutes (Bucy, 2016a). As an example of behavior that, presumably, was more controllable, in the final presidential debate of 2008 John McCain was criticized for rolling his eyes and scowling in reaction to Barack Obama's comments (McAuliff, Saltonstall, & Katz, 2008).

Undermining Images of Others

Over two decades ago, Seiter (1999, 2001) argued that the study of impression management "should be expanded to include not only the ways in which people manage impressions of themselves, but also the ways in which people strategically attempt to construct impressions made of others" (Seiter, 2001, pp. 234–235), a process that he and his colleagues later referred to as "other-presentation" (see Scharp, Seiter, & Maughan, in press). In addition, Seiter (1999, 2001) argued that politics provide an especially rich context for such an understanding because politicians are not only interested in promoting and defending images of themselves, they are in the business of managing impressions of others as well. What's more, debaters' nonverbal behavior is one of the primary means for accomplishing this goal (Seiter 1999, 2001). With that in mind, it is clear that understanding nonverbal behavior in political debates must not only address the ways in which such behaviors serve to promote and defend images of the self, but also the ways in which they function to undermine images of others as well.[1] In Chapter 4, for example, we will examine the 2012 vice presidential debates, in which Senator Joseph Biden's background laughter, which departed from his polite behavior in previous debates, was interpreted as an intentional attempt to undermine his opponent, Paul Ryan, through ridicule (Weger, et al., 2019).

We should also note that other third parties can potentially play a role in undermining debaters' images, whether intentionally or otherwise. In Chapter 5, for example, we will see that pre-debate negotiators, producers, directors, camera crews, and others may play a role in when and what manner debaters' nonverbal behavior is shown. As a humorous illustration, following the first 1960 presidential debate, the fact that Nixon appeared so haggard and Kennedy so composed had some viewers joking that "the cameraman was a Democrat" (Goethals, 2005, p. 102).

Enhancing Images of Others

Of course, this joke also illustrates that other-presentation—in this case, Kennedy's representation—is not always limited to undermining images. It can also function to enhance them. Debaters, for instance, presumably attempt to instill positive impressions of their running mates, and vice versa, perhaps with a smile or confident demeanor when discussing the other. Alternatively, a candidate might enhance his or her opponent's image. In Chapter 4, for example, we discuss the effects of nodding in agreement while one's opponent is speaking.

Defending Images of Others

According to the *New York Times,* then Governor Mike Pence's "go to move" in the 2016 vice presidential debate was "to ruefully shake his head in the split screen," while his running mate, Donald Trump's, unsavory comments were slammed by Senator Tim Kaine. "That's not technically a 'statement,'" *The Times* continued, "but on TV, body language can be more powerful than words. A shake of the head, to the lay viewer, says, 'That's silly, he never said that'—says it, possibly more powerfully than a spoken denial" (Poniewozik & Rutenberg, 2016, para. 4). In other words, nonverbal communication clearly functions to defend others.

Although increasingly rare in today's aggressive political climate, candidates might also use nonverbal communication to defend their opponent's images. To illustrate, consider an example outside of political debates. Specifically, during a rally in the final weeks of the 2008 presidential campaign, a woman, with microphone in hand, told Senator John McCain, "I can't trust Obama. I have read about him, and he's not, he's not—he's an Arab," at which point McCain shook his head in disagreement. He gathered the microphone, took several steps to distance himself, and, before turning his back on her, gestured for emphasis and said, "No ma'am. He's a decent family man, a citizen that I just happen to have disagreements with on fundamental issues, and that's what this campaign is all about" (Associated Press, 2008).

Nonverbal Communication Creates Emotional Bonds with Audiences

Although relationships are typically conceptualized as mutual, actual, face-to-face affiliations, Horton and Wohl (1956) introduced the notion of "parasocial relationships," in which media users experience a psychological bond with media personalities, including political candidates, even though they have never interacted. As noted above, the close-up nature of television is particularly well suited for conveying, through nonverbal behavior, relational information about a candidate, which, in turn, creates psychological connections with viewers. In short, as linguist George Lakoff noted, "Debates are not about scoring points. They are about emotional identification" (Fallows, 2004, para. 14).

Nonverbal Communication as Argument

Bolstering Arguments

Thus far, we have noted that visual images, including nonverbal communication and physical appearance, can be a source of heuristics cues. This, however, is not to suggest that politicians' verbal messages are only processed systematically. To be sure, what politicians say can also serve as heuristic cues. As an example, Nagel et al. (2012) noted that the issues candidates talk about can be viewed as shortcuts used by viewers for evaluating those candidates. Similarly, politicians' nonverbal messages are not only processed heuristically. In fact, research in the area of visual rhetoric illustrates that visuals cues can be a source of rich, substantive information (see Hoffman, 2011).

While conceding that verbal communication allows for more precise and elaborate forms of argumentation, Gelang and Kjeldsen (2011) asserted that nonverbal communication functions argumentatively because it can be taken as signs for spoken or unspoken propositions and premises. Although their analysis focused on the ways in which nonverbal communication performs argumentative functions in acclaiming, defending, and attacking debaters' ethos, they noted that such propositions and premises might be about policies and issues of controversy as well. Similarly, Groarke (2015) makes a compelling case that visual images, sounds, smells, tastes and other nonverbal phenomena can be employed as modes of argument. Chapter 7 will be devoted to exploring these ideas in more detail.

Refuting Arguments

Likewise, Chapter 7 will discuss the ways in which nonverbal communication can function to refute opponents' arguments. For now, and at a very basic level, suffice it to say that the use of reaction shots in debates afford politicians the opportunity to refute an opponent without ever saying a word. To be sure, examples abound of candidates shaking their head, smirking, deeply sighing, and throwing their hands to the heavens in rebuttal to opponents' arguments. We will examine many such examples in later chapters.

Nonverbal Communication Affects Viewers' Cognitive Processing

Up to this point, our framework has treated nonverbal cues as a source of information (or premises) upon which impressions of candidates might be managed and made, and upon which arguments might be refuted or bolstered. In addition, consistent with dual process theories of persuasion (Petty & Cacioppo, 1986; Chaiken, 1987), we have noted that such impressions and/or arguments can be cognitively processed with varying degrees of scrutiny, ranging from heuristic to systematic processing. That said, the role of nonverbal communication in political debates is not confined to being a source of information (or premises). To be sure, nonverbal communication can function to affect the processing of information as well.

Nonverbal Communication Can Affect Viewers' Ability to Process Messages

Previous research indicates that attorneys sometimes rely on nonverbal "red herrings" (e.g., yawning in the background, fist slamming, huffing) in order to distract from the presenting counsel's message (Ubel, 2008). To the extent that such behavior hinders jurors' *ability* to think about strong arguments, thereby diminishing those arguments' persuasiveness, it may be an effective tactic. Likewise, in debate contexts, nonverbal distractions—including audience members who heckle (see Beatty & Kruger, 1978), opponents who wander (Bucy & Gong, 2018), and candidates' own facial expressions (Nagel et al., 2012)—can divert attention away from the meat of an argument. As Weger et al. (2019, p. 155) noted, "When one candidate distracts the audience from the speaking debater's verbal message, the audience is called on to process both a verbal message and nonverbal message simultaneously, which potentially limits the impact of the speaking debater's argumentation." Alternatively, nonverbal behaviors might function to improve people's ability to process messages. Woodall and Folger (1981), for instance, found that people recall messages that are accompanied by emblematic gestures better than those that are not.

Nonverbal Communication Can Affect Viewers' Motivation to Process Messages

In addition to affecting an audience's ability, nonverbal behavior might influence an audience's *motivation* to attend to a message. Imagine, for example, what your response might be to a long debate that featured exceptionally monotone and expressionless speakers. Likewise, consider how you might react to a debater who, as a result of nonverbal behavior, seems especially credible. According to Benoit and Strathman (2004), "Here, belief that the source is an expert on the topic of the message could encourage receivers to 'relax their guards,' or feel less motivation to scrutinize the message. . . . In contrast, if the source is thought to be disreputable, that belief may lead receivers to be more wary, subjecting the message to more scrutiny" (p. 101). Once again, to the extent that the arguments in a message are strong, nonverbal communication that decreases one's motivation to scrutinize that message would also, theoretically, diminish the persuasiveness of that message (see Petty & Cacioppo, 1986). On the other hand, nonverbal communication that increased one's motivation to scrutinize strong arguments, should serve to bolster persuasion.

Nonverbal Communication Can Bias Viewers' Processing of Messages

Nonverbal communication can serve to bias cognitive processing (see Guyer et al., 2019). In one study (Ottati, Terkildsen, & Hubbard, 1997), for example, actors posing as political candidates displayed various facial expressions in a televised clip. The results indicated that happy expressions, compared to angry ones, biased viewers, leading them to generate more favorable thoughts about the speakers' message.

Nonverbal Communication Can Fluster Opponents

In addition to affecting audiences, debaters might use nonverbal actions to affect their opponents' performance, for better or worse. According to Schroeder (2016), for example, by the time the third 2008 debate came around, Barack Obama figured out that looking directly at John McCain was the best way to rattle him. In addition, as we'll see in Chapter 4, Donald Trump's use of proxemics in a 2016 debate with Hillary Clinton purportedly made her uncomfortable and was interpreted by some as an attempt to rattle her. At the same time, research suggest that viewers perceived such behavior as hostile and obnoxious (Bucy & Gong, 2018).

Nonverbal Communication Can Regulate the Flow of Debates

One of the most important functions of communication involves the management, regulation, and coordination of conversations. In political debates, this notion probably applies most to moderators, who rely on a combination of verbal and nonverbal behaviors to interrupt verbose candidates, signal who's turn it is to speak, and so forth. Likewise, debaters themselves attempt to regulate debates, as Barack Obama did in his second 2012 contest with Mitt Romney. According to Ortega (2019), when Romney asked questions, Obama stood up to answer, looked at the audience but not Romney, and moved past his opponent, thereby upstaging him. We'll have more to say about this function of nonverbal communication in Chapters 4 and 5.

Interestingly, and on a side note, verbal communication can be used to regulate nonverbal behavior as well. As one example, at the sixth Democratic primary debate in 2019, while Joe Biden was speaking, Senator Bernie Sanders waved an arm, presumably trying to catch the moderators' attention. "Put your hand down for a second, Bernie," Biden said. "Okay?"

"Just waving at you, Joe," Bernie replied. "Saying hello."

Additional Functions

The preceding sections sketched a descriptive framework of the aims, functions, and effects of nonverbal behavior in political debates. Clearly, however, our list is not exhaustive. Indeed, we can think of additional roles that nonverbal behaviors can play in political debates.

First, nonverbal communication might signal the nature of candidates' relationships with each other. As a case in point, consider a moment immediately following the January 14, 2020, Democratic primary debate, at a time when it is typical to see candidates exchanging pleasantries. While still on stage, Senator Elizabeth Warren shook hands with two opponents, but then apparently refused to shake Senator Bernie Sanders's extended hand. By the looks of Sanders's reaction and the fading smile of a third candidate, Tom Steyer, who found himself between the two senators, the resulting conversation was intense.[2] "I'm not sure what she said," Sanders's campaign co-chair noted on CNN, "but you can read the body language. Obviously their conversation was not pleasant" (Cillizza, 2020, para. 5). Not surprisingly, the apparent spat not only raised questions about what had been said, it served as attributional fodder. The next morning, for example, snake emojis and the hashtag "#neverWarren" were trending on Twitter (Cillizza, 2020). Perhaps more importantly, to some voters, the relationship candidates have with each other matters. Indeed, in the event that an ardent supporter's preferred primary candidate lost or dropped out of a race, which substitute candidate would presumably cause the least dissonance when supported instead: the losing candidate's enemy or friend? With that in mind, at the time of this writing, it is not surprising that the apparent wrinkle in Senator Warren and Sanders's long-time friendship is worrisome to Democratic leaders. As Cillizza (2020, para. 10–12) wrote,

> There are real consequences to all of these raw feelings. Sanders and Warren are the two most prominent liberals in the race. . . . After Tuesday night, however, the idea of the Sanders people rallying around Warren if, after the first few primaries and caucuses, she looks like the most viable liberal candidate, now seems fanciful. And, vice versa for the Warren people being cool with the idea of Sanders as the liberal choice for 2020. And that is true no matter what the two principals say (or don't say) about that now-famous December 2018 meeting and/or the no-handshake moment in Tuesday night's debate.

Second, nonverbal elements of the environment might influence debates. Consider color and lighting, for instance. In the first 1960 presidential debate, Richard Nixon appeared so haggard and pale that Chicago Mayor Richard Daley exclaimed, "My God, they've embalmed him before he even died" (Smith, 2012, p. 79). Keep in mind, however, that although Nixon had been sick and refused to wear makeup, the stage's gray backdrop probably contributed to his washed-out appearance (Jamieson & Birdsell, 1988; Kraus, 2000; Seltz & Yoakam, 1979), a topic we return to later in this book.

Third, nonverbal communication can function as a topic in and of itself. Chapter 5, for instance, reviews research examining the ways in which newscasters discuss political debaters' nonverbal behavior and appearance. As we saw earlier in this chapter and revisit later in this book, politicians themselves are not above making an issue out of their opponents' appearance. Trump, after all, said of Hillary Clinton, "Does she look presidential, fellas?," and later, "Well, I just don't think she has a presidential look, and you need a presidential look" (Parker, 2016, para. 2 and 3). Similarly, in a series of tweets, Trump gave a potential 2020 rival—former New York mayor Michael Bloomberg—the nickname "Mini Mike," and later, in a Fox News interview, accused Bloomberg of making special requests to stand on a box if he qualified for future presidential debates (Sandler, 2020). To this, Bloomberg's campaign spokeswoman, Julie Wood, fired back, calling Trump "a pathological liar who lies about everything: his fake hair, his obesity, and his spray-on tan" (Colvin, 2020, para. 10). Finally, as we also saw earlier in this chapter, politicians might refer to their own appearance. In a 2019 Democratic primary debate, for example, Minnesota Senator Amy Klobuchar, one of the shortest candidates on stage, drew laughter from the audience when, after referring to James Madison, she noted, "and by the way, I think he's a pretty good size for a president; he was five-foot-four" (Fix Team, 2019, para. 23).

CONCLUSION

During a 2007 Democratic primary debate, after expressing concern about then senator Joseph Biden's reputation for talking too much, a moderator asked, "Can you reassure voters in this country that you would have the discipline you would need on the world stage, Senator?" Biden's answer was a simple, "Yes," followed by "a long, pregnant silence," and then laughter from the audience (Tumulty, 2007, para. 2). Far be it from us to step on a good line, but we can't help wonder whether a quiet nod on Biden's part might have served him just as well or perhaps even better. Either way, this story underlines an important point. Specifically, Biden's silence was "pregnant" with *meaning*.

Although we take interest in conversations surrounding the relative importance or influence of verbal over nonverbal communication (or vice versa) in political debates (e.g., see Koppensteiner, Stephan, & Jäschke, 2015; Maurer, 2016; Wasike, 2019), and are sympathetic with academics who desire more substantive deliberation in such events, as scholars in a discipline that occupies itself, to a significant degree, with understanding the ways in which meaning is created and shared, when all is said and done, we find ourselves pointing to what may be the most basic of observations: political debates embody verbal *and* nonverbal messages, both of which, either alone or in tandem, contribute to the perception, interpretation, creation, and sharing of meaning. As Denton (2017) wrote, "For communication scholars, the essence of politics is 'talk' or human interaction. The interaction may be formal or informal, verbal or nonverbal, public or private, but always persuasive, forcing us as individuals to interpret, evaluate, and act" (p. x).

By implication, a complete understanding of communication in political debates, requires more than an examination of verbal elements, which may have sufficed in the days before television. However, in an era where visual images, nonverbal communication, and physical appearances serve to emphasize, contradict, provide context, and, at times, substitute for words spoken, it is our belief that we miss out on too much by neglecting to consider them. To this end, in addition to offering a rationale for understanding such features of political debates, this chapter provided an introduction to understanding them and a framework for chapters to follow.

NOTES

1. The notion that nonverbal impression management involves defending and promoting images of the self (Tedeschi & Norman, 1985) and undermining images of others (Seiter, 1999, 2001) is consistent with the work of William Benoit (Benoit, 2007; Benoit & Wells, 1996). Specifically, based on his analyses of verbal messages in political advertisements, debates, and campaigns, Benoit (2007) created functional theory, which asserts that candidates try to appear

preferable to their opponents through the use of acclaims (making positive statements about themselves), defenses (refuting opponents' attacks), and attacks (criticizing their opponents).

2. Although the senators' exchange originally aired without audio and was followed by widespread media speculation about what was said, CNN's microphones picked up the sound and made it public the next day. "I think you called me a liar on national TV," Warren told Sanders, who replied, "You know, let's not do it right now. . . . You called me a liar" (Blaine, Zeleny, & Cohen, 2020, para. 7–9). The spat resulted from an earlier claim, made by Warren prior to the debate, that Sanders told her a woman could not win the presidency in 2020. When asked in the debate, Sanders denied saying it.

Chapter Two

A Primer on Nonverbal Communication

The visual aspect of televised political debates has provided candidates an opportunity to reach voters and manage their impressions beyond their policy arguments. Ever since the 1960 Kennedy-Nixon debate, scholars, media analysts, and political pundits have talked about the importance of the visual image a candidate presents on stage. In this chapter, we take a closer look at the fundamental elements of nonverbal communication in order to establish a common vocabulary and conceptual basis for the study of nonverbal behavior in televised debates. As an introduction to nonverbal communication in political debates, we necessarily provide more breadth than depth in discussing candidates' nonverbal behavior with deeper discussions of these concepts to follow in later chapters. We start by presenting a working definition of nonverbal communication to help identify the sorts of behaviors that are of most interest to communication researchers. Second, we discuss some general characteristics of nonverbal communication with an emphasis on the role those characteristics play in televised debates. The final part of this chapter presents the key elements of nonverbal behavior that underlie messages candidates communicate through visual and audio channels.

A WORKING DEFINITION OF NONVERBAL COMMUNICATION

For the purposes of this book, we define nonverbal communication as messages sent using nonlinguistic means. Apart from words, any part of a message, including how the verbal message is delivered, can be counted as a nonverbal element. Vocal aspects of the way a message is delivered such as regional accents, volume, pitch, and rate, even though they are spoken and are linked to words, are all nonverbal to the extent that these elements have meaning independent of words. In addition, sign language, texting, and email messages are all verbal (or mostly so) even though they are not spoken. We further narrow our definition of "messages" to mean behaviors or elements of the situation that are typically, but not always, intended as meaningful and that have generally agreed upon meanings within a speech community. A growling stomach or a sneeze might provide information about the person who is emitting those signals, but not all behaviors that are informative are necessarily communicative. A message, in our way of thinking, includes typically symbolic behavior, or behaviors that stand for meanings beyond the inherent physiological or biological functions of the behaviors themselves.

However, messages typically involve packages of both intentional and unintentional meanings. We would not want to ignore the unintentional behaviors/meanings as they are sometimes the most interesting aspect of a message. For example, physical appearance plays an important role in the way candidates for public office are perceived by audiences (e.g., Olivola & Todorov, 2010), yet, a candidates' height and facial structure are completely out of their control and are difficult to intentionally manipulate (although, as we will see, candidates shorter in stature often request accommodations to limit the visual difference in height while on stage with a taller opponent). Scholars studying nonverbal communication in political debates would be remiss to ignore the influence of such cues. Nonverbal elements of a communication situation, such as the setting in which an interaction takes place, is sometimes out of the speakers' control but can also have important impacts on the communication that takes place. For example, the technical aspects of the broadcast medium itself, such as camera angles, backgrounds, split screens versus single shots, and other attributes of televised debates potentially influence audience perceptions of the candidates as they can emphasize or downplay various aspects of a candidate's performance. As communication researchers it would be ill-advised to ignore the ways in which the medium bears on the audience's perceptions of candidates' messages. Finally, in keeping with our framework from Chapter 1, which considers message sources' intentions alongside the ways in which audience members process messages (i.e., automatic v. controlled cognition), we will see in this chapter that unintentional cues are, at times, not only mistaken as intentional, but carry the potential to bias audience members' perceptions. As such, examining the influence of such cues is essential to understanding political messages in debate contexts. With those details out of the way, we turn our attention to four characteristics of nonverbal communication.

CHARACTERISTICS OF NONVERBAL COMMUNICATION

Nonverbal Messages are Polysemous

Nonverbal behavior is ambiguous and lends itself to multiple interpretations. Although this is true for verbal behavior too, the meanings of words can be narrowed to dictionary meanings and common usage interpretations. Nonverbal behavior, on the other hand, is open to far broader interpretation, partly because it is harder to determine what is intentional and what is not, but also because of pervasive, but unfounded, cultural beliefs. For example, a popular belief in the United States is that people who fold their arms across their body are closed off to either a conversation partner or to their ideas. Although there is no social scientific evidence to support this belief, it does not deter the media from propagating such myths. In the popular television series *Lie to Me*, for instance, the protagonist, a fictional character loosely based on Stanford professor Paul Ekman (Lie to Me, n.d.), solves crimes, often by concluding that suspects' nonverbal behaviors are clear indications of guilt or innocence. Although Dr. Ekman is among the top scholars of nonverbal communication in the world, other so-called "body language" experts abound on news programs to provide insight into candidates' behaviors and even psyches during election cycles. For example, a well-known "expert" told hosts of a national morning television program during the 2016 election campaign that Donald Trump's hand gestures, which visually mimic playing the accordion, were a sign of a person who "thinks outside the box" (Today, 2016), a conclusion that is absolutely unfounded in scientific research. At least part of what we hope to accomplish in this book is to differentiate such unfounded speculation from current state of the art conclusions in scholarly humanistic and social scientific research.

Not surprisingly, the ambiguous nature of nonverbal messages interacts with cognitive biases to influence perceptions of others. For instance, the "confirmation bias" (Westen, Blagov, Harenski, Kilts, & Hamann, 2006) leads people to interpret behaviors in ways that match their preconceived impressions of a person. As a result, different interpretations of the same nonverbal behaviors might vary dramatically. As a case in point, consider these two interpretations of U.S. president Barack Obama's rhetorical style. The first was written by Ron Ross (2010) of the conservative publication *American Spectator*:

> Even if messages were put on Mr. Obama's teleprompter I doubt he could pull it off. His teleprompter could say, "Show passion now," or "Be angry here," and it still wouldn't happen. He is a cold fish, not a cool dude. He shows no passion because he has none to show. He could try to fake it, but he has no acting ability. (para 10).

Compare Ross's assessment of Obama's charisma as a speaker with 2016 presidential candidate and former Florida Governor Jeb Bush (also a conservative) while he was on the campaign trail in 2015:

> If I could speak like Barack Obama. If I could light up a room like he does. You know, charisma is not a bad thing. It's a pretty effective tool to be able to take a message to a broader audience, and he is gifted beyond belief in that regard. . . . To be elected and re-elected in the kind of turbulent times that we're in is to be admired for someone that's running for president, trust me. (as quoted in O'Keefe, 2015, July 16, para. 4).

Despite the inherent ambiguity of nonverbal messages, scientific research has still been able to identify some behaviors that audience members generally associate with perceptions of charisma, credibility, likeability, dominance, and a host of other assessments (e.g., Burgoon, Birk, & Pfau, 1990; Nagel, Maurer, & Reinemann, 2012). In later chapters we identify and discuss a variety of theoretical explanations for the effects of nonverbal behavior on audience appraisals.

Nonverbal Communication Is Culture Bound

Although some nonverbal behaviors seem to be universal (e.g., certain facial expressions of emotion), research and practical experience indicate the trouble we can get into by interpreting another culture's nonverbal behaviors from our own cultural viewpoint. For example, gestures that mean one thing in one culture can mean something else entirely in a different culture. The "peace" or "V for victory" gesture involves raising the hand palm out and extending the first two fingers to form a V shape. U.S. President George H. W. Bush, while visiting Australia, mistakenly performed this gesture with his palm facing inward (called "the fork" in Australia), which is equivalent to the meaning of extending the middle finger in the United States. Even nonverbal behavior with physiological roots, such as eye pupil dilation, trembling when anxious, or nearly universal facial expressions such as joy and surprise can vary in intensity, meaning, and appropriateness across cultures (Gudykunst & Ting-Toomey, 1988). There is also dispute over the exact number of universal emotions. Although many scholars agree on seven (happiness, sadness, disgust, anger, surprise, contempt, and fear; Ekman, 1972), new disputes have emerged over the number and the degree to which they are truly universal. For example, Benetiz-Quiroz, Wilbur, and Martinez (2016) claim to have discovered a new universal expression they label the *not face*. The not face is an indication of disagreement made by a combination of elements from anger and disgust and appears to be interpreted as expressing skepticism or disbelief across English, French, Spanish, and American Sign Language users.

Even when nonverbal expressions are nearly universal in their meaning, the norms for appropriate expressions of emotion differ according to each culture's rules for displaying them (Ekman & Friesen, 1982). These display rules guide the cultural norms for evaluating and displaying particular sorts of nonverbal behavior. One example from the political arena involves displaying intense emotions such as sadness, grief, and/or frustration through shedding tears. In the United States, the ability to control intense emotions, especially sadness and fear, is associated with social competence (e.g., Zawadzki, Warner, & Sheilds, 2013). During the 1972 presidential election campaign, Edmund Muskie became visibly upset and reportedly shed tears while defending his wife against a smear campaign initiated by the editor of the *Manchester Union Leader* newspaper (Remembering Ed Muskie, 1996, March 26). Because of the cultural display rules of the time, any appearance of crying by a male leader was perceived as a sign of weakness and incompetence. News that Muskie violated the display rule, along with other factors, helped undercut his campaign for president.

In the 44 years that followed Muskie's doomed press conference, display rules have changed in the United States to the extent that at least restrained displays of emotions appear to be perceived more positively than negatively when expressed in an appropriate context (e.g., Zawadzki, et al., 2013). Politicians seem to routinely shed tears in public with either no negative, or in some cases positive, public response (e.g., Benedictus, 2016, January 9) as long as they appear to remain in control otherwise. As an example of how display rules can change over time, while announcing proposed legislation regulating firearms, tears began to flow down then–President Obama's cheeks as he began to speak about the 2012 Sandy Hook elementary school shooting, which claimed the lives of 20 school children as well as six school employees. Although there was some criticism from opponents of the legislation, media responses were mostly positive. As an example, Jerald Podair, an associate professor of history at Lawrence University was quoted by CNN: "This is the most emotion an American president has ever shown on camera. . . . I can almost guarantee that when there is some sort of collage shown of this president's presidency, this one moment will be in there" (Blake, 2016, January 8, para. 7). Likewise, Chris Cillizza, a Washington Post political reporter wrote,

> I don't have any sort of personal position on Obama or his gun control executive orders. But, I do have a strongly held belief in favor of men—including male politicians—crying in public if necessary. . . . Being moved to tears is a good thing—for people and for politicians, who, it's important to remember, are people too, at least most of the time. (Cillizza, 2016, January 5, paras. 4 and 8)

Nonverbal Communication Expands Lexical Meanings

Perhaps the most widely misused research result in social science suggests that nonverbal behavior accounts for 93% (or any other set portion) of the meaning of a message. Now termed "the Mehrabian myth," this canard was based on research by Albert Mehrabian and his colleagues (Mehrabian & Ferris, 1967; Mehrabian & Wiener, 1967). In one of their studies, female college students were asked to judge the feelings of a male speaker by listening to audio recordings of the speaker saying single words (e.g., "terrible" and "love") in different vocal tones. It comes as no surprise, of course, that more "feeling" was attributed to the speaker's tone of voice than the words themselves, especially considering there was no real meaningful verbal message, just single words, to interpret. Mehrabian himself now cautions against the use of his formula for generalizations about the relative importance of verbal and nonverbal elements of a message (Mehrabian, n.d. para. 5).

That said, there is little doubt that nonverbal behaviors play an important role in helping people understand message meaning. Indeed, research reveals the meaning of a message is more reliably understood when nonverbal cues are available than when they are not (e.g., Skipper, Goldin-Meadow, Nusbaum, & Small, 2009). Sarcasm and other ironic meanings rely on nonverbal cues such as the speaker's facial expression and vocal tone to interpret correctly. However, nonverbal cues can potentiate misunderstanding as well given that discrepancies between verbal and nonverbal meanings can trigger perceptions of deception or confusion (e.g., Seiter, 1997). Nonverbal behavior can also function independently as substitutes for verbal messages. Certain behaviors, such as facial expressions of ridicule, disbelief, surprise, or disagreement can function on their own to communicate with the audience. Physical distance between debaters, differences in height, attractiveness, (un)coordinated movements, particular gestures, facial expressions, and other cues can also communicate messages independently of verbal messages to audiences. We will return to this topic in more detail in future chapters.

Observers' Own Nonverbal Behaviors Potentially Influence Their Perceptions of Televised Debaters

A relatively new and popular theoretical approach to studying nonverbal behavior involves embodied accounts of cognition. An embodied approach suggests that people's somatic (bodily) experiences when encountering a stimulus object (such as a candidate debating on television) influence the reception, storage, retrieval, and processing of emotional, social, and attitudinal responses toward the stimulus object (Niedenthal, Barsalou, Winkielman, Krauth-Gruber, & Ric, 2005). Online embodied cognition occurs when a person directly interacts with a stimulus. For example, one study found that participants who stood while listening to a persuasive message had more negative attitudes toward the message than participants who listened to the message in a reclining posture. The discomfort or bodily effort required to stand while listening to the message may have interfered with the person's ability to fully process the message making the receiver less agreeable to the position advocated by the speaker (Briñol & Petty, 2008).

Offline embodiment occurs when the stimulus object is not present but the perceiver responds nonverbally during recall. For example, Andersen, Reznik, and Manzella (1996) asked participants to write descriptions of a person close to them that they either liked or disliked. The researchers then constructed descriptions of fictious people that contained elements of the participants' earlier descriptions. When participants unknowingly read descriptions of liked others, they were judged to have expressed happy/pleasant emotions but displayed more negative facial expressions when reading descriptions with elements taken from their disliked descriptions. That is, their body responded in ways that indicated an automatic embodied response to their cognitive processing of information about a person.

Considering such research, it is possible that, in the context of political debates, television audiences' nonverbal behavior might influence their responses to candidates' performances. For example, as discussed below, research indicates that motor neurons and associated cognitive structures tend to produce mimicked responses to candidate behavior. That is, when seeing a candidate smile, an observer's facial muscles react by either smiling or preparing to smile. Furthermore, research indicates that authentic smiles produced during online embodied processing function to bias information processing in a positive way toward the stimulus (Wallbot, 1991). As such, when a candidate on screen is seen smiling, partisan audience members who mimic that smile may construct or reinforce positive beliefs about the candidate. Alternatively, when a partisan voter mimics a favored candidate's display of disgust during an opponent's speech, the voter's disgusted expression might reinforce his or her own negative emotional response to the candidate's opponent.

To explain the seemingly automatic connection between physiological expressions of pleasure (i.e., smiling) or disgust and cognitive responses to a stimulus, Zajonc and Markus (1984) introduced hard interface theory (HIT), which argues that certain cognitive states and physiological responses are hardwired together. More specifically, when thinking about or interacting with social stimuli (i.e., people), people have sets of automatic physiological reactions that have the potential to influence their emotional and attitudinal reactions toward the stimuli. Throughout this book, when relevant, we will point out ways in which audience member's own embodied responses to candidates and their message can influence audience member's processing of attitudes, beliefs, and emotions toward the debaters.

Although the embodied approach to cognition has led to intriguing results, it is not without controversy. Perhaps the most famous example to the general public involves the concept of "power posing" made famous by Amy Cuddy's Ted Talk on the subject. In the original study, Cuddy and her colleagues (Carney, Cuddy, & Yap, 2010) asked college-aged participants to pose in either a power position (e.g., standing or sitting with expansive positions and open limbs) or in a more submissive, less powerful position (standing or sitting in contractive positions with closed limbs). The study results suggested that participants in the power positions experienced, "elevation of the dominance hormone testosterone, reduction of the stress hormone cortisol, and increases in behaviorally demonstrated risk tolerance and feelings of power" (p. 1366). A second study (Cuddy, Wilmuth, Yap, & Carney, 2015) found that participants who power posed in preparation for a mock interview were judged to perform better in the interview and were more likely to be "hired" than participants who engaged in less powerful poses.

These results were intriguing and provided a compelling example of how one's own somatic experience might influence physiological, behavioral, and psychological processes. Unfortunately, at least 11 attempts by other researchers have failed to reproduce results related to hormonal and behavioral differences (e.g., Cesario, Jonas, & Carney, 2017; Michigan State University, 2017, September 11). In addition, although some research has replicated the finding that participants in power poses felt more powerful, such replication may be difficult to claim as a success. Indeed, it is not difficult to imagine how instructions to engage in a high versus low power pose might have cued research participants to guess the true purpose of the study, and respond accordingly (i.e., behave in a way that was consistent with researcher's hypothesis). In fact, recently, doubt has been raised on the reliability of several studies related to the embodied approach. For instance, 17 independent studies, conducted at 17 different locations, failed to replicate Strack, Martin, and Stepper's (1988) facial feedback study (Wagenmakers et al., 2016). The facial feedback hypothesis predicts that facial expressions directly affect one's emotional experience. The basic idea is that the brain receives somatic input from the contraction of a person's facial muscles, which helps the brain determine the person's emotional state. Strack et al.'s (1988) study found participants who held a pen in their mouth to simulate the muscle movement of a smile perceived cartoons to be funnier than those who held a pen in their lips mimicking a frown. Such failure to replicate, of course, does not verify that the embodied approach is misguided or has been disproven, but rather that we must take caution in applying such research to televised debates, a topic which, up to this point, has not been a significant focus of embodied research.

A TAXONOMY OF NONVERBAL BEHAVIORS

In order to study a phenomenon as complex as nonverbal communication, scholars often reduce people's multidimensional and multifunctional behavior into smaller, easier to analyze, units of analysis. Some scholars criticize this approach to communication research in general as overly atomistic because it decontextualizes behavior from its original setting and purpose. Although this is true to some extent, it is necessary, especially in this chapter, to develop a common vocabulary that can be used across the book. That said, much of the social scientific research reported throughout the remainder of this monograph considers simultaneously, as well as in isolation, a variety of nonverbal behaviors that account for effects on audience responses. This allows researchers to consider the effects of a constellation of behaviors simultaneously as well as specific behaviors in isolation. Furthermore, we integrate social scientific research with rhetorical scholarship and contemporary accounts from media and other eye-witness reports of debates, and, in so doing, often consider an array of nonverbal behaviors, sometimes in isolation, but more often in overall patterns that lead to different effects (e.g., an array of rhetorical acts, production techniques, and "immediacy" behaviors might contribute to perceptions of a candidate's relatability). As such, in this chapter, we rely on a number of distinct categories of nonverbal behavior that will assist us in analyzing their features and functions in candidates' debate performances.

Facial Expression

Messages involving movements in facial muscles, head position, smiling, and eye contact or gaze are the most studied nonverbal behaviors, perhaps because they are primary among all other nonverbal behavior in the impressions we form of others (Knapp & Hall, 2002). In fact, humans' perceptual system for recognizing faces is so powerful that they sometimes interpret vague images as familiar faces (Jesus, Elvis Presley, etc.) in slices of toast, tortillas, and the surface of Mars, a phenomenon known as *pareidolia*.

Humans have evolved to recognize each other visually, primarily based on facial features that are processed in a specialized section of the brain labeled the *fusiform face area* (Kanwisher & Yovel, 2006). Some evidence for the evolved nature of facial expressions and emotional recognition suggests that there are a limited number of prewired facial expressions across cultures (e.g., Ekman, 1972). However, whether these emotional categories are universal has become debatable (e.g., Jack, Blais, Scheepers, Schyns, & Caldara, 2009). Ekman hypothesized six, and later seven, universally recognized facial expressions of emotion that include surprise, anger, disgust, fear, happiness, contempt, and sadness (e.g., Ekman, 1972; Ekman & Cordaro,

2011). More recent research suggests that there may be some variation among cultures but that most people are able to automatically identify most facial expressions (Gendron, Roberson, van der Vyver, Barrett, 2014; Matsumoto & Hwang, 2019).

Given limited visual access to the majority of a candidate's body, and because of facial primacy, facial expression potentially plays a critical role in perceptions of candidates during televised debates. Smiling and facial pleasantness (not to be confused with attractiveness) are positively related to perceptions of attractiveness, competence (Hess, Beaupre, & Cheung, 2002; Matsumoto & Kudoh, 1993), likeability (Palmer & Simmons, 1995), conviviality, and warmth (Miles, 2009). In addition, research suggests that inappropriate facial expressions (for example, smiling while talking about the death of American combat troops) during televised presidential debates attract more visual attention and create more negative impressions on audience members than context appropriate expressions (Gong & Bucy, 2016). Indeed, even inappropriate microexpressions (facial expressions that last only milliseconds) can influence audience responses to a speech (Stewart, Waller, & Schubert, 2009).

Along with expressing emotions, perceptions of politicians' attractiveness plays an important role in how they are perceived. In general, attractiveness often prompts a bias known as the "halo effect," which causes weaknesses to be overlooked and strengths to be highlighted. As such, attractive people are perceived to be more intelligent, trustworthy, and socially skilled than less attractive people (Canary, Cody, & Manusov, 2008). This effect has led researchers to identify a "what is beautiful is good" heuristic that people use to make fast and favorable judgments about others (Dion, Berscheid, & Walster, 1972).

Research suggests that perceptions of facial attractiveness are driven by bilateral symmetry, average size and shape of facial features, and markers of sex-consistent masculinity (e.g., prominent eyebrow ridges, facial width) or femininity (e.g., prominent cheek bones; Thornhill & Gangestad, 1999). Facial shape is one cue people use to interpret speaker credibility and several studies emphasize the importance of voters' perceptions of candidates' attractiveness (e.g., Benjamin & Shapiro, 2009; Rosenberg, Bohan, McCafferty, & Harris, 1986). For example, "baby-faced" speakers (speakers with rounder and narrower faces with larger than average eyes) were more persuasive than more mature-faced speakers when both speakers' trustworthiness was in question (Brownlow, 1992). This is consistent with research suggesting that people view baby-faced people as more trustworthy (e.g., Berry & McArthur, 1985). However, when both speakers' expertise was in question, the mature-faced speakers garnered greater agreement with their arguments, perhaps because maturity and age are associated with greater knowledge or wisdom (Brownlow, 1992).

Although facial aging increases perceptions of dominance and power, this relationship becomes curvilinear so that very mature faces are perceived as less trustworthy, less warm, and less dominant (Keating, Randall, & Kendrick, 1999). The degree to which a candidate's face appeared dominant influenced voters' perceptions of the candidate's competence which turned out to be more important in predicting actual election results than voter's perceptions of a candidate's attractiveness, familiarity, or youthfulness (Olivola & Todorov, 2010). However, a study by Verhulst, Lodge, and Lavine (2010) suggested that voters' perceptions of candidate attractiveness also influences their judgments about the candidate's competence and ultimately, voters' decisions about whom to cast their ballot.

Besides recognizing emotions and evaluating attractiveness, people tend to mirror or mimic facial expressions as well. In fact, research suggests that the tendency to mirror other people's facial expressions occurs automatically (Hess & Fischer, 2013), and often outside of conscious awareness (Dimberg & Thunberg, 1998). What's more, this reflex is so robust that people have a hard time suppressing it, even when told to do so (Dimberg et al., 2000). The tendency to mirror facial expressions extends beyond interacting face-to-face to other contexts such as watching people on television. One study, for example, found that people watching video clips of Ronald Reagan and Gary Hart tended to mirror the emotions the candidates were expressing (McHugo, Lanzetta, & Bush, 1991). Interestingly, however, people's attitude toward the politicians moderated these effects. Specifically, positive attitudes toward the candidates made people more likely to mimic the candidates' expressions of happiness while negative attitudes muted people's mimicry responses (McHugo et al., 1991). This, considered alongside research on embodied cognition discussed above, suggests that managing one's facial expressions can be critical to succeeding in televised debates.

Eye Contact

Among the most important facial cues related to social judgment involves the eyes. Eye contact, also called *facial gaze,* provides information about what a person is paying attention to (Baron-Cohen, 1995) and combines with emotional expressions to influence judgments about a person's intentions as friendly or hostile (Adams & Kleck, 2003; Hietanen, Leppanen, Peltoal, Linna-aho, & Ruuhiala, 2008). Interestingly, depending on the facial emotion being displayed, direct gaze can be perceived as affiliative and welcoming (e.g., Kwampe, Frith, Dolan, & Frith, 2001) but also as hostile and dominant (Adams, Gordon, Baird, Ambady, & Kleck, 2003). Research suggests that increased eye contact with audience members is associated with perceptions of a speaker's character, veracity, sociability, and persuasiveness (Burgoon et al., 1990; Kleinke, 1986). Further, direct gaze into a camera on the part of a speaker can increase audience members' belief in statements that are not obviously true or false (e.g., "Dogs can sniff the difference between twins," which happens to be true) (Kreysa, Kessler, & Schweinberger, 2016). Paradoxically, speakers are less persuasive when audience members return an extended, direct, gaze at speaker's faces when hearing counter attitudinal speeches on controversial topics (Chen, Minson, Schöne, & Heinrichs, 2013). The study's authors suggest that persuasive situations are often adversarial in nature. Adversarial situations cue dominance motivations in audience members, making direct eye contact feel hostile rather than affiliative. Unfortunately, little research has been conducted on televised debates and facial gaze perhaps because candidates in televised debates tend to maintain their gaze on the camera rather than the opponent. Some evidence suggests that maintaining gaze on the camera provides some advantage (Tiemens, 1970), although, as we will see in Chapter 5, this may depend on a number of factors.

Kinesics

Kinesics, as a general class of nonverbal behavior, involves messages communicated through body movement. Our discussion focuses on three categories of body movement: gestures, gait, and posture. Below, we discuss these categories and present a sampling of research related to all three. Because these movements often occur in concert, we finish this section with a discussion of more general research on holistic bodily movement.

Gestures

Gestures refer to arm and hand movements and can be broken into two subtypes. First, *emblems* are gestures that substitute for verbal messages and communicate meaning independent of speech. Examples include the American "OK" symbol (in which the tips of the index finger and thumb touch to create a circular shape) and waving a hand to communicate leave taking or greeting to someone in the distance. Second, *co-speech* gestures generally reinforce the linguistic portion of a message. Examples include *deictic* gestures, which involve pointing or other behaviors that connect what is said to a referent, *metaphoric* gesture, such as moving the hand right to left to indicate passage of time, and *beat* gestures that convey no specific meaning but add emphasis and keep the rhythm of the speech (such as pounding on a table in rhythm with emphasized words during a speech or chopping the air in a rhythmic fashion). Research indicates that both emblems and co-speech gestures, although nonlinguistic, are at least partially processed in the area of the brain that handles semantic information (e.g., Andric, Solodkin, Buccino, Goldin-Meadow, Rizzolatti, & Small, 2013). Moreover, people understand a speaker's meaning better when gestures are present rather than absent (e.g., Skipper, et al., 2009). Research also suggests that people who use more co-speech gestures are perceived as more credible and persuasive than people who do not (Maricchiolo, Gnisci, Bonaiuto, & Ficca, 2009).

Posture and Position

The topic of body posture and position includes forward/backward/sideways leaning, body orientation (facing toward or away from another), the location of the body within the communication setting, and transitions from one body position to another. Body movement communicates dominance, dynamism, energy, composure, and involvement. For example, taking up space with an open body position and hands extended from either side communicates dominance that generally creates an impression of greater credibility to an audience (e.g., Poggi & D'Errico, 2010). A direct body position (i.e., squarely facing an audience or opponent) communicates interest, attention, and involvement (Guerrero, 2005). Likewise, a moderately composed posture (neither ramrod straight nor slouching forward) and slight forward lean is associated with perceptions of both dominance and involvement. Research has also found that body rigidity is associated with lowered perceptions of speaker persuasiveness and speaker credibility (e.g., Burgoon et al., 1990; Maslow, Yoselson, & London, 1971).

Gait

Gait refers to a person's walking motion, which is related to a host of impressions. For example, people with a youthful and energetic gait are perceived to be more powerful and happier than people with older appearing walking styles regardless of the walker's apparent age (Montepare and Zebrowitz-McArthur, 1988). Moreover, a person whose gait is characterized by swinging limbs and expanding torso is judged to be more adventurous, extroverted, trustworthy, and warm, whereas a person with a more relaxed and leisurely walking style is perceived to be calm, relaxed, and even tempered (Thoresen, Vuong, & Atkinson, 2012). In U.S. presidential debates, gait probably plays a less important role than other nonverbal cues because only one format, the town hall, allows candidates to freely walk about the stage. However, the beginning and end of each debate typically features the candidates walking to the center of the stage, shaking hands, and then taking their places on the stage.

Gait, posture, and gesture movements are rarely observed in isolation. Most often, all three occur as parts of a behavioral package. Overall kinesic movement plays a role in the impressions speakers make on an audience. A number of studies indicate that people extract information from speakers' body motion that lead to impressions of biological sex (Koppensteiner & Grammer, 2011), personality (Koppensteiner & Grammer, 2010), and physical health (Kramer, Arend, & Ward, 2010). For example, two experiments (Kramer et al., 2010) examining the second 2008 presidential debate used visual editing techniques to reduce candidates' physical behavior to stick figure motion. As a consequence, study participants could not identify the candidates (i.e., Barack Obama and John McCain) from the stick figure movements. Results indicated that candidates' physical movements influenced perceptions of their health, which, in turn, predicted participants' voting behavior. A similar study (Koppensteiner, 2013) involving perceptions of Australian politicians' body movement found that study participants' perceptions of speakers' emotional stability were lower when speakers engaged in fast, jerky movements and higher when movements were slower and smoother.

Vocalics

Vocalic behaviors, sometimes called prosody or paralanguage, refer to the sound of a speaker's voice and include elements such as volume, rate of speech, pitch, vocal quality (i.e., "raspy" v. "smooth" sounding voice), pronunciation (which includes regional accent), enunciation (i.e., clarity), pauses, hesitations, and silences (e.g., Guerrero, Hecht, & Devito, 2008). Such cues provide information about the meaning of a message such as whether it should be interpreted as a statement or question. Moreover, the constellation of vocal variation across pitch, rate, pronunciation, etc., can be used to construct impressions of a speaker's social group membership. Research suggests, for example, that listeners can reliably identify information about a speaker such as sex, ethnicity, geographic origin, and age based on the speaker's vocal cues (e.g., Docherty & Foulkes, 2001). What's more, vocal cues can provide information about speaker's attitudes such as skepticism, doubt, enthusiasm, and boredom (Mitchell & Ross, 2013) and emotions such as sadness, happiness, fear, joy, and so on (e.g., Blanc & Dominey, 2003).

Vocal pitch is also associated with perceptions of social dominance (e.g., Klofstad, Anderson, & Peters, 2012). To examine this relationship, Klofstad (2016) conducted two studies. In the first, he manipulated the vocal pitch of purported political candidates and measured participants' voting preferences in each of five randomly created matchups between candidates of the same gender (i.e., male v. male and female v. female). Results of the study indicated that both male and female participants preferred candidates with lower-pitched voices. Interestingly, the preference for lower voice pitch was stronger for participants over 40 years of age and for participants who were more interested in politics in general.

In the second study, Klofstad (2016) asked participants to listen to vocal recordings of candidates who ran for U.S. House of Representative seats in the 2012 election. Although the general finding of the first study held (i.e., lower-pitched candidates won more elections), the effect was more complicated when the sex of the opponent was considered. Specifically, when male candidates faced male opponents, candidates with lower-pitched voices tended to prevail, as in the first study. However, when facing female opponents, males with the *higher*-pitched voices performed *better*. In other words, males with higher-pitched voices, compared to males with lower-pitched voices, were 25% more likely to win the election when their opponent was female.[1] In contests between two females, the effect of pitch was smaller, with just a .5% greater chance of winning the election for the higher pitched candidate. Klofstad suggested that the contrast between an especially low-pitched male competing against a female opponent may create an impression that the male is overly aggressive. Future experimental studies pitting male and female candidates against each other might help resolve this puzzling finding.

In addition to vocal dominance, people use vocalic cues to infer personality characteristics of communicators. For example, people perceive smaller variations in tone to be associated with higher competence and trustworthiness (Brooke & Ng, 1986; Helfrich & Wallbott, 1986). Research also finds perceived speaker confidence to be associated with infrequent, short pauses, faster speaking rate, and louder volume (Brown, 1980). Additionally, channel discrepancies (differences between what people say and how they say it) result in perceptions of anxiety (Bugental et al., 1976) and deceptiveness (e.g., Zuckerman et al., 1981). Interestingly, Baril and Stone (1984) found that legislators who were high in self-esteem and high in self-complexity were also more likely to engage in channel discrepant communication. Perhaps as a result, these legislators were less successful in being reelected and their careers were perceived to be less promising by fellow legislators.

Artifacts

Another way candidates' appearance is evaluated includes the artifacts that adorn them. As such, objects including jewelry, patriotic lapel pins, and other adornments can influence audience members' perceptions of a speaker's honesty, power, and status (Bickman, 1971; Burgoon, Dunbar, & Segrin, 2002). Although the influence of such artifacts has not been systematically studied in the context of televised political debates, it goes without saying that candidates attempt to take advantage of such appearance-based persuasive strategies. As an example, consider Andrew Yang, a Democratic candidate in the 2020 presidential election cycle. During one of the primary debates, rather than donning the usual American flag on his lapel, he wore a pin that simply read "MATH." Yang's pin became the subject of intense discussion on social media platforms, news programs, and newspaper coverage, helping him to draw attention to his candidacy in a crowded field of hopefuls. The pin, an acronym for "Make America Think Harder," served as Yang's rebuttal to President Trump's slogan, "Make America Great Again." In fact, in an earlier debate, Yang quipped, "We need to do the opposite of much of what we're doing now, and the opposite of Donald Trump is an Asian man who likes math" (Mazzara, 2019, October 15, para. 4). As part of the hoopla following these debates, Chris Cillizza (2019, October 19), a CNN political correspondent tweeted, "Andrew Yang 'MATH' pin deserves more attention." Likewise, the hashtag "MATH" trended on Twitter during the debate and the news site *Huffington Post Politics* called his pin, "The Surprise Star of the Democratic Debate."

Contact Cues

Scholars have examined two general types of contact cues. The first, proxemics, refers to physical distance between people as well as the way communicators claim territory. Edward Hall (1968) identified four interpersonal "zones" customarily employed by North Americans when communicating. These zones range from intimate distance (a radius of less than 18 inches) to public distance (a radius of 12 feet or further) and signal both relationship and status information. In general, the level of intimacy between the communicators decreases as space increases. Relatedly, immediacy is a constellation of behaviors that communicate attention, liking, and interest during interaction (Richmond, McCroskey, & Payne, 1987). Forward lean, reduced physical distance, and touch are proxemic indicators of immediacy. Proxemic cues also communicate social status. People with higher status tend to claim more space for themselves (Leffler, Gillespi, & Conaty, 1982; Lips, 1991), use more expansive gestures (Andersen & Bowman, 1999), and are more likely to invade the personal space of others (Burgoon, et al., 2002). Intruding into another's space is an attempt to communicate dominance in primates, both human and nonhuman.

The second contact cue, haptics, or physical touch, is a subset of proxemics. The most common form of touch between political candidates is the handshake. Before, and usually following, televised debates in the United States, the candidates are expected to engage in the handshake ritual. This tradition, running since the Carter-Ford debates in 1976 (Waxman, 2016, October 20), was broken in 2016 in the second and third debates when Clinton and Trump did not shake hands at the opening of the proceedings. The absence of handshakes seemed to communicate that the candidates' differences may be insurmountable and that the climate of the campaign had become historically acrimonious.

Over the years, at least two presidential debate handshakes have garnered public attention, suggesting that it is not simply their presence or absence that is important, but also their nature. The first was in 1980 when Ronald Reagan crossed the stage to shake Jimmy Carter's hand, catching Carter off-guard. A second instance involved speculation that George Bush strategically held the closing handshake a few beats longer following his debate with Michael Dukakis in 1988 as a way to emphasize his six-inch height advantage (Stanton, 2016, September 24).

Unfortunately, the social scientific literature on handshakes is sparse and what does exist mostly involves the point of view of the person shaking hands rather than observers' perceptions of others' handshakes (e.g., Chaplin, Phillips, Brown, Clanton, & Stein, 2000); none of the research examines perceptions of debaters specifically. The two studies that do examine observers' impressions suggest that seeing people shake hands (in business or social situations) increases ratings of trust, receptivity, and competence compared to observing people who do not shake hands (Burgoon et al., 1990; Dolcos, Sung, Argo, Flor-Henry, & Dolcos, 2012).

SUMMARY

Candidates' nonverbal behavior during presidential debates often catches the attention of viewers and media critics and can help create, maintain, or change voters' impressions and voting decisions. Whether we talk about Michael Dukakis's lack of emotional expression or Donald Trump invading Hillary Clinton's personal space, candidate nonverbal behavior plays an important role in viewers' perceptions of candidates. In this chapter we identified several characteristics of nonverbal communication and described a taxonomy of nonverbal behaviors that we will discuss throughout the rest of the book. In the following chapters we'll delve deeper into explanations and models for interpreting nonverbal behavior in presidential debates.

NOTE

1. There were no cases in which the male candidate had a higher-pitched voice than his female opponent. Therefore, the analysis looked at male candidates' pitch compared to the average pitch across all male candidates.

Chapter Three

Nonverbal Behavior of the Speaking Candidate

As the contest for United States president heated up in early days of September 2012, the incumbent, Barack Obama, had reason for optimism. His party's nominating convention not only provided a significant "bounce" in his polling numbers, by most indications, his projected lead in Electoral College votes was substantial (Obama ahead, 2012). By September's end, however, the Republican challenger, Willard "Mitt" Romney, was edging up on his rival. The election, it seemed, was approaching a dead heat (Whitesides, 2012). By early October, with just 30 days until the election, Romney hoped to capitalize on his momentum in the first of three televised debates. Meanwhile, during preparations, Obama revealed to his advisors a disdain for the televised election ritual. He went into the debate tired and irritable (Heilemann & Halperin, 2012).

    The evening's format, a "dual press conference," positioned the candidates at separate podiums, where each fielded questions from the moderator, Jim Lehrer, executive editor of PBS's television news program "NewsHour." As the debate progressed, Obama failed to conceal his annoyance with the spectacle; he seemed defensive, tired, and passive compared to Romney, who came across as energized and charming. When all was said and done, polls confirmed what Obama's advisors had feared. The president had been trounced. In fact, Obama's performance was so lackluster that viewer polls had Romney winning the debate by as much as a 40-point margin (CNN Poll, 2012). The overwhelming sentiment by viewers and media analysts alike involved the performative aspects of the debate rather than any argumentative knock-outs scored by Romney. "It was, in fact, one of the most inept performances I've ever seen by a sitting President," opined Joe Klein (2012, para. 1). Chris Cillizza, political analyst for the *Washington Post*, wrote,

"Obama's facial expressions seemed to alternate between grimly looking down at his podium and smirking when Romney said something with which he disagreed" (Cillizza, 2012, October 3, Para 3). An editorial in the *Chicago Tribune* was more pointed: "Romney was alert, energized and confident. Obama slumped his shoulders, smiled mostly to himself, and for some reason kept staring down. He was that guy at the meeting who's surreptitiously checking his email" (as quoted in The 2008 candidate, 2012, Para 2). Election forecasts trended accordingly, with some showing a small, but significant lead for Romney (Jones, 2012a).

Deeply concerned about their candidate's showing, Obama's advisors set sights on the second debate, working to improve both the substance of his message and nature of his delivery, a process described by John Heilemann and Mark Halperin as an "intervention." The debate's format, a town hall in which audience members pose questions, most likely played to the president's advantage. That said, judging by the turn-around in his demeanor, the coaching and practice proved transformative. As Timothy Stanley (2012, October 17) noted, "The difference between the two men was obvious in body language. Romney walked stiffly about the stage, as if in flip flops; Obama slid across the floor like he was skating on ice" (para. 1). To this, Bob Moser (2012, October 17) added, "The aggressiveness that served Romney so well against a listless Obama in Round One became a liability against a fired-up and focused president in the town hall format. Romney sneered and smirked through the president's answers. He bullied the moderator (though she refused to be cowed). He invaded Obama's space" (para 1 & 2). A Gallup poll following the debate confirmed a win for Obama by a 51% to 38% margin, reversing his devastating loss in the first debate (Jones, 2012b).

This example is but one of many in which press commentary and opinion polls illustrate the important role of nonverbal behavior in shaping voters' perceptions of political debaters. In the case of Obama and Romney, as in almost all televised presidential debates, split-screen and/or wide-angle shots enabled viewers to watch as candidates occupied the roles of speaker and non-speaker. As we will see in the next chapter, although candidates in the latter role are typically expected to bide their time in silence, they frequently, and sometimes effectively, upstage their opponents through the use of nonverbal behavior. In this chapter, however, we focus on the debater in the spotlight. Specifically, and consistent with our framework presented in Chapter 1, we consider several key functions of nonverbal behavior in debates. These include an examination of the ways in which speaking candidates create emotional bonds with their audience. In addition, we discuss how candidates create favorable impressions of themselves, and, alternatively, how candidates' nonverbal impression management can go wrong. Finally, we examine how speaking candidates might leverage their nonverbal behavior to attack an opponent's image. Although, as noted in Chapter 1, nonverbal behavior serves a number of additional functions, (e.g., nonverbal behavior can influence the audience's evaluation of candidates' arguments), because the lion's share of relevant research focuses on self-presentation, impression management, and relational messages, we limit this chapter to a discussion of those topics while reserving Chapters 6 and 7 for an examination of nonverbal behavior's persuasive and argumentative functions.

CREATING EMOTIONAL BONDS WITH AUDIENCES

A fundamental postulate of communication suggests that messages (verbal and nonverbal) have content and relational dimensions (Watzlawick, Bavelas, & Jackson, 1967). The content dimension involves the propositional substance or the "what" that is being communicated. The relational dimension involves cues that "indicate how two or more people regard each other, regard their relationship, or regard themselves within the context of the relationship" (Burgoon & Hale, 1984, p. 193). Although nonverbal messages can help understand the content level of a message's meaning (as we have seen in Chapter 2), its main role is relational in nature. Moreover, although people can say how they feel about others, nonverbal messages accompanying verbal messages offer multiple simultaneous cues that people use to make inferences about the relationship (Pfau & Kang, 1991) regardless of whether the topic of the verbal message is related to the relationship (e.g., Burgoon, Buller, & Woodall, 1989). For example, a greeting accompanied by a smiling face implies a different sort of relationship than a greeting accompanied by a pained expression.

In the context of political debates, relational messages play a key role in establishing a sense of connectedness between voters and candidates whether the relationships are real or imagined. As noted in Chapter 1, parasocial relationships form when audience members feel attached or close to a candidate (or celebrity) simply because they have come to know the candidate through the media (Horton & Wohl, 1956). Such relationships are one-sided yet powerful because they create an attachment between a candidate and a voter (Pfau, Diedrich, Larson, & Van Winkle, 1993). With this in mind, although televised debates are generally considered a one-to-many mass communication medium, candidates communicate para-interpersonal messages that build and maintain parasocial relationships with their audience (Johnson-Cartee & Copeland, 1997). Indeed, voters' parasocial relationships with candidates can have a powerful influence on voting behavior (e.g., Cohen & Holbert, 2018). Below, we discuss the ways in which candidates' nonverbal behaviors create impressions upon which such parasocial relationships are based.

CREATING AND UNDERMINING FAVORABLE IMPRESSIONS OF THE SELF AS SPEAKER: STRATEGIES OF SELF-PRESENTATION

Although candidates' verbal messages play an important role in impression formation and management, people are particularly influenced by nonverbal behavior when forming impressions. Indeed, in political contexts, visual stimuli can create powerful impressions in milliseconds (Olivola & Todorov, 2010), and people tend to believe that nonverbal behavior is more reliable in judging others' character than what people say, especially when a person's words and nonverbal behavior seem inconsistent (Mehrabian, 1968). Based on a review of several studies, Philpott (1983) suggested that nonverbal communication is a powerful influence on the meaning people extract from interactions. Perhaps more importantly, DePaulo (1992) highlighted the strategic nature of nonverbal behavior in how people present themselves in public:

> People try to regulate their nonverbal behaviors. They are rarely content to allow their nonverbal behaviors to be spontaneous and unselfconscious expressions of their dispositions or feelings or other internal states . . . Attempts at nonverbal regulation are often guided by self-presentational goals. That is, people use their nonverbal behaviors in attempts to claim identities that they find desirable and that they think others will find believable. (p. 211)

Five strategies of self-presentation identified by Jones and Pittman (1982) comprise particular impression management goals along with specific behaviors associated with each goal. The first strategy, *ingratiation*, aims to create an impression of likeability. Ingratiators try to present themselves as warm, humorous, reliable, and charming. Nonverbally, their strategies include smiling, warm vocal tones, relaxed posture, direct eye contact, and trying to appear physically attractive. Using these behaviors to induce liking can be tricky. Indeed, if the audience perceives them as inauthentic, the strategy can backfire, creating the impression of pandering to the audience.

Intimidation, a second strategy, is aimed at appearing serious, feared, and dangerous. A successful intimidator will communicate a willingness and ability to inflict psychological, physical, or some other kind of pain. Nonverbal behaviors that communicate intimidation might include dominance cues such as taking up space, violating another person's space, low vocal pitch, loud vocal volume, emphasizing physical size, and a furrowed brow. In addition, nonverbal expressions of anger are typical of this strategy. By way of example, Jones and Pittman (1982) noted,

> When the potential intimidator has enough power to be a credible aggressive threat, incipient anger is a very common controlling device in his relations with others. . . . President Eisenhower had a very mobile face whose expres-

sions ranged from the famous grin to a dark forbidding glower. The latter often appeared when a particular line of questioning began in a press conference, and we are tempted to speculate concerning the controlling potential of such "incipient rage," especially in view of our knowledge of his blood pressure problem. (p. 239)

Supplication, a third strategy, is the opposite of intimidation. Communicators using supplication attempt to create an impression of weakness, helplessness, or dependence. A stooped posture, indirect eye gaze, facial expressions of fear or sadness, and making oneself appear as small as possible are behaviors that can communicate weakness and dependence. Supplication as a self-presentation strategy is based on social norms obliging the provision of assistance to people who are infirmed, disabled or in some other way unable to obtain a resource held by the target of the supplication strategy (Jones & Pittman, 1982).

A fourth strategy, labeled *self-promotion*, includes behaviors aimed at appearing competent, qualified for a particular task, and respected. Self-promotion can include elements of both intimidation and ingratiation as competence can be both intimidating to some people and attractive to others. Adornment that suggests high social status such as tailored clothing, expensive jewelry, dominance cues, and ingratiation behaviors can all be strategically used to appear competent (Jones & Pittman, 1982).

The fifth self-presentation strategy is termed *exemplification*. Exemplification might be described as a form of self-promotion when the desired impression is integrity, honesty, charitableness, and moral worthiness (Jones & Pittman, 1982). Some aspects of Ralph Nader's (a six-time candidate for U.S. president) Spartan style of adornment and rejection of modern conveniences lent themselves to cultivating such impressions. Indeed, Nader's style of dress and self-denial was consistent with his desire to present himself as a frugal advocate for the common person, the environment, humane working conditions, and ending economic disadvantage. His exemplifying behaviors included driving himself to campaign events in an economy car, using public transportation whenever possible, wearing the same six pairs of shoes he had purchased for almost 20 years because he bought them at a discount, and dressing in suits he purchased at sales or outlet stores. Nader's ascetic approach to personal style earned him the moniker "conscientious objector to fashion" (Cornwell, 2016). Similarly, after law school, Senator Cory Booker, a Democratic candidate for 2020 presidential election, lived in a Newark housing project with the goal of helping fellow tenants. Donald Trump's campaign pledge to donate his salary to a variety of charities serves as another example of exemplification.

The five strategies identified by Jones and Pittman (1982) are not necessarily mutually exclusive and the behaviors communicators use to create impressions can serve dual purposes. For example, successful exemplification requires at least a modicum of self-promotion to be fully effective—a person's behaviors cannot serve as an example to others if no one knows about them. Self-promotion, at least in terms of communicating authority or power, requires some level of intimidation because with authority comes responsibility to enforce obligations. Moreover, ingratiation and intimidation are not necessarily incompatible. According to Goethals (2005, p. 96), John F. Kennedy's communication style with the press was "friendly-dominant," firm with a smile, inviting friendly and submissive responses in return. Likewise, despite what many referred to as his "honeyed voice," Ronald Reagan could speak "in a stern, forceful manner" (Goethals, 2005, p. 100). Below, we examine more closely how such strategies help candidates achieve their goals in creating and managing their identities in the minds of voters.

Candidate Impression Management Goals

Depending upon the formulation, several dimensions of character traits seem critical to candidates' overall impressions with voters. For example, Pfau (1987) suggested that three are most important, including "immediacy/affection (e.g., warmth, involvement, enthusiasm, and interest in receivers), similarity/depth (e.g., caring and friendliness), and receptivity/trust (e.g., sincerity, interest in communicating, and willingness to listen)." Similarly, Prysby (2008) utilized National Election Study data to analyze perceptions of the 2004 candidates, George W. Bush and John Kerry, along four dimensions: leadership (strong and decisive), competence (knowledgeable and intelligent), integrity (moral and honest), and empathy (perceptions that the candidate cares about them).

Based on our own review of literature, alongside our approach to the strategic use of nonverbal behavior in creating impressions, we organize the literature below based on three impressions shown to influence person perception and electoral success. These dimensions are similar to other formulations and are consistent with the self-presentation strategies listed above. The first dimension, *likeability/warmth,* is communicated via ingratiation strategies and aimed at creating perceptions of friendliness, likeability, and approachability. The second dimension, *competence,* is communicated through self-promotion and intimidation (or dominance displays), and aimed at creating perceptions of leadership, intelligence, and the capability to accomplish goals. The third dimension, *trustworthiness,* is communicated via exemplification and ingratiation strategies and aimed at creating perceptions of honesty and sincerity (e.g., Abele, Cuddy, Judd, & Yzerbyt, 2008; Brambilla, Rusconi, Sacchi, & Cherubini, 2001; Cuddy, Fiske, & Glick, 2008). Importantly, perceptions of these dimensions are significantly influenced by a source's nonverbal behavior. Three facial expressions, for example, have received considerable scholarly attention, including displays of happiness-reassurance, anger-threat, and fear-evasion (see Stewart, Salter, & Mehu, 2013, for a review). In the sections that follow, we examine perceptions associated with these expressions and other forms of nonverbal behavior.

Nonverbal Behaviors Associated with Candidate Impression Management

Impressions of Likeability/Warmth

Ever since Sam Adams/Roper Starch conducted a poll in October of 2000 asking which presidential candidate "would you rather have a beer with," the issue of candidate likeability has been seen by political analysts as an important issue (Steinhorn, 2015)—and rightly so. Indeed, appearing likeable is a particularly important impression management goal for political candidates and can make or break a candidate's relationship with voters. By way of example, a Barbara Lee Family Foundation (2016) survey of more than 1,000 likely voters in 2016 indicated that 84% of men and 90% of women said liking a candidate is important in deciding whom to support. Interestingly, respondents who were Latina, women living in the Southern United States, people holding strong partisan views, and less educated respondents were most likely to say that liking a candidate was very important in their voting decisions.

Candidates can employ several ingratiation strategies in creating an impression of likeability/warmth. Generally speaking, political candidates who are perceived as friendly, sincere, and similar to voters represent the positive side of this dimension, whereas candidates who are perceived as bellicose, aloof, pretentious, and indifferent to the needs of voters represent the negative side (Hall, Coats, & Smith LeBeau, 2005). In addition, leaders who communicate positive emotions not only tend to be perceived favorably, their positive emotional displays spread like a contagion to followers (Bono & Ilies, 2006).

The most studied nonverbal channel associated with perceptions of the warmth/likeability dimension involves candidates' facial expressions, which provide a rich source of information about a person's emotional experience (Ekman, 1985). In fact, one of the best predictors of liking a person is an assessment that the person is friendly (i.e., that the person has positive attitudes toward others). People who appear friendly tend to be more approachable, well liked, admired, and trusted than people who appear threatening (Sofer, Dotsch, Wigboldus, & Todorov, 2015).

How, then, might friendliness be signaled? Previous research indicates that ratings of friendliness are positively associated with facial displays of happiness-reassurance, which involve moving the corners of one's mouth upward and to the sides, a loose jaw, and engagement of the orbital muscles (which control facial muscles around the eye) that signal a genuine (Duchenne) smile. In contrast, simulated (i.e., fake or masking) smiles lack orbital contraction and lead to lower ratings of friendliness (e.g., Stewart & Ford Dowe, 2013). In addition to these cues, raised eyebrows and a raised chin also signal affiliative intentions.

In political contexts, previous research and polling data are consistent with the notion that friendly, affiliative facial cues are positively associated with voters' impressions of candidate likeability. In one study, for example, Wasike (2019) examined nonverbal behaviors, particularly facial expressions, in the second of three debates between 2016 presidential candidates Donald Trump and Hillary Clinton. Clinton was found to have engaged in a significantly higher frequency of smiling, head raising, and eyebrow lifting (all signs of affinity) than Trump. In contrast, although Trump displayed a relaxed mouth (another sign of affinity) at a higher frequency than Clinton, he also displayed more hostile behaviors (e.g., showing his lower teeth and hostile stares). Although Clinton's facial expressions were probably not the sole cause of audience reactions, a Gallup poll (Saad, 2016, October 13) of about 1,000 debate viewers found Clinton to be relatively more likeable than Trump based on the survey item "Was more likeable" (59%–31%) (although both candidates' overall poll numbers indicated they were perceived unfavorably coming into the debates). In another study, the official campaign photos of 672 Japanese candidates for Lower House seats and 286 Australian candidates for lower house found that candidates pictured with full smiles garnered 2% (Japan) to 5% (Australia) more of the vote when controlling for incumbency, gender, and number of candidates in the race (Horiuchi, Komatsu, & Nakaya, 2012).

In addition to facial expressions, gestures play an important role in the development of a leader's affective valence. For example, Talley and Temple (2015) examined people's perceptions of leaders based on hand gestures. Three types of positive hand gestures were identified. Specifically, "community hands" position the palms up or vertical to the ground; "humility hands" are clasped in front of the person at waist level; and "steepling hands" form a triangle with the fingertips of both hands touching and pointing up. In addition, the study identified three types of defensive hand gestures, including the "hands in pockets," "crossed arms," and "hands behind the back" gestures. Results of the study indicated that leaders who exhibited either no hand gestures or defensive hand gestures were perceived to be less involved, warm, and socially attractive than leaders who exhibited positive hand gestures.

Despite the value of such research, it is important to note that facial expressions and gestures are not perceived in isolation. To be sure, nonverbal messages are typically displayed in packages. With that in mind, the concept of nonverbal immediacy refers to a group of behavioral cues, which, together, communicate the "directness and intensity of interaction" (Burgoon, Birk, & Pfau, 1990; Mehrabian, 1967, p. 325), while also signaling warmth, availability, involvement, and decreased psychological or physical distance between communicators (Pfau, Diedrich, Larson, & Van Winkle, 1993). For instance, speakers who have an expressive face, friendly sounding voice, make eye contact, and smile frequently communicate warmth and approachability, which, in turn, makes them more likeable in the eyes of the audience (Burgoon, Dunbar, & Segrin, 2002). Given what we have learned so far, it is not surprising that a speakers' level of immediacy predicts his or her success in changing an audience's attitudes and behaviors (Burgoon, Coker, & Coker, 1986; Segrin, 1993).

In the wider literature on message effects, research suggests that immediacy is an important dimension for speaker success (As such, we revisit the concept in Chapter 6). Likewise, in the history of political communication, some candidates have clearly been more immediate in their behaviors than others. By way of example, consider Bill Clinton's response to a question during the 1992 town hall presidential debate. A woman in the audience asked each candidate to discuss how the national debt and lagging economy personally affected them. After his opponents answered, Bill Clinton directly approached the woman, standing only a few feet from her, and made strong eye contact. In a warm and conversational tone, he talked about how being governor of a small state made him feel connected and personally affected by events in the lives of his constituents. His nonverbal connection with the woman both visually and vocally reinforced his verbal message, making him appear relatable and compassionate. Clinton's response is widely recognized as one of the key dramatic moments in the debate (e.g., see Pfau, 2002; Zakahi & Hacker, 1995).

As another example, consider Sarah Palin, the Republican's 2008 nominee for vice president as described by Schroeder (2016):

> For one brief moment, before her public image hardened into self-parody, Sarah Palin stood poised to infuse something fresh into American presidential politics: a down-to-earth, next-door-neighbor sensibility that prized common sense over calculation, the wisdom of the people over the wisdom of the elites. Unfortunately . . . as she made her debut on the vice presidential debate stage, Sarah Palin had degenerated into a national punchline. Even a face-saving performance against Joe Biden could not wipe away the negative perceptions that clung to her like barnacles. . . . In predebate coverage on NBC, Chuck Todd put it more bluntly: "The goal, really, is for Sarah Palin to survive." Survive she did, with an ease that belied her previous tribulations. Palin's performance against Biden brought back echoes of the perky hockey mom who enthralled the Republican convention. Winking, grinning, dropping her *g*'s, and pointedly ignoring the moderator. (pp. 197–198)

According to Schroeder (2016), in preparation for that debate, Biden's sparring partner, Jennifer Granholm, challenged and baited Biden, accurately impersonating Palin with all but one exception. "I missed the wink," she confessed (p. 107).

Although ingratiation strategies can be effective in building voters' parasocial rapport with candidates, inauthentic, or "illicit," ingratiation has the potential to do more damage than good (Jones & Pittman, 1982). One drawback to using ingratiation behavior is the *ingratiator's dilemma*. As described by Jones and Pittman, the dilemma occurs when ingratiation behavior appears inauthentic, suggesting that the ingratiator might have ulterior motives for creating a friendly relationship. For example, compliments from students might appear inauthentic to a professor who controls their grades. An important indicator of authenticity involves the consistency of verbal and nonverbal behaviors. For example, smiling while delivering a verbal attack, faking a smile, or masking (e.g., using a smile to hide another emotion) can create perceptions of inauthenticity in a person's ingratiation behavior (Jones & Pittman, 1982) which, in turn, can damage voters' perceptions of candidates' sociability and trustworthiness (Gong & Bucy, 2016).

As a case in point, consider Mitt Romney's behavior in 2012. Although Obama's performance in the first presidential debate was a debacle (see Chapter 4 and above), Romney faced criticism as well. Not only had he flip-flopped on certain issues (e.g., opposing a federal healthcare plan that resembled his own plan while governor in Massachusetts), some critics suggested that his nonverbal behavior seemed inauthentic as well. Judis (2012), for example, referenced a video that was produced by James Lipton (Lipton, n.d.), host of the television show "Inside the Actor's Theater." In it, Lipton pointed to examples from Republican primary debates in which Romney's behavior looked forced and inauthentic. According to Lipton, for instance, Romney's laugh seemed "mirthless," and his smile, "inauthentic" because his lips and mouth expressed joy but his eyes displayed "no pleasure." Lipton's analysis is consistent with previous research. Specifically, Ekman (e.g., Ekman, 1985; Ekman & Friesen, 1982) reported that posed smiles (covering neutral affect) and masking smiles (covering an emotion such as fear or anger) are characterized by a lack of movement in the muscles surrounding the eyes, and are often longer or shorter in duration and intensity than smiles that reflect actual enjoyment. In general, people can detect posed/masking expressions from authentic ones with better than chance accuracy (e.g., DePaulo, Lanier, & Davis, 1983).

Impressions of Trustworthiness

Trustworthiness refers to how sincere candidates appear to be about the assertions they make, and whether they appear to believe those assertions are valid (Hovland, Janis, & Kelley,1953). Previous research indicates that trustworthiness, and the related concept of integrity, are important to voters. In fact, during voter interviews, candidate honesty is among the most frequently mentioned character judgements (Garber, 1984), and integrity has been among the most mentioned character traits of U.S. presidential candidates in the National Election Studies (Miller, Wattenberg, & Malanchuck, 1986). That said, research indicates that trustworthiness and integrity are important perceptual criteria beyond U.S. borders. Indeed, in one examination of national election data, perceptions of trustworthiness reliably predicted election results across several Western democracies, including Australia, Germany, Sweden, and the United States (Ohr & Oscarsson, 2005). A similar study reported integrity to be an important factor in survey respondents' judgments of politicians across the U.K., Canada, and the United States (Pancer, Brown, & Barr, 1999). The implications of these results seem especially clear when considered alongside additional research, which indicated that debate performances can change an audience's predebate perceptions of a candidate's character (Wanzeried, Powell, & Franks, 1989). Specifically, voters' perceptions of candidates' trustworthiness is an important element in a candidate's image management strategy.

Although not always accurate in their appraisals, people use several nonverbal cues to judge candidates' trustworthiness, including exemplification strategies that communicate sincerity, honesty, and authenticity. There are many examples of candidates engaging in photo opportunities or using advertisements to cultivate an image of moral integrity by serving meals to homeless people, attending religious services, building houses for the poor and so forth. In televised debates these qualities are often communicated by combining self-promotional verbal statements that highlight candidates' exemplary behavior along with attempts to appear sincere in their delivery. In addition, wearing artifacts that symbolize patriotism (e.g., flag pins on lapels) communicates dedication to the country while stoking feelings of nationalism among some audiences (Kemmelmeier & Winter, 2008).

Above all, creating perceptions of trustworthiness requires candidates to avoid behaviors that audience members associate with deceptiveness. Cues such as averted eye contact, strained facial expressions, and nervous movements are among the most often used signs for inferring deceptiveness (e.g., see Granhag, Giolla, Sooniste, Stromwell, & Lui-Jonsson, 2016; Riggio, Tucker, & Throckmorton, 1987). In addition, vocalic qualities such as increased speech errors, hesitations, higher pitch, misarticulation, and slower speaking rate are associated with perceived deceptive communication (Zuckerman, DePaulo, & Rosenthal, 1981). In contrast, maintaining eye contact with the audience, pleasant rather than nervous facial expressions, facial expressiveness, calm rather than nervous body movements, and avoiding self and object adapters (such as nervously pulling at clothing, touching the face, handling objects like pens) have been found to increase audience perceptions of speaker trustworthiness (e.g., Beebe, 1974; Burgoon, Birk, & Pfau, 1990; Bond, Omar, Mahmoud, & Bonser, 1990; Kreysa, Kessler, & Schweinberger, 2016). Of course, in televised contexts, what counts as "eye contact" is tricky. For example, according to Sauter (1994), in the 1976 vice-presidential debates, Bob Dole addressed his remarks to the panelists when answering questions, which, to television viewers, gave him "an off-camera focus rather than creating a sense of eye contact with the viewer" (p. 62). In contrast, his opponent, Walter Mondale, directed his remarks to the television audience and the camera.

In addition to face and body movements, a person's physical appearance and attractiveness also influence perceptions of trustworthiness. A study examining speaker's persuasiveness found that a baby-faced speaker (i.e., a face with neonate characteristics such as rounded face and comparatively large eyes) was perceived to be more trustworthy than a speaker with a mature face, even when participants were induced to believe both speakers' credibility was in question (Brownlow, 1992). Additionally, politicians with younger looking faces were judged to be more honest than candidates with older, more mature looking faces (Keating, Randall, & Kendrick, 1999). That said, there could be a tradeoff between perceptions of honesty and experience. Specifically, in political contexts, babyfacedness is positively associated with honesty, but negatively associated with perceptions of males' political sophistication (Lee, 2013).

Second, research indicates that typical-looking faces (e.g., around the mean level of attractiveness) evoke stronger perceptions of trustworthiness than faces that are either very attractive or very unattractive (Sofer, Dotsch, Wigboldus, & Todorov, 2015). Similarly, faces that remind us of ourselves are perceived to be more credible, likeable, and persuasive than faces that do not (Richards & Hample, 2016). Finally, a study by Bucy (2000) found that politicians displaying inappropriate facial expressions in reaction to news events (such as smiling in response to a tragic story) were rated lower in credibility than politicians with expressions that matched the tone of the story.

Several features related to vocalics have also been associated with audience perceptions of speaker credibility. By way of example, speakers whose rate of speech is faster than average are perceived to be less trustworthy (although more dynamic, extroverted, and competent) than speakers whose rate is closer to average (Burgoon, et al., 1990). Similarly, pauses that are too long, vocal volume that is too quiet, vocal pitch that is monotone, and incorrect tonal inflections can negatively influence comprehensibility of the verbal message and perceptions of a source's character (Burgoon et al., 1990: De Meo et al. 2011; Rodero, Mas, & Blanco, 2014; Rognoni 2012).

Before concluding this section, it is important to note that the influence of trustworthiness may be moderated by additional factors. First, discrepancies between verbal and nonverbal communication can lead to positive or negative perceptions of candidates depending on the underlying motives attributed to such discrepancies. For example, Grebelsky-Lichtman (2016) identified four functional combinations of verbal and nonverbal messages in three Israeli televised debates occurring in 1996, 1999, and 2009. "Supportive nondiscrepancies" consisted of a supportive verbal behavior (agreement, encouragement, appreciation, etc.) combined with a supportive nonverbal behavior (e.g., open hands, head nods, leaning forward, etc). "Challenging nondiscrepancies" consisted of challenging verbal (accusations, rejections, threats, etc.) and challenging nonverbal behaviors (folding arms, clenched fists, sharp cutting motions, etc.). The combination of a challenging verbal message with supportive nonverbal message was labeled "adaptive discrepancy" while the combination of a supportive verbal message with a challenging nonverbal message was labeled "leakage discrepancy." Losers in these debates were more likely than winners to engage in leakage discrepancies. Grebelsky-Lichtman suggested that audiences believe nonverbal behavior reveals a person's true feelings, which results in interpreting candidates' supportive verbal behaviors as inauthentic and deceptive when they "leak" their true negative feelings nonverbally.

On the other hand, winners in these debates were more likely than losers to engage in adaptive discrepancies. Perhaps viewers saw the supportive nonverbal behavior as mitigating face threats in a civil and composed way compared to employing both verbal and nonverbal challenges. Finally, winners were more likely than losers to engage in supportive nondiscrepancies while both winning and losing candidates engaged in challenging nondiscrepancies about equally. In general, it is interesting to see that channel discrepant messages can be perceived positively when it appears that the intent of the discrepancy is to soften the blow of an attack, but not when the discrepancy is perceived as an untrustworthy attempt to conceal candidates' actual opinions about their opponents.

Second, the influence of trustworthiness on voting decisions may be moderated by perceptions of competence. In one study (Chen, Jing, & Lee, 2014), for example, perceptions of trustworthiness only factored into participants' voting decisions if the candidate was perceived to be competent. Trustworthiness, however, did not play a role if the candidate was perceived to be low in competence. To voters, an incompetent but trustworthy voter may not inspire confidence in the candidate's ability to lead. We now turn our attention to the third important image component of successful candidates, competence.

Impressions of Competence

Research suggests that voters' perception of a candidate's competence is among the most important impressions they consider in elections (Kinder, Peters, Abelson, & Fiske, 1980; Miller, Wattenberg, & Malanchuck,1986; Trent, Mongeau, Trent, Kendall, & Cushing, 1993). With that in mind, how might such impressions be fostered? According to Jones and Pittman (1982), self-promotion strategies aim to create an impression of competence, expertise, and leadership ability. Verbally, this is accomplished by discussing accomplishments, experience, and claiming traits related to competent leadership. The danger, of course, is that self-promoters risk being perceived as fraudulent, conceited, or defensive (Jones & Pittman, 1982). By way of example, few candidates for U.S. president have utilized verbal self-promotion as pronouncedly and brazenly as Donald Trump, who, during the 2016 Republican primary debates, boasted about his billionaire status, his success in business, and his education at an elite business school. Trump, however, is not the only candidate to tout accomplishments. Indeed, it is common to find candidates pointing to previous achievements such as distinguished military service or policy successes. In a more recent example, Democratic candidate Pete Buttigieg demonstrated his ability to speak Spanish when he engaged in a brief interaction in Spanish with debate moderator Jose Diaz-Balart from the Telemundo network at the beginning of the first Democratic primary debate in June of 2019 (Rocha, Merica, Krieg, Bradner, Wills, & Blaine, 2019, June 28).

Nonverbally, self-promotion can bolster such claims or convey success more indirectly by helping candidates look, sound, and move like a leader. According to Jones and Pittman (1982), creating the appearance of competent leadership often requires some degree of strategic intimidation. Previous research supports this notion, indicating that people often infer competence from observing candidates' nonverbal social dominance cues (e.g., Chen, Jing, & Lee, 2014; Lord, de Vader, & Alliger, 1986; Todorov, Mandisodza, Goren, & Hall, 2005). In the paragraphs that follow, we discuss how perceptions are related to candidates' height, faces, vocalics, and kinesics.

First, with regard to height, anecdotal accounts of previous political debates suggest that candidates' physical stature plays an important role in how they are perceived. By way of example, consider Goethals's (2005) account of the 1976 presidential debates:

> One immediate impression from the outset of the first Carter-Ford debate was that Ford was favored by the stage setting. The candidates stood behind large wooden podiums, unlike the simple orchestra director-style podiums used by Nixon and Kennedy. Gerald Ford, a large former football player at the University of Michigan, leaned over his podium and seemed to dominate it. Carter, a smaller man, stood behind his podium, and looked more like a choirboy than

an athlete. The initial visual impression favored Ford. He appeared more commanding than Carter. (p. 104)

With this in mind, it is not surprising to find candidates attempting to compensate for differences in height. As we'll see in Chapter 5, for example, pre-debate negotiations have frequently focused on the design of podiums and/or lifters that make presidential candidates appear taller, perhaps for good reason. Indeed, empirical research indicates that taller people are perceived to be more competent leaders (Stulp, Buunk, Verhulst, & Pollet, 2013), more convincing (Young & French, 1996), and more physically intimidating (Carrier, 2011) than shorter people. In U.S. presidential elections, taller candidates receive more votes and are more likely to be reelected than their shorter opponents (McCann, 2001; Murray & Schmitz, 2001; Stulp et al., 2013). In fact, according to Judge and Cable (2004), no presidential candidate shorter than the average U.S. citizen has been elected since 1896. Interestingly, social dominance is itself associated with the perception of height. Winning politicians are perceived to be taller than losing candidates (Higham & Carment, 1992) and people tend to perceive their favored candidate to be taller than the opponent (Sorokowski, 2010).

In addition to candidates' height, judgments about candidates' facial shape and expressions are especially important in televised debates. As we'll see in Chapter 5, the visual structure of debate broadcasts emphasize candidates' faces. As Shah et al. (2016) pointed out regarding television coverage using split-screen technology, "Consistently and prominently filling the screen with candidates' faces allows viewers to monitor expressions, demeanor, and gaze, details individuals naturally account for when evaluating politicians' self-presentation" (p. 1812). Considering this alongside what this chapter has already said about the importance of candidates' perceived competence, a question that naturally follows asks, what specific features of candidates' faces are associated with such perceptions?

One of the more interesting lines of research on candidate faces and voters' impressions of competence involves research participants' ability to predict election winners, and their inclination to cast votes, based on competence assessments of candidates' faces. Todorov and others (Hall et al., 2009; Hassin & Trope, 2000; Todorov, Said, Engell, & Oosterhof, 2008; Todorov, Said, & Verosky, 2011) suggest that, as a survival skill, people make spontaneous judgements about people based on physical appearance, particularly, facial features. What's more, these judgements occur in just milliseconds after exposure to candidates' faces (Olivola & Todorov, 2010). Remarkably, people reliably identify winning candidates and predict vote share in actual elections from pairs of photos in U.S. Senate (Todorov et al., 2005), U.S. House (Atkinson, Enos, & Hill, 2009; Hall et al., 2009), Finnish (Poutvaara, Jordahl, & Berggren, 2009), and French elections (Antonakis & Dalgas

2009).[1] In most of these studies, researchers statistically controlled other, potentially confounding, perceptions such as attractiveness and sociability.

Such research provides a compelling example of the connection between attributions of candidates' competence and social dominance displays. As Riggio and Riggio (2010) suggested,

> We propose that individuals are not seeing facial characteristics that directly indicate competence in terms of experience, or specific skills, knowledge, or qualifications (including intelligence) when they are asked to pick the more "competent" face. . . . Instead, it seems that such competence judgments are based on a rapid assessment of facial cues indicating two factors: the "strength" of the target, reflected in cues of dominance/threat, and the degree to which one may safely approach/interact with a new person. (p. 120)

In short, then, perceptions of dominance (and approachability) contribute to overall impressions of a person's competence. In addition, research indicates that perceptions of a person's competence/dominance are influenced by the person's facial structure as well as the person's facial expressions. First, the structure of competent appearing faces is characterized by greater jaw angularity, less distance between eyes and eyebrows, facial maturity (older looking faces), thin lips, broad chins, a receding hairline, and attractiveness (facial symmetry), all features that were judged to be more masculine, dominant, and characteristic of leadership (e.g., Keating et al. 1981; Little, Burriss, Jones, & Roberts, 2007; Olivola & Todorov, 2010). Similarly, as noted earlier, baby-faced and feminine appearing faces are judged to be less competent (although more trustworthy) than masculine and mature-looking faces. Finally, preferences for socially dominant-appearing faces may depend upon the contextual problems confronting the world that candidates will govern. For example, Little et al. (2007) found that participants favored a candidate who appeared more masculine and dominant to govern during wartime, but a candidate who appeared less dominant to govern during peacetime.

Second, candidates' facial expressions of emotions are also associated with perceptions of social dominance/competence. Anger-threat expressions involving lowered eyebrows, less smiling, showing lower teeth, and frowning are associated with perceptions of social dominance and masculinity (Bucy, 2016; Stewart, Salter, & Mehu, 2013). Happiness-reassurance displays (i.e., expressions related to ingratiation cues) combined with anger-threat cues tend to be associated with more positive impressions of candidate competence (Bucy, 2016). Expressions of fear or evasion communicate submission or weakness and include raised eyebrows, lip compression, and averted gaze. Although the valence of anger-threat expression evaluations depends on both context and partisan alignment, fear-evasion displays are almost universally perceived negatively by audiences (Lanzetta et al., 1985).

Before concluding our discussion of competence as it relates to candidates' faces, it is important to note, as we have in previous chapters, that nonverbal behaviors, including facial features and expressions, are not perceived in isolation. In addition, research (Spezio, Loewsch, Gosselin, Mattes, & Alvarez, 2012) indicates that people's automatic judgments of candidates' competence are also influenced by information contained in photographs of candidates' faces such as hairstyle, clothing, and background objects. In short, attributions of competence are based on a variety of cues, suggesting that more research is needed to determine which cues are most influential.

In addition to height and characteristics of the face, another set of social dominance cues involves the vocal channel. Specifically, speech that is louder and faster, with shorter response latencies, and greater pitch variety is perceived as more dominant than speech that is slower, softer, and more monotone (Burgoon, Dunbar, & Segrin, 2002). Likewise, dysfluencies (audible vocal stumbles) negatively affect perceptions of speakers' competence and, in turn, speakers' persuasiveness (Carpenter, 2012). A similar pattern of results has been found in studies of presidential debates. Boulton (2006), for example, analyzed vocalic behavior in the 2004 U.S. presidential debates between incumbent George W. Bush and challenger John Kerry. Kerry, who was judged to be the winner in viewer polls, engaged in significantly fewer instances of speech dysfunctions. In the candidates' initial 120-second responses to moderator questions, 30% of Bush's time and about 17% of Kerry's time consisted of silent pauses. In the 30-second follow ups, about 21% of Bush's time, and 17% of Kerry's time consisted of silent pauses. Bush also engaged in more filled pauses (e.g., "er," "uh"), more phonetic repetitions ("b-but"), and non-stylistic repetitions (e.g., "it's it's it's it's not what the American people thought they were getting") than Kerry. In polls following the debate, 60% of viewers thought Kerry expressed himself more clearly than Bush (Poll: Kerry tops Bush, 2004). In the second presidential debate, a virtual tie in viewers' minds (Poll: Bush, Kerry Even, 2004), Bush significantly decreased the number of speech dysfunctions, which might reflect his greater confidence in dealing with the topics of the second debate: foreign policy and the wars in Iraq and Afghanistan. In any case, Bush was perceived to be more likeable than Kerry in both debates. Perhaps Kerry's more structured, formal sounding speech increased perceptions of his competence but also made him appear less relatable. As Julian Coman (2004, September 4, para. 17) wrote, "Sen Kerry was a champion debater in his youth but his reputation for public speaking has plummeted; . . . he has come across as aloof and aristocratic."

As we discussed in Chapter 2, vocal pitch is another vocalic cue related to perceptions of social dominance and competence. Unlike simple vocal pitch, research suggests that some vocal cues related to perceptions of social dominance are processed, at least in part, automatically. Consider, for example, investigations of fundamental frequency (F_0), or vocal pitch below .5 kHz. F_0 communicates important social information even though the verbal content is muffled and not processed consciously. Consistent with the general trend in studies of vocal pitch, Gregory and Gallagher (2002) compared candidates' F_0 in presidential debates between 1960 and 2000. Their study found that candidates with the lower pitch in the F_0 range won six out of eight debates (according to post debate polls) and won all the elections in that time frame.

In addition to comparisons of overall F_0 between candidates, Kalkhoff and Gregory (2008) examined the degree to which candidates adapt F_0 to each other. Earlier research based on communication accommodation theory found lower status individuals tended to adapt their vocal pitch on the F_0 frequency toward that of higher status people (Gregory & Webster, 1996). Specifically, Kalkhoff and Gregory (2008) examined patterns of adaptation in F_0 during the 2008 debate between Barack Obama and John McCain. They found that McCain had a small advantage in overall vocal dominance (i.e., lower F_0) for each of the three debates. Over time, however, McCain's vocal dominance seemed to peak around the middle of each debate while Obama's vocal dominance started lower, then increased and overtook McCain's in each debate. Given that the most recent information about a person tends to be best remembered and most influential (Fang, van Kleef, & Sauter, 2018), Kalkhoff and Gregory suggested that Obama's approach may reflect a rope-a-dope strategy, whereby he waited patiently for McCain to make mistakes and then, with increasing force, responded verbally and nonverbally, helping him to win the debates according to post debate polls (e.g., Jones, 2008).

This is not to say that changes in vocal dominance necessarily reflect a conscious decision by candidates. To be sure, although vocal dominance can modulate over the course of a debate, research suggests that dominance differences, as well as adaptations during a conversation, reflect status or power differences between communicators (Gregory & Webster, 1996). An embodied approach might suggest that cognitive processing will translate into bodily (i.e., nonverbal behavior) responses that reflect a candidate's beliefs about the situation. Consequently, holding the lead in an election potentially creates a sense of who is in control at the time, which, in turn, is reflected in each candidate's embodied response, in this case, vocal dominance. At the time, both candidates were likely aware that based on a number of polls, Obama had a six- to ten-point lead heading into the 2008 debates (RealClear Politics, n.d.). With that in mind, McCain's early advantage in vocal dominance in each debate may reflect an unconscious attempt to gain control. In contrast, Obama's measured, yet escalating vocal dominance may reflect not only his status as front runner in the election, but also his (and perhaps McCain's) belief that he was winning the debate (as viewer polls later confirmed), thereby taking control in the power ritual.

In addition to the nonverbal behaviors discussed thus far, research suggests that kinesic behaviors such as bodily motion, posture, and gestures also communicate competence and social dominance. That said, in the context of political debates, politicians' display of such behaviors is undoubtedly affected by the format of the specific event. Because most U.S. primary and general election presidential debates involve candidates standing at a podium, there are fewer opportunities to observe candidates' kinesic behavior outside of gestures, whereas town hall formats provide more opportunities for movement.

With regard to gestures, in general interactions, finger pointing, steepling hands, and expressive gestures tend to be perceived as dominant (Burgoon, et al., 2002). In political contexts, Grabe and Bucy (2009) identified gestures related to affinity and defiance. Affinity gestures, which are used to ingratiate, communicate friendliness. Examples include showing approval with a "thumbs up" or displaying an open palm rather than a pointed finger when making a case. Defiance gestures, which are used to intimidate, communicate opposition. Examples include finger wagging, shaking one's head, or pounding a fist.

With regard to the body, research suggests that, in general interactions, people displaying relaxed postures and expansive body orientations are perceived as more dominant than people displaying rigid postures and closed body orientations (Burgoon et al., 2002). Similarly, in political contexts, Koppensteiner, Stephan, and Jäschke (2016) found that speakers exhibiting expansive body posture and expansive body movements (e.g., arms held wide apart) were judged to be more dominant, but less trustworthy, than politicians with less expansive nonverbal behavior. Of course, candidates who use dominance displays during debates, and intimidation strategies in general, risk being perceived as bullies, and even worse, perhaps, if they fail to appear threatening, topics we'll discuss in Chapters 4 and 8.

Another way candidates can damage their impressions is by failing to engage in social dominance displays when they are expected. By way of example, Gong and Bucy's (2016) analysis of the 2012 presidential debates indicated that at least some dominance, as opposed to submissiveness, is expected in debate contexts. In the first debate, for example, Barack Obama's infrequent use of defiance gestures (and facial expression) were interpreted as inappropriate.

Besides their link to impressions of competence, dominance displays are in and of themselves an important element in televised political debates. As Kalkhoff and Gregory (2008) frame them, televised debates are "power rituals" in which candidates vie to control the tempo and tone of the event by exerting social dominance both verbally and nonverbally. In other words, the competitive nature of debates places a premium on social dominance and control, suggesting that candidates gather support and "win" contests, in part, by appearing more powerful and capable than their opponents. Although verbal communication is important in contesting such power, the influence of nonverbal dominance displays is particularly potent because audience members are often less aware of how these cues influence their decisions (Gregory & Gallagher, 2002).

MANAGING IMPRESSIONS OF THE OPPONENT

Thus far, we have seen that nonverbal behavior can be leveraged strategically to create and manage a candidate's impression on an audience during televised debates. Along with managing one's own impression, however, nonverbal behavior can be used to attack or undermine an opponent's image (see Chapter 1). One memorable example occurred moments before the 1980 U.S. presidential debate between Ronald Reagan (the challenger) and Jimmy Carter (the incumbent). Given this was only the second time since 1960 that debates were held during the general election campaign season, few norms or rituals had been established. As the candidates prepared, rather than stopping at his podium, Reagan strode across the stage and shook his opponent's hand, eliciting a surprised look from Carter. At the end of the debate, and against agreed-upon rules, it happened again: "Reagan marched over and shook hands with Carter, this time on camera, under the watchful eye of perhaps the largest television audience ever assembled for a presidential debate. The move served a dual purpose: making Reagan look amiable and flummoxing Carter" (Schroeder, 2016, p. 51).

Although it is unclear whether Reagan's greeting and farewell were designed to "flummox" Carter,[2] there is no doubt that candidates can use emotion evoking behaviors to cast their opponents as weak, uninformed, or untrustworthy. By way of example, Poggi, D'Errico, and Vincze (2011) identify several discrediting moves made by Italian politicians that are either purely nonverbal or combine nonverbal with verbal behavior. Exhibiting behaviors of social dominance, are by themselves, sometimes attempts to make a candidate appear strong and as a correlate, make the opponent look weak. Sarcasm and contempt, for example, are communicated nonverbally as modifiers of the verbal message through prosodic features such as emphasis and tone (e.g., "*yeah, riiiiight*") and communicate to the audience that the candidate does not believe an opponent and neither should the audience. Facial expressions such as sneering or contempt and head movements such as shaking one's head as if to indicate negation while verbally attacking an opponent's argument are also discrediting strategies. Gestures such as finger wagging, stabbing at an opponent with a pointed finger, and throwing up one's arms in exasperation during a speaking turn are further examples.

Although Reagan's surprise handshakes worked well in helping define himself and his opponent, not all attempts to attack an opponent using nonverbal behavior have been successful. An example of a failed strategy can be observed in the 2008 presidential debate. In an attempt to cast his opponent, then Senator Obama, as inexperienced and naïve, Senator John McCain attacked verbally and nonverbally, using eye rolls and a condescending, dismissive tone while addressing Obama's views on the economy and the Iraq and Afghanistan wars. Dan Kennedy of *The Guardian* summarized the tone of McCain's performance this way, "Obama, calm and cool, presented himself well. McCain, grumpy and lumpy, sneering and condescending, refusing even to look at his opponent, did not" (Kennedy, 2008, para 4). In the second debate, while arguing about an energy bill, McCain, again with a condescending, sarcastic tone, pointed toward Obama and said, "Who voted for it? You might never know—*that one.*" He followed up, again with patronizing superiority, "You know who voted against it? *Me.*" In the final debate, McCain continued on the offensive. As Spillius wrote, "US newspapers noted Mr. McCain's unappealing range of facial reactions to his opponent, including condescending smiles, thinly concealed grimaces and at least one roll of the eyes" (Spillius, 2008, para 8). Unfortunately for McCain, the tactic backfired and instead of showing Obama to be naïve and inexperienced, his behavior stood in contrast to a cooler, though sometimes professorial sounding, Obama.

A final way that candidates can strategically use nonverbal cues against their opponents is by verbally mocking or in some other way calling into question the appearance and/or self-presentation behaviors of their opponents. Although the strategy is verbal, it is of interest here because nonverbal behavior is at issue. As described in Chapter 1, a well-known example occurred in 2016 and resulted in Donald Trump defending the size of his hands and other parts of his anatomy in a Republican primary debate. A more recent example took place during a heated exchange in one of the Democratic primary debates of the 2020 presidential campaign season. Specifically, Senator Bernie Sanders raised his arms in despair while former Colorado Governor John Hickenlooper accused him of being too extreme and radical to beat President Donald Trump in the next election. Noticing it, Hickenlooper yelled, "No, throw your hands up." Sanders obliged, this time with more verve. "Oh ho, I can do it," Hickenlooper responded, throwing his own arms in the air. The exchange went viral, becoming an instant meme (Van Hagen, 2019). In our view, Hickenlooper's attempt to mock Sanders's behavior ultimately failed and perhaps even damaged his own image by making him seem less composed. Even so, the exchange exemplifies another strategy for discrediting opponents via their nonverbal behavior and appearance. We'll have more to say about the strategy in chapters to come.

SUMMARY

This chapter identified several ways the speaking debater can strategically deploy nonverbal cues to create and maintain a positive identity with an audience. Nonverbal cues largely communicate relational messages that help define and build connections between the candidate and voters. Nonverbal communication can function to build an image of a warm, trustworthy, and competent leader when those cues are managed carefully during a debate. They can also backfire and create perceptions of incompetence, bellicosity, and deceptiveness when managed haphazardly. Finally, nonverbal communication can be used to negatively affect perceptions of an opponent.

NOTES

1. The study of French elections used school children as the research participants.
2. As noted in Chapter 1, our framework includes flustering opponents as a potential function of nonverbal behavior in political debates. As this example illustrates, such behavior need not be intended to flummox an opponent in order to effectively do so.

Chapter Four

Background Nonverbal Behavior in Political Debates

The Role of Nonspeaking Candidates

Although civility suggests that candidates in political debates should remain silent while their opponents are speaking, it is not always easy fading into the background, especially when you are under attack. Take the legendary Lincoln-Douglas debates of 1858, for instance. In the fourth debate, Abraham Lincoln announced that until Stephen Douglas "gives a better or more plausible reason than he has offered, I suggest to him it will not avail him at all that he swells himself up, takes on dignity, and calls people liars" (Guelzo, 2008, pp. 200–210). The audience laughed and applauded, but Douglas did not take the comment lightly. He jerked up, paced the platform, and erupted to some of his friends in bursts of profanity so loud that Robert Hitt of *The Chicago Tribune* reportedly had trouble hearing Lincoln (Guelzo, 2008, p. 201).

It is fortunate for Douglas, perhaps, that his reaction occurred well over a century before the arrival of the Internet and the 24-hour news cycle. Indeed, as this chapter will show, coverage of debates is not always kind to politicians who show strong reactions while their opponents are speaking. By way of example, the first 2004 presidential debate between John Kerry and George W. Bush was followed by days of coverage speculating on whether Bush's apparent disgust and annoyance proved damaging to his image. The Democratic National Committee capitalized on the moment by producing and posting to its website a video titled "Faces of Frustration," which featured a montage of Bush's expressions. Not surprisingly, the video made its rounds through the press. Critical assessments of President Bush's behavior came from scholars, viewers, the media, and the First Lady alike (Edwards, 2012). Gourevitch (2004) wrote, "The President held his head slightly cocked and low to his shoulders, and his expressions kept shifting, in increments of wincing aggravation . . . through a range of attitudes: impatience, boredom, indignation, sourness, imperiousness, contempt" (p. 10). When asked later about his own behavior, Bush said, "I guess I didn't learn any lessons from the first debate in 2000" (Lehrer, 2011, p. 129), in which both he and his opponent, Al Gore, were likewise criticized for their nonverbal reactions to each other's remarks.

Despite the abundance of media attention that such incidents receive, there has been comparably little research on the topic of background nonverbal behavior in political debates. In the same way that debate scholars tend to prioritize verbal over nonverbal communication (see Chapter 1), those who have studied the latter, tend to focus on the behavior of the speaking debater rather than the behavior of the nonspeaking opponent (Seiter, Abraham, & Nakagama, 1998). That said, production techniques such as the use of split screens has become more common, thereby providing TV viewers with more access to debaters' nonverbal reactions, and, consequently, political debaters, who are often short on time, more opportunities for silent influence. As a result, scholars have devoted more attention to this topic, providing important insights into the nature of nonverbal behavior in political contexts.

With that in mind, the purpose of this chapter is to explore this topic in detail. We begin with a brief discussion on the controversy surrounding the use of reaction shots in presidential debates, and then, guided by the framework outlined in Chapter 1, examine the primary aims and functions of behavior that appears in such shots. Next, we review several experimental studies that explore the specific effects of background nonverbal behavior and the ways in which candidates might respond to such behaviors. Along the way, we examine key moments in political debates where background nonverbal behavior played an important role.

THE CONTROVERSY OVER REACTION SHOTS

According to Hellweg, Pfau, and Brydon (1992), "One of the hottest issues involving camera techniques, and a persistent subject for negotiation prior to debates and complaints following debates, involves the use of reaction shots, depiction of one candidate while the other is speaking" (p. 91). Before the first televised presidential debate in 1960, for example, Richard Nixon's chief production advisor "argued for a long time" with CBS director Don Hewitt, "objecting strenuously" to the use of reaction shots (Seltz & Yoakam, 1979, p. 89). Similarly, after the first Clinton-Dole debate of 1996, campaign advisors approached producer Bob Asman "very upset" that split screens had been used (Schroeder, 2000, p. 166).

Considering that presidential campaigns spend millions of dollars buying airtime for their candidates, it might seem strange to learn of protests such as these. On the other hand, considering the history of nonverbal blunders captured through reaction shots, it is hard to blame candidates who might feel a little camera shy. While Richard Nixon's disregard for personal appearance and George H. W. Bush's glances at his wristwatch during their respective debates come to mind, Al Gore's performance in the first 2000 presidential debate is one of the best examples of how damaging background nonverbal behavior can be to a candidate. Jim Lehrer (2011), the debate's moderator, called Gore's behavior "the most important story of that debate" (p. 94) and summarized the event this way: "Vice President Al Gore debated Texas governor George W. Bush at the University of Massachusetts in Boston last night and sighed himself to death" (p. 93). Televised in split screen, Gore was caught rolling his eyes, sneering, frowning, shaking his head, and sighing boisterously in response to Bush's answers. According to Lehrer (2011), "Gore was judged the clear loser in the debate, based almost entirely on his body language" (p. 94). One analysis found that Gore's nonverbal behavior provoked considerable negative reactions from viewers, particularly regarding issues related to character, image, and style (Carlin, Vigil, Buehler, & McDonald, 2007).

Several authors (e.g., Scheufele, Eunkyung, & Brossard, 2007; Lehrer, 2011; Weissman, 2014) have suggested that, at least in part as a result of this incident, the two major presidential candidates in the election that followed agreed on a "memorandum of understanding," which, among other things, provided instructions to broadcasters on how candidates were to be shown on television. Specifically, the memo insisted that coverage would be limited to the speaking candidate only. No cut-away or split-screen shots of nonspeaking candidates were to be shown.

Carlin and her colleagues (2007) pointed out that the 2004 memorandum of understanding is proof that candidates recognize the power of the camera to influence audiences, yet also noted that attempts to reach such agreements are nothing new. In 1988, for example, representatives of George H. W. Bush and Michael Dukakis signed a similar agreement regarding reaction shots (Kraus, 2000), as did aides to Bush and Clinton in 1992 (Peters, 2012). Despite that, broadcasters, who are not party to such memos, tend to ignore candidates' stipulations and show what they want to show however they want to show it (Carlin et al., 2007). In 2004 and since then, for example, major networks tend to cast the debates using split screens. In the next chapter, we explore this controversy from the perspective of television producers in addition to examining the ways in which certain production techniques (e.g., close ups, camera angles, number of reaction shots) might affect perceptions of candidates' nonverbal cues. For now, though, we confine our examination to behaviors enacted by candidates themselves. We also note that reaction shots in political debates seemed destined to stay.

THE STRATEGIC AND NONSTRATEGIC NATURE OF BACKGROUND NONVERBAL BEHAVIOR IN POLITICAL DEBATES

In Chapter 1, we presented a framework that outlined the aims, functions, and effects of nonverbal communication in political debates. With reference to that framework, Chapter 3 examined the ways in which the nonverbal messages and characteristics of debaters who have the floor influence the process and outcomes of debates. The following sections apply the framework to debaters in the *background*. Beforehand, however, it is important to note that, although we generally focus on the functions of background nonverbal behaviors in isolation, such behavior can serve multiple functions simultaneously. Consider, for example, Joe Biden's overblown performance in the 2012 vice presidential debates with Paul Ryan. Although Biden later claimed, "I wasn't laughing at him, I was laughing at some of the answers coming forward" (Schroeder, 2016, p. 196), from the moment his opponent, Paul Ryan, began speaking, Biden expressed ridicule, feigned shock, mocking disbelief, headshaking, or derisive laughter at least 50 times (Weger, Hinck, & Seiter, 2019). According to Olson (2015, p. 220), "As Ryan answered a follow up question, Biden shook his head side-to-side, mouthed 'that's not true,' laughed silently, then smirked and rolled his eyes heavenward. . . . Sometimes Biden chuckled until his shoulders visibly shook or covered his mouth with his hand, as if trying to suppress his derisive hilarity." Considering this, it is easy to see how Biden's behavior might have served several functions. According to Weger et al. (2019), in addition to attacking Ryan's image and arguments, Biden's behavior supported his running mate, became a talking point in social and mainstream media, was distracting, and depending on whom you ask, bolstered or damaged his own image. Besides that, it is easy to see how Biden's behavior might have, among other things, rattled Ryan, affected the flow of the debate, and communicated something about his relationship with Ryan (e.g., a possible lack of respect). With that in mind, we turn now to a more detailed examination of these ideas with accompanying insights and illustrations from theory and history.

Enhancing and Defending Images of the Self

As we saw in Chapter 1, political debates are as much, if not more, about projecting images as they are about arguing positions on policy. On this subject, Exline (1985) noted that candidates' nonverbal behavior might, under some circumstances, override the importance of their verbal utterances. Research beyond debate contexts supports the notion that people rely more on nonverbal than verbal communication for social meaning (see Andersen, 2008), perhaps because of the perception that nonverbal behavior is spontaneous, uncontrolled, and therefore, more authentic (Burgoon, 1985; Burgoon, Guerrero, & Floyd, 2010). In many cases, of course, such perceptions are naïve. In fact, a fundamental principle of impression management theory (Goffman, 1959) is that self-presentation is often planned, controlled, and inauthentic, regardless of the communication channel. Indeed, impression management theory argues that people "attempt to exercise conscious control over selected communication behaviors and cues—particularly nonverbal cues—for purposes of making a desired impression" (Leathers, 1997, p. 195). With regard to political debates, this notion underlines the importance of reaction shots, where verbal utterances are scarce, while opportunities for nonverbal self-presentation are abundant.

In addition, impression management theory argues that techniques for presenting the self can be either assertive, which aim to promote positive images, or defensive, which seek to avoid negative images (Tedeschi & Norman, 1985).[1] With regard to political debates, it is clear that background nonverbal behaviors can function in both ways. In preparation for his 1980 debate with Jimmy Carter, for example, Ronald Reagan and his team devised a strategy for reacting to attacks. On the one hand, Reagan was advised to show righteous indignation (i.e., a defensive tactic). On the other, he was told to temper his reaction with restraint, good humor, and smiles (Ritter & Henry, 1994), presumably in order to project an image of composure and likeability (i.e., an assertive tactic). On the night of the debate, an advisor handed Reagan a 3-by-5 card with one word written on it: "Chuckle"—which, of course, Reagan did. When it was his turn to speak, he added his now iconic phrase, "There you go again" (Kraus, 2000).

Obviously, split-screen technology affords both speaking and non-speaking debaters an opportunity to project favorable images. To be sure, regardless of their role in the spotlight or otherwise, debaters can smile or frown appropriately. On the other hand, it seems that *defensive* nonverbal behaviors are predominantly germane to non-speaking debaters in response to their opponents' verbal attacks, which, according to Democratic strategist Paul Begala, is "one of a debater's most important skills" (Schroeder, 2016, p. 90), and a topic we cover later in this chapter.

Undermining Images of Self

In the third presidential debate of 2000, Al Gore, in what moderator Jim Lehrer (2011, p. 96) called "a most bizarre move," walked across the stage with a scornful expression, stopped, and stood physically close to George W. Bush, who paused, smirked, and nodded at Gore. At the time, Lehrer was thinking, "Oh, my God! Gore's going to physically attack Bush! Do a body block, a head butt—something" (p. 107). When interviewed later, Bush remarked, "I couldn't tell if he was trying to threaten me . . . All I can tell you is that, I think if you review the tape you will see a bemused expression on my face" (Lehrer, 2011, p. 109).

Based on these and other examples in this chapter, it should come as no surprise that viewers often perceive background behavior in political debates as inappropriate. In Carlin et al.'s (2007) study, for instance, one woman said of Gore, "He was belligerent and petty. That sort of worries me a little in terms of diplomacy. If this is how he acts against an adversary, it sort of concerns me that he tends to zero in on some type of tiny detail and lose the big picture" (p. 76). This, and reactions like it, point to the fact that, through their background nonverbal behavior, debaters often undermine themselves.

As noted in Chapter 1, we suggest that such behaviors can be categorized as either strategic and intentional behaviors gone wrong, or as nonstrategic behaviors that debaters inadvertently "leak." Al Gore's bizarre proxemic behavior is an apparent example of the former. As for the latter, the notion that images can be undermined by behaviors that are nonstrategic and unintentional intersects a longstanding principle from theory and research on the topic of deception. For example, interpersonal deception theory (Burgoon & Buller, 2004, 2008) asserts that, to avoid detection, liars control some behaviors, yet remain unaware of others that might slip out and betray them. To the extent that presidential candidates attempt to mask certain feelings, the principles of interpersonal deception are applicable to the context of political debates. Consider, for example, a candidate who tries to come across as composed but appears uncontrollably nervous. According to Minow and Lamay (2008, p. 8), debate audiences watch for "demeanor evidence" such as blinks or being flustered to make judgments about candidates' abilities. As evidence, Carlin et al. (2007, p. 78) found that in both the 1996 and 2000 elections, viewers relied on visual cues to assess candidates' "grace under fire."

Along these lines, previous research and media coverage indicates that appearing nervous is associated with negative perceptions of candidates. In 1960, for example, reaction shots showed a pale and perspiring Richard Nixon (Seltz & Yoakam, 1979), whose behavior was widely interpreted as anxious and frequently blamed for contributing to his defeat in the election (Scheufele et al., 2007).[2] A study by Exline (1985) found that Jimmy Carter's high levels of blinking, gaze shifts, and other tense behaviors early in the first 1976 debate, and Gerald Ford's tense behaviors later in the debate were related to lower ratings of competency for both candidates. In reaction shots, however, Carter appeared less tense and more pleasant, smiling in 11 of 53 shots and frowning in none, compared to Ford, who frowned in 7 of 41 shots and smiled in only 3 (Tiemens, 1978). Four years later, however, the tables were turned; Carter appeared tense, failing to coordinate his verbal and nonverbal behavior, while his opponent, Ronald Reagan, looked more relaxed and smiling (Ritter & Henry, 1994). According to Wingerson (cited in Hellweg et al., 1992), Carter's tension contributed to his perceived loss to Reagan in that debate. In more recent contests, anecdotal accounts suggest that John McCain and Mitt Romney were perceived as less relaxed than their opponent, Barack Obama, in 2008 and 2012, respectively (see Dumitrescu, Gidengil, & Stolle, 2015; Lehrer, 2011).

It is important to keep in mind, of course, that background nonverbal communication can be ambiguous and subject to multiple interpretations. For example, as mentioned above, in the course of a town hall debate versus Bill Clinton and Ross Perot in 1992, George H. W. Bush was caught looking at his wristwatch, a behavior that occurred four times. While some pundits viewed his behavior as signaling boredom, others interpreted it as a sign of his impatience with discussing domestic issues (Zakahi, 2004). When interviewed later, Bush said, "They made a huge thing out of that. Now, was I glad when the damn thing was over? Yeah. And maybe that's why I was looking at it—only ten more minutes of this crap" (Lehrer, 2011, p. 53).

What's more, at times, similar behavior has been interpreted differently across candidates. For example, neither Jimmy Carter in 1980 nor John McCain in 2008 spent much (if any) time looking at their opponents in their respective debates. While Carter's behavior was, in part, interpreted as a sign that he was trying less than Reagan to engage in direct confrontation (Tiemens, Hellweg, Kipper, & Phillips, 1985, p. 40), many pundits interpreted McCain's behavior as a sign of his disdain or lack of respect for Obama. This, according to Schroeder (2016), is what Obama's team had hoped for. "Their mission was to make McCain come off like Mr. Wilson, the grouchy next-door neighbor on *Dennis the Menace*" (Schroeder, 2016, p. 59).

Finally, sometimes candidates' background nonverbal behavior is misinterpreted and, therefore, misleading (Jamieson & Birdsell, 1988). In the first 1960 debate, for example, Richard Nixon's gaze darted, making him appear shifty-eyed, thereby reinforcing the label "Tricky Dick" that an opponent had given him years earlier (Weissmann, 2014). He repeatedly shifted his weight, and was pale and perspiring, which made him appear uncomfortable, nervous, and unsure of himself (Seltz & Yoakam, 1979). In reality, however, Nixon's shifting gaze could be explained by the location of the timer off stage, which Nixon kept checking. Similarly, he had recently undergone knee surgery, and just before the debate, reinjured himself while exiting his car. The pain probably accounts for his shifting weight and complexion. Finally, a fever, the bright studio lights, and the makeup used to cover his emerging whiskers probably account for his perspiration (Jamieson & Birdsell, 1988; Kraus, 2000; Seltz & Yoakam, 1979). In short, nonverbal behaviors are not always what they seem to be.

Undermining Images of Others

Although voters claim to dislike negativity in campaigns (Lau & Sigelman, 2000), elections are political contests and, as such, are inherently aggressive (Seiter & Gass, 2010). This is not to say that political aggression is necessarily unsavory. Indeed, despite the prevalence of views that political attacks are unethical (Lau & Sigleman, 2000), we share the opinion of some scholars (e.g., see Felknor, 1992; Geer, 2006; Jamieson, 1992) that political aggression can be desirable, depending on the nature of the attack. By way of example, Seiter and Gass (2010) proposed three criteria—veracity, relevancy, and decorum—which may be used to evaluate the acceptability of political aggression.

Consider, for instance, what Donald Trump told *Rolling Stone* magazine about Carly Fiorina, one of his rivals for the 2016 Republican presidential nomination: "Look at that face. Would anyone vote for that? Can you imagine that, the face of our next president?" (LeBlanc, 2018, para. 5). Although "beauty is in the eye of the beholder," we not only disagree with the veracity of Trump's comment, we fail to see how a candidate's attractiveness is relevant to being president or appropriate to the context of political campaigning. On the other hand, depending on the manner in which it is done, questioning an opponent's ability to withstand the stresses of office—as some did in 1972 when Thomas Eagleton, who had been hospitalized several times for depression became a Democratic vice-presidential nominee—seems closer to meeting the criteria.

According to Seiter and Gass (2010), previous research suggests that these criteria are also relevant to perceptions of nonverbal communication, including background behaviors displayed by nonspeaking candidates in political debates. Importantly, however, because nonverbal behavior is frequently off-the-record and ambiguous, holding candidates accountable to any criteria can be tricky business. As DePaulo (1992) argued, many nonverbal behaviors are

> off-the-record to all parties to an interaction: the actor, the interaction partner, and any other observers. In commenting on an interaction, it is more difficult to describe a facial expression or a tone of voice than it is to recount the words spoken. Parties to a social interaction might ask each other to repeat their words, but never ask each other to repeat facial expressions, voice tones, or body movements or gestures. Furthermore, even if they did "catch" the nonverbal expression the first time and could hold it in their minds, they still could not seek further clarity about its meaning by looking it up in a dictionary. To the self-presenter, this elusiveness of nonverbal behavior contributes further to

the flexibility with which it can be used. People might take a chance at expressing something nonverbally that they would be reluctant to express verbally; should pangs of regret set in, they can deny that the behavior ever occurred or that it had the meaning being attributed to it. (p. 206)

Considering this, it is clear that nonverbal communication provides political debaters a potentially powerful instrument for third-person impression management (Seiter, 1999, 2001) or, correspondingly, what we referred to in Chapter 1 as "other-presentation" (also see Scharp, Seiter, & Maughan, in press), which can function to enhance, defend, and/or undermine another person's image. With regard to the latter, D'Errico, Poggi, and Vincze (2012) examined verbal and nonverbal behaviors aimed at discrediting opponents in political contexts (see also D'Errico & Poggi, 2012). Based on a qualitative analysis of Italian, Swiss, and French debates, these researchers suggested that typical attacks target three aspects of the opponent's image. First, they might be aimed at the *competence* of an opponent. For example, during a 2007 presidential debate in France, Ségolène Royal verbally highlighted Nicholas Sarkozy's ignorance of nuclear power plants while tilting her head and pointing her finger to emphasize her superior knowledge. Second, discrediting moves might target an opponent's (lack of) *dominance*. In one Italian debate, for instance, the moderator defended a debater because he kept getting interrupted, at which point the opponent, protruded his lips and mocked the speaker by saying, "Ma povero, poverino" (Oh poor, poor thing!) (D'Errico et al., 2012, p. 167). Third, the attack might target an opponent's *benevolence*. For example, during a mayoral debate in Naples, when one candidate denied his connections to the Neapolitan Mafia, his opponent tried to discredit him by skeptically raising the external part of one eyebrow and making a praying hands gesture as if to convey "how the hell can you say so?" (D'Errico & Poggi, 2012).

Enhancing and Defending Images of Others

Who knows why Richard Nixon was nodding in the background during John F. Kennedy's closing statement in the first televised presidential debate? Perhaps he actually agreed with his opponent. Perhaps he was taking the advice of his running mate, who reportedly advised him to erase his assassin image (Windt, 1994). Whatever the case, it is interesting to speculate on the possible effects of such behavior. Weissman (2014), for example, surmised that the apparent agreement expressed by Richard Nixon, Al Gore, Barack Obama, and Mitt Romney in their respective debates fueled negative perceptions of their performances. Relatedly, in 1976, Jimmy Carter was advised to beware of appearing too agreeable (Schroeder, 2000).

Sometimes, of course, debaters might not be able to help themselves. As an illustration, compare Joe Biden's guffaws in 2012, which seemed intentional and strategic, with Walter Mondale's reaction to Ronald Reagan in their second 1984 presidential debate. Specifically, after Henry Trewhitt, a moderator, raised concerns about Reagan being too old to function as president. Reagan, then 73, replied, "I want you to know that I will not make age an issue of this campaign. I am not going to exploit, for political purposes, my opponent's youth and inexperience." At this, Mondale, age 56, broke into laughter, as did the audience. When asked about it later, Mondale admitted to knowing that Reagan was scoring big points with the audience, but could only respond naturally to the funny remark (Goethals, 2005).

Bolstering and Refuting Arguments

In addition to managing images of communicators, politicians use background nonverbal behavior to affect perceptions of messages as well. As Morello (1992) noted, reaction shots afford the opportunity to refute an opponent without ever saying a word. Gelang and Kjeldsen (2011) extended this idea by demonstrating the *argumentative* dimensions of nonverbal communication in political debates, a topic we discuss at greater length in Chapter 7. For now, however, consider part of their analysis, which centered on the background nonverbal behavior of Hillary Clinton in her 2008 Democratic primary debates versus Barack Obama. In one exchange, Clinton stands still and expressionless until Obama accuses her and her husband of playing political games, to which she protests, "Now wait a minute, wow, wait a minute!" She stretches an opened palm toward Obama as if to stop him and, when he continues, takes a step toward him to contain the attack. According to Gelang and Kjeldsen, Clinton's behavior can be seen an implicit argument about Obama's ethos, which can be rendered as such (p. 573):

	Obama's behaviour is unreasonable,
because	I react strongly to his behaviour,
and	when behaviour is unreasonable, people react strongly.

Although Clinton's argument is created both verbally and nonverbally, Gelang and Kjeldsen noted that both the *what* (stopping palm and stepping forward) and *how* (dynamic, intense, and sudden) of the response creates Clinton's nonverbal argument and makes it believable. Such behaviors, they argued, can affect viewers' perceptions of debaters' character, thereby advancing an argument for or against that debaters' ability to be president (Gelang & Kjeldsen, 2011).

Affecting the Audience's Processing of Messages

Despite this ability to advance arguments, a nonverbal attack might also, as Weger et al. (2019, p. 155) pointed out, "be reconstructed as fallacious because it potentially diverts attention away from the argument being made, thereby denying the debater a fair opportunity to advance arguments uninterrupted." Likewise, Remland (1982) suggested that such behavior could be seen as a special type of *ad hominem* fallacy. Specifically, nonverbal behavior can be used to degrade an adversary, thereby, distracting the audience's attention away from substantive issues to characteristics of the message target (in much the same way that name-calling does). Remland recognized such behaviors as "implicit *ad hominem* fallacies." Examples include laughing or smiling to ridicule an opponent's claims, displaying signs of displeasure (e.g., disgust, frustration, impatience, boredom, indignation) to emphasize disagreement or disrespect, and degrading the presence of an adversary (e.g., by invading the space or ignoring the other person; Remland, 1982). Another study identified no less than 51 different types of aggressive nonverbal behaviors, including frowning, rolling the eyes, sighing, and shaking the head from side-to-side (Rancer, Lin, Durbin, & Faulkner, 2010).

Of course, background nonverbal behavior need not express disagreement to be distracting. Consider the second 2016 presidential debate, a town hall format, which found Donald Trump wandering around the stage during Hillary Clinton's speaking turns, sometimes looming closely behind her. As described by Bucy and Gong (2018),

> While cued more to the body and Trump's imposing size than his facial displays, focus group comments confirm Trump's ability to divert attention and visually interrupt Clinton during her speaking turns by hovering over her, invading her personal space, and walking through the camera frame during her speaking turns. During these visual interruptions, Trump maintains an ambiguous facial expression, slightly disapproving at times, and disinterested and bored at others. Through a combination of bodily maneuvering and expressive signaling, Trump appropriates viewer attention, distracts from Clinton's carefully constructed arguments, and casts aspersions without uttering a word. (p. 75)

Flustering Opponents

This example also illustrates the potential role of background nonverbal behavior in rattling opponents, or, at the very least, audience members' perceptions that debaters are attempting to do so. In fact, one study indicated that viewers interpreted Trump's behavior as an intended attempt to knock Clinton "off her game," "make her stress," or "mess with her delivery" (Bucy & Gong, 2018, p. 90). Clinton (2017) herself recounted not only how Trump's behavior made her feel but also the dilemma it created in not knowing how to respond:

> Now we were on a small stage, and no matter where I walked, he followed me closely, staring at me, making faces. It was incredibly uncomfortable. He was literally breathing down my neck. My skin crawled. It was one of those moments where you wish you could hit Pause and ask everyone watching, "Well? What would *you* do?" Do you stay calm, keep smiling, and carry on as if he weren't repeatedly invading your space? Or do you turn, look him in the eye, and say loudly and clearly, "Back up, you creep, get away from me, I know you love to intimidate women but you can't intimidate me, so *back up*." I chose option A. (p. 136)

EXPERIMENTAL STUDIES ON THE EFFECTS OF BACKGROUND NONVERBAL BEHAVIORS

Up to this point, we have discussed the functions of background nonverbal behavior in broad strokes, primarily with regard to candidates' images. In this section, we explore this issue in finer detail by describing several experiments that have focused on particular aspects of candidates' images.

Credibility

As long ago as 380 B.C., Aristotle wrote that credible orators possess "good sense, good moral character, and good will" (p. 1378). More recently, researchers have used statistical techniques (i.e., factor analysis) to identify the dimensions of public-figure credibility. Echoing Aristotle, McCroskey and Teven (1999) found three factors: competence, trustworthiness, and goodwill. Berlo, Lemert and Mertz (1969) identified safety, qualification, and dynamism as components of credibility. McCroskey, Hamilton, and Weiner (1974) found that credibility is composed of five dimensions, including competence, character, sociability, composure, and extroversion.

The first experimental study (Seiter et al., 1998) to manipulate debaters' background nonverbal behavior relied on McCroskey et al.'s (1974) dimensions. The purpose of the study was to examine whether background nonverbal disagreement (e.g., shaking the head, frowning, mouthing the word "What?") affected viewers' perceptions of a speaking debater. Participants in the study were asked to watch one of four televised versions of a hypothetical political debate. All four versions showed the same footage of two male candidates standing at their respective rostrums while a moderator introduced them, followed by the incumbent candidate making his opening statement. One version of the debate was shown in a single-screen format, where, after the introductions, only the speaker was seen. The other three versions were shown using a split-screen format, in which the speaker's opponent remained "stone-faced" or displayed occasional or nearly constant nonverbal disagreement with the content of the speaker's message. After watching the videos, participants rated the speaker's competence, character, sociability, composure, and extroversion.

Results of the study indicated that the opponent's behavior had a significant influence on viewers' perceptions on four of the five dimensions. Specifically, the speaker received significantly higher competence and character ratings when his opponent displayed nearly constant disagreement compared to the other conditions in the study. Moreover, the speaker was perceived to be significantly more composed and sociable when his opponent displayed nearly constant disagreement than when his opponent was not shown or when his opponent remained stone-faced. With regard to the fifth dimension, extroversion, no significant differences were found. In a later study (Seiter, Weger, Jensen, & Kinzer, 2010), however, participants rated a speaker as significantly *less* extroverted when she was confronted with background nonverbal disagreement than when she was confronted with neutral expressions. Overall, then, with the exception of extroversion, background nonverbal disagreement seemed to bolster the credibility the speaking debater.

The question that naturally followed asked whether and how different nonverbal reactions affect the credibility of the debater in the background (Seiter, 1999). Historical incidents indicate that both expressive and unexpressive reactions might be judged harshly. As noted earlier, for instance, both candidates in the 2004 debates were criticized for excessive background nonverbal displays. On the other hand, Michael Dukakis may be the best example of a candidate coming across as too wooden. In the first 1988 presidential debate, for example, Dukakis was asked whether he would favor the death penalty if his wife were raped and murdered. One of the debate panelists described his reaction as "flat" and "bloodless." Another said, "It was like he had just turned into a block of ice" (Lehrer, 2011, p. 45). The incident is often cited as a "defining moment" in presidential debates (see Zakahi, 2004).

To examine whether nonverbal behaviors affect perceptions of political candidates in the background, Seiter (1999) replicated the procedures of the earlier study (Seiter et al., 1998), only this time, participants were asked to rate the credibility of the nonspeaking opponent. Results of the study indicated that background nonverbal behavior had a negative influence on perceptions of four out of five credibility dimensions. First, displaying *any* nonverbal disagreement led the nonspeaking opponent to be perceived as less competent and sociable, while displaying constant nonverbal disagreement led the opponent to receive lower composure and character ratings.[3] On the other hand, the opponent was perceived as more extroverted when he showed *any* nonverbal disagreement, especially when the disagreement was constant.[4] In short, displaying nonverbal disagreement was generally damaging to the credibility of the opponent in the background. These results are consistent with a later study (Seiter et al., 2010), which found that neutral facial expressions, compared to expressions of nonverbal disagreement, were associated with significantly higher ratings of a nonspeaking debater's sociability, competence, and character.

In a third study, Seiter (2001) examined the role of background behavior on perceptions of both speaking and nonspeaking debaters' veracity. We discuss the study here because, presumably, perceptions about whether a person is behaving truthfully or deceptively should be related to perceptions of that person's character (i.e., a dimension of credibility). As before, participants watched four versions of a debate, but this time, rated the degree to which they believed the candidates were behaving truthfully or deceptively. Results suggested that constant disagreement on the part of the nonspeaking opponent seemed to backfire. Not only was he perceived as significantly more deceptive when displaying such behavior (compared to the other conditions in the study), his opponent, the speaker, was perceived as significantly more truthful. On the other hand, displays of moderate disagreement were associated with higher ratings of deceptiveness for *both* debaters.[5] In other words, from the nonspeaking debater's perspective, moderate disagreement might be a double-edged sword. You might use it to undermine an opponent's image, yet, in the process, undermine your own image as well.

Likeability

According to Sauter (1994, p. 46), Bob Dole lost the 1976 vice presidential debate "by appearing mean and often contradictory." His remarks seemed witty enough—for example, there were three presidential debates that year because Jimmy Carter "has three positions on everything" (Schroeder, 2000, p. 26)—but he didn't smile, so he came across as caustic and unlikeable. Similarly, Geraldine Ferraro's steely persona may have lost her the 1984 vice presidential debate (see Hellweg et al., 1992). Indeed, Nimmo and Savage (cited in Kraus, 2000, p. 215) reported that candidates' likeability was the single most important explanation for voting behavior.

To examine whether background nonverbal behavior influenced audience perceptions of likeability, Seiter, Weger, Kinzer, and Jensen (2009) asked research participants to view one of four versions of a hypothetical televised debate. Each version featured two female debaters. While one spoke on the main screen, subscreens showed her nonspeaking opponent displaying a neutral expression or various levels of nonverbal disagreement with what the speaker was saying.[6] After watching the debate, participants rated both of the debaters' likeability. Results indicated that the nonspeaking opponent was perceived as significantly more likeable when maintaining a neutral expression compared to when displaying disagreement. On the other hand, perceptions of the speaker's image were not associated with her opponent's background behaviors, suggesting that she was judged on the merits of her own behavior.

Appropriateness

Alan Schroeder (2000) wrote that

> the nakedness of the clash is a distinguishing feature of TV debates. Presenting one's own case will not suffice; one must also bash the opposition, and do so in a way that passes the smell test of tens of millions of viewers. Each debater walks a tightrope between disparaging the competition and being properly respectful. (pp. 49–50)

Indeed, voters tend to frown on negative attacks by politicians (Lau & Sigelman, 2000; Mark, 2006; Swint, 2008). That said, although political debates usually involve written rules about who gets to speak and for how long, guidelines regarding candidates' *nonverbal* behaviors are not so explicit. What's more, because nonverbal behaviors can be so ambiguous, they are subject to different interpretations. On one hand, background nonverbal behaviors might be perceived as intentional and inappropriate attempts to attack an adversary's image. On the other, they might simply be perceived as natural, unintentional reactions to whatever a speaker is saying.

To examine the issue of perceived appropriateness, Seiter and Weger (2005) followed the procedures of an earlier study (Seiter et al., 1998), only this time, participants were asked to rate the appropriateness of speaking and nonspeaking debaters who encountered or displayed various levels of background disparagement. Results indicated that increasingly conspicuous nonverbal disagreement resulted in negative perceptions of the nonverbal communicator's appropriateness. What's more, the speaking debater was perceived as significantly more appropriate when his opponent displayed constant, as opposed to moderate or no disagreement, perhaps because a speaker who is able to keep from reciprocating attacks from a rude opponent is seen as especially respectful (Seiter & Weger, 2005).

Finally, a study by Bucy (2016a) sought to explain the popular perception of Richard Nixon and Barack Obama "losing" the first 1960 and 2012 U.S. presidential debates, respectively. Analysis indicated that, consistent with expectancy violations theory (see Chapter 6), Nixon and Obama, compared to their respective opponents, displayed more behaviors that were inappropriate to the context. Evasive facial expressions, particularly in response to an opponent's statements, seemed particularly relevant to Nixon and Obama's losses. Relatedly, focus groups in another study (Gong & Bucy, 2016) judged Obama more harshly when he was shown in split-screen format smirking and glancing downward while being verbally attacked by Mitt Romney in their first debate; he was judged more positively when he was shown continually staring at Romney while being verbally attacked in their third debate.

Tempering Disagreement with Agreement

Given the apparent negative effects of displaying nonverbal disagreement, Seiter et al. (2010) wondered whether showing some agreement with one's opponent might be effective. On one hand, the nonverbal communicator might be seen as less antagonistic and, consequently, more appropriate. On the other, the behavior could backfire, making the speaker seem more credible and persuasive. To underline this point, following the first 2008 presidential debate, the linguist George Lakoff suggested that, to improve his performance, "Instead of saying 'I agree with Senator McCain . . . ,' Obama should try 'Senator McCain agrees with me that . . . '" (Lakoff, cited in Schroeder, 2016, p. 74).

To examine the effects of agreement, Seiter et al. (2010) asked research participants to view a hypothetical televised debate, featuring two female opponents. While one spoke, the other was shown displaying (1) a neutral expression, (2) occasional disagreement, (3) nearly constant disagreement, or (4) both agreement and disagreement with what the speaker said. Afterward, participants were asked to share their perceptions about the debaters and who won the debate. Results indicated that, in terms of credibility and appropriateness ratings, agreement-plus-disagreement showed no advantage over expressing disagreement alone, and fared worse when compared to maintaining a neutral expression. In terms of debate outcomes, expressing agreement-plus-disagreement, compared to the other nonverbal expressions, was associated with being judged by more viewers as the debate loser and with losing by a substantially larger margin. Finally, although expressing agreement-plus-disagreement, compared to expressing disagreement only, was associated with higher objectivity ratings for the nonverbal communicator, it also boosted objectivity ratings for the speaker. In short, from a practical and strategic standpoint, displaying agreement-plus-disagreement is probably a debater's worst option (Seiter et al., 2010).

Live Contexts

Do background nonverbal behaviors play a role in non-mediated debates? Seiter, Kinzer, and Weger (2006) examined this question by asking students to attend live debates, where one of the debaters remained stone-faced or displayed nonverbal disagreement with her speaking opponent. Afterward, the participants completed surveys regarding their perceptions. Results indicated that, when displaying disagreement, the debater received lower ratings of appropriateness and delivery skills (but higher ratings of extroversion) than when she remained neutral. What's more, displays of nonverbal disagreement boosted perceptions of the speaking opponent's sociability and delivery skills.[7]

RESPONDING TO OPPONENTS' NONVERBAL BEHAVIOR

One question that follows from Hillary Clinton's dilemma discussed above and the research we have discussed so far is what should a speaker do when confronted with disparaging nonverbal behavior? This question was addressed in two studies conducted by Weger, Seiter, Jacobs, and Akbulut (2010, 2013). Based on politeness theory (e.g., Brown & Levinson, 1987; also see Chapter 6), these researchers suggested that an opponent's background behavior and a speaker's response to it could be conceptualized as face-threatening acts. That is because both have the potential to interfere with people's desire for social approval (positive face wants) and autonomy (negative face wants), which translate into debate contexts as the desire to maintain a positive image and the desire to hold the floor (i.e., not be interrupted).

Relying on politeness theory (Brown & Levinson, 1987)—which suggests a hierarchy of strategies for engaging in face-threatening behavior—Weger et al. (2010) imagined several ways that speakers could respond to the background nonverbal behavior of their opponent. Ranging from most to least polite, these behaviors include avoidance (e.g., saying nothing), going off the record (e.g., shaking one's head), going on record but being conventionally indirect (asking the moderator to stop the opponent's behavior), going on the record with redress (e.g., asking the opponent politely to stop his or her behavior by saying "please"), going bald on record (i.e., demanding that the opponent stop), and attacking the opponent (e.g., ridicule). To examine perceptions of such responses, the researchers asked participants to watch one of six versions of a hypothetical mayoral debate. Each version featured the same video footage of a speaker faced with strong disagreement (e.g., rolling eyes, smirking, head shaking, pained expressions) from his male opponent. The opponent, in turn, is responded to in one of six ways (see above). After watching the debate, participants completed questionnaires.

In general, results of these studies (Weger et al., 2010, 2013) indicated that the speaker was perceived more favorably as he became increasingly more direct, but only up to a point. For example, compared to saying nothing, directly requesting that the opponent stop the behavior resulted in higher ratings of speaker's effectiveness, appropriateness, expertise, and character. Ridiculing the opponent, however, fared no better than saying nothing with regard to appropriateness, expertise, and character ratings, and significantly worse than direct requests with regard to appropriateness ratings.[8]

SUMMARY AND FINAL THOUGHTS

According to Meadow (1987, p. 209), "because of the focus on the blooper, candidates tend to be overly rehearsed, cautious, and uncreative." That said, although history indicates that candidates have little control over when and how reaction shots will be used by television producers, some scholarship suggests that reaction shots can provide powerful opportunities to candidates (e.g., Morello, 1992). Along these lines, this chapter followed a descriptive framework of the objectives candidates might be aiming for when they display background nonverbal behavior in debates. For better or worse, however, we have seen that the desired effects of background nonverbal behavior do not always match the effects that are observed. To be sure, a recurrent theme in the experiments we reviewed was that background nonverbal disparagement tends to backfire, damaging the image of the nonverbal communicator while benefiting the speaking opponent. This finding is consistent with other research in political contexts which shows that audiences are turned off by aggressive, negative, and impolite attack strategies (e.g., Dailey, Hinck, & Hinck, 2008; Schrott & Lanoue, 1992), and by theory and research suggesting that nonverbal communicators who violate expectations in a negative way are judged harshly (e.g., Burgoon 1978, 2009).

On the other hand, we have seen that audiences are relatively tolerant of direct, aggressive responses from speakers who face nonverbal disagreement from their opponents. Perhaps, as Seiter et al. (2006) suggested, viewers expect debaters who are confronted in such a way to stand up for themselves. This notion is consistent with literature in interpersonal contexts, which suggests that people feel justified in reciprocating verbally aggressive attacks (Martin, Anderson, & Horvath, 1996) and may even expect them to be reciprocated (Martin, Dunleavy, & Kennedy-Lightsey, 2010). Moreover, people who do not reciprocate verbal aggression are perceived as less credible than those who do (Infante, Hartley, Martin, Higgins, Bruning, & Hur, 1992).

Reflecting on the 2004 presidential debates, Bob Shrum (2006) wrote that one of the reasons the press waited until polls started rolling in to declare a winner is that "press room reporters were seeing the Debate Commission feed. Viewers at home were seeing the network split screen" (p. 119). Considering the material covered in this chapter, we understand why members of the press, and especially candidates, might have been wary about the influence of reaction shots.

In the aftermath of the first presidential debate in 2000, Al Gore blamed camera operators for breaking the rules and focusing on him while Bush was speaking (Burns, 2008). If it is true, however, that nonverbal behavior is as, if not more, important than verbal communication in the process of persuading others (see Andersen, 2004), a more prudent approach, perhaps, would have been to assume that the spotlight is sometimes shining brightest on those who are *not* speaking. Indeed, if participants in political debates are to take one lesson from this chapter, it should probably be that *the cameras are always watching*. As such, they would be well advised to consider the ways in which their background nonverbal behavior affects perceptions, not only of their opponents, but of themselves as well.

NOTES

1. The notion that nonverbal impression management involves defending and promoting images of the self (Tedeschi & Norman, 1985) and undermining images of others (Seiter, 1999, 2001) is consistent with the work of William Benoit (Benoit, 2007; Benoit & Wells, 1996). Specifically, based on his analyses of *verbal* messages in political advertisements, debates, and campaigns, Benoit (2007) created functional theory, which asserts that candidates try to appear preferable to their opponents through the use of acclaims (making positive statements about themselves), defenses (refuting opponents' attacks), and attacks (criticizing their opponents).

2. The first debate in 1960 is widely cited as evidence that people who saw the debate on television thought Kennedy won, while those who heard it on radio thought Nixon won. After an extensive review of the data, however, Vancil and Pendell (1987) found little support for this claim, reporting that most of the evidence was anecdotal and impressionistic in nature. A more recent study (Druckman, 2003) involving an experiment that required some participants to watch the debate and others to listen to it, supported the earlier reports, i.e., television viewers were more likely to think Kennedy won the debate. After the election, Nixon (1962, p. 340) confessed, "I had concentrated too much on substance and not enough on appearance, while Kennedy noted, "It was TV more than anything else that turned the tide" (White, cited in Windt, 1994, p. 1).

3. Both moderate and constant displays of disagreement led to lower competence and sociability ratings when compared to the stone-faced and single-screen conditions. Displaying constant disagreement led to lower composure ratings when compared to the single-screen condition and lower character ratings when compared to all three of the other conditions (i.e., moderate disagreement, stone-faced, and single-screen conditions).

4. The opponent received significantly higher extroversion ratings when displaying constant disagreement compared to all other conditions (i.e., moderate disagreement, stone-faced, and single-screen conditions), and when displaying moderate disagreement compared to the stone-faced and single-screen conditions.

5. When facing moderate disagreement, the speaker was perceived as more deceptive than when he was pictured alone (single-screen condition). When displaying moderate disagreement, nonspeaking debater was perceived as more deceptive than when he displayed no disagreement (i.e., remained stone-faced).

6. In the three remaining conditions, the opponent displayed (1) occasional disagreement, (2) nearly constant disagreement, or (3) both agreement and disagreement with what the speaker said. The effects of the last condition (i.e., expressing agreement plus disagreement) will be discussed later in this chapter.

7. It is informative, perhaps, to note that there were fewer statistically significant differences found in this live-debate study than in televisions studies on the same topic. According to the authors, one possible explanation for this could be that nonverbal behaviors are less salient in live debates than on television, thereby lessening the attention paid to the nonspeaking debater (Seiter et al., 2006). This assumption is consistent with the notion that television magnifies the importance and influence of political candidates' nonverbal behavior (e.g., see Atkinson, 1984; Jamieson, 1988; Pfau & Kang, 1991).

8. The results of both studies were moderated by the level of participants' trait verbal aggressiveness.

Chapter Five

Mediated Nonverbal Communication and Political Debates

During the first presidential debate of 1960, while Senator John F. Kennedy and Vice President Richard Nixon sparred before a television audience of 70 million Americans, a contest of a different kind was taking place in the WBBM-TV control room (Schroeder, 2000). There, Don Hewitt, the debate's director, had his hands full. According to Alan Schroeder (2000, p. 6), with the debate in progress, Kennedy's advisor "chided Hewitt that he 'owed' Kennedy more reaction shots." Hewitt, argued back, apparently misunderstanding what was being asked. Kennedy's advisor, it turns out, was not seeking additional screen time for his own candidate; he wanted more reaction shots of Nixon (Schroeder, 2000).

And it is not difficult to guess why. Indeed, much has been written about Nixon's unkempt appearance and anxious demeanor during the telecast. In fact, perhaps the most common claim associated with that debate is that people who watched it on television thought Kennedy won, while radio listeners—with no access to visual cues—went with Nixon. Although that claim has been called into question (Vancil & Pendell, 1987), at least some evidence suggests that the mode of presentation influences debate outcomes. For example, more than 40 years after the debate, Druckman (2003) asked some research participants to watch it on television while others listened to an audio-only version. Results indicated that television watchers believed Kennedy won. What's more, other studies suggest that the mode in which a debate is presented makes a difference. Exline (1985), for instance, found that Gerald Ford and Jimmy Carter benefited from the visual (versus auditory) modality during different times in their first 1976 debate; while Patterson, Churchill, Burger and Powell (1992) found that Ronald Reagan's 1984 advantage over Walter Mondale was greater in the visual (versus the audio) modality.[1]

One implication of all this, as we saw in the previous chapter, is how important being aware of appearances and behaviors can be to a politician. That said, even when they attempt to manage their nonverbal behavior, other factors remain beyond their control. Before the 1960 debate, for example, Richard Nixon requested and was promised that he not be shown wiping sweat from his face. One shot, however, caught him doing so (Seltz & Yoakam, 1979; Windt, 1994).

This example suggests that a complete understanding of the role of nonverbal behavior in political debates is not possible without examining a large number of significant "behind the scenes" factors that influence not only whether such behavior is presented, but also the manner in which it is received, interpreted, and evaluated by viewers. With that in mind, the purpose of this chapter is to review and discuss research that has investigated these "behind the scenes" factors. Specifically, we examine the role of those who control the visual presentation of debates (e.g., camera persons, directors, producers). We also explore the effects of non-candidates' (e.g., the audience, the moderator) nonverbal behavior and the ways in which post-debate coverage (e.g., photos and commentary) influences viewers' perceptions of debates and candidates. First, though, we revisit a topic we discussed in the previous chapter: negotiations prior to debates.

PRE-DEBATE NEGOTIATORS

Despite his history as an all-star athlete who declined two offers to play professional football, Gerald Ford had a reputation for being clumsy, leading some to joke that "Vice President Rockerfeller was just a banana peel from the presidency" (Schieffer, 2006, p. 1). Not surprisingly, in preparation for the 1976 presidential debate, Ford's negotiating team insisted that their candidate's podium be equipped with a brace for securing the president's glass of water (Schroeder, 2000). In 1988, to compensate for Michael Dukakis's height disadvantage, his team demanded a podium equipped with a riser, and Dukakis took heat for it. *Saturday Night Live*, for example, parodied the debates by showing Dukakis (played by Jon Lovitz) raising himself behind the podium alongside the whine of a hydraulic lift (Franken, 2016). Before that, George H. W. Bush's team, referring to the riser as a "pitcher's mound," tried to sneak a softball onto Dukakis's podium ahead of the second debate but was unsuccessful (Schroeder, 2016, p. 46). In 1992, Dan Quayle's team did not try to sneak props into the vice-presidential debate. Instead, they negotiated, wanting Quayle to read passages from Al Gore's controversial book, until, that is, Gore's team threatened to bring a potato, "the vegetable

Quayle had misspelled in a widely publicized incident earlier in the year" (Schroeder, 2000, p. 34).

Although no contracts existed in 1960, 1976, and 1980, negotiations since then have resulted in "memos of understanding," quasi-legal documents that detail what will, and will not, be permitted during debates. Although such agreements are created, signed, and often concealed by campaign representatives (Schroeder, 2016), they represent an integration of three agendas, including the candidates', the media's, and the voters', who, theoretically, voice their opinion through the Commission on Presidential Debates (Self, 2017). Discussions among representatives of these often-competing agendas have not always been characterized by cooperativeness. The 2004 memo of understanding is a case in point. Besides being the only memo released to the public in advance of the debates, it was unique in its demands. Specifically, prompted by George W. Bush's team, the memo demanded that debate sponsors and moderators become signatories to the document. Both refused (Schroeder, 2016).

According to Self (2017), pre-debate negotiations, or "debate about debates," are important because, among other things, they influence the format of debates, thereby lending insights into characteristics of politicians. For instance, candidates who attempt to avoid a town hall format might lack the interpersonal skills necessary to deal with such an audience (Self, 2017). Perhaps even more relevant to the topic of this book, such negotiations can influence if, when, and in what manner a politicians' nonverbal behaviors are displayed. As such, and consistent with the functional framework we presented in Chapter 1, pre-debate negotiations play an important role in the ability of nonverbal communication to affect images, refute arguments, regulate conversations, and so forth.

As we saw in the last chapter, pre-negotiated agreements have often attempted to control production elements of debates, including those that involve nonverbal reactions shots. In 1960, for example, although Kennedy's advisers wanted reaction shots, Richard Nixon's team protested unsuccessfully, both before, and during, the debate (Self, 2017). Considering the ensuing, widespread spanking that Nixon took from the press, it is not surprising that subsequent campaigns were gun-shy about reaction shots. Although 1976 found Ford and Carter's negotiators in long, heated, and, ultimately, successful arguments with members of the media about the prohibition of audience reaction shots, the issue of reaction shots has continued to vex candidates. Moreover, despite candidates' persistent efforts to have such shots banned, the media has prevailed on the issue and continues to televise them, primarily as a matter of principle. Indeed, media representatives have argued that attempts to prohibit camera shots are not just a form of censorship, but an insult to their journalistic integrity (Lampl, 1979). As Robert

Chandler, vice president of CBS News noted when commenting on the 1976 dispute,

> We were put in a position that was intolerable for us. Had we gone to Russia and shot some sort of event there, and had the Russians said . . . you will not shoot in this direction, . . . everybody would have been horrified. And yet, here we are in the same kind of position, . . . we've been invited to cover a news event and suddenly we're told that we cannot cover part of the event. Now, that is a matter of principle and it is quite important to us and it was an intolerable situation. (Kraus, 2000, p. 45)

What's more, members of the media have described their role as one that provides an objective account of what takes place in political debates. Don Hewitt, for example, saw himself as a "surrogate" for viewers watching the Kennedy-Nixon exchange. "I didn't try to catch the candidates in a grimace," he said. "I listened to the comments and tried to anticipate the public—to switch to a reaction shot when I thought viewers would expect one" (Schroeder, 2000, p. 6). Richard Salant (1979) echoed this perspective when he wrote of the 1976 bans on audience shots that, unlike newspaper reporting, television could have reflected the debate directly, permitting viewers to see and hear the debate "first hand" (p. 184). Likewise, in 2004, networks argued that the mode of coverage (i.e., shape of split screen) did not make a difference in viewers' judgments of debates (Scheufele, Eunkyung, & Brossard, 2007).

Others, however, have disputed the notion that the media treats televised debates objectively. There is, in fact, a long history of scholarship that critiques the media, accusing it of distorting coverage of political events. As Tiemens (1978, p. 363) noted, "The television medium does more than merely transmit pictures and sounds. It selects and transforms visual and auditory information for the viewer." In the case of debates, there is certainly potential for editorializing. Indeed, although the Commission on Presidential Debates, a nonpartisan organization, determines where cameras are placed, other decisions (e.g., the timing of reaction shots) are left entirely up to the network that directs and produces the debate. This "pool network" provides footage from its cameras to other networks, which, in turn, can direct the debate as they see fit. With so many versions of a debate being broadcast, the potential for bias becomes a concern. Specifically, by broadcasting (un)flattering reactions of candidates or by showing audience members rolling their eyes or nodding their heads in response to candidates' comments, an individual or network might be able to put its own spin on a debate. What's more, through the use of various camera techniques, individuals or networks might be able to influence an audience response to debaters, a topic we examine later.

Considering such possibilities, it is no surprise that campaigns work painstakingly to control debates through negotiation. As a result, perhaps, since 1984, campaigns have kept memos of understanding on the down-low, not wanting to appear overly petty about their obsession to detail (Schroeder, 2016). That said, from 1984 to 1992, memos of understanding grew from three to thirty-seven pages of precise instructions (Self, 2017), including minute details that might affect perceptions of nonverbal appearance or behavior. As just one example, because of the candidates' height differences, the "belt buckle" compromise in 1976 prescribed that Gerald Ford and Jimmy Carter's lecterns would be built to intersect their torsos two-and-a half versus one-and-a-half inches above their belt lines, respectively (Schroeder, 1996).

IMAGE EXPERTS

In modern elections, image experts have become a priority, and include the likes of coaches and consultants, pollsters and press assistants, "spin doctors" and sparring partners, all with the goal of shaping images. According to Grabe and Bucy (2009), "Image handlers now rank among the elite of contemporary politics, and top consultants, such as Karl Rove, James Carville, and Frank Luntz, have become media celebrities in their own right" (p. 97). What's more, such image experts have a strong influence on how politicians present themselves, both verbally and nonverbally. By way of example, upon noticing that Barack Obama had spoken several fewer words in several more minutes than did Mitt Romney in 2012, coaches ran drills to hurry the president's speaking rate along (Schroeder, 2016). In contrast, to prepare for the 1984 vice presidential debates, Geraldine Ferraro's coach urged her to speak slower (Schroeder, 2016). In 2004, George W. Bush was consulted about his poor eye contact, which improved in subsequent debates (Eaves & Leathers, 2018).

Although it is tempting to believe that Al Gore's disastrous performance in presidential debates resulted from a lack of good advice, his problem was probably more attributable to his unwillingness to follow his team's recommendations. In Chapter 4, for example, we found Gore invading his opponent's space on stage. It turns out, in fact, that Gore had tried the maneuver in a rehearsal debate, apparently with the goal of appearing dominant and in charge. His advisors, however, warned him not to, concerned that it would come across as too aggressive. They even drew a line on the rehearsal stage, so Gore could practice not crossing it. Against their advice, he did it anyway, undermining his image along the way (Grabe & Bucy, 2009; Stanton, 2016).

In contrast, ahead of the first ever U.S. presidential town hall debate in 1992, Bill Clinton's team not only worked to improve his posture and facial expressions, they carefully choreographed his movements around the stage. Why? In an effort to undermine images of Clinton's opponents, they hoped that cameras would catch George H. W. Bush and Ross Perot in the background with unfavorable facial expressions. It turns out, they caught something more damaging: Bush checking his watch several times (Schroeder, 2016). Meanwhile, Perot may have appeared uncomfortable because, reportedly, before the debate and without permission, Clinton's team had secretly swapped the debate stools with stools that Clinton had been practicing with, which also were too tall for the 5-foot-5 Perot (Stanton, 2016).

Image experts not only play a role in rehearsing for debates, they can be important afterward as well. Indeed, press assistants and public relations specialists have a history of defending or explaining candidates' actions and appearances, including those that are nonverbal in nature. Consider, for example, responses to questions that have been raised about possible cheating. Specifically, in the first 2004 presidential debates, certain camera angles revealed a rectangular bulge under the back of George W. Bush's suit jacket, leading critics to speculate that he had been wearing an electronic prompting device. By the time the story percolated into mainstream and social media, Republican spokespeople were dismissing the bulge as a wrinkle, a rumple, or a poorly tailored suit. "I'm not sure what it was," one of them claimed, "but the gentleman responsible for the tailoring of that suit is no longer working for this administration" (Schroeder, 2016).

Similarly, in 2012, Mitt Romney was accused of sneaking notes into a debate, which would have been a violation of negotiated rules. Romney's campaign, however, came to the rescue, arguing that the object was a handkerchief, a claim that was later supported by camera shots (Schroeder, 2016).

PRODUCERS, DIRECTORS, CAMERA CREWS, AND THE EFFECTS OF VISUAL PRESENTATION

In his debates, George H. W. Bush preferred the right side of the stage because it made his receding hairline less visible (Schroeder, 2000). Even so, when it comes to manipulating camera angles, there is only so much a candidate can do. To be sure, for at least a century, film directors have established an impressive repertoire of visual conventions involving camera techniques that are believed to influence viewers' responses to onscreen characters (Messaris, 1994). Given the large number of such techniques, our review here is not comprehensive. Instead, we focus briefly on the three techniques most pertinent to political debates: camera distance, camera angles, and reaction shots. In addition, we ask whether such techniques are effective.

Camera Distance: Close-ups and Long-shots

In Chapter 2, we saw that the physical space between people can affect the nature of their communication. Specifically, closer distances are more typical in intimate, interpersonal interactions (see Burgoon, Guerrero, & Floyd, 2010). Similarly, Meyrowitz (1986) coined the term para-proxemics to describe the ways in which cameras might be used to simulate social distance, affecting how people (or characters) on screen are perceived and responded to. According to Messaris (1994, 1997), tight, close-up shots might encourage audiences to identify and sympathize with a protagonist. Empirical research supports the general conclusion that simulated distances affect audiences' responses. That said, the findings are not always consistent. For example, while Baggaley (1980) found that a fictional administrator was perceived as less nervous in close-up versus mid-shots, Reeves, Lombard, and Melwani (1992, cited in Lombard, 1995) found that the effects of close-up shots were mixed. Specifically although people in close-up shots, compared to long shots, were evaluated more positively in some respects (i.e., on passive adjective pairs such as happy/sad and interesting/boring), they were evaluated more negatively in others (i.e., on active adjective pairs such as violent/gentle and competitive/cooperative). Finally, a study by Mutz and Holbrook (cited in Cho, 2009) manipulated the level of incivility displayed by politicians in a hypothetical debate. Their findings indicated that incivility increased audience viewers' cynicism toward government and politicians, but only when a close-up shot was used.

Camera Angles: Being Shown from Above, Below, or Sideways

One of the most pervasive examples of using camera angles to convey impressions of dominance comes from the German propaganda film *Triumph of the Will*. In it, Adolph Hitler was filmed with the camera positioned below him, thereby portraying a person of power. In contrast, using high camera angles is commonly used in films to portray a person as powerless and submissive (Messaris, 1994; Tiemens, 1970). As an interesting side note, Hitler was keenly aware of the importance of nonverbal behavior in stirring the emotions of an audience. Recently a trove of photos has emerged, some depicting Hitler in a variety of strange poses, displaying wild gestures and facial expressions that he used to determine which nonverbal behaviors might enhance his verbal messages at public rallies. Hitler had ordered these photos destroyed, but, unbeknownst to him, they were saved by his personal photographer (Nevitt, 2016).

Although several studies have examined the use of high and low camera angles (e.g., Kraft, 1987; Mandell & Shaw, 1973; McCain, Chilberg, & Wakshlag, 1977; Tiemens, 1970), a consistent picture of their effects in political debates/political-news contexts has not come into focus. Mandell and Shaw (1973), for example, found that a fictional politician was perceived as more powerful when seen from a lower (versus higher) camera angle, while McCain and Wakshlag (cited in McCain et al., 1977) found that newscasters were perceived as more credible when seen from higher rather than lower camera angles. Moreover, Tiemens (1970) found that low camera angles boosted credibility ratings for just one of three speakers who were editorializing on political topics. Following closer analysis, he suggested that the positive effects of low camera angles might be confined to speakers who are discussing less controversial topics. On the other hand, based on a review of literature, Messaris (1997) suggested that low camera angles might enhance judgments of people who are recognized as authorities and diminish judgments of people who are not, particularly in cultures where egalitarianism is the norm:

> Americans have traditionally been ambivalent about according superior status to political figures, and any obvious attempt to display authority or power is a risky move for an American politician—hence, the success, in American political life, of people who are able to combine the look of leadership with convincing evidence of being just plain folks in other ways. (Messaris, 1997, p. 35)

An additional camera angle that has received far less attention is the "talking head" shot in which a person is shown facing the camera directly. Baggaley and Duck (1975) compared the effects of this type of shot to a half-profile shot. Contrary to their expectations, a speaker received significantly higher ratings on reliability and expertise when shown in half-profile.

Regardless of camera angle, of course, candidates can choose whether to look at moderators or, alternatively, whether to simulate eye contact with viewers by looking directly at the camera. Such choices, according to Davis (1978), may be important. Nimmo (cited in Davis, 1978), for example, asserted that John Kennedy's strategic use of simulated eye contact with the television audience was a key factor in his success. Empirical research, however, suggests that additional factors must be considered. Davis (1978, p. 433), for instance, hypothesized that in 1976, Jimmy Carter, whose campaign promoted him as "somewhat of a peer" to the public, would benefit from simulated eye contact with viewers, whereas Gerald Ford, with "the aura of the Presidency visually attached to him," would benefit from maintaining eye contact with moderators. In fact, prior to the first debate, Ford was advised not to look at the cameras (Davis, 1978). Results of Davis's (1978) study, which examined candidates' eye contact alongside polling data, supported the hypotheses in two of the three debates. Specifically, for the first debate, which featured both candidates spending large proportions of their speaking time looking at moderators, polls indicated that Ford won. In the second debate, which featured both candidates spending more time looking at the camera, polls indicated that Carter won (Davis, 1978).

Reaction Shots and Split-Screen Coverage

If it is true, as we saw at the beginning of this chapter, that people's responses to debates are influenced by the mode in which they are presented, it stands to reason that the use of split screens, which provide nonverbal information above and beyond what is available in a single-screen format, should influence viewers as well. To test this assumption, several studies (Cho, 2009; Cho, Shah, Nah, & Brossard, 2009; Scheufele, et al., 2007) asked research participants to watch part of a debate (i.e., the first 2004 presidential debate between George W. Bush and John Kerry) in either a single- or a split-screen format. Results indicated that split-screen (compared to single-screen) coverage, encouraged viewers to rely on party attachment and candidates' character when forming their opinions about debate issues. This was especially true when viewers' attentiveness was low (Cho, 2009). In addition, perceived incivility between candidates was higher in the split-screen versus the single-screen format (Cho et al., 2009). Moreover, viewing the debate in split-screen (versus single screen) format led Bush supporters to become more extreme in their negative judgments about Kerry and in their positive judgments about Bush (Scheufele et al., 2007).[2] Finally, a study by Wicks (2007) found that viewers' perceptions of John Kerry were dependent upon which network they had used to view the 2004 presidential debates. For instance, watching networks that used split-screens either rarely (PBS) or constantly (C-SPAN) was associated with more liking for John Kerry than watching networks (ABC, CNN, FOX) that used sporadic split-screen coverage.

In a conceptual replication of these studies, this time examining the 2016 debates, Stewart, Svetieva, Eubanks, and Miller (2018) found that perceptions of Donald Trump and Hillary Clinton varied depending on which network was watched (Field study 1) and depending on whether the debates were viewed in split- or single-screen format (Field study 2). In the latter study, both candidates were evaluated more critically in the split-screen format.

Taken together, these experimental studies indicate that the manner in which the media presents political debates has the potential to affect viewers' responses (Cho, 2009). A question that naturally follows is whether the media, intentionally or not, has given unequal treatment to some candidates over others, a topic we discuss next.

Do Candidates Receive Equivalent Coverage?

Equal Time? The Role of Chronemics in Debates

The first Democratic primary debate leading up to the 2016 election found former Virginia Senator Jim Webb doing a lot of complaining—not about his rivals, mind you. Instead, over 5 percent of the words Webb spoke were devoted to griping about his limited opportunities to speak (Hanrahan, 2015). Comedian, Seth McFarlane joked, "That poor guy. His whole debate strategy was, 'Excuse me, we haven't gotten our salads yet!'"

Senator Webb, of course, is not the first person to be concerned about equal coverage in political debates. Originally, broadcast stations were legally required to provide equal time and opportunities to any and all qualified candidates running for political office. Because there were just too many smaller parties with candidates, broadcasters refused to host debates, until, that is, the law was amended, allowing coverage of bona fide news events, including presidential debates. Even so, for many years, the National Association of Broadcasters provided guidelines to foster equal treatment of candidates within a debate (Milavsky & Zhu, 1996). Despite that, empirical research suggests that televised coverage of debates may provide advantages to some candidates over others.

With respect to time, some debates have been more equitable than others. For example, Tiemens (1978) found that the time and duration of shots were roughly equal for Carter and Ford in 1976, while other analyses (Hellweg, 1984, cited in Milavsky & Zhu, 1996; Hellweg & Phillips, 1981) found considerable time disparities in a 1980 primary and all of the 1984 primary and general election debates. The most comprehensive study on this topic was conducted by Milavsky and Zhu (1996), who analyzed twenty-two debates from the 1980, 1984, and 1992 elections. Results of their study indicated that the degree of speaking and camera time provided to candidates varied substantially across debates, depending on three factors. Specifically, inequality of time occurred more often when the stakes were lower (i.e., in primary versus general election debates and in vice-presidential versus presidential debates), when the debates were sponsored and moderated by television networks rather than non-networks, and when candidates were more, rather than less, aggressive.

In more recent general elections, although Obama and Biden received more speaking time than Romney and Ryan in 2012, Trump and Clinton received nearly equal speaking time over the course of their general election debates (Voth, 2017). Moreover, an analysis of six Republican primary debates in the 2012 election found that front-runners received significantly more speaking time than their underdog opponents (Stewart, 2015), and an analysis of both Republican and Democratic debates in the 2016 elections found that, in their respective primary debates, Hillary Clinton and Donald Trump received significantly more air time than their opponents (Stewart, Eubanks, & Miller, 2019; Stewart, et al., 2018). Interestingly, Voth (2017) observed that Trump probably benefited from RNC rules, which permitted candidates 30 additional seconds to respond if attacked:

It is likely that planners thought this might help the many Republican candidates attacked by Trump. If that was the logic—it backfired. The rule helped Trump consistently emerge with the most speaking time. Ben Carson in one desperate moment begged one of his rivals to attack him so he could have more speaking time. (p. 90)

That said, although networks structure primary debates in ways that benefit frontrunners, frontrunners do not always use their time wisely. Indeed, although Wisconsin governor Scott Walker was one of the frontrunners in the 2016 Republican primaries, he received less camera time than Donald Trump, Jeb Bush, and the remaining seven candidates, largely due to his comparatively terse responses to the mediators (Stewart et al., 2019).

Comparable Camera Angles?

When Hans Kepplinger (1982) asked whether it was possible to make a person appear positive or negative by using only optical means, 78% of expert camerapersons answered definitely, while 22% said maybe. When asked "how," the majority of camerapersons said that, to leave a positive impression, they would shoot at or about a subject's eye level. This finding is interesting when you consider the results of an analysis that followed. In it, news coverage of Germany's 1976 campaign for chancellor featured camera angles that favored one candidate (Helmut Schmidt) over the other (Helmut Kohl). In contrast, a content analysis of TV news media's visual coverage of candidates in the 2000 U.S. presidential election found no bias in camera angle, distance, or movement (Banning & Coleman, 2009).

Similar analyses have examined the use of camera angles in televised debates. Tiemens (1978), for example, found that visual treatment in the 1976 presidential debates favored one candidate over the other. Specifically, Carter received a significantly greater number of tight shots (larger image size), close-ups, and balanced shots than did Ford. Moreover, in the second debate, the frame placement made Carter appear taller. In contrast, Frye and Bryski (1978) found very little difference in the camera treatment of Ford or Carter in any of their three debates (but see below for reaction shots). Moreover, an analysis of the 1980 Reagan-Bush primary debate reported that although Reagan was given more close-ups, the camera treatment was roughly comparable for both candidates (Hellweg & Phillips, 1981).

In an analysis of 2016 Republican and Democratic primary debates, Stewart et al. (2019) found evidence that the camera shots chosen by the networks benefited some candidates more than others. Specifically, they noted,

> Whether visually priming viewers to perceive a candidate as a viable leader by placing him or her in the visual center of contentiousness, as was the case with

Trump throughout the Fox News and CNN debates, or visually framing contenders as leaders by limiting camera shots to mainly head-and-shoulder shots and competitive shots with other viable candidates or diminishing their leadership potential through multiple-candidate shots that either emphasize their being just another pack member, the visual choices made by the networks influence public perceptions. (p. 27)

Finally, in the 2016 election, Donald Trump was accused by Hillary Clinton's campaign of "menacingly stalking" their candidate by moving around in front of the cameras rather than sitting. NBC reported that "Camera angles gave Trump a looming presence as he moved around in the background behind Clinton" (Jamieson, 2016).

Candidate Reaction Shots and the Stories They Tell

Every great writer knows that conflict is essential to a good story, and they are not alone. According to some critics, members of the media not only know this principle, they exploit it at the cost of objectivity. In the case of debates, Swerdlow (1984) argued that, because networks are for-profit organizations, they might be drawn toward using reaction shots to maximize drama rather than to reflect objectively what truly happens. Likewise, Morello (1992) wrote, "'Good television,' in the case of presidential debates, creates a sense of confrontation. While the task of visualizing clash in debates presents the television director with limited options, the cutaway to a reaction shot . . . offers the best choice for showing the combative nature of the debate" (p. 207).

Several studies conducted by John Morello (1988a; 1988b; 1992, 2019) examined the use of reaction shots in political debates. The first (Morello, 1988b) compared the frequency of switching between shots in the 1976 Carter-Ford and 1984 Mondale-Reagan presidential debates. Results indicated that shot pacing was faster in 1984, perhaps to prevent the debates from appearing "dull to an audience conditioned to a world of fast-paced programming" (Morello, 1988b, p. 236). The implication, of course, is that a faster visual pace might impede people from comprehending what is said in a debate (Morello, 1988b).

The second study (Morello, 1988a) compared instances of actual verbal clash (e.g., attacking or defending ideas, statements, and policies) with visual depictions that implied clash (i.e., close-ups or shots showing reactions to what was being said) in the 1984 Mondale-Reagan debates. Results indicated that over one-fourth of reaction shots that implied clash occurred when candidates were not arguing with one another. Moreover, visual depictions favored one candidate over the other, portraying Reagan as having initiated more verbal clash when, in fact, Mondale did.

The third study (Morello, 1992) examined the 1988 Bush-Dukakis debates and found similar results. Specifically, compared to the 1976 and 1984 debates, the number of reaction shots increased. Moreover, Bush may have been advantaged in several ways. First, although Dukakis initiated more verbal clash, the visual record suggested that Bush did. Second, considering Dukakis's reputation for lacking emotion, the fact that the pace of his reaction shots was slower than Bush's did not help him. Finally, reaction shots frequently followed *ad hominem* attacks, thereby magnifying their impact by "making the speaker's opponent a visual anchor for the name-calling" (p. 216). Because Bush resorted to using more *ad hominem* attacks in the debates, reaction shots may have benefited him over Dukakis.

The fourth study (Morello, 2019) examined the 1992, 2004, 2008, and 2012 town hall debates, and, again, found similar results. In 2012, for example, despite a nearly equal number of attacks and defenses by Obama and Romney, cameras featured more close-ups of Obama while he was speaking, and more reaction shots of Romney while Obama was speaking, creating a visual sense that Obama was "landing more arguments on his opponent" (Morello, 2019, p. 332).

Additional studies by other researchers are sometimes consistent and sometimes inconsistent with Morello's (2019) findings. Messaris, Eckman, and Gumpert (1979), for example, agreed that visual depictions of the 1976 debates portrayed them as more "gladiatorial" than they really were. Tiemens, Hellweg, Kipper, and Phillips' (1985) analysis of the 1980 Carter-Reagan debates, however, reported that camera shots did very little to portray the debates as confrontational. Such discrepancies might be due to different debate cycles or different methodologies. For instance, Morello compared verbal and visual clash, but Tiemens et al. did not. Finally, just because a candidate receives more reactions shots does not necessarily mean that the candidate was advantaged. Indeed, in his analyses of the 1992 vice-presidential debates, Devlin (1994) argued that Al Gore had an advantage over Dan Quayle and James Stockdale because his larger number of reaction shots provided more opportunities for nonverbal disagreement. As we saw in Chapter 4, however, nonverbal disagreement is not always received well by viewers.

THE AUDIENCE

The 1988 U.S. presidential debates found Michael Dukakis responding to a hypothetical question involving his wife: "Governor, if Kitty Dukakis was raped and murdered," Bernard Shaw, one of the moderators, asked, "would you favor an irrevocable death penalty for the killer?" As noted in Chapter 4, Dukakis's response—"No, I don't," followed by a lesson on crime rates and the war on drugs—came across as wooden, contributing to his nickname the "Ice Man." And what was Kitty Dukakis's reaction in the moment? It is difficult to know. Indeed, according to Schroeder (1996), although it would have been logical for cameras to cut briefly to Kitty, "because the campaigns prohibited reaction shots of family members, viewers were deprived of the full context of the coverage" (p. 68).

Depending on the year, candidates and commissions have not only attempted to keep debate audiences, including family members, from being seen (e.g., in reactions shots), but also from being heard, as evidenced by this excerpt from veteran debate moderator Jim Lehrer (2011):

> One of the rules that the commission adopted after 1992 was strict silence from the audience in the hall. So after being introduced to the audience of six hundred people . . . , I laid down the law. I reminded everyone that they were not to participate. This was not a talent show. Applause, cheers, hisses, and/or boos to demonstrate approval or disapproval were not only not permitted; they were mortal sins. I told them that if this rule was ever violated, I would stop the debate, turn around, and point to the culprit before a national television audience that would most likely include everyone they had ever known in their lives. I said it all with a smile, but I meant every word. (p. 123)

Debate audiences, however, often participate paralinguistically through laughter, applause or other means. In a 2007 Republican primary debate, for example, Senator John McCain, a former prisoner of war, pointed out that Hillary Clinton had tried to spend $1 million on a museum memorializing 1969's Woodstock music festival, a monumental event for members of a counterculture described as "hippies." "Now, my friends," McCain quipped, "I wasn't there. I'm sure it was a cultural and pharmaceutical event. I was tied up at the time" (Rutenberg, 2007, para. 1). The audience laughed, cheered and, eventually rose to their feet.

Similarly, as described in Chapter 4, when asked if, at age 73, he was too old to be president, Reagan's answer—"I will not make age an issue of this campaign. I am not going to exploit, for political purposes, my opponent's youth and inexperience"—received a boisterous response. The audience could not be seen, but their laughter and applause continued for nearly 20 seconds. Walter Mondale, Reagan's opponent, joined in, as did the moderator, Henry Trewhitt. In contrast, Judy Woodruff, moderator of the 1988, vice-presidential debates, admonished the audience for its applause, cheers, and boos following a "zinger" from Senator Lloyd Bentsen. Specifically, after his opponent, Dan Quayle, compared himself in age and experience with John F. Kennedy, Bentsen said, "Senator, I served with Jack Kennedy. I knew Jack Kennedy. . . . Senator, you're no Jack Kennedy." Moreover, when replying to a concern about his inexperience in government matters, Ross Perot said in the 1992 debates, "I don't have any experience running up a four trillion dollar debt." To this, the audience roared (Schroeder, 2000).

Finally, during the first general election presidential debate between Hillary Clinton and Donald Trump, the audience repeatedly applauded, cheered, and sometimes booed, despite being reminded by the moderator, Lester Holt, to refrain from doing so. "This isn't like the primary debates," Holt said. "There's no clapping. There's no cheering. There's no booing." (White, 2016). Analysis of the debate revealed that while Trump and Clinton drew four episodes each of applause and cheers from the audience, Trump was more polarizing, eliciting five additional responses made up of laughter and/or boos. Additionally, only applause/cheers seemed to increase viewers' liking for whichever candidate was speaking (Stewart, Eubanks, Dye, Gong, Bucy, Wicks, & Eidelman, 2018).

According to Stewart (2015), such boisterous responses from audiences are most characteristic of primary debates. To be sure, his analysis of the 2008 election found nearly four times the amount of laugher in primary versus general election debates (Stewart, 2012). This pattern, he argued, is important considering that one goal of primary debates is to mobilize ingroup support, and candidates who elicit laughter and applause are more likely gain support. As "speculative evidence," an analysis of a 1984 Democratic primary debate found that the two candidates who were judged to have won the debate were also those who were most interrupted by applause and laughter (Lanoue & Schrott, 1989, p. 305). Interestingly, another study found that, compared to frontrunners, candidates with lower electoral status tend to induce more audience laughter in debates (Stewart, 2015).

Of course, not all political debaters have received such reactions, or stated more accurately perhaps, *been seen or heard* receiving such reactions. Sauter (1995), for instance, discussed the ways in which Bob Dole may have suffered in his 1996 vice-presidential bid because his debate with Walter Mondale included no shots of or sounds from the audience. During the debate, Dole used humor several times. He was interested in the vice presidency, he claimed, because "it's indoor work and no heavy lifting." "But we'll give him the bunny vote," he said of Jimmy Carter, whose reputation had taken a recent hit after admitting in a *Playboy* interview that "I've looked on a lot of women with lust." According to Sauter (1995), Dole's humor was a strong point in his campaign. Audience reaction shots—like laugh tracks on situation comedies—might have served him well. Without them, however, Dole, more than likely, came across as sarcastic and less funny.

Several experimental studies support the notion that audience reactions influence viewers' perceptions. In two studies (Baggaley, 1980; Duck & Baggaley, 1975), for example, research participants viewed a video in which an audience was shown responding either positively or negatively to a lecture. Results indicated that the lecturer was perceived as significantly less popular, less interesting, less expert, more confusing, and more shallow in the negative condition than in the positive one. Other studies have found that audience reactions influence people's responses, but only under certain conditions. Specifically, audience reactions were influential when the people seeing or hearing those reactions (1) thought they shared attitudes with the audience (Davis, 1999); (2) were uninvolved in the issue at hand (Axsome, Yates, & Chaiken, 1987); and (3) perceived the audience as attractive (when favoring a politician) or unattractive (when not favoring a politician) (Weigman, 1987).

In the context of political debates, Fein, Goethals, and Kugler (2007) conducted several experiments examining the effects of audience reactions. In two, research participants were shown, in part or whole, the second 1984 Mondale-Reagan debate. For some participants, the debate was not altered. For others, two of Reagan's quips (e.g., "I won't exploit my opponent's age") were deleted. For a third group, the quips remained but the audience's positive reaction to them was deleted. Results of the study revealed that deleting audience reactions had an especially strong effect on perceptions of both candidates, helping Mondale and hurting Reagan. Specifically, while Reagan was perceived as winning the unedited debate, he was perceived to have lost in the other two conditions, particularly when audience reactions were deleted. In short, people's judgments about debates were strongly influenced by audience reactions.

Such findings are particularly concerning when considered alongside research that reports uneven use of audience reaction shots by the media. Kepplinger (1982), for example, found that news coverage of Germany's 1976 campaign for chancellor featured unbalanced positive and negative audience reactions toward the candidates. To our knowledge, such findings have not been investigated with regard to political debates.

Up to this point we have discussed the ways in which audience reactions might function heuristically—that is, audience approval or disapproval might serve as a type of "social proof" (see Cialdini, 1993), indicating that a candidate is worthy or unworthy in some way. Presumably, however, audiences might have other effects. Hecklers, for instance, might distract viewers from processing verbal arguments (Ware & Tucker, 1974). Additionally, approving audiences might appease candidates, while disapproving audiences might rattle them. In fact, prior to the second 2016 debate, the Trump campaign sought to intimidate Hillary Clinton by inviting four women who had accused Bill Clinton of sexual misconduct to sit in the family area, close to the stage. The Commission on Presidential Debates thwarted the plan, however, and the women were seated alongside regular audience members (Mitchell & Jamieson, 2016).

Finally, although, so far, we have seen that politician's behavior might *elicit* responses (e.g., laughter) from audiences, it is also possible for politicians to *solicit* responses. For example, during their runs for the presidency in 2016 and 2020 respectively, former Florida governor Jeb Bush and former South Bend mayor Pete Buttigieg asked silent audiences at campaign events to clap for them (Riotta, 2020). Both candidates received disparagement from the media, pointing to the apparent risks of such solicitation. A more recent event, however, suggests that soliciting audience response can be effective. In a Democratic primary debate leading up to the 2020 election, for instance, former vice president Joe Biden asked the audience to show support for Lt. Col. Alexander Vindman, who had testified at Donald Trump's impeachment trial, and was subsequently removed from his position at the White House in what many believed was an act of retaliation (e.g., Rogan, 2020; Santucci, 2020). "Stand up and clap for Vindman! Get your, get up there!" Biden beseeched members of the debate audience, and most of them did, which we believe benefited Biden. Indeed, as Rogan (2020, para. 3) argued,

> In this case, just about the whole room stood up and applauded for Vindman. It will suggest to primary voters that Biden is capable of bringing together an increasingly disparate Democratic Party. And the translation on TV cameras will be one of the former vice president finding his mojo again.

MODERATORS AND PANELISTS

Near the end of the second 2012 presidential debate, soon after Governor Mitt Romney disputed a claim by President Barack Obama, the moderator, Candy Crowley stepped in, pointing out that Romney was wrong. It is no surprise that she was criticized by conservatives, who claimed that she had violated "the sacred role of impartial moderator" (Platt, 2012, p. 1). That said, moderators and panelists are not required to be impartial. In fact, Morello (1992) wrote of the 1988 debates, "Candidates not only clash with one another but also with the panel of reporters. . . . The 'questions' from the panelists often served not as neutral openers for debate but as pointed critiques to which the candidate had to reply" (p. 208).

The 2016 election found moderators playing a larger role as "fact checkers," consuming 15% of speaking time in the general election debates compared to 10% in 2012 (Voth, 2017). According to Voth (2017), this was largely due to the idea that Donald Trump was "so improvisational in his abuse of 'facts' that he would need moderators who could control and correct him" (p. 88).

Such antagonism between candidates and panelists can and has been portrayed visually. Morello (1988), for example, found that, compared to the 1976 presidential debates, those in 1984 featured more shots of panelists. As a result, broadcasts in 1984 "visually emphasized much more of the contest of each candidate *against* the panel" (Morello, 1988, p. 237). Considering this, we find it quite possible that the nonverbal behaviors of moderators and panelists affect viewers' perceptions of political debates. Although we are unaware of any studies that examine this issue, there is supporting evidence from research conducted in other contexts. One study, for example, found that mock jurors were influenced by judges' positive and negative nonverbal diplays (Burnett & Badzinski, 2005). A second study found that shots of an interviewer's nonverbal behaviors affected viewers' perceptions of an interviewee (Baggaley, 1980). A third study found that a talk show host's positive facial expressions led to attitude change in viewers (Nabi & Hendricks, 2003). In short, then, the influence of moderator/panelist nonverbal behavior seems ripe for examination.

Beyond visual clash and attacks, recent criticism aims at moderators' questions as focusing on, and instigating, conflict among candidates. In the 2016 Republican debates, moderators often pitted candidates against each other, creating an atmosphere of personal conflict. As an example, the CNN-sponsored Republican debate in September of 2015 featured questions from moderators such as "Carly Fiorina, would you be comfortable with Mr. Trump in charge of the nuclear arsenal?," "Chris Christie, what do you think of Ben Carson's criticisms of professional politicians like you?," and "Jeb Bush, are you a puppet under the control of your donors, as Mr. Trump says?" (Poniewozik, 2015, September 17, para. 5). Not to be outdone, productions of the 2019–2020 Democratic primary debate have also faced such criticism. Consider a question from Jake Tapper to Bernie Sanders early in the first round of debates that seemed purposely phrased to encourage conflict:

> You support Medicare for All, which would eventually take private health insurance away from more than 150 million Americans, in exchange for government-sponsored healthcare for everyone. Congressman Delaney just referred to it as bad policy. And previously, he has called the idea "political suicide that will just get President Trump re-elected." What do you say to Congressman Delaney? (Galgano, 2019, August 8, para. 4)

POST-DEBATE COMMENTATORS: PUNDITS, NEWSPAPERS, EDITORIALISTS, AND NEWSCASTERS

Sometimes the most influential debate is the one that comes *after* the debate. Indeed, people's perceptions about who won a debate may depend on what network they tune into for post-debate coverage (Brubaker & Hanson, 2009). And anyone who has watched post-debate commentary knows that a common topic among pundits, editorialists, and newscasters is the meaning behind political candidates' nonverbal behavior. Communication scholars have dubbed these types of conversations "metadiscourses of nonverbal behavior," and argue that such conversations can influence the ways in which nonverbal behavior is interpreted, judged, and framed (Manusov & Jaworski, 2006; also see Jaworski & Galasinski, 2002).

Previous research, for example, has examined choices the media has made when discussing Bill Clinton's nonverbal behavior during the Clinton-Lewinsky ordeal (Jaworski & Galasinski, 2002), and Hillary Clinton's tears when asked by another woman about the personal challenges of campaigning (Manusov & Harvey, 2011). In their analysis of latter case, Manusov and Harvey identified two common frames used by the media. Specifically, an "informative frame" treated the behavior as an authentic reflection of the candidate, while a "performative frame" implied that Hillary Clinton's tears were strategically manufactured for political gain.

In the context of political debates, Joseph Biden's smirking and laughter in the 2012 vice-presidential debate was framed by some pundits as a controlled strategy involving a nice balance of aggressive belittlement and politeness, while others suggested that Biden's behavior resulted from a lack of control and professionalism (Flock, 2012). That said, we know of only one empirical study focusing on the ways in which media framed nonverbal behavior. Specifically, Cummings and Terrion (2020) used qualitative content analysis to examine how newspapers assessed Hillary Clinton's credibility and likability through her use of nonverbal immediacy cues. Consistent with the argument that female politicians face a double bind—in which they are expected to display traditionally feminine qualities (e.g., be cooperative and nurturing), yet are judged unfit for office for not displaying traditionally masculine qualities (e.g., acting assertive and tough) (see Jamieson, 1995, and Chapters 7 and 8)—Cummings and Terrion identified several themes in commentary, columns, opinion pieces, and editorials in the *Boston Globe* and/or *Houston Chronicle*. For instance, Clinton was portrayed as stiff, cold, and unable to connect with others. As a case in point, she "was penalized in coverage for refusing to shake Trump's hand before or after most debates" (Cummings & Terrion, 2020, p. 7). In addition, although on one hand Clinton was portrayed as an emotional deviant and was criticized for displays of anger and excitement, on another she was criticized for appearing weak.

In addition to influencing their audience by talking about nonverbal behavior, people in the media might influence others by way of their own nonverbal behavior. One study of the 1976 election, for instance, found that four out of the five news anchorpersons (Walter Cronkite, David Brinkley, Harry Reasoner, and John Chancellor) showed greater facial positivity when talking about one candidate over the other (i.e., Chancellor favored Ford and the others favored Carter) (Friedman, Mertz, & DiMatteo, 1980). A related study found that news anchor Peter Jennings's positive facial expressions when talking about Ronald Reagan may have affected viewers' voting behavior (Mullen et al., 1980). Finally, an investigation of Israeli television found evidence that interviewers displayed nonverbal bias that favored one candidate over another (Babad, 1999).

PHOTOGRAPHERS AND EDITORS OF IN-PRINT (OR COMPUTER SCREEN) MEDIA

Earlier in this chapter, we examined the role that "moving" pictures play in political debates. Many of the same principles and findings from that research apply to the presentation of "still" pictures on the page or computer screen as well. For example, camera angles are considered important, although the size and placement of photos may come into play too. Specifically, larger and front-page photos may be seen as more important than smaller photos placed elsewhere (Wanta, 1988; Moriarty & Popovich, 1991).

As with moving pictures, a number of studies have demonstrated that photographs in newspapers, magazines, and on television have the power to convey certain images of candidates and influence voter preferences (e.g., Rosenberg, Bohan, Mccafferty, & Harris, 1986; Rosenberg & McCafferty, 1987). Moreover, studies of photographs in past elections have raised concerns about visual bias and preferential treatment of candidates (e.g., Graber, 1987; Kenney & Simpson, 1993; Moriarty & Garramone, 1986; Moriarty & Popovich, 1991; Waldman & Devitt, 1998; but also see Banning & Coleman, 2009). Moreover, as with moving pictures, the media has been criticized for using still pictures to exaggerate the confrontational nature of debates. According to Edwards (2012), this can be achieved visually through what he labels "oppositional positioning," which juxtaposes characters in an inherently adversarial association. As Edwards (2012) noted,

> Although oppositional positioning is not generally a feature of campaign news coverage, it is periodically used as an editing or montage technique to illustrate contested political relationships in debates. News photographs may lend themselves to this configuration through various editorial interventions such as cropping and placement involving two separate images. In debate coverage, a photo editor may place separate profile or semi-profile shots of the two candidates in a profiled oppositional juxtaposition, as Joe Biden and Sarah Palin were in a story about the 2008 vice-presidential debate in a New Haven *Register* story. The words "Face to Face" are superimposed over their profiles to emphasize a sense of conflict, one that often characterizes the headlines assessing the debate performances. (pp. 686–687)

Following her analysis of news photographs from the 2016 debates, Conners (2017) concluded that, although conflict was reflected more in headlines than photos, oppositional positioning in the photos was quite common. This was particularly true when photos were positioned to show Clinton and Trump facing each other, possibly suggesting conflict to readers.

SOCIAL MEDIA

According to Gutgold (2017), political debates are especially important today, considering that YouTube and other Internet sites have given them media immortality. Indeed, the Internet has not only provided the means for watching debaters and their associated gaffes and triumphs repeatedly, it has changed the nature of *how* political debates are watched and talked about. Research indicates, for example, that millions of viewers not only watch debates (sometimes distractedly) on the "second screen," but also use social media to discuss the events before, during, and after they air (Stroud, Stephens, & Pye, 2011; Shah, Hanna, Bucy, Lassen, Van Thomme, Bialik, Yang, & Pevehouse, 2016). Twitter, for example, recorded 17 million tweets related to the second 2016 presidential debate, setting a record for the most-tweeted debate in history (Peck, 2019).

Apparently, candidates' nonverbal communication plays an important role in such Internet activity. Indeed, one study found that candidates' nonverbal behaviors in the 2012 presidential debates—especially their facial expressions, gestures, and blinks—predicted the volume and valence of viewers' Twitter use, more so than candidates' rhetorical strategies and comparable to memes (i.e., virally transmitted units of culture) that reflected politicians' verbal utterances. For example, memes from the 2012 debates included Obama telling the moderator, "I had five seconds before you interrupted me," and Romney declaring "I love Big Bird," though promising to cut funding for public television (Shah et al., 2016).

According to Peck (2019), such memetic practices matter because, in aggregate, they not only function as "large-scale inside jokes," but as framing devices that help understand political debates, constructing and reifying candidates' images. Of course, memes are not confined to candidates' verbal utterances; they can reflect nonverbal communication as well. Three examples come from the 2012 and 2016 elections. First, the "laughing Joe Biden" meme emerged five minutes into the 2012 vice presidential debate in response to Biden's repeated background smiling and guffawing during his opponent's speaking turns. According to Dewberry (2019), the meme not only suggested that Biden was dismissive and derisive, but possibly inappropriate too.

Second, the "Clinton shimmy" meme emerged out of the first 2016 presidential debate. During one of many interruptions from Donald Trump, Hillary Clinton said, "Whoo . . . okay!," smiled, and literally shook off Trump's claims (Carter, 2019, p. 243). According to Carter (2019), that shimmy, which was captured and circulated as a meme, functioned to encapsulated the elation Clinton felt over her strong performance in the debate, and, more generally, the joy people feel over everyday victories, as evidenced by subsequent memes featuring basketball star Shaquille O'Neil or cats performing similar shimmies. Some memes, in turn, featured Shaq, cats, and Hillary competing in a three-way "shimmy-off" (Carter, 2019, p. 247).

Third, the second 2016 presidential debate inspired memes that drew attention to Donald Trump, who lurked behind Clinton as she responded to questions. A popular iteration, according to Carter (2019), transposed the scene onto a movie poster of the horror movie *It Follows*. In so doing, the meme functioned to frame Trump's behavior as nefarious, while providing networked debate viewers an opportunity to influence others and participate in a non-traditional form of democracy (Carter, 2019).

SUMMARY AND FINAL THOUGHTS

Following the first 1960 presidential debate, Kennedy said of television, "We wouldn't have had a prayer without that gadget" (Mackay, 2000, para. Goethals, 2005, p. 51). Regardless of whether that was the case, or whether anyone intentionally introduced bias into the broadcast, the material reviewed in this chapter illustrates that debate effects are not simply a matter of what goes on between two or more candidates on a stage. Indeed, the ways in which debates are negotiated beforehand and talked about afterward influence not only what nonverbal behaviors viewers will be exposed to, but also the ways in which those behaviors are interpreted and judged. Likewise, television (and photography) does not necessarily reflect the reality of debates. The media is not merely a channel for transmitting what happens in front of a camera. Instead, it can and does filter and transform information, constructing and representing something beyond the debate itself. As such, even when political candidates manage their nonverbal behaviors, the ways in which those behaviors are viewed depend, to a large extent, on factors beyond candidates' control. With that in mind, the importance of understanding the media's role in political debates cannot be emphasized enough. In fact, we would argue, it is essential to being an informed citizen and a competent consumer of visual messages.

NOTES

1. An examination of the 1976 Dole-Mondale vice-presidential debate found that people's judgments were more affected by verbal comments (transcript) than visual or audiovisual stimuli (Krauss, Apple, Morency, Wenzel, & Winton, 1981).
2. Kerry supporters were not affected by mode of presentation.

Chapter Six

Applying Principles of Persuasion to the Social Scientific Study of Nonverbal Behavior in Political Debates

"The heart of politics," wrote W. Lawrence Neuman, "is persuasion" (1998, p. 319), an observation reflected in the first handbooks of social influence, or rhetoric. Penned in ancient Greece by teachers known as sophists, these handbooks instructed students in the art of persuading fellow citizens in the context of political gatherings. During that same era, Aristotle wrote *On Rhetoric*, his landmark treatise, which, likewise, pointed to politics as a fundamental context for persuasion. These teachers, along with Roman rhetoricians such as Cicero and Quintilian, divided the study of rhetoric into five "canons," including invention, arrangement, elocution, memory, and delivery (Corbett, 1971). The last of these categories focused largely on gestures and facial expressions, thereby underlining the important role of nonverbal communication in political persuasion.

Today, the legacy of these classic scholars resonates not only in humanistic approaches to the study of rhetoric and argumentation, but also in social scientific research on political persuasion, which emerged in the 1920s with the work of Walter Lippmann, and blossomed in the 1950s with experiments conducted by Carl Hovland and his colleagues at Yale University's Communication and Attitude Change Program (Perloff, 2013; Seiter, 2017). With regard to the latter, although these and other early efforts to articulate persuasion processes from a social scientific perspective "relegated nonverbal behaviors to second class status" or "ignored them altogether" (Burgoon, Birk, & Pfau, 1990, p. 140), the important role of nonverbal behavior in the process of social influence has become apparent. With that in mind, while the next chapter focuses on humanistic/argumentation/rhetorical approaches, the purpose of this chapter is to examine a number of social scientific theories, models, concepts, and processes, largely from the field of persuasion, that speak to the role of nonverbal behaviors in political debates. Although many of these have been mentioned in other parts of this book, they are extended in this chapter alongside the presentation of principles not yet considered.

THE SOCIAL MEANING MODEL AND DIRECT EFFECTS MODEL OF IMMEDIACY

In communication, the term "immediacy" is used to describe behaviors that simultaneously signal warmth, friendliness, availability, psychological closeness, involvement, and positive affect (Andersen, 2004). Verbally, such behaviors might include calling people by name, complimenting them, and/or using plural ("we") rather than individual ("I" and "you") pronouns. Nonverbally, examples of such behaviors include eye contact, touch, and smiling.

According to the direct effects model of immediacy (Andersen, 2004) and the social meaning model (Burgoon, Coker, & Coker, 1986; Burgoon, Manusov, Mineo, & Hale, 1985), people who engage in such behaviors are better liked and/or more trusted than those who do not signal immediacy. Moreover, because people tend to comply more with people they like and trust, both models predict that communicating immediacy is positively associated with successful persuasion. Indeed, a significant body of research conducted in non-political contexts indicates that immediacy behaviors are influential. By way of example, in retail and service contexts, customers who were complimented or called by name made more purchases or left higher tips than customers who received no such messages (e.g., see Dunyon, Gossling, Willden, & Seiter, 2010; Jacob & Guéguen, 2014; Seiter, 2007; Seiter & Dutson, 2007; Seiter, Givens, & Weger, 2016; Seiter & Weger, 2010, 2013). Similarly, a meta-analysis of 49 nonverbal studies across several contexts indicated that the use of direct eye contact (versus averted gaze), appropriate touch, and vocal pleasantness were positively associated with greater compliance (Segrin, 1993).

Evidence for this same pattern of results can be found in debate contexts. One study, for example, examined audiences' responses to debaters' nonverbal behavior across 37 televised debates on political issues in Denmark (Jorgensen, Kock, & Rorbeck, 1998). Results indicated that debaters who gazed intensely at their audience, displayed open (vs. closed) body postures, spoke enthusiastically, and gestured energetically won more than they lost. Debaters who displayed a combination of closed posture and unfriendly facial expressions fared particularly poorly (for research with similar findings, see Chapter 3).

Finally, previous literature suggests that the impact of immediacy, alongside other types of relational messages, may carry more impact in political debates than do verbal utterances. As Michael Pfau (2002) wrote nearly two decades ago,

> Television communication features both visual and verbal content, but the visual overpowers the verbal. . . . As a consequence of television's visual dominance, television magnifies the role and impact of relational messages, which rely heavily on the nonverbal stream for transmission. . . . This new language embodies softer persona dimensions, such as: immediacy/affection, which consists of involvement, warmth, enthusiasm, and an interest in the receiver; receptivity/trust, which comprises sincerity, honesty, interest in communicating, and willingness to listen; similarity/depth, which includes friendliness and caring; and lesser dimensions. I maintain that political debaters who communicate these relational cues are more persuasive, and that relational messages overpower content messages in televised debates. (p. 254)

In support of this argument, Pfau and Kang (1991) analyzed the first Bush-Dukakis presidential debate and found that positive relational cues—especially displays of immediacy, affection, similarity, and trust—had more persuasive impact than did the verbal content of the debate.

EXPECTANCY VIOLATIONS THEORY

Alternative approaches suggest that the direct effects model of immediacy may be too simplistic to explain the role of nonverbal behavior in the process of persuasion. One such approach, known as expectancy violations theory (EVT; Burgoon, 1978, 2009; Burgoon & Hale, 1988; Burgoon & Jones, 1976; Burgoon & Aho, 1982), originated as an explanation for inconsistencies in research on the topic of proxemics. Specifically, while some studies found that people react negatively to sources who invaded their personal space, others found that space invasions resulted in positive outcomes (e.g., space invaders were perceived as more credible than their non-invading counterparts).

How might such inconsistencies be accounted for? According to EVT, based on social norms, people have expectations about appropriate interaction distances that should be maintained in various contexts. When a communication source violates such expectations, the receiver's attention shifts to the source's behavior, which, in turn, is evaluated either positively, which facilitates persuasion, or negatively, which hampers persuasion. Alternatively, if the violation is interpreted as ambiguous, the receiver evaluates characteristics of the source. As such, highly valued sources (e.g., attractive, credible, likeable people) are more persuasive when they violate expectations (within reason), while low valued sources are most persuasive when abiding by social norms.

Although EVT was originally conceived as an explanation for the effects of proxemic violations in interpersonal settings, subsequently, it has been applied to a wide array of other verbal and nonverbal behaviors, including eye contact, touch, and body orientation (e.g., see Burgoon & Walther, 1990), and in a variety of communication contexts, including political debates. By way of example, Bucy and Gong (2018) noted,

> Political competition requires challenges and, at times, a certain degree of combativeness. But how attacks are delivered, and the rhetorical context in which they are delivered, determine their acceptability and ultimate impact. Whether attacks are conveyed verbally or nonverbally, political audiences ultimately expect appropriate reason and action, which for all but the most extreme partisans entails not committing violations of well understood boundaries and social norms. (p. 76)

Examples of such violations occur throughout this book. Consider, for instance, the behavior of Al Gore and Donald Trump, who suffered criticism after invading the personal space of their respective opponents, George W. Bush and Hillary Clinton, in the 2000 and 2016 presidential town hall debates (see Chapter 4, and Bucy & Gong, 2018). Similarly, research indicates that viewers not only paid more attention to Barack Obama's violation of nonverbal expectations, they also responded negatively, especially to his disengaged and downcast style in the 2012 presidential debates versus Mitt Romney (Gong & Bucy, 2016).

POLITENESS THEORY

In the wake of a poor performance in his first Democratic primary debate of the 2020 presidential campaign season, former vice president Joe Biden pledged not "to be as polite" in the second debate (Frazin, 2019, para. 1). Considering our discussion of expectancy violations, however, the prudence of such a pledge seems questionable. Indeed, the history and format of debates has prompted a norm that candidates should treat their opponents with courtesy and respect (Rowland, 2019). Based on this notion, Dailey, Hinck, and Hinck (2008) extended Brown and Levinson's (1987) politeness theory to an analysis of political debates.

Specifically, politeness theory (Brown & Levinson, 1987) argues that people are motivated to maintain two kinds of face. The first, positive face, is maintained when a person is well regarded (i.e., liked and respected) by others. The second, negative face, is maintained when a person does not feel constrained or impeded on by others. Previous analyses of politeness in presidential debates suggests that audience members notice impolite, face-threatening behaviors (e.g., character attacks) and use them as a criterion for judging candidates' performances (Dailey, Hinck, & Hinck, 2005; Dailey et al., 2008; Dailey, Hinck, Hinck, & Hinck, 2017).

Although such analyses are based on transcripts of political debaters' *verbal* communication, previous research (Weger, Seiter, Jacobs, & Akabulut, 2010; Weger, Seiter, Jacobs, & Akabulut, 2013) has argued that politeness theory can be applied to debaters' nonverbal actions as well. By way of example, nonverbal behaviors that communicate disapproval (e.g., head shaking) or derision (e.g., eye rolling) during an opponent's speaking turn threaten the speaker's positive face. Alternatively, attempting to interrupt an opponent's turn via strong nonverbal expressions violates the turn holder's autonomy to complete the speaking turn unhindered, thereby threatening the speaker's negative face. Of course, the consequences of such face threatening behavior extends beyond the speaker:

> Whether verbal or nonverbal, egregious interruptions during political debates create a politeness dilemma for both debaters. When choosing whether to interrupt, a debater must weigh the costs of appearing impolite with the costs of allowing an opponent to complete an argument that can potentially hurt the interrupting debater. . . . Having been interrupted, the speaker with the floor also must choose among turning over the floor, ignoring the interruption, or using some strategy to call out the interrupter's impolite behavior. Nonverbal expressions of disagreement are interruptions that implicitly, rather than explicitly, challenge the speaker's right to the floor, so in this case, the speaker's main decision is whether to ignore the nonverbal interruption or call out the norm violation. (Weger et al., 2013, p. 184)

In other words, speakers can respond to impolite behaviors with varying levels of politeness themselves. Such research suggests that, generally, speakers are most effective if they directly address (rather than ignore) their opponents' nonverbal behaviors, as long as they do not personally attack their opponents in the process (Weger et al., 2010). Indeed, as Gong and Bucy (2016) noted, "In the television era, effectively performing leadership requires a delicate balancing act, however, between politeness, interruption, and argumentation, especially when a rival attempts to assume the mantle of leadership through verbal assertion and aggressive debate tactics" (p. 350).

ETHOLOGICAL AND EVOLUTIONARY PERSPECTIVES

This notion—that effective leadership requires a balance of appropriate behaviors—is consistent with ethological and other evolutionary approaches to the display of emotion. Specifically, ethological approaches, rooted in the study of rivalry and alliances between and among primates, suggests that nonverbal displays of emotion play an important role in the communication of dominance and affiliation. In addition, perceptions regarding the appropriateness of such nonverbal displays depend on the competitiveness or noncompetitiveness of a situation as well as the relative social rank held by interactants (see Salter, Grammer, & Rikowki, 2005). As Stewart, Salter, and Mehu (2013) explained,

> Therefore, potential leaders must exhibit not just the ability to dominate others, whether in response to internal threats to the group's peace or external threats to its well-being, but also the ability to affiliate with group members. Facial display behavior of leaders, and those who hope to wear the mantle of leadership, therefore must be able to communicate with both agonistic and hedonic intent. However, circumstances determine which type of display behavior is appropriate and should predominate. (p. 168)

In short, then, a variety of expressions, adapted appropriately to fit a given situation, appears to be an effective approach to displaying emotions, assuming that the source is not perceived as contradictory in his or her behavior. In fact, a substantial body of research supports the general argument that leaders—and by extension, political debaters—are most effective when their affiliative (i.e., expressions of happiness/reassurance or sadness/appeasement) and agonistic (i.e., expressions of anger/threat or fear/submission) displays of emotion are perceived to be appropriate (see Salter et al., 2005; Stewart et al., 2013). That said, in an analysis of major party candidates in the general elections of 1992, 1996, 2000, and 2004, Bucy and Grabe (2008) found that when voters supported a candidate, they responded most positively to the candidate's happiness/reassurance displays and some anger/threat displays. In contrast, when voters were critical of a candidate, they responded negatively to the candidate's anger/threat displays. Finally, both critics and supporters of candidates responded negatively to displays of fear (Bucy & Grabe, 2008).

THE DOUBLE BIND

Although politeness theory and ethological perspectives support the notion that displays of dominance are sometime appropriate, many politicians find themselves at distinct disadvantages when attempting to assert themselves in debates. Indeed, a considerable amount of persuasion theory and research points to the pervasiveness of inaccurate gender stereotypes, which lead to perceptions that males are more competent than females, and that females should be warmer, kinder, and more likeable than males (see Carli, 2004). As a consequence, females face a double bind. As Jamieson (1995, p.125) noted,

"Women are penalized both for deviating from the masculine norm and for appearing too masculine." In debate contexts, this double bind undoubtedly influences perceptions of female candidates' verbal and nonverbal behaviors. Hillary Clinton, after all, was accused by her opponent, Donald Trump, of "lacking a presidential look," of being a "nasty women," and for lacking the stamina of her male opponents (Kitsch & Hinck, 2019). Moreover, commentators on both sides of the political aisle critiqued her, but not her opponent's, laughter and smile (Tonn, 2019), a topic we return to in Chapters 7 and 8.

ROBERT CIALDINI'S PRINCIPLES OF SOCIAL INFLUENCE

Strategic self-presentation is the process through which people attempt to augment their power by influencing the impressions that other people have of them (Jones & Pittman, 1982). In other words, self-presentation is, by its very nature, a form of persuasion. In previous chapters, we saw how theoretical work on the topic of self-presentation and, more generally, impression management (Goffman, 1959), could be applied to the study of political debates. According to Verser (2007), the basic aims of impression management in political contexts include creating perceptions of likeability, attractiveness, and credibility. A question that naturally follows is whether such impressions, once formed, are persuasive. To address this question, we turn to the work of Cialdini (1993, 2016), who presented a framework of several underlying principles related to effective social influence. Four of those principles seem especially pertinent to our discussion.[1]

First, the *principle of authority* asserts that people are more readily influenced by sources who are thought to be credible (Cialdini, 1993). Previous research indicates that credibility is composed of several characteristics that people perceive in a source. Examples include expertise (also known as competence or qualification), trustworthiness (also called character or integrity), goodwill, extroversion, composure, dynamism, and sociability (Berlo, Lemert, & Mertz, 1969; McCroskey Hamilton, & Weiner, 1974; McCroskey & Teven 1999; McCroskey & Young, 1981). Additionally, as we saw in Chapter 3, perceptions of these characteristics, particularly a source's competence, are influenced by the source's nonverbal behaviors (Barak, Patkin, & Dell, 1982; Newman, 1982). Not surprisingly, this holds true in the context of politics as well. By way of example, Bob Dole's shifty-eyed behavior in the 1996 presidential debates was associated with perceptions of lower competence (Eaves & Leathers, 2018). Moreover, as we saw in Chapter 4, the background behavior of nonspeaking debaters affects perceptions of both their own and their opponents' credibility.

Cialdini's (1993) second principle asserts that people are persuaded by sources whom they perceive to be likable. Previous research not only indicates that people who are asked to make other people like them change their nonverbal behavior (e.g., by smiling more, nodding, and making more eye contact) (Godfrey, Jones, & Lord, 1986), but also that these and other nonverbal behaviors (e.g., forward lean, touch, gestures) do, indeed, lead to increased liking for sources (Barak et al., 1982).

Cialdini's (2016) third principle, *unity*, asserts that audiences are more easily persuaded by people with whom they share identities (i.e., people they feel "at one" with), which, in politics, might be applied through a quintessential "person of the people" approach to politics. It is ordinary, for example, to find political debaters sharing stories about their conversations with "real" people facing difficult problems, all the while displaying appropriately empathetic nonverbal expressions. In 1992, Bill "I-Feel-Your-Pain" Clinton was considered by some to have benefited from "The Bubba factor," which characterized him as "a 'good old boy,' comfortable in the company of common folk and someone you would like to have a beer with" (Talbert, 2012, para. 1). Similarly, it is common to find candidates dressed like regular-folk on the campaign trail, though formal attire is still the norm in debates. Indeed, 2020 Democratic presidential candidate Andrew Yang, best known for his proposal to provide all Americans with a universal basic income, drew criticism for not wearing a tie in a primary debate. "Sartorial update: Once we pass universal health care," former U.S. attorney Prett Bharara tweeted, "Andrew Yang can purchase a tie" (Lemon, 2019, para. 9). "Do you look at Mr. Wang and say, 'Would it kill you to wear a tie?'" asked MSNBC's chief anchor, Brian Williams (Tschorn, 2019, para. 4).

Cialdini's (1993) fourth principle, *social proof*, suggests that people tend to look to others for clues about what is correct, worthwhile, or appropriate. As such, people are more likely to visit popular restaurants, read best-selling books, or purchase trendy merchandise. In political debates, we suspect that this tendency might translate into relying on others' nonverbal behavior as a means of deciding which candidate's position is best, or more generally, which candidate is winning a debate. Some primary debates, for example, feature a large number of candidates. If most of them display nonverbal disapproval for the same opponent, we wonder whether the audience might be influenced.

A more likely scenario is that the nonverbal behaviors of other sources have such effects. Indeed, as we saw in Chapter 5, viewers perceptions of debates change depending on the absence or presence of audience laughter. Similarly, although we are unaware of any research on this topic, we suspect that reaction shots showing approval and/or disapproval from debate moderators might influence viewers' perceptions of candidates as well. This notion is consistent with the predictions of social comparison theory (Festinger, 1954), which assumes that people not only learn about and evaluate themselves by comparing themselves to others, they tend to assimilate group opinions. According to Haumer and Donsbach (2009), this tendency to use others as a decision-making heuristic may be especially prevalent when forming impressions via television given that the criterion for making judgments is often ambiguous.

THE HALO EFFECT

The term "halo effect" (Thorndike, 1920) refers to a cognitive bias in which one positive attribute of an individual leads people to perceive additional attributes of that individual in a positive light. Attractive people, for instance, are perceived more positively in general than are unattractive people (Dion, Berschid, & Walster, 1972). As a consequence, attractive people tend to be more persuasive (Cialdini, 1993). Because they are viewed as more "rewarding," their persuasiveness extends to situations in which they violate expectations of persuasive targets (see Burgoon & Aho, 1982, and expectancy violations theory above). This bias, it turns out, extends to political contexts as well, providing attractive politicians, compared to unattractive ones, more favorable ratings of effectiveness, more media coverage, and an electoral advantage, among other things (see review by Lev-on & Waismel-Manor, 2016). As Lev-on and Waismel-Manor (2016) noted,

> While functioning as a heuristic, the "beauty premium," as it has been called, has real implications. If better looking candidates are able to raise more money, secure more endorsements, or even win elections at least in part due to their physical attractiveness, then these qualities are not merely variables we need to control for in electoral models; they may have a direct and substantive effect on candidates' electability. (p. 1758)

FRENCH AND RAVEN'S POWER BASES

In what is now considered a seminal work, French and Raven (1960) identified five bases of power that leaders might draw upon when attempting to persuade others. These include reward (i.e., the power to control valued resources), coercive (i.e., the power to inflict punishments), expert (i.e., power based on knowledge, experience, and/or skill), legitimate (i.e., power that is based on one's formal rank or position), and referent (i.e., power based on an ingroup's respect or liking for a leader). Previous research indicates that a person's nonverbal behavior affects perceptions of these power bases. In one study, for example, people with relaxed, as opposed to nervous, facial expressions were rated as higher on all of the power bases except for coercive (Aguinis, Simonsen, & Pierce, 1998).

THE MERE EXPOSURE EFFECT

Two days after his wife was accused of plagiarizing a speech delivered eight years earlier by Michelle Obama, Donald Trump tweeted, "Good news is Melania's speech got more publicity than any in the history of politics, especially if you believe that all press is good press!" (Kruse, 2016, para. 2). As absurd as this claim sounds, it is not entirely inconsistent with what is known as the *mere exposure effect*, which indicates that things we are familiar with (e.g., songs, faces, or other objects we've seen or heard repeatedly) are perceived more favorably than unfamiliar things (Zajonc, 1968).

Although we find ourselves skeptical of Trump's claim and of the similar claim, often attributed to P.T. Barnum, that "There's no such thing as bad publicity," Voth (2017) speculated that Donald Trump's success in the 2016 election was due, in part, to his outlandish moments on the debate stage:

> Initially, the offensive comments and remarks of Trump inverted the media pattern for diminishing candidates through an attrition of attention. As candidates conventionally adapt to "expected" norms of political rhetoric—attention from the media declines. The media appears to be looking for mistakes. Trump's "mistakes" created spectacles that by almost any account led to billions of dollars in free advertising for his campaign. That was an important concept that was incorporated in the RNC primary debates. (p. 90)

As discussed in Chapter 5, candidates have also reaped potential advantages based on the relative number of times they are called on to speak, the amount of time they are permitted to speak, and how often they appear in reaction shots. At times, these numbers have been quite lopsided. During Dan Quayle's speaking turns in the 1992 vice-presidential debates, for example, Al Gore appeared in 59 two-headed reaction shots, compared to James Stockdale, who appeared in zero (Devlin, 1994).

MOTIVATED REASONING

As we have seen throughout this book, nonverbal behavior not only plays a critical role in shaping the images of candidates, it also helps to foster one-sided, yet powerful "parasocial" relationships that some voters feel they have with candidates (Horton & Wohl, 1956; also see Chapters 1 and 3). Nonverbal behaviors, especially early in campaign events such as primary debates, are especially likely to help foster these parasocial relationships. Whether positive or negative, the affective valence of parasocial relationships can bias viewers' cognitive processing of candidates' arguments via motivated reasoning (Redlawsk, 2002). Unlike cold, controlled, and effortful searches for evidence and reasoning in support of a position, motivated reasoning begins with experiences and attitudes toward a particular issue or communicator and then moves to evaluations of the argument based on these prior attitudes (Taber & Lodge, 2016). In other words, rather than being most concerned with accuracy in forming attitudes and beliefs about issues, theories of motivated reasoning suggest that people are most concerned with maintaining their identities, values, and attitudes (Chaiken, Liberman, & Eagly,1989), and in doing so, "ignore or devalue contrary information, bias the perception of credibility, or overlook important factors" (Taber, Lodge, & Glathar, 2001, pp. 208–209).

By way of example, one study examined the neural responses of partisan participants' (i.e., voters who are biased toward a particular candidate), who were asked by the researchers to complete reasoning tasks during the 2004 U.S. presidential elections. Results of the study indicated that motivated reasoning occurred in brain areas associated with emotional responses rather than in areas associated with the conscious processing of evidence and arguments (Westen, Blagov, Harenski, Kilts, & Hamann, 2006). Similarly, other studies have found that parasocial relationships motivate viewers to reach conclusions based on their experience "with" candidates rather than motivating viewers to draw accurate conclusions about the quality of arguments based on evidence and reasoning (e.g., Kunda, 1990; Mutz, 2007).

One prescient example of a candidate drawing on his relationship with supporters occurred in the 2016 campaign when Donald Trump, then a presidential candidate, famously said, "I could stand in the middle of 5th Avenue and shoot somebody and I wouldn't lose voters" (Diamond, 2016, para 2). In this quote, Trump suggested that the devotion his followers have for him outweighs any negative behavior he might engage in. Trump's comment squares with research by Redlawsk (2002) who found that people became more, rather than less, supportive of a favored candidate when presented with negative information about the candidate.

GAINING AND HOLDING AUDIENCE ATTENTION

Classic persuasion theory, including William McGuire's (2001) input-output framework, argues that an audience must pay attention to a message in order for the message to be persuasive. With that in mind, attention arousing nonverbal behavior might include any unexpected or particularly vivid behavior on the part of a debater. For example, an especially pleasant voice, attractive face, or bodily movement can attract attention to the speaker and perhaps to the message as well. In political contexts, beat gestures may be particularly useful in providing emphasis and maintaining a compelling, interesting, and memorable cadence during speech. For example, Streeck (2008) conducted an in-depth analysis of hand gestures used by Democratic candidates during primary debates leading up to the 2004 election. The analysis identified both hand shape and arm movement as elements of each gesture. For example, a *slice* gesture occurs with an open hand and a downward stroking movement of the arm, which performs two functions. First, when strokes correspond with peak vocal emphasis on particular words, they function to stress particular elements of a message, presumably drawing attention from the audience. Second, when strokes occur on every accentable syllable, they can be used to change the cadence of the speech. Similarly, Maricchiolo, Gnisci, Bonaiuto, and Ficca (2009) found that gestures linked to beat and rhythm increased audience perceptions of a speaker's credibility and persuasiveness compared to speakers who did not use such gestures.

On the other hand, nonverbal behavior that garners *too much* of the audience's attention may decrease the persuasiveness of a candidate's verbal message if the behavior inhibits the audience's ability to cognitively process the candidate's arguments or if the behavior violates expectations for behavior in a negative way. As noted above, when expectations are violated, people tend to focus on the unexpected behavior more than the message itself. For example, behaviors such as rapid eye blinking, seemingly random gestures, and low volume may be so distracting that audience members are not able to pay attention to the verbal message. Indeed, Gong and Bucy (2016) found that inappropriate facial displays by Barack Obama and Mitt Romney in the 2012 presidential debates drew viewers' attention away from their messages.

Other examples of distracting behavior abound. For example, in the Vermont Gubernatorial debate in 2014, all of the candidates running for office were invited to participate in the televised debates regardless of voter support. The debate featured Bernard Peters, an Independent, whose appearance was unconventional. He wore a long, rather unkempt beard and a camouflage hunting cap. Similarly, the 2014 Idaho Gubernatorial debates featured candidates with distracting looks or mannerisms. Harley Brown, for example, wore a leather hat, leather vest, and weight lifting gloves. Two cigars were tucked into the breast pocket of his shirt, and, while speaking, he engaged in nearly constant angry and threatening facial expressions. Not to be outdone, another candidate, Walt Bayes, with eyeglasses perched atop his head, spent much of his debate time reading Bible verses and other religious messages from a small piece of paper. He also used finger-jabbing gestures toward the incumbent governor. Interestingly, although the looks and behavior of such candidates presumably distracts from their messages, the elaboration likelihood model (Petty & Cacioppo, 1986) suggests that, under some conditions, distraction can increase a debaters' persuasiveness. We examine that model next.

THE ELABORATION LIKELIHOOD MODEL OF PERSUASION

In Chapter 1, we considered the ways in which dual process theories of persuasion inform the study of nonverbal behavior in political debates. Here, we extend that discussion by focusing on one specific model's predictions about the influence of context and audience characteristics on the processing of persuasive messages. The elaboration likelihood model (ELM; Petty & Cacioppo, 1986) proposes that social influence can be conceptualized as following one of two basic routes to persuasion, each entailing different amounts of thought, or elaboration. The first, known as the *central route*, involves attitude change that requires an audience to carefully scrutinize a persuasive message, weighing the relative strengths and weaknesses of arguments in order to reach an informed decision. The second, known as the *peripheral route*, entails little effort, thought, or critical attention to the relative merits of the information presented in a persuasive message. Instead, attitude change via the peripheral route is based on cues that are not directly related to the substance of a message. In addition, the model acknowledges that attitude change might involve using both routes at the same time (known as *parallel processing*), although Petty and Cacioppo (1986) suggest that there is typically a trade-off, such that either the central or the peripheral route has the most impact at any given time.

Whether the central or peripheral route predominates hinges on two factors. First, the central route requires the *ability* to process substantive arguments in a persuasive message. Voters, however, might not always be able to do so. They might, for example, be distracted from the message (see above) or lack the requisite skills. As Lubell (1977) noted,

> In my interviewing during the [1960] campaign I systematically asked each voter, "Did you listen to any of the TV debates?" and "What do you think of them?" The overwhelming majority responded in terms of how the candidates looked and handled themselves rather than in terms of the issues that were argued about. Many voters explained that they tried to make sense of the arguments of the candidates "but the more we listened the more confused we got." (p. 152)

To this point, Berquist (1994, p. 37) added,

> Most American television viewers are not expert in argumentation, skillful in following an extended argument, or adept in judging the precise merits of a debater's case. . . . What Americans feel confident in doing, what each of us does day-in and day-out, in both face-to-face and televised encounters, is to size up the quality of a stranger. (p. 37)

Second, the central route requires that people have the *motivation* to scrutinize arguments in a persuasive message. Such motivation, however, is not always present in those who view debates. Consider, for example, the effects of issue involvement, i.e., the degree to which the outcome of a particular issue is relevant to an audience. Specifically, when people have low involvement with an issue, the ELM predicts that they are less inclined to engage in central processing.

Although central processing has more impact when ability and motivation are high, the ELM predicts that peripheral processing has more impact when motivation is low and/or ability is hindered. Thus, for example, when the outcome of an issue has no personal relevance, people are more likely to rely on peripheral, message irrelevant cues to make decisions (Petty & Cacioppo, 1986). Finally, when persuasion occurs via the central route, attitude change tends to be more persistent than persuasion that is brought about via the peripheral route (Petty & Cacioppo, 1986).

Because persuasion via the central route entails processing and evaluating messages, and because visual information is traditionally considered less substantive than verbal argument, it is tempting to consider nonverbal behaviors as nothing more than peripheral cues to persuasion. According to Guyer et al. (2019), and as noted in Chapter 1, however, a source's nonverbal behavior potentially plays multiple roles in the persuasion process. Indeed, working within the ELM's framework, one means by which nonverbal behavior might affect attitude change is by influencing the amount of effortful thinking that an audience engages in when considering a persuasive message. Specifically, nonverbal behavior or appearance might heighten an audience's motivation and ability to think about strong arguments, in which case persuasion should increase (Guyer et al. 2019). A source who appears competent, for example, might increase an audience's motivation to listen to a persuasive message. On the other hand, if a source's nonverbal behavior or appearance hinders an audience's ability and/or decreases an audience's motivation to think carefully about a message that contains strong arguments, persuasion could be reduced. In the 1960 presidential debates, Ted Rogers, Richard Nixon's chief production advisor, seemed to understand this point, objecting to the use of reaction shots on the basis that it would draw the audience's attention away from what was being said (Seltz & Yoakam, 1979).

In addition to influencing the degree to which people engage in issue-relevant thinking, nonverbal behaviors can also bias people's thoughts, serve as arguments themselves, or act as peripheral cues to persuasion (Guyer et al., 2019; also see Chapter 1). According to Eaves and Leathers (2018, p. 64), it is in the latter of these roles, that nonverbal behaviors "take center stage." Specifically, when an audience's motivation and ability to engage in effortful thinking is low, a source's nonverbal behavior and appearance can function as a simple heuristic for making a decision. As such, the peripheral route not only magnifies the importance of nonverbal style, appearance, and personality, it emphasizes the expression of emotion, which is a strong predictor of voter preference (see De Landtsheer, De Vries, & Vertessen, 2008).

Previous experimental studies support these predictions. By way of example, Hart, Ottati, and Krumdick (2011) found that, when evaluating political candidates, distracted research participants were more influenced by candidates' attractiveness than were non-distracted participants, presumably because distraction lessened participants' *ability* to process information critically (i.e., via the central route) while simultaneously increasing their reliance on heuristics. Moreover, several studies have found that informed voters, compared to their counterparts, are less likely to use candidates' attractiveness as a decision-making heuristic, presumably because informed voters are *better able* to critically scrutinize information (Ahler, Citrin, Dougal, & Lenz, 2007; Hart et al., 2011; Johns & Shephard, 2011; Lenz & Lawson, 2011; Stockemer & Praino, 2015).

Similarly, previous research is consistent with ELM's predictions regarding message recipients' *motivation* to scrutinize information. As one example, consider research suggesting that people differ in the *need for cognition* (Cacioppo & Petty, 1982). Specifically, compared to their counterparts, people high in the need for cognition are especially *motivated* to engage in effortful thinking. With this in mind, it is not surprising that, when evaluating political debates, people who were high in the need for cognition were less swayed by heuristics than people who were low in the need for cognition (see Kugler & Goethals, 2008). Similarly, evidence suggests that people who are issue involved (see above), should be particularly *motivated* to engage in effortful thought. Lubell's (1977) examination of the 1960 debates supports this notion, indicating that the issues attended to most "were those which listeners could translate into their own personal and even selfish calculations" (p. 153). Not surprisingly, then, previous research indicates that high-involved participants are less influenced by candidates' physical appearance than are low-involved participants (e.g. Bailenson, Iyengar, Yee, & Collins, 2008).

According to Hacker (2004), who applied the ELM to political campaigns, the degree and nature of cognitive elaboration might not only explain the process of attitude change, but the emergence of political images as well. Specifically, he wrote,

> Testing the utility of the ELM for candidate image research might begin with these types of hypotheses. First, when elaboration is low for the voter, more persona information or impressions will become content in the candidate image. When elaboration is high for the voter, more issue impressions than persona impressions will become content in the candidate image. In the case of parallel processing where elaboration is fluctuating or middle-range in elab-

oration, the candidate image will have both issue and persona content in nearly equal amounts. (p. 116)

COMMUNICATION ACCOMMODATION THEORY

Communication accommodation theory (CAT) (Giles & Wiemann, 1987; Street & Giles, 1982) predicts that because listeners perceive communication styles that are similar to their own as pleasant and attractive, sources are more persuasive when they adjust their communication style to match the style of their listeners. Of course, in televised debate contexts, mirroring a diverse national audience's communication patterns would prove impossible. That said, CAT provides a potentially interesting explanatory lens. By way of example, Andersen's (2004) review of research suggests that rapid rates of speech are more persuasive in geographical regions where faster speech is the norm, while the opposite is true in regions where slower speech is normative.

CONSISTENCY THEORIES

A central postulate for a host of classic persuasion theories—including balance theory (Heider, 1958), cognitive dissonance theory (Festinger, 1957), and congruity theory (Osgood & Tannenbaum, 1955)—is that people strive to be consistent.[2] As such, when their attitudes and/or behaviors are incompatible, they experience psychological discomfort, which, consequently, they are motivated to resolve. Consider, for example, a vegetarian who falls in love with another vegetarian. The congruity of loving someone who shares your attitudes should feel comfortable. Alternatively, imagine that the vegetarian falls in love with an avid carnivore. According to consistency theory, having a negative attitude toward eating meat, yet a positive attitude toward someone who persistently eats meat, should lead to psychological angst, which might be resolved in various ways. The vegetarian, for instance, might change his or her negative attitude toward eating meat or his or her positive attitudes toward the carnivore.

To the extent that nonverbal expressions reflect a person's attitudes, it is easy to see how the principle of consistency is pertinent to our discussion. In Chapter 1, for example, we suggested that nonverbal communication might signal the nature of candidates' relationship with one other. With that in mind, how might voters who hold positive attitudes toward two political candidates react when the candidates express nonverbal disregard for a rival, as Senator Elizabeth Warren did when refusing to shake Senator Bernie Sanders's hand following a 2020 Democratic primary debate? Might their positive attitudes toward one or both candidates dampen? Might they be less willing to vote for one candidate after the other drops out of the race? Alternatively, how might voters who hold positive attitudes toward one candidate and neutral attitudes toward another respond when one candidate expresses positive regard for another, as former vice president Joe Biden did when putting his arm around Bernie Sanders after the latter candidate had been accused in a 2020 Democratic primary debate of being liked by no one? Finally, how might voters who hold positive attitudes toward one candidate and negative attitudes toward another candidate react when the candidates express nonverbal disregard, as Hillary Clinton and Donald Trump did when refusing to shake hands with each other before and after their 2016 presidential debates? Might voters' attitudes toward one or both candidates change for better or worse? Clearly, such questions provide promising avenues for future research.

FRAMING EFFECTS

Erving Goffman (1974), one of the earliest contributors to framing theory, argued that people organize and interpret their world through frames, which are mental representations that function heuristically. In public opinion research, attention has focused on a phenomenon known as "framing effects," which, according to Chong and Druckman (2007),

> occur when (often small) changes in the presentation of an issue or event produce (sometimes large) changes of opinion. For example, when asked whether they would favor or oppose allowing a hate group to hold a political rally, 85% of respondents answered in favor if the question was prefaced with the suggestion, "Given the importance of free speech," whereas only 45% were in favor when the question was prefaced with the phrase, "Given the risk of violence." (Sniderman & Theriault, 2004, p. 104)

In other words, the ways in which messages are presented (i.e., framed) influence the ways in which people respond to issues. As such, in media studies, considerable attention has focused on the ways in which television and other media create, build, perpetuate, reinforce, and maintain frames. More specifically, in political contexts, evidence indicates, among other things, that frames influence the attributions that voters make about candidates (see Perloff, 2013). Considering this, it is not surprising that political campaigns are motivated to frame candidates in the most favorable of lights. Furthermore, considering that image-based political frames represent a primary focus of media coverage in U.S. elections (Nitz, Koehn, & McCarron, 2017), and considering the essential role of nonverbal behavior in creating favorable impressions (see above), there is little doubt that campaigns that disregard the value of such behavior do so to their own detriment.

SUMMARY AND FINAL THOUGHTS

The social scientific study of persuasion provides meaningful contributions to our understanding of the role and functions of nonverbal behavior in political debates. This chapter not only explored the ways in which several prominent theories and concepts from the field of persuasion might be applied to debate contexts, it extended ideas discussed in previous chapters.

The commonly understood purpose of political debates is to allow the electorate to weigh and compare candidate's arguments in support of their positions and their vision for the direction of the country. In an ideal world, the outcome of this process would be based on the quality of candidates' reasoning and evidence. In the real world, however, candidates' nonverbal behaviors also influence the evaluation of verbal arguments. Specifically, messages that are primarily based on viewers' affective impressions of candidates' nonverbal performance can influence the way audience members evaluate accompanying verbal arguments. Being persuasive requires both what a candidate says and how the candidate delivers the message.

As such, we should note that although the theories we have presented in this chapter are diverse, it is clear that, in many respects, they are compatible.[3] Consider, for example, that the images politicians (and others) attempt to create (see impression management, self-presentation, mere exposure, and framing theories) might serve to bias the processing of messages, affect receivers' motivation or ability to pay attention to or scrutinize messages, and/or serve as heuristic/peripheral cues to persuasion (see the elaboration likelihood model; distraction models; and motivated reasoning). Specifically, audiences might be swayed, biased, or otherwise affected by sources who are credible, likable, similar, popular, powerful, and attractive (see Cialdini's principles of authority, liking, unity, and social proof; communication accommodation theory; the five power bases; and the halo effect). Similarly, audiences might rely on heuristic cues such as the degree to which sources communicate warmth and sociability (see the direct effects model of immediacy and the social meaning model) and the degree to which they perceive debaters as having acted "appropriately" (see expectancy violations theory, the double bind, ethological perspectives, and politeness theory). In short, we hope this chapter serves not only as a useful resource, but as an invitation to compare, contrast, and integrate. Indeed, this is the value, we believe, of considering an array of principles side by side and all in one place.

NOTES

1. Cialdini's (1993) principles of social influence that were not featured in this chapter include (a) the principle of *reciprocity*, which suggests that we should repay, in some form or another, what other people have given us (e.g., when someone does us a favor, we feel indebted

and more likely to repay with compliance); (b) the principle of *scarcity*, which states objects or opportunities in short supply are perceived as more valuable (e.g., when something is a "limited edition" or on sale for a "limited time," we are more motivated to buy it); and (c) the principle of *consistency/commitment*, which says that the more someone becomes committed to an idea, the more likely he or she will be to behave consistently with it (e.g., after committing time and resources to shopping for a particular car, you'll feel more committed to buying it).

2. In their presentation of the elaboration likelihood model, Petty and Cacioppo (1986) note that it is compatible with a number of persuasion theories that, previously, had been considered at odds with one another.

3. The notion that people strive for consistency is yet another of Cialdini's (1993) principles. We treat that principle separately here in order to highlight other theories and perspectives.

Chapter Seven

Humanistic Theories for Analyzing Nonverbal Behavior in Televised Debates

The practice of rhetoric (essentially, persuasion) is almost certainly as old as the earliest human settlements, and so vitally important to participating in the civic lives of ancient Athenians and Romans that citizens often pursued formal training. The first people we know of to write a systematic treatment of rhetoric were the Sicilians Corax (the teacher) and Tisias (a student of Corax) sometime in the 5th century B.C.E. (Hinks, 1940). Later, the Attic orator Isocrates, credited with introducing the first academy devoted to teaching rhetoric (Usher, 1999), wrote that rhetoric is "that endowment of our human nature which raises us above mere animality and enables us to live the civilized life" (as quoted in Johnstone, 2009, p. 53).

Although, historically, the study of rhetoric has focused largely on the topics of style, arrangement, and logical properties of verbal utterances, nonverbal elements of delivery have also been recognized as key to successful persuasive speaking. In fact, Demosthenes, another of the classic Greek orators and a contemporary of Aristotle, argued that delivery was the quintessential persuasive factor in rhetoric: "[T]he management of the voice and gesture, in Public Speaking ... is intimately connected with what is, or ought to be, the end of all Public Speaking ... and therefore deserves the study of the most grave and serious Speakers" (Demosthenes as quoted in Blair, 2005, p. 363). Echoing this notion, the Roman orator Quintilian wrote with exquisite detail regarding the effective use of gestures, vocal style, and other elements of delivery. For example, when discussing the use of voice in oratory, Quintilian (ca. 95 C.E./1968) wrote,

> For the voice is like the strings of a musical instrument; the slacker it is the deeper and fuller the note produced, whereas if it be tightened, the sound becomes thinner and shriller. Consequently, the deepest notes lack force, and the higher run the risk of cracking the voice. The orator will, therefore, employ the intermediate notes, which must be raised when we speak with energy and lowered when we adopt a more subdued tone. (XI.III.42)

Rhetoric as a scholarly discipline continued through the middle ages and enlightenment (McKeon, 1942), as reflected in the European education system, which centered on what became known as the trivium (rhetoric, grammar, and logic) and the quadrivium (arithmetic, geometry, astronomy, music). Likewise, colleges created in the English colonies of America, such as Harvard, followed the Elizabethan statutes of 1571–1576, which required the study of rhetoric in the first-year curriculum (Forsyth, 2019; Kraus, 1941). About this same time, the elocutionary movement of the 17th and 18th centuries renewed interest in techniques of delivery, at least partially, out of concern for the decline of English oratory practices, particularly in delivery (Mohrmann, 1966). As Goring (2017) noted, "Indeed the figure of the dull orator speaking to a drowsy audience—the type of preacher depicted in Hogarth's 'The Sleeping Congregation' (1736)—became a recurrent topos within eighteenth-century culture" (p. 562).

For a number of reasons, the elocutionary movement eventually withered, and, once again, the linguistic components of public oratory became, and, with a few exceptions, have remained the dominant form of study in the fields of rhetoric and argumentation. That said, in this chapter we demonstrate that, despite such scholarly focus, many prominent humanistic theories of rhetoric and argumentation serve as useful analytical models for understanding nonverbal behavior in televised political debates.[1] Specifically, this chapter demonstrates that there is much to be gleaned about the nonverbal behavior of rhetors, including debaters, from an examination of classical and modern humanistic approaches to communication. We begin by discussing rhetorical theories, starting with Aristotle, and then move through Bitzer's rhetorical situation, Fisher's narrative paradigm, and the gendered double bind. Finally, we examine contributions from theories of argumentation, including multimodal argument, strategic maneuvering, and the design approach to argumentation.

ARISTOTLE'S THEORY OF RHETORIC

Perhaps the most influential classical treatise regarding public speaking, *On Rhetoric*, was penned by Aristotle (born about 384 B.C.E.), a student of Plato and teacher of Alexander the Great (Kennedy, 2008). Aristotle defined rhetoric as the art of discovering the available means for persuading an audience.

Of most interest to our project are his classification of artistic proofs and the enthymeme, which are important concepts in the rhetorical theories discussed later in this chapter. To begin, however, it is important to consider Aristotle's view of delivery as a persuasion strategy. Although Aristotle was not fond of using nonverbal behavior to sway an audience, he recognized its power to do so:

> [F]or [those who study delivery][2] consider three things, and these are volume, change of pitch, and rhythm. Those [performers who give careful attention to these] are generally the ones who win poetic contests; and just as actors are more important than poets now in the poetic contests, so it is in political contests because of the sad state of governments. But since the whole business of rhetoric is with opinion, one should pay attention to delivery, not because it is right but because it is necessary . . . but, nevertheless, [delivery] has great power, as has been said because of the corruption of the audience. (Aristotle/ Kennedy, 2007, 3.1.3–4)

In the three books comprising *On Rhetoric*, two were devoted to methods of inventing arguments and one was devoted to linguistic style. The quote above opens the third book and represents almost the entirety of Aristotle's comments concerning rhetorical delivery in *On Rhetoric*. Like most argumentation and political communication scholars (e.g., Hayes, 2019), as well as political pundits (e.g., Ventre, 2008; Weil, 2012), Aristotle considered it shameful that audiences can be persuaded by a polished delivery rather than the strength of a speaker's argument. Below, with all apologies to Aristotle's sensibilities, we discuss how his methods of proof might be related to elements of a speaker's nonverbal behavior.

Aristotle differentiated among two main types of rhetorical argument. Inartistic proofs are those forms of evidence that exist outside the speaker's own creation such as witnesses and documents; artistic proofs are persuasive strategies invented by the speaker for a particular occasion. The three classes of artistic proofs consist of ethos, pathos, and logos. *Ethos* refers to the character of the speaker. Aristotle was careful to point out that his conception of a speaker's character was the result of the speaker's performance rather than the speaker's reputation with an audience preceding a speech. Although Aristotle posited that ethos should be built on the quality of a speaker's verbal arguments and analysis, Chapters 3 and 4 demonstrated the powerful role that nonverbal delivery plays in an audience's perception of a speaker's character. Especially for undecided voters, debates are an opportunity for candidates to look "presidential," maintain composure under fire, and to manage attacks on their persona.

The second proof, *pathos*, refers to a speaker's use of emotions in persuading an audience. Although Aristotle focused on verbal strategies of emotional appeals, there is strong evidence that nonverbal behavior can arouse emotions in an audience. First, as discussed in Chapters 1 and 2, nonverbal communication is well-suited to communicating emotions. Likewise, the emotional tone set by debaters' nonverbal behavior can influence the emotional experience of the audience as evidenced by audience members' mimicry of the speaker's affective displays (e.g., Lanzetta et al., 1985; McHugo, Lanzetta, & Bush, 1991). Although not set in a debate context, Consenza (2014) suggested that the gestures, movements, and facial expressions of Beppe Grillo, an Italian comedian turned political activist, play an essential role in creating humorous moments and emotional connections with his audience.

Along these lines, applause functions to connect speakers and audiences emotionally by signaling approval of the speaker's message. Even more to the point, research indicates that an audience's applause can be prompted by a speaker's nonverbal behavior. Indeed, Atkinson's (1984) work on charismatic political speakers underlined the importance of coordinating verbal strategies with vocal intonation and gestures in order to successfully arouse an audience to applause. As a case in point, consider speakers' use of three-part lists (see Atkinson, 1984), as illustrated by a line from Ronald Reagan's nomination acceptance speech at the 1984 Republican National Convention. "Our tax policies," Reagan said, "are and will remain *pro-work, pro-growth, and pro-family*" (Cannon, 1984, para. 28). According to Atkinson (1984) such three-part lists can be used as a strategy for generating applause or cheering from an audience. In addition, research by Heritage and Greatbatch (1986) found that delivery features such as eye contact with audience members, pausing at the end of the three-part list, gesturing rhythmically, and vocally stressing the final element in the list is essential. Indeed, only 5% of applause generating strategies succeeded when none of these delivery components were present, while almost 60% of the three-part lists generated applause when all the elements were included. Similarly, an investigation of applause during British political party meetings found that speakers use gestures to control and calm applause as well as to signal when applause is expected (Bull, 1986). For example, Bull found that speakers raised their arm with an open palm facing the audience as a gesture to calm applause.

The third proof, *logos*, or persuasion by use of reasoning, is probably the least amenable to being communicated by nonverbal behavior as it is not well-suited for communicating propositional content. However, as discussed above, gestures, vocal tone, and facial expressions potentially make the verbal component of a message more understandable. Moreover, any argument made using satire or irony require nonverbal cues, such as vocal tone and facial expression, for audiences to understand the meaning beneath the words. Finally, nonverbal behavior can play an important role in the process of enthymematic reasoning.

Aristotle identified the enthymeme as the primary means of persuasion and as a form that arguments often take in constructing proofs by logos. Enthymemes are characterized by two features. First, the enthymeme is often described as a truncated syllogism. Unlike a formal syllogism, which states both premises explicitly, the enthymeme omits a premise (or sometimes a conclusion). For example, the argument "Pete carries a gun, so he is probably a member of the National Rifle Association" includes only one premise, followed by a conclusion. The premise—"Most people who carry guns are members of the National Rifle Association"—is omitted. As such, the audience must fill in the missing premise on their own. As Bitzer (1959) noted, "the enthymeme succeeds as an instrument of persuasion because its premises are always drawn from the audience" (p. 408). The abridged nature of the enthymeme was useful in rhetoric, according to Aristotle, because he believed the typical citizens comprising audiences in legal proceedings and political assemblies were not trained well enough in logic to follow long chains of syllogistic reasoning characteristic of more elaborate dialectical argumentation.

The second feature of an enthymeme concerns the probabilistic nature of rhetoric. The goal of enthymematic reasoning in rhetoric is persuading an audience that a legal or policy action is *probably* correct rather than demonstrating a conclusion to be certainly true or false as in dialectic. Further, premises in enthymemes are based on *doxa*, that is, the current state of knowledge held by an audience, rather than logically established truths as in syllogisms. Therefore, besides being shorter versions of syllogisms, enthymematic reasoning offers less certainty than syllogisms (Aristotle/Kennedy, 2007). Thus, in the example above, the first premise is stated enthymematically, as "*Most* people who . . ." rather than "All people who . . ." As we elaborate below, visual and acoustic elements of delivery can function as signs in enthymematic reasoning about a speaker's emotional experience, the intensity with which the speaker holds a belief, and as an argument about the speaker's character.

Finally, a more comprehensive analysis of how Aristotle's artistic proofs can be communicated via nonverbal behavior in political debates is found in the work of Poggi and Vincze (2009), who used both qualitative and quantitative methods to analyze nonverbal behavior in political debates during the national Italian elections of 1994 and 2006. Specifically, these researchers identified several functions of nonverbal behavior related to Aristotle's concepts of ethos, pathos, and logos (see above). For instance, gestures of benevolence (e.g., holding a hand over one's heart to communicate sincerity) convey that a speaker is morally worthy (ethos), while gestures displayed with various degrees of intensity convey a speaker's emotion (pathos). As an example, Romano Prodi, one of the candidates, roused voters and conveyed his pride in being Italian by "moving his forearm with short and jerky movements of high power and velocity" (Poggi & Vincze, 2009, p. 81). Finally, gestures that communicate a speaker's certainty can function to amplify a verbal enthymeme (logos). One example includes the precision grip gesture in which the index finger touches the thumb with the other fingers of the hand either balled in a fist or extended as in the American "OK" gesture (see the more detailed description below), which, according to Poggi & Vincze (2009) indicates that a precise argument is being made.

THE RHETORICAL SITUATION

Communication theorists have long held that the meaning of messages is contextual, which is to say that people use contextual information to interpret the intention and goals of a speaker. Lloyd Bitzer (1968) likewise argued that the meaning of rhetorical acts are inextricably tied to the situations in which they occur. As such, understanding a rhetorical act requires understanding the situation from whence it came. A rhetorical act, such as participating in a televised political debate, according to Bitzer (1968, p. 5), "comes into existence as a response to a situation" and is given significance in terms of how the act responds to the situation. Rhetoric is successful when it serves as a "fitting response" to the situation that calls it forth. Indeed, as Bitzer wrote, "Not the rhetor and not persuasive intent, but the situation is the source and ground of rhetorical activity" (p. 6).

According to Bitzer, the rhetorical situation includes three elements: exigence, audience, and constraints. *Exigence* is an identifiable problem or obstacle that calls forth rhetorical action as an "imperfection marked by urgency." An exigence is rhetorical when communicative action is capable of addressing, and potentially modifying, the imperfection in the situation. For example, the failing United States economy in 2008 motivated both John McCain and Barack Obama to address the degree to which the real estate and banking collapse was a problem and what might be done to make matters better.

The *audience* forms a second element of a rhetorical situation and includes the intended or unintended recipients of a persuasive message. The audience can be present or not and can be addressed through written or spoken communication. The rhetorical audience, writes Bitzer (1968), "must be distinguished from a body of mere hearers or readers: properly speaking, a rhetorical audience consists only of those persons who are capable of being influenced by discourse and of being mediators of change" (p. 7).

Constraints, the third element of the situation, serve to open opportunities for some strategies while closing off others. The beliefs, attitudes, and values of an audience, cultural norms, societal rules for behavior in the situation, larger cultural systems of belief, and the like all act as constraints on the speaker's communication strategies. One constraint on behavior in U.S. presidential debates stems from cultural norms that favor "appearing presidential" during debates, in part, by exercising emotional control. At least at the time of this writing, no presidential candidate has wept during a general election debate.

In response to Bitzer's concept of the rhetorical situation, Richard Vatz (1973) suggested that rhetoric is not driven by any objectively real and identifiable exigence. Rather, he contended, situations are defined by rhetorical acts rather than the other way around. For Vatz, there are no exigencies that are objectively real without the meaning created by the rhetorical act that defines them. Specifically, Vatz wrote, "Thus rhetoric is a cause not an effect of meaning. It is antecedent, not subsequent, to situations" (p. 160). For Vatz, rhetorical acts bring attention and meaning to a chaotic world filled with an infinite number of potentially meaningful events, facts, actors, calamities, and so forth, which become salient by talking about them. A speaker's choice of which facts to share, how to interpret the chosen facts, and what remedies, if any, are required bring the exigence into being.

The dueling conceptions of the rhetorical situation as conceived by Bitzer and Vatz was bridged by Scott Consigny (1974), who wrote, "I argue that Bitzer correctly construes the rhetorical situation as characterized by 'particularities,' but misconstrues the situation as being thereby determinate and determining. I show that Vatz correctly treats the rhetor as creative, but that he fails to account for the real constraints on the rhetor's activity" (p. 176). For Consigny, then, rather than requiring a particular response, the situation is an instrument for the rhetor to use in the creation of a message. Moreover, rather than being simply of the rhetor's own making, rhetors must be receptive to features of situations, whether established or novel, in constructing effective messages. Consigny skillfully argued that although exigencies and situations are most often real and create some constraints on speakers, the speaker's ability to apply universal themes, such as freedom-tyranny, war-peace, or possible-impossible (and many others) to a heteronomous situation is the driving factor in how situations find meaning.

With these conceptualizations in mind, televised political debates occur in situated contexts with a particular set of identifiable and meaningful exigencies facing the electorate. Candidates for office must not only skillfully argue for policies aimed at alleviating problems and creating new opportunities, they must also convince the audience to adopt their perspective on the nature of the exigencies facing them. Of course, the candidates also face the exigence of the debate situation itself in terms of the obstacles they face in creating an electable persona. These exigencies interact in constraining the types of verbal and nonverbal behaviors that will overcome the obstacles.

Understanding the exigencies and audience dynamics of televised debates is especially important because it can help make sense of puzzling candidate behavior, both verbal and nonverbal. One such puzzle involves the dramatic difference in vice presidential candidate Joe Biden's performance in debates with Sarah Palin in 2008 and Paul Ryan in 2012. In the first of these debates, the Obama-Biden ticket was slightly ahead in the polls, and the press had already created a narrative that Palin was more folksy than policy wonk and somewhat of an issues lightweight. The traditional approach to vice presidential debates was for candidates to attack the lead person on the ticket rather than the opposing VP candidate. As such, Biden's preparation for that debate centered on communicating the Obama campaign's message while attacking John McCain, the Republican candidate for president. Biden's obstacles were to avoid being distracted by Palin's attempts to get under his skin and to add a voice of experience to the ticket (Schroeder, 2016). He also had to avoid looking patronizing given both the difference in debate experience and the gender dynamics involved in debating Palin. Indeed, as Charlotte Alter (2016) wrote,

> So many male candidates have floundered when they found themselves going man-to-man with a female opponent. Most voters don't like to see women candidates get attacked or patronized by men. And since debates are often the only moments where candidates share the same physical space, the gender dynamics can be more obvious—and more precarious. (para. 2)

In other words, appearing overly aggressive or overly patronizing toward the less experienced Palin might have, to some voters, seemed inappropriate for the more experienced, and male, life-long politician, Biden. Known for making occasional, and sometimes inappropriate, gaffes in stump speeches, Biden's team prepped him for the situational constraints associated with gender norms and audience expectations. According to Schroeder, Biden consulted with Hillary Clinton, Barbara Boxer, and the first woman to participate in a vice presidential debate, Geraldine Ferraro. As a result, perhaps, Biden indicated that he understood, and rejected, sexist beliefs regarding female candidates' skill in competing with men in the political arena when he said to reporters, "It seems like the only people in the room that think that debating a woman is going to be fundamentally different are people who don't hang around smart women" (as quoted in Schroeder, 2016, p. 107). Throughout the debate, Biden maintained an even and well-composed performance with restrained facial expressions and gestures and was not unexpectedly condescending. Although he engaged directly with Palin's ideas, he did not engage in verbal, or nonverbal, attacks on her character. This was not to be the case in his debate with Ryan.

The situation Biden faced in the 2012 debate was entirely different. First, rather than a relative political newcomer, Ryan, Biden's opponent, was touted by many in the media as a Republican rising star: young, energetic, and declared by his running mate, Mitt Romney, as the "intellectual leader" of the Republican party (Mehta, 2012, para 1). Second, the debates took place shortly after Obama's devastating loss to Romney in the first presidential debate and a narrowing in the polls that showed the race to be a dead heat. Given these exigences, Biden faced the obstacle of changing the media narrative from one of a potential upset in the making as well as the narrative that Ryan, though young, was an intellectual heavyweight with new ideas for dealing with the country's problems. From this perspective, Biden's continual condescension and use of ridicule both verbally and nonverbally functioned as attacks on Ryan's intellectual stature and as fireworks to distract the media from Obama's performance.

Biden's performance against Ryan, compared to his subdued behavior against Palin, highlights the important influence of rhetorical situations as seen from the perspective of the Obama campaign. To be sure, considering the problems that the campaign faced (ahead in the polls in 2008, even or slightly behind in 2012), the constraints on Biden's behavior (an opponent who was female and not well prepared in 2008, compared to a fit, young male with formidable intellect in 2012), and the audience to which Biden mostly appealed (voters in 2008 and the media in 2012). Biden's behavior, both verbal and nonverbal, in each debate was less about his personality or style and more about his ability to adjust his rhetorical strategy in responding to different situations given the obstacles he faced in achieving campaign goals.

NARRATIVE PARADIGM

The narrative paradigm, developed by Walter Fisher, argues that narrative is the natural mode of thinking and reasoning. In fact, as an essential metaphor for describing humans, Fisher used the term *homo narrans*, or humans as storytellers. Specifically, Fisher (1987) wrote,

> When I use the term "narration," I do not mean fictive composition whose propositions may be true or false and have no necessary relationship to the message of that composition. By narration I mean symbolic actions—words and/or deeds—that have sequences and meaning for those who live, create, or interpret them. (p. 58)

Later in the same book, Fisher clarified,

> The idea of humans as story teller . . . holds that symbols are created and communicated ultimately as stories meant to give order to human experience and to induce others to dwell in them in order to establish ways of living in common, in intellectual and spiritual communities in which there is confirmation for the story that constitutes one's life. (p. 63)

The narrative paradigm was Fisher's reaction to the traditional "rational world paradigm," which suggested that logic and reasoned argumentation were the *sine qua non* of rationality. In other words, from the traditional, rational world approach, methods of formal and informal logic, and constructing proofs that embodied particular propositional structures are considered superior to other forms of communication in resolving disagreements or in coming to policy decisions. As such, only specialists who are trained in these methods of reasoning are considered rational, and only by using these methods could one's decision be considered a rational one. As noted in Chapter 1, adherence to this rational perspective is common in political science and political communication. Indeed, scholars in such fields have decried the decline of reasoned decision making in the electorate's voting behavior, bemoaning the influence of non-discursive elements, including visual presentations and charismatic speaking styles that make personality and character perceptions equal to or more important than policy arguments in voters' evaluations of candidates.

In contrast to breaking arguments into constituent patterns of formal logic as was often the case in traditional rhetorical analyses, Fisher's narrative approach requires a critic to use the same interpretive processes as the people who create, and who serve as the audience of, a rhetorical act. Thus, rather than assessing the logical validity of an argument, Fisher identified two alternative standards for evaluating rhetorical messages. The first, known as narrative coherence, refers to how internally coherent a story is judged to be. It answers the question of whether the story holds together. Does it make sense and seem probable? Of course, this standard includes rational-world-paradigm reasoning, as a speaker might employ evidence and structural relationships among propositions as part of the message. It is left to the audience and critic, however, to determine whether such reasoning holds together with the larger narrative in which it resides.

Fisher's second standard, known as narrative fidelity, refers to whether the message is consistent with other narratives an audience already holds to be true. As such, narrative fidelity resides as much in the values held by an audience as in any facts or evidence that might be presented to an audience. Indeed, people build narratives to help make sense of where they exist in the world. Considering this, imagine an audience of people who regularly watch true crime shows and sensationalized news stories. Convincing them that violent crime in the United States has been decreasing for 20 years could prove difficult because the facts might violate their sense of narrative fidelity.

In the context of televised political debates, narrative rationality can be useful for understanding the persuasiveness of verbal and nonverbal behavior. To see how, consider the ways in which candidates' words and behaviors might be analyzed in terms of narrative fidelity and coherence. We have seen in previous chapters, for example, that candidates who display contradictory verbal and nonverbal behavior are perceived less positively than candidates whose behavior is consistent. Conflicting verbal and nonverbal behavior is detrimental to establishing narrative coherence because it creates inconsistencies in the speaker's storyline.

That said, there are times when interrupting the fidelity and coherence of an ongoing narrative might benefit candidates during televised debates. This is especially true when the predominant narrative might damage a candidate's image. As a case in point, general election debates occur at the conclusion of a long campaign season where both media sources and the campaigns themselves construct narratives about the candidates. One popular narrative from the 1988 Presidential campaign centered on whether the Democratic candidate, Michael Dukakis, was likeable enough to be elected. In it, Dukakis was depicted as a person who lacked human emotions and frailties, yet took pride in his own self-control. In one widely circulated story, his wife, Kitty, recounted a trip to Las Vegas where Dukakis played one coin in a slot machine, won a small sum, and left without ever playing again. She also shared that her husband was the kind of person who could open a can of peanuts, eat one, and put the lid back on without eating a second (Reid, 1988). And although Dukakis had begun integrating more heart-warming stories into his campaign narrative, he resisted advisors who urged him to appear warm and likeable nonverbally, especially in his upcoming debates with then Vice President George H. W. Bush (Reid, 1988). Such advice put Dukakis in an unenviable position. As Shogan (1988) noted,

> Unlike front-runner Bush, whose managers figured he only had to avoid making a serious mistake, Dukakis entered the encounter with a double-barreled mission: To force Bush into making an error and at the same time to present the human side of his own political personality. (para 15)

Unfortunately for Dukakis, his demeanor in the debates did little to disrupt the fidelity and coherence of the narrative. During the second debate, moderator and *Newsweek* reporter Margaret Warner summarized the media narrative surrounding Dukakis's lack of warmth in her first question for Dukakis, "Governor, you won the first debate on intellect and yet you lost it on heart. . . . The American public admired your performance, but didn't seem to like you much. Now, Ronald Reagan has found his personal warmth to be a tremendous political asset. Do you think that a president has to be likable to be an effective leader?" (Debate Transcript, 1988, October 13, para. 27). Dukakis's response to the question first circled back to the issue of taxes before he lamely said, "I think I'm a reasonably likeable guy" (Debate Transcript, para. 28) and changed the topic back to tax policy. As noted in previous chapters, Dukakis also delivered an emotionless response to a question regarding the hypothetical rape and murder of his wife. Unfortunately for Dukakis, calm and composed responses such as these both "rang true" and were consistent with the audience's beliefs about his lack of emotion and seeming inability to express warmth or passion.

THE GENDERED DOUBLE BIND

People confronted with a *double bind* face a dilemma in which the available behaviors for resolving the dilemma all carry negative consequences—a "damned if you do and damned if you don't" situation. One early conceptualization of the double bind was presented by Gregory Bateson (1963), who pointed to a behavioral dilemma faced by children in the form of conflicting messages from parents (usually the mother), which resulted in punishment regardless of the child's response. Extending the concept, Jamieson (1995) described the gendered double bind as "a rhetorical construct that posits two and only two alternatives . . . constructed to deny women access to power and, where individuals manage to slip past their constraints, to undermine their exercise of whatever power they achieve" (p. 14).

Jamieson's concept is based on earlier feminist scholarship that identified the duality of language as a source of structural inequality. This duality suggests that words are often understood in reference to their opposites (such as male/female; father/mother; inside/outside, power/submission, etc.). As Jamieson (1995) wrote when exposing the power of this duality,

> (Double) binds draw their power from their capacity to simplify complexity. Faced with a complicated situation or behavior, the human tendency is to split apart and dichotomize its elements. So we contrast good and bad, strong and weak, for and against, true and false, and in so doing assume that a person can't be both at once, or somewhere in between. . . . This tendency drives us to see . . . choices available to women as polarities and irreconcilable opposites, those differences become troublesome. (p. 5)

The feminist legal scholar Catherine Mackinnon (1979) explained that the duality itself is less a problem than the tendency to arrange the terms hierarchically, with one part of the dichotomy ascribed a higher social rank than the other. Feminist rhetorical theory goes on to suggest that hierarchical structures tend to favor the group in power (males most everywhere) and overwhelmingly favor terms associated with masculine roles (Foss, Foss, & Griffin, 2006). As such, although the terms "breadwinner" and "homemaker" do not in their definitions assign greater social rank to one role or the other, American social norms attribute greater prestige and power to "breadwinner" than to "homemaker." The "father/mother" dichotomy, at least nominally, likewise recognizes the father role as the leadership position in the home.

Indeed, the oppositional nature of language also assumes that one cannot occupy opposing roles simultaneously. That is, one cannot be both strong and nurturing or both masculine and feminine.

Because stereotypically feminine roles tend to occupy a lower tier than masculine roles in the social hierarchy, women who assume traditionally male leadership positions must take on masculine traits in order to be accepted. At the same time, power-seeking women must also behave consistently with their historical and culturally sanctioned roles as mother, nurturer, caregiver, and so forth. As we will see below, women whose behavior is discordant with feminine norms are often penalized for being too masculine. As an illustration of the rhetorical double bind faced by women in politics, Jamieson quoted long-time California Senator Barbara Boxer:

> In 1972, to be a woman in politics was almost a masochistic experience, a series of setbacks without a lot of rewards.... If I was strong in my expression of issues, I was strident; if I expressed any emotion as I spoke about the environment or the problems of the mentally ill, I was soft; if I spoke about economics I had to be perfect, and then I ran the risk of being "too much like a man." (as quoted in Jamieson, 1995, p. 6)

The quote above serves as an example of the double bind faced by female leaders. The rhetorical double bind expands the dualist nature of language from simply identifying oppositional concepts, such as feminine/competence, to the idea that a person can be one or the other but not both. In other words, "Women who are considered feminine will be judged incompetent, and women who are competent, unfeminine," either of which can doom a female's political fortunes (Jamieson, 1995, p. 16). Along those lines, the gendered double bind is particularly challenging to female candidates because the framing of the president is inherently and historically masculine. As Anderson (2017) explained, "The U.S. presidency . . . is the Catch-22's (i.e., double bind's) last outpost—fortified by the thorough masculinization of the office of U.S. president" (p. 527). Stated differently, leadership, for many people, is understood culturally as a masculine trait, thereby creating a challenge for women seeking leadership roles because "men fit cultural construals of leadership better than women do and thus have better access to leadership roles and face fewer challenges in becoming successful in them" (Koenig, Eagly, Mitchell, & Ristikan, 2011, p. 638).

Fortunately, women who cultivate an impression of gravitas on national and international issues can garner significant support from voters. As Bolton (2010) concluded from her study of 1,039 American adults, "People who see women as competent to deal with things like the economy and terrorism are dramatically more likely to voice a willingness to support them for office.... This would suggest that attention to bolstering credibility on these issues, or even working to neutralize the stereotypes, would serve women candidates well" (p. 85). Unfortunately, developing such an image may be easier said than done. To be sure, females who occupy, or aspire to, leadership positions in traditionally male-dominated arenas such as government or business risk negative evaluations that include being labeled "bitchy," "selfish," an "ice-queen," and so on (Okimoto & Brescoll, 2010, p. 924). Indeed, females who openly seek power and status face potential backlash for taking traditional male roles. As an example, one study (Okimoto & Brescoll, 2010) found that participants were less likely to say they would vote for a female candidate who indicated a clear desire for power and status. In addition, power-seeking women were "seen as less caring and sensitive than the non-power seeking female," a perception linked to participants' voting decisions (Okimoto & Brescoll, 2010, p. 931). However, male candidates' desire for power did not influence participants voting decisions nor were power seeking males perceived to be less sensitive or caring.

Media and the Double Bind

Whatever they are called, double binds, role incongruities, Catch-22s, and the like are features of language that emerge over time, through interaction, and as a consequence of continued use, which reinforces them as a rhetorical strategy. Given their reach and influence, broadcast and social media criticism grounded in the double bind not only finds a large audience but functions to present candidates in particular ways. Although Hillary Clinton was the first woman to participate in a general election presidential debate, both Sarah Palin (a Republican) and Geraldine Ferraro (a Democrat) had previously participated in vice presidential debates. And, like Clinton, both vice presidential candidates were subject to a gendered double bind that highlighted aspects of their verbal and nonverbal behavior. In contrast to Clinton who was deemed "not feminine enough," media attention to Sarah Palin's physical appearance contributed to her disqualification as a serious candidate, even though she had relevant political experience as the governor of Alaska. By way of example, Carlin and Winfrey (2009) pointed to early news coverage of Palin's beauty pageant background as the beginning of the media's focus on Palin's appearance. Indeed, many media pundits remarked on Palin's overtly feminine appearance in sexual terms (Perks & Johnson, 2014). As an example of sexualizing Palin's looks, Tucker Carlson, now a Fox News host, took to Twitter to voice his impression of her sexual appeal (which he later deleted from his account). "Palin's popularity falling in Iowa," he wrote, "but maintains lead to become supreme commander of Milfistan" (MILF is a sexually explicit term for a woman who is a mother) (Tucker Carlson, n/d). Not to be outdone, Erick Erickson, then conservative blogger, now L.A. Times Opinion writer, wrote of the controversy surrounding Carlson's tweet: "Maybe my sense of humor needs to be recalibrated, but when I heard Tucker Carlson's MILFistan comment, I laughed then got out my passport" (Shahid, 2011, March 3, para. 10). Joe Biden was also criticized for commenting on Palin's appearance before their vice presidential debate in 2008 when he remarked, "There is a gigantic difference between . . . me and my Vice Presidential opponent. She's good-looking" (Newton-Small, 2008, September 1, para. 2). In addition to sexualizing Palin, such banter was problematic in that it redirected audiences' attention away from substantial issues in a debate. Indeed, research consistently indicates that focusing on appearances diminishes people's evaluations of candidates' competence and qualifications (e.g., Funk & Coker, 2016), an effect that tends to be larger for female candidates (Lizotte & Meggers-Wright, 2018). More specifically, one study found that participants rated Palin as less competent and were less inclined to cast their vote for the McCain/Palin ticket when they were instructed to focus on Palin's physical appearance as opposed to the more general instruction to think of Palin as a person (Heflick & Goldenberg, 2009). Media commentary, therefore, can redirect voters' attention away from issues that matter to running a government and, at least in the case of women, function to discredit a candidate.

This is not to say that attractiveness is necessarily deleterious to a candidate's electoral fortunes. As noted in Chapter 6, research related to the halo effect suggests that there may be a political advantage for conventionally attractive candidates of both sexes. That said, the requirement for females to wear makeup and dresses; to be well-coiffed and physically appealing (i.e., feminine); *and* to display masculine traits associated with leadership competence is key to the double bind. To be sure, scholarship involving mock U.S. presidential elections suggests that perceptions of competence are critical for both male and female candidates but attractiveness is especially important for females (Chiao, Bowman, & Gill, 2008).

As another example of the feminine/competence paradox, Geraldine Ferraro, the first female major party nominee for vice president, faced the double bind in her vice-presidential debate with George H. W. Bush in 1984. Indeed, Ferraro, a third-term member of congress, was not immune from shaded sexist remarks, even from other women, including her opponent's wife. As Heinemann (2011) wrote, "And during the run-up to the debates, when it came out that the Ferraros had substantial net worth and several houses, Barbara Bush remarked that Geraldine Ferraro was a 'four million dollar. . . . I won't say it but it rhymes with rich.' Mrs. Bush later 'clarified' that she meant 'witch'" (Heineman, 2011, March 27, para. 9). As if that wasn't enough, coverage of Ferraro's campaign was laden with sex role stereotypes. As an illustration, Baird (2008, September 13) reported that "(Ferraro) was described as 'feisty' and 'pushy but not threatening,' and was asked if she knew how to bake blueberry muffins. . . . When she stood before the Democratic National Convention in San Francisco, anchor Tom Brokaw announced: 'Geraldine Ferraro . . . The first woman to be nominated for vice president . . . Size 6!'" (para. 1).

Meanwhile, in trying to negotiate the political tightrope of appearing competent without violating stereotyped expectations, Ferraro's demeanor during her debate with Bush was lackluster. As Sullivan (1989), in her analysis of Ferraro's debate performance wrote, "One polltaker even suggested that 'She was trying too hard not to be brassy and she ended up just plain dull.' An analysis of her style suggested she 'had given up some of her normal fire on the campaign stump in the effort to convey a more serious image'" (p. 329). Others criticized Ferraro for being too sedate and uninspiring (Trent, 1994). Even then, "Peter Kelly, George Bush's press secretary, termed Geraldine Ferraro 'bitchy'" (as quoted in Sullivan, 1989, p. 329), a reaction that certainly sexist, may have come in response to Ferraro's willingness to tangle verbally with Bush. In one exchange, for example, Bush said, "'Let me help you with the difference, Ms. Ferraro, between Iran and the embassy in Lebanon.' Ferraro shot back, 'Let me first of all say that I almost resent, Vice President Bush, your patronizing attitude that you have to teach me about foreign policy'" (Heinemann, 2011, para. 12).

More recently, in their race for the 2020 Democratic presidential nomination, Joe Biden and Pete Buttigieg were accused of characterizing their opponent Senator Elizabeth Warren as angry and antagonistic (Viser & Linskey, 2019), a strategy which, according to Viser and Linskey, could backfire,

> The new attacks, marking a more vigorous phase of the race, get at something far beyond her [Warren's] policy positions, and into one of the most fraught areas for a female candidate: Is she likable? Pushing that argument is treacherous given that many Democrats remain upset over what they view as sexist treatment of Hillary Clinton, the party's last nominee. Warren's allies view the language being used against her as constructed to be particularly devastating for female candidates and beyond the policy divisions between her and her rivals. (para. 3 and 4)

In short, the gendered double bind functions to contain female candidates' rhetorical choices by essentially forcing women running for office to choose between a more stereotypically masculine or feminine style of communication. As we have seen, trying to engage in both risks drawing negative interpretations from observers. This is especially true for women running for their nation's highest office because the person in that position is often responsible for leading the military—a responsibility stereotypically associated with masculine traits and behaviors. In this case, females are expected to engage in nonverbal behavior that creates an impression of competence in leading a country, possibly, to war. However, a female leader must not violate expectations for feminine behavior either. The leader must be dressed well, in a feminine style, and smile while on the camera. A telling example of how this dilemma can play out during television debates was discussed in Chapter 4 specifically, while Trump was invading Clinton's space by hovering over her. The risk of appearing too aggressive and "bitchy" limited her rhetorical choices for responding to him. Clinton might have wanted to stop what she was saying and call him out on his aggressiveness. Instead, she ignored him and kept speaking—a passive response to an aggressive attack.

MULTIMODAL ARGUMENT

Until the 20th century, argumentation scholarship existed mostly in departments of philosophy, English, and only later in departments of Speech (following speech teachers' break from English departments in 1910). Considering the state of communication technology at the time, it is understandable why arguments expressed nonlinguistically, including pictures, sounds, and the like were not of much interest. Indeed, visual messages were primarily confined to paintings, early photographs, and illustrations printed in newspapers and books. Because audio and video reproductions of speeches are an historical novelty, the analysis of rhetorical artifacts focused almost entirely on the written manuscripts of speeches and the focus of rhetorical theory and criticism remained on analyzing verbal arguments, linguistic style, and the structure of written rhetorical artifacts. As often happens, habits of analysis eventually became doctrine, and argumentation came to be studied as the propositional structures of reasons and claims almost exclusively. In more recent years, many rhetoricians, communication scholars, and philosophers refocused their attention from formal logic to informal systems of logic as defeasible or practical reasoning, but the practice of reconstructing messages into component propositions was (and mostly remains today) a popular approach to studying rhetorical argumentation.

As the newly mediated landscapes of the 20th and 21st centuries unfolded, it became clear that argumentation and rhetoric were not exclusively verbal phenomenon. Following communication scholars who recognized the analogical nature of communication (Fisher, 1978) and that meaning occurs, "in people and not in words" (Watzlawick, Bavelas & Jackson, 1967), Wayne Brockriede (1975) wrote, "Arguments are not in statements but in people. Furthermore argument isn't a thing to be looked for but a construct people use, a perspective they take. Human activity doesn't usefully constitute an argument until some *person* perceives what is happening is an argument" (emphasis in original, p.180). As a result of such thinking, by the mid-1990s, argumentation scholars were coming to see that visual, audio, and other elements of messages could function argumentatively. As Gronbeck (1995) wrote, "If we think of meanings as called up or evoked in people when engaged in acts of decoding, then not only words but also pictures, sounds, and other sign systems certainly can offer us propositions of denial or affirmation, and can, as Locke understood trueness and falsehood, articulate empirically verifiable propositions" (p. 539).

As a result of such thinking, many argumentation scholars began explicating just how nonlinguistic elements of messages might evoke propositional meanings in audiences. To be sure, pictures, sounds, nonverbal behavior, and other multimodal elements of an argument often combine with verbal elements, although occasionally they can exist purely as nonlinguistic messages. Our earlier example of Biden's throwing his hands up and rolling his eyes in response to Paul Ryan during their vice-presidential debate serves as but one purely nonlinguistic argumentative move. Moreover, multimodal elements can function to reinforce the verbal meaning of a message or contribute additional meaning to an argument by signaling ironic, emotive, metaphoric, or other communicator intentions (Groarke, 2003). For example, an aggressive slashing gesture delivered with the rhythmic cadence of the speech can both reinforce the speaker's position as an intensely held belief (i.e., "I am passionate about this issue") and as a strategy for arousing an emotional response in the audience ("I want to see that you are passionate too").

Despite a growing consensus among argumentation scholars that arguments can exist in multiple modalities, some critics take the position that visual and other nonverbal modes of communication are too ambiguous to reliably extract propositional content for proper analysis (e.g., Johnson, 2000). In response to such criticism, Gronbeck (1995) and others (e.g., Kjeldsen, 2015) point out that extracting propositional content from real-world, multimodal messages requires the same interpretive processes as extracting meaning from purely verbal message modalities. In fact, it is often because of its ambiguity that communication, as we now understand it, requires making inferences in order to interpret the intentions and goals of a message source, rather than simply decoding the meaning of the words (Jacobs, 2002). To be sure, what is meant by any speaker is almost always more than what is said (e.g., Grice, 1989). As a consequence, understanding the meaning of messages requires an understanding of context as well as the way in which people go about communicating intentions with symbols and signals whether verbal or nonverbal (Jacobs, 2002). Echoing Willard's (1988) analysis of arguments as interactions in which all moves made during the discussion can be interpreted as part of the communicators' argumentation, Kjeldsen (2007) pointed out, "The elements of an argument do not need to be presented explicitly as long as the audience is aware that they are faced with argument-making and in turn understand the argument being communicated" (p. 125).

As scholars who study argumentation in televised debates, our interest lies in understanding *rhetorical* argument, which advocates for action under conditions of uncertainty, rather than logical argument, which is aimed at judging the truthfulness of claims. As such, we find the topic of multimodal argumentation an especially appealing and fruitful avenue of study. Research in this area has analyzed rhetorical argumentation in several message modes such as sound as argument in radio programs (Eckstein, 2016); spatial argument in community events (Endres, Senda-Cook, & Cozen, 2014) and national monuments (McGeough, Palczewski, & Lake, 2015); visual argument in television advertisements (e.g., Gronbeck, 1995), political cartoons (e.g., Groarke, 2017), newspaper photographs (Kjeldsen, 2017); and most important to the current project, nonverbal behavior as argument in televised political debates (e.g., Gelang, 2013; Seiter, Weger, Kinzer, & Jensen, 2010).

As one example, Gelang and Kjeldsen (2011) took a multimodal approach to analyzing the 2008 Democratic primary debates, focusing on the ways in which Barack Obama and Hillary Clinton's verbal and nonverbal behavior worked in tandem to function as argumentation. According to Gelang and Kjeldsen, arguments in televised debates are necessarily multimodal by virtue of the medium that is used to transmit debaters' messages. In other words, television makes candidates' appearance, vocalics, facial expressions, and body movements available for interpretation. In their analysis, Gelang and Kjeldsen identified three qualities of delivery (*actio*) that contribute to this argumentative function. The first, *energy*, describes the intensity and focus of a debater's behavior. The second, *dynamism,* refers to the variation in a debater's actions. And the third, *tempo and rhythm*, describes the flow, speed, and timing of a candidate's nonverbal behaviors.

As part of their analysis and consistent with the framework we presented in Chapter 1, Gelang and Kjeldsen (2011) argued that nonverbal behavior can function to attack another debater, to defend against an opponent's attack, and to claim political successes or policy superiority. In addition, nonverbal behavior can function as a sign argument scheme in which debaters use their behavior to signal the acceptability of their position on an issue. To illustrate, consider the following hypothetical example provided by Gelang and Kjeldsen (p. 570), "Politician A's nonverbal communication is energetic and energetic nonverbal communication is a sign of an involved and passionate person, therefore, Politician A is an involved and passionate person."

From this perspective, audiences make inferences about character traits of candidates based on the candidates' debate behavior. Stated differently, candidates' nonverbal behaviors function as signs or evidence for assessing the validity of character inferences made by the audience. In this respect, multimodal argument can be thought of as a type of enthymematic reasoning (see above) in which one element of the argument form is missing a piece. In the example above, for instance, the bottom line, which represents the minor premise of the overall argument, must be inferred by the audience. Similarly, Gelang and Kjeldsen argue that in the 2008 primary debates Hillary Clinton used nonverbal behavior in acclaiming her own ethos (character) by smiling, maintaining eye contact with the audience, and engaging in energetic vocal and gestural communication, "The qualities in (Clinton's) actio, energy and tempo, together with a multimodal activity, face, posture, gesture and voice in simultaneous use, create a dynamic actio that indicates resoluteness and determination" (p. 571).

In another study that examined how visual displays can be reconstructed as argumentation, Lempert (2011) analyzed Barack Obama's use of the *precision grip* gesture. The precision grip is made by touching the index finger, or multiple fingertips to the tip of the thumb. The index-finger-thumb (IFT) grip resembles the act of holding a very small object and functions in one way to communicate exactness, precision, or the need to be delicate in making a point. In his analysis of the 2007–2008 Democratic primary debates, Lempert reported that all of Obama's initial gestural strokes were IFT grips, perhaps to nonverbally communicate that his arguments were specific and precise. Obama also used the IFT to communicate that he was making sharp or important points, perhaps inviting the inference that he himself is sharp or that his arguments were precise. Interestingly, by Lempert's count, Obama's use of the precision grip occurred about three times as often in televised debates than in campaign stump speeches. Moreover, Lempert suggested that Obama's "making a sharp point" use of the gesture occurred often in debates as a way to emphasize his argument as a counterpoint to his opponents' attacks. Lempert did not suggest that Obama was alone in using this gesture, but instead evaluated Obama's use of the gesture rhetorically. In so doing, Lempert demonstrated the careful analysis required to examine the possible meanings of nonverbal behavior in specific situations, a welcome contrast to the unfounded and often careless interpretations of candidates' nonverbal behavior by so-called "body language experts."

In presidential debates, instances in which a candidate's delivery style can be interpreted as evidence for or against a standpoint abound. One such example occurred in the 1988 vice presidential debate between Lloyd Bentsen and Dan Quayle. Lloyd Bentsen was a mature and experienced legislator of 24 years while Dan Quayle was much younger and had served in the U.S. Senate and U.S. House for just 12 years total (Oreskes, 1988, August, 19). Thus, one obstacle facing Quayle in the debate was proving to voters that his youth and lack of experience was adequate to equip him to handle the stress and crises he might face if his running mate, George H. W. Bush, became unable to continue as president. A key to alleviating voters' concerns would be an actio demonstrating his ability to remain poised under stress. Bentsen heightened pressure on Quayle's performance by arguing that the debate was about whether Quayle was ready to be president (Decker, 1994). When the time came and he was asked by a moderator what he would do if he suddenly became president, Quayle, in a somber tone of voice hesitated several times in his answer, "Fir—first, I'd say a prayer (1 second pause) for myself (3 second pause) and the country that I'm about to lead (3 second pause) and then I would (2 second pause) assemble (1 second pause) his people and talk." In the first half of his answer Quayle stared with a blank expression to his left before turning his attention back to the moderators and camera. Quayle was later asked to clarify his response and once again hesitated in several places. As a result, Quayle's hesitant delivery did not dispel people's concerns about his ability to lead. As Decker (1994) noted "the hesitations were critical for the viewer, whereas, a reader of the debate would not get the same impact out of his statement. The nonverbal behaviors were critical to the outcome of the statement" (p. 178). From a multimodal argumentation perspective, Quayle's hesitations and false starts, rather than providing a demonstration of being calm under pressure, provided support for Bentsen's argument that he was not yet ready to take on the position of president should he be required to do so.

STRATEGIC MANEUVERING

Strategic Maneuvering (e.g., van Eemeren, 2010) represents a model of argumentation that extends the pragma-dialectical model of argumentation (van Eemeren & Grootendorst, 1984, 1992). Pragma-dialectics conceptualizes argument as a complex speech act that functions to resolve differences of opinion. Rather than locating rationality in arguers, or in arguers' messages, pragma-dialectics locates rationality in the procedures that guide and/or regulate interaction. Legal decisions, for example, are not reasonable because attorneys, juries, or judges are reasonable people, or because they make deductively valid arguments, but rather because law courts have highly defined procedures for what sorts of messages are and are not allowable. Likewise, pragma-dialects proposes a set of 10 rules or "commandments" aimed at resolving disagreements based on the merits of the case each arguer makes. The rules prohibit behaviors that threaten to disrupt the orderly progression of an argumentative discussion.

1. Freedom rule: Parties must not prevent each other from advancing standpoints or from casting doubt on standpoints.
2. Burden of proof rule: A party that advances a standpoint is obliged to defend it if asked by the other party to do so.
3. Standpoint rule: A party's attack on a standpoint must relate to the standpoint that has indeed been advanced by the other party.
4. Relevance rule: A party may defend a standpoint only by advancing argumentation relating to that standpoint.

5. Unexpressed premise rule: A party may not deny a premise that he or she has left implicit or falsely present something as a premise that has been left unexpressed by the other party.
6. Starting point rule: A party may not falsely present a premise as an accepted starting point nor deny a premise representing an accepted starting point.
7. Argument scheme rule: A party may not regard a standpoint as conclusively defended if the defense does not take place by means of an appropriate argumentation scheme that is correctly applied.
8. Validity rule: A party may only use arguments in its argumentation that are logically valid or capable of being made logically valid by making explicit one or more unexpressed premises.
9. Closure rule: A failed defense of a standpoint must result in the party that put forward the standpoint retracting it and a conclusive defense of the standpoint must result in the other party retracting its doubt about the standpoint.
10. Usage rule: A party must not use formulations that are insufficiently clear or confusingly ambiguous and a party must interpret the other party's formulations as carefully and accurately as possible.

Argumentative moves that violate one or more of these rules is considered fallacious. Notice most of the rules govern allowable contributions by arguers rather than identifying logical and illogical argument structures. Given the rules, it is easy to see how nonverbal communication is relevant to the pragma-dialectical model. Indeed, nonverbal behavior, as part of the overall message, has the potential to violate several of these rules. For example, background disagreement, as we have discussed in an earlier chapter, has the potential to constitute a "nonverbal ad hominem" argument. In fact, Remland (1982) suggested that, to the extent that nonverbal behavior could belittle an opponent, it could be characterized as a type of "implicit ad hominem" argument. Abusive ad hominem arguments, in which the speaking debater's character is called into question can be interpreted as violations of rules 1 and 2 (e.g., Mohammed and Weger, 2017).

Strategic maneuvering extends pragma-dialectics beyond its focus on reasonableness by adding a theoretical understanding of persuasive effectiveness in rhetorical settings. Strategic maneuvering provides a system of analyzing the reasonableness of arguments (in terms of the pragma-dialectical obligations of speakers) as well as an argument's effectiveness in persuading an audience. In televised debates, this extension seems especially relevant. Rather than seeking a resolution to a disagreement, candidates for office in televised debates defend their own positions, and attack the positions of other candidates, in order to persuade an audience to elect them to office. That said, ideally, effective leaders should also be reasonable.

Somewhat akin to Bitzer's (1959) rhetorical situation, van Eemeren (2010) points to three elements of the situation that guide an arguer's strategic choices. The first, known as "topical potential," includes all of the arguments available for defending a standpoint. The second, "audience demands," includes the attitudes, beliefs, and values held by the audience(s) that the arguer may appeal to. The third, "presentational devices," includes an arguer's range of strategic choices for arranging the arguments, the linguistic choices the arguer makes in articulating a message, and the nonverbal choices the arguer makes in delivering the message.

Importantly, the topical potential, audience demands, and presentational devices in any situation are limited by the "activity type" in which the disagreement takes place. An activity type is identified by the institutional purposes of the activity. In identifying the institutional purpose of televised debates, we largely follow Rowland and Voss's (1987) analysis. First, debates should educate citizens about the policy positions candidates hold on major issues. Second, debates demonstrate character traits required to fulfill the position of chief executive, to wit, the ability to remain composed under pressure while offering persuasive arguments in favor or in opposition to policy issues raised in the debate. And finally, Rowland and Voss argue that debates function to support the democratic institution because "the process of seeing candidates together reinforces faith in the viability of the system" no matter who ultimately wins the election (p. 283). Public debates provide voters an opportunity to evaluate candidates' leadership potential as they attack and defend each other's policy positions and character. One implication that follows from the purpose of the activity type includes candidates' obligation to answer the questions posed by the moderator and to conform responses to the time limits. Without some semblance of following this obligation, televised debates would be derailed into chaotic disorder in which candidates could deliver nothing but prewritten speeches allowing them to evade responding to their opponent or by limiting opponents' ability to advance standpoints by refusing to give up the floor. This obligation limits the topical potential of a speaker to the subject of the moderator's (or in town hall debates, audience members') question. Although not an example of nonverbal behavior, a failure to adhere to preconditions can be seen in the 2008 vice presidential debate when Sarah Palin, responding to Biden's accusation that she was not answering the moderator's questions, said, "And I may not answer the questions the way that either the moderator or you (referring to Biden) want to hear, but I'm going to talk straight to the American people and let 'em know my track record also." In this case, Palin's suggestion that she will ignore the moderator's question can be assessed as an argumentation fallacy in the context of strategic maneuvering because her response is at odds with the institutional purpose of the activity.

A clear nonverbal violation of reasonableness in strategic maneuvering can be identified in Joseph Biden's exaggerated nonverbal disparagement of Paul Ryan in the 2012 vice presidential debates (Weger, Hinck, & Seiter, 2019). Biden's behavior framed Ryan as a clown and so ridiculous in his opinions that he was unworthy to be seen as an equal to Biden in a serious discussion of the nation's problems. By extension, Biden's behavior also effectively defined Ryan as unworthy of the audience's attention. Besides potentially preventing Ryan from offering particular arguments out of concern for being discredited in the background (violation of Rule 1), the off-the-record nature of nonverbal behavior essentially freed Biden from having to defend the ad hominem attack (violation of Rule 2). This put Ryan in a tough position because if he counterattacked verbally, Biden could deny that his intention was derisive, possibly making Ryan look overly sensitive. If, on the other hand, Ryan decided not to acknowledge the attack, Biden could continue attacking unimpeded, possibly damaging Ryan's image in the eyes of the audience. Although Biden's behavior was effective at deflecting media attention away from Obama's dreadful performance, his behavior was none the less unreasonable given that he put Ryan in an impossible argumentative position.

DESIGN APPROACH TO ARGUMENTATION

All argumentative situations are designed to some extent. Courts of law, for example, have clear guidelines for the types of talk that are allowed or prohibited. Although rarely formally discussed or codified, marital disagreements are loosely governed by the rules couples informally establish through talk over time (e.g., Weger & Canary, 2010). Theorizing about argumentation (and communication in general) as a design enterprise motivates research examining how interaction design influences the quality of deliberation (e.g., Aakhus & Jackson, 2005; Jackson & Aakhus, 2014; Weger & Aakhus, 2003). Much like pragma-dialectics, the design approach recognizes that rules and/or procedures for conducting deliberative discussions impact the quality of deliberative dialogue. Analyzing interaction design allows the critic to uncover problematic design issues and identify possibilities for redesign. As Aakhus (2007) stated,

> A central puzzle that people face, from a design perspective, is how to make communication possible that was once difficult, impossible or unimagined. Communication design happens when there is an intervention into some ongoing activity through the invention of techniques, devices, and procedures that aim to redesign interactivity and thus shape the possibilities for communication. (p. 112)

One aspect of argumentation design receiving attention from scholars and media commentators has centered on the design of televised debates (e.g., the length of speaker turns, the number of candidates competing on one stage, the sorts of topics covered by moderators, etc.). From the beginning, journalists have complained that the visual medium of television along with the question/answer format of presidential debates emphasized style, nonverbal delivery, and rehearsed responses over thoughtful argumentation. For example, CNN's Greg Botelho reported reactions to the 1960 presidential debates:

> Historian Henry Steele Commager, in a subsequent *New York Times* piece, said he hoped "TV debates will be eliminated from future presidential campaigns" after the 1960 affairs. "The present formula of TV debate is designed to corrupt the public judgment and, eventually, the whole political process," he wrote. "The American presidency is too great an office to be subjected to the indignity of this technique." (Botelho, 2016, paras. 12–13)

Commager's comment is not so different from Plato's (and later Aristotle's) complaints about the ostentatious delivery of the sophists, who emphasized style over substance 2,500 years ago.

Until 1992, debate formats remained similar to 1960, which saw candidates responding to discussion prompts from journalists. In 1992, the town hall format was introduced with audience members asking questions instead of journalists. Later, the "meet the press" format with a single moderator and candidates sitting around a desk was introduced. Although each format requires adaptations in delivery, all of them continued to have either formal, or informal, speaking time guidelines. These relatively short time limits, abrupt changes in topics, and limitations on follow-up questions from journalists limit the opportunities that candidates have for deep discussions of issues. As Soma Golden, a panelist for the 1980 debate between candidates Carter and Reagan put it,

> I was surprised to learn just how much the format IS the debate. Ideally, the candidates should have locked horns in a direct debate of substantial length on one or two important subjects. But they refused that and agreed instead to a series of very brief mini-debates kicked off by reporters' questions. Worst of all, reporters were not allowed to follow up on their questions. We fought to change the format. Without follow-up questions, we said, one could not pursue an evasive response. (Berquist & Golden, 1981, p.136)

Candidates and their campaigns are sensitive to the issue of debate formats and their efforts to control them are discussed in Chapter 5. Considering the high stakes gamble involved in participating in debates when a verbal gaffe can cost an election, candidates are much safer repeating themes from campaign speeches and looking for opportunities to use "zingers" rather than providing thoughtful answers to journalists' questions (e.g., Schrott & Lanoue, 2008). Given the limits on meaningful discussions of policy, emphasizing style is a rational adaptation to the debate format for candidates and their campaigns. Creating an image of being both a likeable and dominant leader has become as important as scoring debating points.

The related design problems associated with meager time limits have become worse in recent years, particularly in primary debates. For example, the 2012 Republican primary began with eight candidates, and the 2016 Republican primary began with 17. The 2020 Democratic primary began with 27 candidates (20 of whom participated in the first televised debates, split into two separate nights), and at the time of this writing, has narrowed to seven candidates participating in a single February 25 debate in Charleston, South Carolina. This sheer number of candidates necessitates very short speaker turns and relatively few opportunities to speak. Because many candidates are not well known nationally, a key goal is to use the visual medium to build a favorable impression with viewers, and perhaps more importantly, appear in news coverage following the debates. Paul Hayes, the director of the collegiate debate team at George Washington University described the format problem in the 2019 Democratic primary this way:

> Unfortunately, the approach for presidential primary debates might be described as worst practices, ones that usually emphasize flash over substance. The chosen format for the first Democratic debate on Wednesday and Thursday night, as has been true in previous years, strongly favors candidates already doing well in the polls by actively impeding the types of exchanges that might be most informative to potential voters. (Hayes, 2019, para. 2)

Several collegiate debate coaches and scholars have suggested strategies to improve the information value of both primary and general election debates. Hayes (2019) suggested limiting each debate to a single topic, thereby allowing candidates to thoroughly explore plans and policies. Bob Bordone (2019), a Harvard Law School professor, suggested increasing the number, but reducing the size of debates. For example, instead of two debates with ten candidates each, there might be five discussions with four candidates each. Alternatively, Robert Rowland and Gary Voss (1987) suggested that permitting multiple rebuttals rather than the typical single rebuttals allowed in most debate formats offered several advantages. Specifically, multiple rebuttals would create an incentive to respond to opponents' arguments, and limit candidates' ability to memorize a few canned lines, thereby discouraging endless repetition of talking points. In addition, "The inclusion of multiple rebuttals in the debate format would test the creativity, intellectual quickness, and skill in rhetorical adaptation possessed by the candidate and therefore might reveal a great deal of interest to the public" (Rowland & Voss, 1987, p. 244). As multiple rebuttals push candidates to think on their feet, candidates would have to work harder to maintain the appearance of composure, likeability, and rationality under higher cognitive load than current formats require. In any case, an examination of the constraints and opportunities afforded by the design of televised debate as a communication activity can help us understand, and possibly alter, the way candidates and campaigns pursue their goals in televised debates.

SUMMARY

This chapter reviewed a number, but certainly not all, of the humanistic approaches available to researchers interested in studying nonverbal behavior in televised debates. The issue of style over substance in persuasive speaking is an old one, dating back at least to Plato's *Gorgias* (ca. 380 B.C.E./1987) and continues to be a point of controversy today in televised debates. The ubiquitous nature of visual media in the 20th century has reignited scholarly interest in the rhetorical power of nonverbal behavior and illuminates how style can have a substance all its own. As we pointed out in this chapter, nonverbal behavior *is* argumentative behavior, especially as it offers evidence of both ethos and pathos in persuasive appeals. A reconsideration of how nonverbal behavior can function as argumentation breathes new life into more traditional humanistic approaches, including Bitzer's rhetorical situation and Fisher's narrative paradigm. Finally, when we understand that the rationality of an activity, at least in part, is a function of the constraints and opportunities built into its design, there emerges the possibility of redesigning debate formats to better facilitate reasoned voting decisions. Although critics tend to focus on improving verbal argumentative features of debate formats, audiences will always consider the nonverbal behavior of candidates. Indeed, regardless of how much time for arguing is built into a format, the research reviewed in the pages of this book suggests that nonverbal behavior offers important information to voters about candidates' character and their fitness for office.

NOTES

1. Humanistic approaches are somewhat different from the social scientific theories that we examined in the previous chapter. Specifically, social scientific theories of communication tend to focus on creating descriptions of reality in the form of cause-and-effect relationships. Such approaches rely on scientific methods, particularly, the experiment as a strategy for verifying theoretical statements, predictions, and explanations of communication phenomenon. Humanistic theories, on the other hand, focus more on establishing normative standards for evaluating and critiquing the quality of human activity. Additionally, rather than examining cause and effect relationships, humanistic approaches focus on understanding how humans find meaning in their experiences. Finally, humanistic approaches often search for deep, underlying structures that create and maintain values, beliefs, and cultural understandings.

2. Square brackets within the translated text supply words and phrases implied but not stated in the text that may elucidate the meaning.

Chapter Eight

Nonverbal Behavior in the 2016 Presidential Debates

Applying Communication Theory to the Debates

When Hillary Rodham Clinton and Donald J. Trump took the stage for the first of three televised presidential debates in late September of 2016, the country had already witnessed several notable "firsts" in U.S. history. First, the Republican primary elections included a record 17 major candidates, more than in any previous primary election (Linshi, 2015). In another first, Hillary Clinton became the only woman ever nominated by either major party as their candidate for president. Although not quite a first, Donald Trump was the only major candidate for president, other than Wendell Wilke in 1940, to have held no government office nor served in any branch of the military. Furthermore, Trump and Clinton reached new lows in voters' evaluations of them. In fact, when discussing the candidates' dismal polling record, one reporter pointed out, "The 2016 election is the only one in Gallup's polling history to feature two broadly unpopular candidates. Further, when factoring in the high percentages viewing each very negatively, Trump and Clinton are the two most negatively reviewed U.S. presidential candidates of the modern era, and probably ever" (Saad, 2016, para 6). In addition, Clinton and Trump may have been the two most experienced debaters to take the stage in a presidential debate as Clinton participated in many debates in 2008 and 2016 while Trump participated in 11 debates and 5 presidential forums during the primary election season.

With that in mind, in this chapter, we summon concepts from previous sections of this book to analyze nonverbal behavior in the 2016 presidential debates. In addition, we examine Clinton and Trump's image goals, and how their behavior may have functioned to manage their impressions. Moreover, we consider the ways in which the candidates' nonverbal behavior functioned as argument, and how their relationship with voters might have been influenced by their nonverbal behavior. We also demonstrate the ways in which scholarly theory and research can provide tools that students, media commentators, and debate scholars might use to develop an understanding of nonverbal behavior in televised debates. We begin by exploring the rhetorical situation facing the candidates in the fall of 2016. We nominally organize the first part of the chapter around Bitzer's (1968) exigence-audience-constraints format presented in Chapter 7. Specifically, we examine the exigence faced by the candidates, the audience(s) that are critical to each candidate's success and some of the main obstacles that constrained each candidate's choices of their verbal, and especially nonverbal, rhetorical strategies."

THE RHETORICAL SITUATION

Exigence

In the words of Bitzer (1968), "Any exigence is an imperfection marked by urgency; it is a defect, an obstacle, something waiting to be done, a thing which is other than it should be" (p. 6). The urgent thing waiting to be done for the candidates in 2016 involved the election scheduled to occur 43 days from the first debate. Elections, almost by definition, are popularity contests and given voters' almost equally unflattering assessments of both Clinton and Trump, the need to manage both their own, and their opponent's, image in the eyes of voters formed one of the more influential exigences of the campaign. The three televised debates provided both candidates an opportunity to ameliorate voters' low opinion of them and to make a case in support of their candidacy for the nation's highest office.

Audience

As noted by Bitzer (1968), rhetors are generally faced with appealing to multiple audiences simultaneously and this is especially true of televised debates. To begin, one audience critical to the fortunes of candidates are late deciding voters who are usually unaffiliated with a major party and are more likely to rely on candidates' images when making voting decisions (e.g., Dalton, McAllister & Wattenberg, 2000; Palfry & Poole, 1987). Undecided voters focus on their impressions of candidates' personality, to be sure, and a passionate delivery can sometimes be enough to sway some of them. As an example, following the December 2019 Democratic primary debate in Los Angeles, the L.A. Times, with pollster Frank Luntz hosting, conducted a focus group composed of 25 undecided Democratic and independent voters.

After asking people if the debate had changed their minds, one woman answered, "I thought I liked Amy (Klobuchar) and Biden." When asked who she liked now and why, the woman replied, "Definitely Bernie Sanders. . . . Because he's on fire, he wants this SO bad . . . he's just feverishly hungry to change the world" (*Los Angeles Times*, 2019, December 20).

A second audience that debaters contend with are members of news organizations, including reporters, political analysts, and, perhaps most importantly, the moderators, who are almost always selected from an array of well-known media news personalities. Receiving positive performance evaluations from political commentators is important, especially because pundits' reactions to candidates' debate performances are often transmitted in real time via Twitter and other digital platforms. As such, media responses to debate performances may be more important in forming voting decisions than the candidates' actual performances (e.g., Hollihan, 2009). As we noted in Chapter 5, media pronouncements of winners and losers can sway voters' perceptions as well.

Finally, candidates must also satisfy their own partisan supporters, whose motivations for watching debates involves reinforcing positive perceptions about their preferred candidate and negative perceptions about other candidates (Mullinix, 2015). Although partisans who decide on a candidate early are more likely to vote than late deciders, candidates must work to deepen their partisans' motivation to vote on election-day (e.g., Finn & Glaser, 2010; Marcus & MacKuen; 1993). Indeed, a spirited, quotable "zinger" can play well with the candidate's voting base, helping to rally supporters' enthusiasm, improve fundraising, and increase voter turnout in the candidate's favor. For example, during the February 19, 2020, Democratic primary debate in Nevada, Senator Elizabeth Warren delighted fellow progressives by launching a withering attack on billionaire Michael Bloomberg. Charles Chamberlain, the chair for the progressive group Democracy for America said after the debate,

> Tonight, Elizabeth Warren ripped Mike Bloomberg's face off on national television exposing his ugly record on women and racial justice. . . . Together, these progressives came in tonight to fight against the billionaires, and the candidates billionaires are backing—and won. (Goldmacher & Herndon, 2020, February 20, para. 14).

At least in part as a result of Warren's impassioned attack on Bloomberg, she raised $52 million in a single day, shattering the top fund-raising day in her candidacy up to that point (Goldmacher & Herndon, 2020, February 20).

Constraints on Candidates' Nonverbal Behavior

Clinton and the Double Bind

In her various roles as the first lady of Arkansas and the United States, senator from New York, secretary of state, and presidential candidate, Hillary Clinton presents an excellent example of how the gendered double bind (discussed in Chapters 6 and 7) constrains women's rhetorical choices. To be sure, Clinton defied gender stereotypes for women who hold or seek office or are married to powerful men. As a result, critics attacked her, not only for her stances on issues, but for nonverbal behaviors and appearances that had nothing to do with politics. For example, after the second debate in 2016, Trump attacked her physical appearance by saying, "The other day I'm standing at my podium and she walks in front of me, right? She walks in front of me and when she walked in front of me. Believe me, I wasn't impressed, but she walks in front of me" (Diaz, 2016, October 15, para. 2). Carlin and Winfrey (2009) noted that media comments about Clinton during the 2008 campaign also took shots at her appearance and assertiveness:

> No one, however, doubted Hillary Clinton's desire to appear powerful and that resulted in negative representations of her feminine side. Clinton was the anti-seductress who reminded men of the affair gone bad and was "likened by national Public Radio's political editor, Ken Rudin, to the demonic, knife-wielding stalker played by Glenn Close in *Fatal Attraction*" (Stephen, 2008, as quoted in Carlin & Winfrey, 2009, p. 331).

Although critics targeted Clinton's appearance and mannerisms, her paralinguistic cues received what may have been the most disparagement. Her laughter, for example, was characterized routinely in the media as a "cackle," conjuring images of witches and derangement (Romaniuk, 2016). Her voice, roundly criticized as "shrill," seemed to be a rallying point, particularly for supporters of Bernie Sanders, who derided her as "Shrillary." Not to be outdone, one-time presidential candidate and conservative political commentator Pat Buchanan, like many male critics, used Clinton's voice and communication style to attack her femininity. On the television program *Morning Joe*, for instance, Buchanan, no fan of the Clintons, alongside the show's cohost, Mika Brzezinski, acknowledged the double bind, but then brazenly proceeded to perpetuate it:

> Buchanan: It's very tough for a woman. You see two men going back and forth at each other, you say, "Boy, they're really going at it." You see two women, or something, and you say, "Boy, what a catfight this is."

Brzezinski: That's what's so unfair. . . . You think about what she said over the weekend, the sound bites that have been isolated, and imagine those coming from the mouth of a male candidate. And he'd look strong, and aggressive—like a fighter. And what's happening here, with Hillary?

Buchanan: Well, frankly, it's the voice. To be—look, Barack Obama's got a very deep voice. He can go out, he can use mockery and ridicule, and he comes off very smooth and pleasant. But when she raises her voice, and when a lot of women do, you know it's, as I say, it's—it makes you support what every husband in America has heard at one time or another. . . . I know that's a sexist comment but there's truth to it. There's truth to it. It's very difficult for women to reach those kinds of levels effectively as it is to make them sort of a rally speech. They're not good at that. (Garber, 2008, February 28 paras.16–18)

Such attacks resurfaced in 2016, as evidenced by a tweet about Clinton's performance in her debates with Donald Trump. Specifically, although Frank Luntz, a Republican consultant, complimented Clinton for coming across as presidential, his tweet made it clear that some critics focused elsewhere: "Text from a GOP friend of mine in Congress: 'She just comes across as my bitchy wife/mother'" (Luntz, 2016, September 26). The point illustrated, of course, is that the double bind creates an impossible situation for female candidates; when they speak with power and assertiveness, they are accused of appearing "bitchy" or sounding "shrill," but when they embrace a feminine style of communication, they are chastised for sounding weak, incompetent, or unauthentic. Echoing this conclusion, Stanley Fish, though talking about Clinton specifically, described the gendered double bind writ large: "If she answers questions aggressively, she is shrill. If she moderates her tone, she's just play-acting. If she cries, she's faking. If she doesn't, she's too masculine. If she dresses conservatively, she's dowdy. If she doesn't, she's inappropriately provocative" (Fish 2008, February 3, para. 8).

Clinton's Likeability Problem

In the midst of the 2016 election, the *Washington Post* (Gearan & Balz, 2016, May 15) summed up Hillary Clinton's image problems this way:

> More than a dozen Clinton allies identified weaknesses in her candidacy that may erode her prospects of defeating Donald Trump, including poor showings with young women, untrustworthiness, unlikability and a lackluster style on the stump. . . . "I bring it down to one thing and one thing only, and that is likability," said Peter Hart, a Democratic pollster who has conducted a series of focus groups for the Annenberg Public Policy Center at the University of Pennsylvania. (paras. 3–4).

This assessment is consistent with what we've noted about the effects of the double bind, which, in Clinton's case, placed her in a complex predicament. Her leadership roles, her seeking and holding political office, and her assertive style of speech were at odds with society's expectations for femininity, resulting in attributions and presentations of her as "bitchy" and unlikeable. In her last chance to address the American public in a live rhetorical performance, her choices for delivery were limited. As such, she needed to focus on rehabilitating her negative image by avoiding behaviors associated with dominance such as angry facial expressions and vocal tone. As we will see later in the chapter, however, her tendency to smile while being attacked by Donald Trump may have registered as weakness, rather than likeability, to an audience of undecided voters.

Along with being characterized as shrill and aggressive, Clinton faced perceptions that she was untrustworthy and involved in criminal activity. These perceptions originated from an investigation of her (and her husband's) alleged financial association in a land deal involving White Water Savings and Loan, her use (and misuse) of a personal email server while she was secretary of state, and a congressional investigation of her role in responding to the attack on the U.S. Embassy in Benghazi, Libya. Eventually, Clinton was cleared in the investigation of White Water and allegations that she called off military support during the Benghazi attack (e.g., Schmidt, 2014, November 22). The investigation of her use of a private email server, however, resulted in a Federal Bureau of Investigation inquiry, which concluded that "there is evidence of potential violations of criminal statues covering the mishandling of classified information" (as quoted in Zurcher, 2016, para. 22). The Justice Department, however, declined to charge Clinton with a crime. On top of these investigations, stolen emails between officials of the Democratic National Committee (DNC) were leaked to the press, indicating that there had been a concerted effort by the DNC to undermine the campaign of Clinton's primary election opponent, Senator Bernie Sanders. This revelation soured Sanders's supporters on Clinton, making it crucial to win back their support. Overall, these accumulated accusations and investigations cast a shadow on Clinton's trustworthiness as she headed into the 2016 debates.

Trump and the Presidential Image

Donald Trump came into the debates with perhaps the lowest favorability rating of any candidate in history (Saad, 2016, November 8). Although, according to many polls (Cillizza, 2016, May 26), he was less likeable than Clinton, likeability appears to be less important in winning elections for men than for women (Barbara Lee Family Foundation, 2016). As such, Trump's major image obstacle centered, instead, on whether he could conform to behavioral norms embodying the dignity, propriety, and decorum expected of the president of the United States. For the most part, Trump's perceived lack of presidential temperament was based on several patterns of behavior, including his habit of insulting and demeaning political opponents and critics; his use of misogynistic language such as "dog," "pig," and "piece of ass" in describing female opponents and critics (e.g., Milbank, 2016, April 29); and his aggressive nonverbal delivery that was perceived as bullying or threatening to some (Abransky, 2016, February 12; Beattie, 2016) and clownish to others (e.g., Hall, Goldstein, & Ingram, 2016).

Overall, critics agreed that such patterns of behavior made Trump seem "unpresidential" (Winberg, 2017). To improve his image, Trump was constrained in his rhetorical choices by the need to avoid nonverbal behavior that appeared demeaning or overly dominant; that is, the situation called for Trump to project an image befitting a U.S. president. As John Hudak (2016, September 25) from the Brookings Institute wrote, "Trump needs to control himself and his emotions. . . . He needs to be calm, in control, presidential, and look more like a statesman than a stage actor" (para. 18).

On the other hand, Trump's propensity for attacking opponents and the political establishment in Washington had not, so far, been a problem with his ardent supporters. As such, one question for candidate Trump was whether his belligerent verbal and nonverbal approach would work when being directly compared to his opponent's demeanor, especially in appealing to his own supporters as well as undecided voters. When asked about how he planned to avoid coming off as too rough, Trump said, "'I'm going to be very respectful of her. . . . I think she deserves that and I'm going to be nice. If she's respectful of me, that'll be nice,' he said" (Schroeder, 2016, September 23, para. 11).

Like Clinton, Trump also had a history of controversy. For example, Trump faced charges of racism after he settled a federal Fair Housing lawsuit alleging that his company purposely refused to rent to black applicants. Compounding the issue, a former president of Trump Plaza Hotel and Casino related a conversation in which Trump said, "Black guys counting my money! I hate it. The only kind of people I want counting my money are short guys that wear yarmulkes every day . . . laziness is a trait in blacks. . . . It's not anything they can control" (as quoted in Lopez, 2019, July 15, para. 15).

Along with allegations of racism, Trump's love life, particularly his numerous alleged infidelities, fueled concerns about his trustworthiness and personal moral compass. This issue came to a head when an audio recording of Trump speaking with a host of the television show *Access Hollywood* revealed that he had made unwelcome advances on a married woman (who he admitted rebuffed him) and that his celebrity status allowed him access to women whether they wanted it or not. On the tape, Trump is heard saying, "when you're a star you can do anything you want, grab them by the pussy" (Full tape, 2016).

Beyond personal failings, Trump also received negative attention to his business dealings. Over the years, for instance, Trump had used bankruptcy court to vacate his business debts on several occasions. He also refused to release his tax returns, a tradition for those seeking the office of president, claiming he was not legally allowed to do so because he was under audit (though there is no legal requirement to withhold tax returns during an audit, Lipman, 2019, April 19). Trump, therefore, needed to engage in behaviors that would project an image of trustworthiness and controlled temperament—characterized by composure, controlled gestures, and the avoidance of derogatory facial expressions when being attacked.

THE FUNCTIONS OF NONVERBAL BEHAVIOR IN THE 2016 PRESIDENTIAL DEBATES

In this section, we examine several major functions of nonverbal behavior in televised debates as described in Chapter 1. We begin by exploring the ways in which candidates' nonverbal communication enhanced and/or undermined images of themselves and of their opponent. We next discuss how nonverbal behavior functioned argumentatively and rhetorically (see Chapters 1 and 4 for a discussion of other functions served by nonverbal behavior in the 2016 debates). Finally, we examine audience reactions to the candidates' overall debate performances to assess their relative successes and failures in overcoming the obstacles they faced at the outset.

Impression Management: Hillary Clinton

Enhancing One's Own Image

As noted throughout this book, leaving favorable impressions may be the most important goal facing televised debaters, and nonverbal cues are a critical element in the process of creating such impressions. Several studies, in fact, indicate that in the 2016 debates Hillary Clinton engaged in several nonverbal behaviors previously associated with perceptions of warmth, trustworthiness, and emotional openness. Such behaviors, in turn, might have been aimed at improving voters' perceptions of her likeability. First, two studies of behaviors by both candidates across all three debates found that Clinton smiled more frequently than Trump (Greblesky-Lichtman & Katz, 2019; Witkower, Tracy, Cheng, & Henrich, 2020) and engaged in more extensive facial expressions (Greblesky-Lichtman & Katz, 2019). In fact, a third study by Wasike (2019) found that Clinton smiled approximately 12 times more often than Trump in the second debate. In addition, Clinton raised her head and eyebrows (both affinity expressions) more often than Trump, although Trump displayed a relaxed mouth (also an affinity expression) more frequently than Clinton (Wasike, 2019). Finally, an analysis of vocal frequency found that Clinton's speech, compared to Trump's, was more regular and rhythmic, a pattern associated with perceptions of charisma and likeability (Bosker, 2017). These studies, taken together, provide triangulated data suggesting that Clinton engaged in a wider range and higher frequency of nonverbal behaviors that are normally consistent with audience impressions of liking and trust.

That said, as noted earlier, candidates' success in televised debates often depends on their ability to appear competent and presidential. Across studies and most media commentary, Clinton more closely conformed to these expectations than Trump. Indeed, although not as aggressively dominant as Trump, Clinton engaged in nonverbal behaviors that led to perceptions in polls that she was able to handle the job and that she appeared presidential (e.g., Saad, 2016, October 24). In addition, Clinton engaged in a mixture of masculine (e.g., including assertive hand movements and sarcastic vocal tones) and feminine stereotyped behaviors (e.g., small gestural movements, round gestural movements, and an emphasis on appearance—feminine appearing clothing and styled hair) (Grebelsky-Lichtman & Katz, 2019), perhaps to maintain a persona consistent with the double bind expectations of looking like a leader while also meeting feminine stereotyped expectations.

Interestingly, however, an important distinction might be made between behaviors that convey dominance and behaviors that convey prestige. Specifically, although dominance and prestige displays are both signals of social rank associated with effective social influence (e.g., Cheng, Tracy, Foulsham, Kingstone, & Henrich, 2013), prestige, "involves the demonstration of knowledge and expertise to earn respect and freely chosen followership," while dominance "involves the use of aggression and intimidation to induce fear and forced deference" (Witkower et al., 2020, p. 2). Moreover, while prestige behavior includes smiling, head tilted up, and an expanded chest, dominance behaviors include head tilted down while making eye contact with the other, gesturing with arms outstretched, and occupying relatively more space. In the 2016 debates, Clinton not only engaged in more prestige, and less dominance, behavior than Trump on each measure (Witkower et al., 2020), debate viewers ranked her higher in prestige and lower in dominance than Trump (Kakkar & Sivanathan, 2017).

Finally, Clinton's nonverbal behavior, especially when she was in the background, fostered an image consistent with the presidential norms of dignity and composure. Specifically, when speaking, Clinton remained calm and restrained. She did not sound angry, even when personally attacked, and rarely engaged in overly animated gestures (except, perhaps, her "shimmy," see Chapter 5). Clinton's nonverbal behavior during the debates demonstrated decorum and dignity as well as her ability to remain calm under pressure.

Undermining One's Own Image

Even though Clinton appeared somewhat personable and presidential, her nonverbal behavior may also have functioned to undermine her image. To be sure, her smile conveyed warmth but it may have also been perceived as inappropriate at times, perhaps because much of it occurred in the background as Trump spoke. In fact, Grebesky-Lichtman and Katz (2019) counted at least 58 Clinton smiles when she was in the background or as she began to speak after a Trump attack. As such, Clinton's background smiling in the second debate during Trump's aggressive verbal and nonverbal attacks might have appeared inappropriate to the audience. Instead of smiling, facial displays of anger, contempt, or maintaining a neutral expression might have appeared a more appropriate response to such attacks because those expressions would be more compatible with the situation. Indeed, research suggests that inappropriate displays of emotion are often perceived negatively. As Gong and Bucy (2016) noted, "For nonverbal reactions to be evaluated as appropriate, they must be compatible with the message and with the tone of the setting in which they occur" (p. 350). However, given the double bind, such displays could risk appearing too aggressive for a female candidate and play into the media narrative that Clinton was shrill and abrasive, thereby inviting the audience to perceive her as a "nasty woman," which was how Trump described her in the third debate.

Beyond her tendency to smile in the background at inopportune moments, maintaining a cool, unruffled demeanor in the face of Trump's interruptions, spatial encroachments, and intimidating presentation style may not have served Clinton well. As CNN legal correspondent and talk show host Mel Robbins (2016, September 27) wrote, "Clinton was too restrained, too smart—and as much as I hate to say it—she was too presidential. . . . She needed to take him out at the knees. We know Clinton is smart, what we needed to see was a woman who is tough and won't take nonsense from anyone. She failed to do that tonight. Tonight, she was nice. Nice won't win the presidency" (paras. 2–5). This comment, of course, encapsulates the double bind, i.e., Clinton needs to both avoid being aggressive but at the same time fight like a mixed martial artist in a cage match—a seemingly impossible task for anyone.

That said, Clinton also missed opportunities to connect with audience members, often delivering messages that came across as scripted or rehearsed rather than personal and "from the heart." One example occurred in the second debate when a Muslim woman asked what the candidates might do to combat Islamophobia. *Washington Post* writer Sarah Kaufman (2016, October 10) identified the shortcoming in Clinton's response:

> Did Clinton relate personally at all to this woman's anxiety? . . . "My vision of America is an America where everyone has a place, if you are willing to work hard and do your part and you contribute to the community," she said, firmly. But to a woman waiting to hear that she was understood, accepted and safe, Clinton betrayed little feeling, offered up none of the vulnerability that the audience member had shown in speaking up. (paras. 11–12)

Although Clinton engaged in more warmth/reassurance behaviors than Trump overall, and although viewer polls indicated Clinton was perceived to be more likeable by a sizable majority (Saad, 2016, October 26), it may have not been enough to overcome her pre-debate negatives. As Bucy (2016) noted, "Except for small glimpses of genuine emotion—the much-heralded "shimmy" towards the end of the first debate, a delightful rallying cry in the rain at the very end of the campaign—her expressive behavior was not a great ally. . . . In part, she struggled to convince because she struggled to effectively emote." (p. 33).

Undermining the Opponent's Image

We now turn to an examination of the ways in which Clinton's nonverbal behavior functioned to undermine the image of her opponent. Clinton, in her 2016 debate performances might best be described as an "appropriate aggressor" which involves an assertive, rather than aggressive, style of confrontation (Germond & Witcover, 1989). "It is aggression without belligerent antagonism" (Bucy & Gong, 2019, p. 77). Although vocally and visually, Clinton often deployed hints of sarcasm and contempt as she quarreled with Trump's policy positions and wrangled with him over his treatment of women and minorities, her behavior was not overly demonstrative. As a case in point, consider the following exchange from the first debate, which features an argument over Clinton's position on the Trans-Pacific Partnership:

Speaker	Verbal Message	Nonverbal Display
Clinton	That is just not accurate. I was against it once it was finally negotiated and the terms were laid out. I wrote about that . . .	Smirk smile; vocal condescension
		Trump in background: Head nod in disbelief; head tilt back, eyes looking down at Clinton
Trump*	You called it the gold standard. You called it the gold standard of trade deals.	Interrupting with increasing volume, almost shouting

Speaker	Verbal Message	Nonverbal Display
		Clinton in background: raising eyebrows; slight non-Duchenne smile; head tilted up
Clinton	And . . . you know what?	Head still tilted up
		Trump in background: hostile stare
Trump	You said it was the finest deal you've ever seen.	Shouting; slashing right hand gesture
		Clinton in background: Clinton raises eyebrows, tilts head up, shakes head side to side; non-Duchenne smile
Clinton	Nooo	Rising intonation; head shake, lips pursed; then sarcastic smile
Trump*	And then you heard what I said about it and then you said you were against it.	Interruption, shouting over Clinton; displays lower teeth
		Clinton in background: continues to shake her head; derisive smile; looks down at podium
Clinton	Well, Donald, I know you live in your own reality, but that is not...	Vocal sarcasm/contempt; raises voice but does not shout, starts precision grip gesture slash on the word "but"
Trump*	Oh yeah? (simultaneous talk starting at "but")	Sarcastic tone; head canted to the side, smirking
Clinton	. . . the facts. The facts are I did say, I hoped it would be a good deal, but when it was negotiated . . . which I was not responsible for. I concluded it wasn't. I wrote about that in my book . . .	Down stroke precision grip gesture for emphasis on the word "the facts" and then again with "hoped it would be" then an index finger pointed up gesture for emphasis on the word "I"; two hand, palms out facing front on the word "book"; contemptuous vocal tone
		Trump in background: Hostile stare, lips downturned; head tilted right
Trump*	So is it President Obama's fault? (simultaneous talk starting at "responsible for")	Simultaneously leans and tilts posture toward the microphone, turns head to face Clinton, blinks eyes, anger/threat facial expression with index finger jab gesture, still shouting

Speaker	Verbal Message	Nonverbal Display
Clinton	... before you even announced.	Two-handed slice gesture rhythmically in time with emphasis on each word
		Trump in background: Anger/ threat facial display, trunk slightly twisted toward Clinton, shoulder dipped.

* Talk over/interruption. Italic font indicates behaviors by a candidate during the opponent's speaking turn.

This exchange depicts an example of how the candidates attacked each other's image both verbally and nonverbally. During this contentious moment, with Trump interrupting Clinton continuously, Clinton remained relatively calm and did not escalate to an angry tone of voice or engage in overtly aggressive nonverbal displays. Her subtly derisive, non-Duchenne, smiles appeared to be an attempt to communicate that his attacks were harmless and fabrications as she tried to complete her response. Clinton's tone and demeanor during these types of exchanges was patient although she insisted on explaining the facts to the audience despite her opponent's attempt to silence her through interruptions and verbal jabs. As her frustration grew from being interrupted, she, at times, employed condescension and sarcasm to make her point. Throughout the exchange, Clinton painted her opponent as inexperienced and unable to sustain the decorum necessary to engage in serious discussions of important issues. For most of the debates, especially when in the background, Clinton remained poised and polite, with few interruptions, a striking counter image to Trump's continual verbal and nonverbal belligerence.

Impression Management: Donald Trump

Enhancing One's Own Image

Under normal circumstances, candidates for office generally attempt to create an impression of warmth and competence in order to connect with voters. However, as noted earlier, males are less burdened with being liked as long as they can appear competent (Barbara Lee Family Foundation, 2016). As an example of the potential upside for males being seen as aggressive leaders, one of the authors was discussing a new department head with a colleague, describing him as "a pit bull" because of his reputation as a pugnacious leader, which was followed by his colleague's response, "Yes, but he is OUR pit bull."

As noted above, nonverbal analyses of the 2016 debates indicate that Trump was aggressively dominant in his nonverbal behavior and largely abandoned attempts to meet traditional standards for "presidential" behavior. For example, in Witkower et al.'s (2020) analysis, Trump's social rank displays were almost entirely reflective of dominance, rather than prestige. Indeed, Trump commanded more space, used more expansive gestures, and deployed more head-tilt down plus eye contact displays (all dominance rather than prestige related moves) than Clinton. He also engaged in more dominance-based verbal strategies (e.g., attacks and interruptions) and fewer prestige-based verbal behaviors (e.g., demonstrations of expertise) (Grebelsky-Lichtman & Katz, 2019; Witkower et al., 2020). Similarly, Wasike's (2019) analysis in the second debate found Trump engaged in more displays of anger related dominance (e.g., revealing lower teeth and hostile stares) than Clinton. In addition, Grebelsky-Lichtman and Katz (2019) reported only stereotypical masculine (i.e., dominance displays), and no stereotypical feminine, verbal and nonverbal behavior by Trump during the three debates. According to Bucy (2016), these dominance displays were exactly what Trump's base wanted to see. "Key to his success: Trump's expressions were unambiguous. His message of defiance and threat came across blunt and clear, even with the sound off. Whether by design or happenstance, Trump's confrontational style of campaigning bonded supporters to his cause" (Bucy, 2016, p. 32).

Remarkably, although most candidates engage in at least some behaviors to appear warm and approachable, Trump did almost nothing to foster such an impression. As we mentioned above, previous analyses of the candidates' nonverbal communication indicated that Trump communicated almost no warmth throughout the debate, especially when compared to Clinton (Grebelsky-Lichtman & Katz, 2019; Bucy & Gong, 2019; Witkower et al., 2020). He rarely displayed a true Duchenne smile, and when he did smile, the expression tended to be derisive or sarcastic, more taunting or discrediting than an expression of happiness. That said, and also noted above, Trump's popularity was not based on his warmth or friendliness. Instead, his base perceived him as a tough, successful businessman willing to fight for them in restoring the economic advantages usurped by government insiders, immigrants, feminists, minorities, and one-sided trade agreements (Griffin & Teixeira, 2017, June). To this point, scholarship details situations in which dominance displays are more persuasive than prestige displays. For example, in a study covering 69 countries, Kakkar and Sivanathan (2017) found that under conditions of economic uncertainty, people are more likely to support a dominance-based leader over a prestige-based leader, especially when people lack a sense of personal control—conditions that map on well to the psychographic makeup of many Trump supporters (e.g., Thompson, 2016, March 1).

Eschewing a debate strategy in which the candidate attempts to foster a presidential and likeable image is normally a risky proposition. However,

Trump was wildly popular with his voting base (Huey-Burns, 2015, June 18), drawing crowds as small as a few hundred at first, yet building to rallies with as many as 20,000 attendees later (List of rallies, n.d.). The partisan debate audience for Trump included a large percentage of people who regularly watched his reality television show *The Apprentice* and noncommitted voters who were doubtful of Clinton's trustworthiness and/or her likeability. As such, a consideration of Trump's parasocial bonds with viewers is relevant to an understanding of the debates.

As discussed in Chapter 5, media consumers often build parasocial relationships with people who receive significant media attention. Donald Trump successfully built a following by starring in the televised reality show *The Apprentice*, his numerous media appearances on television programs such as *Lifestyles of the Rich and Famous*, *Entertainment Tonight*, *Access Hollywood*, his induction into the *World Wrestling Hall of Fame*, his interviews on Howard Stern's nationally syndicated radio program, and in more recent years, his social and political commentary on social media such as Twitter. Over a 30+ year relationship with his publics, his dress, ornamentation, manner, possessions, relationships with women, and the opulence of his residences all communicated wealth and status. His business acumen was portrayed on *The Apprentice* as a tough but fair boss who was bottom line driven and did not give quarter to celebrities that failed to measure up to his expectations. These portrayals of Trump likely worked as an enthymeme (see Chapter 7) with the conclusion that his wealth and status were evidence of his intelligence and business savvy. From there, of course, a political candidacy is not hard to imagine. In fact, Kevin Drum (2015, August 4) explained how the television portrayal of Trump on *The Apprentice* matches an idealized persona of a U.S. President:

> He is running things. . . . The competitors all call him "Mr. Trump" and treat him obsequiously. He gives orders. . . . At the end of the show, he asks tough questions and demands accountability. He is smooth and unruffled while the team members are tense and tongue-tied. Finally, . . . he takes charge and fires someone. Do you see how precisely this squares with so many people's view of the presidency? The president is the guy running things. He tells people what to do. He commands respect simply by virtue of his personality and rock-solid principles. When things go wrong, he doesn't waste time. He gets to the bottom of the problem in minutes using little more than common sense, and then fires the person responsible. . . . That's a president. (paras. 6–7)

Trump's media savvy may have factored into his success in the primary elections despite negative reactions to his debate performances from the Republican party establishment. In a poll of Republican party "insiders" following the first primary debate, Trump received only 1% of the vote while several of his opponents, including Rubio, Kasich, Bush, and Christie, all received double digits (Cornfield, 2017). Viewer polls and responses on Twitter, however, clearly indicated that Trump was favored over the other candidates by those watching his performance in the debate (Cornfield, 2017). To many, Trump seemed at ease on stage, using gestures, facial expressions and pantomime to "roast" his opponents. Such imitations included a "slumped torso with closed eyes to depict Republican competitor Jeb Bush" (Hall, Goldstein, & Ingram, 2016, p. 73). Trump also engaged in dominance displays—especially the L-shaped "pistol grip" hand gesture used by children when pretending to fire a handgun. This gesture was familiar to fans of *The Apprentice* and a signature move for Trump, who pointed his "gun" at contestants whom he "fired" from the show at the end of every episode.

Indeed, by engaging in the same sort of nonverbal behavior he displayed during his role on *The Apprentice*, Trump's aggressively dominant nonverbal behavior likely appealed to his partisan audience and improved, or at least confirmed, their impression of him as a hard-nosed, take-no-prisoners, leader. In fact, research suggests that positive parasocial relationships are, in general, predictive of political support above and beyond traditional variables such as partisanship and demographics (Cohen & Holbert, 2018). More specifically, Gabriel, Paravati, Green, and Flomsbee (2018) found that people who formed a parasocial relationship with Trump were more supportive of him and his candidacy. Gabriel et al. (2018) summarized their findings this way, "These parasocial bonds with Trump predicted believing Trump's promises, disregarding his unpopular statements, and having generally more positive evaluations of him. Parasocial bonds with Trump were also a significant predictor of self-reported voting behavior, even when examined concurrently with other likely predictors" such as party affiliation and gender (p. 299).

Undermining One's Own Image

Although his verbal and nonverbal dominance displays may have rallied his base, Donald Trump's belligerent debate performances might have done as much to undermine his image with undecided voters and political news media reporters as help it. In fact, according to Bucy and Gong (2019), Trump's behavior was perceived as inappropriate and even confusing to some viewers. As one of their focus group participants put it, "Trump sends so many messed up signals. It's very confusing to watch him. Like, I have a hard time reading him as a person—and it scares me. Admittedly, Clinton isn't the most personable [candidate], either" (focus group participant as quoted in Bucy & Gong, 2019, p. 91). However, it was not just Trump's dominance displays that may have been damaging. During the first debate, press accounts discussed his noticeable sniffing that the Democrats used in a later press release with the headline, "Trump Sniffs at Paying Taxes" (Johnson, 2016, September 26, para. 12). In addition, an analysis of vocal delivery found that Trump engaged in significantly more speech dysfluencies than Clinton (Tian, 2017). Finally, although Trump's nonverbal behavior largely demonstrated anger/threat dynamics, he also displayed nervousness through tics and retreat. For example, an analysis of his nonverbal behavior across the three debates also indicated that Trump engaged in numerous nervous tics and signs of distress such as lip moistening, water drinking, sniffing, and head bobbing (Bucy & Gong, 2019). Psychologist Geoffrey Beattie (2016) pointed to an example of Trump signaling discomfort in the second debate during a discussion of the leaked *Access Hollywood* tape:

> Looking tired, he started quietly rocking on his feet as Clinton spoke, a telltale sign of negative emotion leaking out nonverbally. Clearly he wasn't comfortable with the fallout from the leaked tape. He started sniffing when he talked, as he did throughout the first debate. It's a distraction, and it noticeably gets more pronounced when he's on the spot. (p. 30)

Below, we identify media and general audience responses to Trump's performance, and they are far from positive.

Undermining the Opponent's Image

So far, we have examined how Trump's behavior might have functioned to enhance and harm his image. We now turn to a discussion of how Trump used nonverbal behavior to attack his opponent's image. Bucy and Gong (2019) cataloged Trump's nonverbal behaviors occurring simultaneously with verbal issue and character attacks. During these attacks, Trump remained aggressive throughout by displaying slightly more anger/threat and brush-offs during issue attacks. As Bucy and Gong concluded,

> Nonverbal coding shows that regardless of attack type, Trump showed clear disagreement, made threatening displays while on the attack, and used an agentic or energized style characterized by a multitude of perplexing but, some would say, effectively sequenced defiance gestures. . . . The message communicated to partisans, however, was clear: Trump disliked Clinton, could care less about the rules, and sought to roil American politics rather than reassure. (p. 92)

Beattie (2016), in his analysis of the debates, used the term "bully" to characterize Trump, suggesting that Trump's nonverbal behavior is key to his strategy of relentless attacks on Clinton:

> He started gesturing demonstratively for the first time when he talked about his wealth. "Batonic" gestures—stress-timed gestures that have no iconic con-

> tent, such as the up-and-down beat of a hand—tend to mark out content that's highly significant for the speaker, but when Trump begins his personal attacks, the more complex and abstract metaphoric gestures start up in earnest. . . . Their meaning is processed simultaneously with his speech. As he went on the attack in the debate, his use of beat gestures duly increased. He chopped, he pointed, he sliced . . . he heckled, he interrupted, he glowered as Clinton talked, issuing a nonverbal running commentary on what she was saying. All in all, this was a bully's performance, a physical attempt to dominate Clinton and manipulate our interpretation of her words. (p. 30)

As aggressive as Trump was when it was his turn to speak, it might be his behavior in the background during the second debate that received the most attention. As we have noted elsewhere (see Chapters 4 and 5), the freedom to roam the stage during the town hall debate allowed Trump to engage in, what Bucy and Gong (2019) referred to as, "visual interruptions." At several points, Trump followed behind Clinton, invading her space, standing close behind her as she spoke. By inserting himself into the camera shot during Clinton's speaking turns, he could divert audience attention away from what she was saying as well as engage in "background derogation" (e.g., Seiter, Kinzer, & Weger, 2006). This tactic both intruded on Clinton's speaking time and provided Trump with an opportunity to argue in the background. Bucy and Gong discussed the rhetorical advantage this behavior provided Trump in attacking Clinton's image and ideas when they wrote:

> An additional message that Trump effectively communicates by occupying the frame is one of disinterest and boredom. By first stealing Clinton's airtime and then signaling disinterest in what she has to say, Trump hijacks the very process of idea exchange and reasoned expression of contrasting views that televised debates are supposed to enable. (Bucy & Gong, 2019, p. 92)

Normative theories of argumentation, such as strategic maneuvering (see Chapter 7), clearly consider this type of visual argumentation as fallacious. His behavior both put Clinton in a position to call out his visual interruptions (and sacrificing speaking time to do so), or ignore his behavior, thereby allowing him to continue interrupting her and distracting the audience.

Overall, Trump's background behavior was roundly criticized by viewers and media commentators. "Donald Trump was accused by his rival's campaign of 'menacingly stalking' Hillary Clinton on stage at Sunday night's debate, with even a prominent supporter likening the billionaire to a gorilla," wrote NBC reporter Alastair Jamieson (2016, October 10, para. 1). The front page of the *New York Daily* news ran the headline "Grab a seat loser!" with a photo of Trump clutching the back of his chair as Clinton spoke (Grab a seat, 2016, October 10). Former Republican strategist Nicolle Wallace said, "If a man on the street walked behind her the way he skulked behind Clinton, she'd keep 911 dialed on her cellphone, just in case" (Goldberg, 2016, October 10, para. 5). Jamieson provided several tweets from viewers echoing their perception of Trump's behavior as strange and menacing. For example, one tweet from a woman featuring a photo from the debate in which Trump was close behind Clinton read, "When this happens to me on a sidewalk, I basically start running," and another, displaying the same scene said, "Any questions whether Trump understands what invading a woman's personal space means?" Finally, participants in Bucy and Gong's (2018) focus group observed, "He was over her shoulder the entire time and trying to make her stress or trying to apply some pressure to mess with her delivery," and "He hovered over her the entire time. It's a bullying tactic" (p. 90). Of course, not all viewers saw it this way. For example, Nigel Farage, a British politician and broadcaster said Trump "took control, he dominated Hillary Clinton. . . . I don't think he did it in a particularly aggressive way[;] . . . what you saw tonight is the way he is" (as quoted in Jamieson, 2016, October 10, para. 9).

NONVERBAL BEHAVIOR AS RHETORICAL ARGUMENTATION IN THE 2016 DEBATES

Ethos, Logos, and Pathos Appeals

As discussed in Chapter 7, Aristotle classified the means of persuasion into three types: ethos or credibility, logos or the use of logic and reasoning, and pathos or appeals to emotions. To begin, our analysis of the image function of nonverbal behavior presents several ways that candidates' nonverbal displays functioned to argue for their own, and against their opponent's, image and character. Our analysis here also follows from our discussion of multimodal argumentation in which acoustic and visual elements of the candidates' delivery can function argumentatively, primarily through enthymematic reasoning. Clinton's calm, composed demeanor and Trump's aggressive and animated dominance displays serve as enthymematic grounds for the conclusions they hoped viewers would draw about their personality and temperament.

Both candidates also engaged in nonverbal behavior that enhanced the verbal arguments they made. In an example of enhancing both the verbal logos and ethos appeals, we can see Trump's dominance displays, particularly his anger/threat, derisive, and bored facial displays as types of nonverbal discrediting moves (e.g., D'Errico, Poggi, & Vincze, 2012). Through his spatial crowding of Clinton, Trump may have signaled, or intended to signal, that he held higher status, given that higher status people are typically allowed to invade the space of lower status people (Burgoon et al., 2002). His bored facial expressions argued that her positions were nothing new and nothing that he could not handle. Finally, his anger/threat displays operated as background disagreement moves, communicating that he was insulted by, or challenged the truth of, what she said.

Likewise, Clinton's sarcastic and condescending tone communicated that she thought little of Trump's intelligence or understanding of the issues. Consequently, she had to act as a teacher to a child. Additionally, both candidates engaged in different versions of precision grip displays (see Chapter 7). For example, Trump tended to deploy a version of this gesture in which his middle finger touched his thumb with index finger extended skyward and arm pumping vertically like a piston in a rhythmic motion as he spoke. Bucy and Gong (2019) referred to this as a defiance gesture that Trump often used when responding to criticism from Clinton. In addition to defiance, we think the gesture was used at times to communicate that he was "setting the record straight." Trump also often engaged in the middle finger-thumb grip when he wanted to communicate the fine points of an argument. In contrast, Clinton did not use the middle finger-thumb display as much as Trump, but did use the index finger-thumb display. As noted in Chapter 7, this display is used to enhance the verbal message (logos) by emphasizing the precise nature of the argument being made or by emphasizing the importance of the argument.

Finally, both candidates' communication displays served the function of appealing to audience emotions (pathos). As the quote from Beattie (2016) above suggested, Trump's fervently animated gestures and movements communicated his passion for his argumentative positions and signaled to the audience that they should be passionate as well. As we discussed above, the drawback was that the gestures also signaled the loss of composure, thereby countering Trump's own verbal arguments that he had the temperament to be president. In contrast, Clinton's cool and controlled demeanor argued she was presidential, although, again, her lack of anger displays during Trump's invasive behavior may have also argued that she was too timid in provocative situations to act as an effective leader.

Narrative Analysis of the Candidates' Nonverbal Behavior

During the debates, Trump's dominance displays may have been persuasive with his followers because this behavior is consistent with the narrative of Trump's campaign as a fighter for the way America used to be. Throughout the campaign, Trump argued that the system was rigged for political insiders and that their decisions reflected the Washington establishment and big money donors' interests rather than those of the common person. He argued that their interests were not the interests of the factory worker, the farmer, or the business owner. He placed part of the blame for the working class's problems at the feet of negotiations that favored foreign workers and on immigration policies that allowed immigrants to take jobs from rural Americans. From the perspective of narrative rationality (see Chapter 7), Trump's anger and bellicosity at those he, and his supporters, blamed for economic hardship and uncertainty rang true for his audience. His willingness to violate norms for presidential candidates' comportment was faithful to and coherent with how he presented himself as a different kind of candidate. As evidence of his claim as a political outsider, his unconventional communication style, including unapologetic aggressive dominance displays, also created narrative fidelity. His behavior squared with audience members' experience of typical politicians and his position as an outsider given his communication style and lack of political experience. He also did not communicate like the billionaire one typically sees presented in the news or television programs. To working class voters, his anti-immigrant rhetoric seemed consistent with their concerns about being replaced by factories moving to distant countries, losing jobs to immigrant labor, and the portrayals of Hispanic males in the media. To retirees concerned about their economic future, his rhetoric rang true with their fears of increasing taxes, a demographically changing country, and suspicion of Hillary Clinton. In short, his rhetoric hit all the right notes with people who supported him. As Perloff (2016) explained,

> Trump's narrative resonated with the white working class because it addressed the powerlessness and frustration many workers felt in the midst of crushing technological and economic change, experienced tangibly in communities facing joblessness and attendant social decay, manifest in drug addiction and marital strife. He tapped into real fears Americans had, offering policy alternatives that Republican elites had conveniently elided, telling people who felt they were at the bottom of the heap their needs mattered. He was their blue-collar billionaire. But he also was a canny communicator, exploiting their anxieties for political gain. (p. 61)

Clinton's behavior during the debate can also be analyzed as narrative. Much as Michael Dukakis was urged to interrupt the narrative that he was an automaton that lacked human frailties, Clinton needed to disrupt the narrative that she was unlikeable and inauthentic. Her efforts to stay above the fray by remaining calm and composed were attempts to change the narrative by demonstrating her reasonableness. She refrained from raising her voice to avoid sounding shrill. She smiled to enhance her humanity. All these strategies function argumentatively and rhetorically in attempts to disrupt the dominant media narratives of her campaign. As we will see below, Clinton was partially successful in the polls, suggesting that she appeared more likeable and more presidential than Trump among debate viewers in general. However, among independents and voters in general, her performance did little to change the narrative.

VIEWER REACTIONS TO THE DEBATES

Now that we have examined the background forces at play in the debate, and presented a functional analysis of the candidates' behavior, we think it appropriate to briefly review audience reactions to the debate. To begin, both press accounts and scholarly research tend to agree that Clinton won the debates. Based on viewer polls, Clinton won each debate handily. Nate Silver (2016), founder of polling company *Fivethirtyeight*, reported, "Every scientific poll we've encountered so far suggests that voters thought Hillary Clinton beat Donald Trump in Monday night's debate. In fact, some pollsters showed her winning by a wide margin" (para. 1). *Gallup* (Saad, 2016, October 13) reported Clinton winning by 34 points, *CNN* (Agiesta, 2016, September 27) saw a 27-point win, and *Reuters* (Kahn, 2016, September 28) reported a 30-point win. Lydia Saad (2016, October 13) described the polling this way:

> Her (Clinton) confidence in detailing one policy plan after another likely contributed to viewer perceptions that she had a good command of the issues and was more "presidential." And her 36- and 32-point leads, respectively, over Trump on these qualities mirror her 34-point lead in overall perceptions of who did the better job in the debate. The telltale sign that Trump came up short is that barely half of Republicans believe he won, compared with almost all Democrats believing Clinton won. (para. 9)

The second (Agiesta, 2016, October 10), and third (e.g., Saad, 2016, October 24) debates were much like the first with Clinton winning by large margins. After the third debate, an AP-GfK poll of over a thousand voters reported that Clinton won all three debates by a 69% to 29% margin (Swanson, 2016, October 26). An article discussing polling for all three debates showed that Clinton won by large margins on the questions of who was more likeable, had a good understanding of the issues, was inspiring, and appeared presidential (Saad, 2016, October 24). Meanwhile, although reporting suggested otherwise, Trump still claimed victory. "'Every single online poll had me winning,' Trump said at a campaign stop in Council Bluffs, Iowa on Wednesday. 'You sit back and you hear how well she did in the debate. I don't think she did well at all'" (Kahn, 2016, September 28, para. 6).

Certainly, not all commentary favored Clinton. For example, Fox News commentator Richard Grenell (2016, September 27) summarized the debates this way, "In the end, Trump easily proved that Hillary Clinton's multimillion dollar advertising campaign to define him as a two-headed monster was not accurate. Trump was tough, but fair; gracious, but firm. Clinton was prepared but robotic" (para. 20). Another news writer pointed out that Trump performed well enough to meet expectations:

> Lost will be the other real news of debate: Trump is a very fast learner. The difference between his performance in the first head-to-head encounter with Hillary Clinton and the last was vast. Not only did he stay on message, but he clearly has amassed a great deal of information in a very short time. He spoke about Aleppo and Obama Care, the economy and the Supreme Court with confidence. He will never match Hillary's mastery of policy detail; he doesn't need to. He just needs to sound competent, and he did. (Peek, 2016, October 20, para. 11)

Although most of the polls suggested that Clinton was the viewer favorite, the methodology of many polls simply asked viewers to choose which candidate appeared "more likeable" and did not clearly differentiate among supporters and undecided voters. Nor did they ask viewers to rate each candidate on the various traits, nor did many polls determine whether viewers had changed their view of the candidates based on the debates. Fortunately, two studies shed light on the relative effectiveness of the candidates' performances. First, a study by Winneg and Jamieson (2017) consisting of 2,520 debate viewers found that, following the third debate, there was little change in people's perceptions of who was more qualified (though Clinton was about twice as likely to be seen as qualified) or whether either candidate was a threat to the nation's well-being. Although Clinton continued to lead after the debates, only about 50% thought she was qualified (compared to about 25% for Trump) and as many as 50% thought she was a danger to the well-being of the country (about 63.2% for Trump). To be sure, both candidates experienced small, but significant changes in the positive direction; however, their results suggest that voters were not particularly inspired by either candidate. Unfortunately, this study did not ask questions about either candidate's weakest areas of likeability and trust (for Clinton) and presidential demeanor (for Trump).

A second study conducted across all three debates consisted of undergraduate students and community members from 12 colleges across the United States as participants who watched the debates and evaluated the candidates. Warner et al. (2019) surveyed 1,125 community members before and after debates regarding their perceptions of each candidate's character, intelligence, leadership, charm, competence, and homophily (perceived similarity between candidate and participant). Further, the authors separated participants into Republican, Democratic, and independent viewers. In general, both candidates improved audience perceptions of them, but Clinton outperformed Trump on every measure in terms of relative gains from pre- to post-debate. More importantly, Clinton made significant gains in the areas in which she was weakest, specifically character (trust) and charm (likeability). What's more, she made these gains across Democratic, Republican, and undecided viewers. However, for the character trait (a vitally important area for Clinton), her ratings never exceeded the midpoint of the 5-point scale. That is, even though she made gains, her average scores stayed on the negative side of the scale (2.76 out of 5 with 3 representing "neutral"). For the charm trait, her score barely inched above neutral (with an overall post-debate score of 3.22 out of 5). Trump's scores were worse than Clinton's on all traits for Democrats and undecided viewers and only exceeded the neutral score of 3 out of 5 for Republican viewers. Neither candidate was able to shake off the negative perceptions held by those outside their own parties. In the critical group of independents, Clinton improved her score on most traits (including character) and finished the debates above the neutral point on all traits except homophily and character. Trump, on the other hand, improved on many traits but did not finish above the neutral point on any traits in the eyes of the independent voters. Finally, polling data suggests that Clinton received a significant bounce from the debate. According to data from Nate Silver's *FiveThirtyEight*, on the eve of the first debate, the average across polls suggested the race was very tight with about a 1% lead for Clinton over Trump—well within the margin of error. By October 30th, the day after the last debate, Clinton had opened a 7-percentage point lead (45% Clinton to 37% Trump) in the average across state polls (National election polls, 2008, November 8). This sort of bounce from a debate is unprecedented. Although small swings in close elections can influence results, "There's little historical evidence that they've (general election debates) ever swung polls by more than a few percentage points" (National election polls, para. 4). Given post-debate viewer polling, the data gathered in the community debate viewing studies, and the national polling bounce received from her debate performance, we feel comfortable suggesting that Clinton was more successful at avoiding pitfalls and achieving her argumentative and image goals than was Donald Trump.

That said, given the lopsided victory for Clinton in the debates, one vexing question remains: What happened? How did Clinton lose an election in which she had a 7-percentage point lead in the polls a week beforehand? To begin, it is important to remember that Clinton won the popular vote by almost 3 million votes, which indicates that a majority of American voters preferred her candidacy to that of Donald Trump's. Be that as it may, a number of factors potentially played a role in the election's outcome. As one example, consider the release of a letter by FBI Director James Comey, which reported that the FBI had found a set of email messages possibly related to the investigation of Clinton's misuse of an email server during her tenure as secretary of state.[1] Considering that the letter was delivered to Congress and employees of Federal Bureau of Investigation just 11 days before the election, statistician Nate Silver (2017) made a compelling case about the impact of the letter on the election:

> The impact of Comey's letter is comparatively easy to quantify. . . . At a maximum, it might have shifted the race by 3 or 4 percentage points toward Donald Trump, swinging Michigan, Pennsylvania, Wisconsin and Florida to him, perhaps along with North Carolina and Arizona. At a minimum, its impact might have been only a percentage point or so. Still, because Clinton lost Michigan, Pennsylvania and Wisconsin by less than 1 point, the letter was probably enough to change the outcome of the Electoral College. (para. 3)

President Trump won the electoral college by a combined 78,000 votes in the states of Wisconsin, Michigan, and Pennsylvania—all of which voted Democratic in the 2012 election.[2] Given the letter reignited voters' concern over Clinton's trustworthiness, it seems plausible that the Comey letter kept some Democrats home on election day (turnout was lower than 2012 in many reliably Democratic counties) and may have swung independent and white working class voters toward Trump. Of course, we will never know exactly how the Comey letter changed the results of the election, but we cannot ignore it in estimating the impact of Clinton's historic win in the debates.

SUMMARY AND FINAL THOUGHTS

As we put the finishing touches on this book, it is not certain whether there will be general election debates in the year 2020. Indeed, President Trump has expressed misgivings about the Commission of Presidential Debates, a nonprofit and nonpartisan organization that normally sponsors the debates (Haberman & Karni, 2019, December 12). Citing bias on the part of the organization as a cause of debate watchers' negative assessment of his performance, Trump suggested that he is eager to debate the Democratic nominee but will refuse to participate if the debates are organized by the commission. Specifically, Trump said, "As President, the debates are up to me, and there are many options, including doing them directly & avoiding the nasty politics of this very biased Commission" (as quoted by Russel, 2019, December 16, para. 3). Whether a Democratic nominee would agree to some other arrangement is yet to be determined. Of course, as debate scholars, we hope to see candidates compete on stage in the fall of 2020 and future elections. We look forward with great anticipation to the opportunities such contests present for examining, among a vast array of other topics, the ways in which candidates' nonverbal behavior most certainly affects viewers' perceptions and choices.

To be sure, considered alongside the pages that preceded it, this chapter indicates that nonverbal communication plays an essential role in how candidates manage their image in televised debates across their campaign and how their nonverbal behaviors can function rhetorically and argumentatively as well. In this chapter we analyzed nonverbal behavior in the 2016 presidential debate between Hillary Clinton and Donald Trump. Our analysis started by considering the context in which the debate occurred, exploring constraints on candidates' nonverbal behavior (i.e., the gendered double bind) and challenges each faced in managing their impressions with voters. We also made sense of candidates' nonverbal behavior given their verbal argumentation in the debates. Next, we analyzed how each candidate's nonverbal behavior might have functioned in enhancing and undermining their own image and in undermining the image of their opponent. Finally, we examined how the candidates' behavior functioned as multimodal argumentation, creating ethos, pathos, and logos appeals as well as providing fidelity and coherence in building rhetorical narratives.

Throughout this book, we have built a case for the importance of understanding the functional qualities of nonverbal communication in televised political debates. In doing so, we presented the results of hundreds of social scientific and humanistic studies, and outlined several theoretical approaches supporting our assertion that a deeper understanding of nonverbal behavior in political communication is a significant area of study. Even with an abundance of existing research, there is still so much we do not know. Given this, we look forward to new research and emerging theories that contribute to our understanding of this phenomenon. In writing this book, we hope to have demonstrated the importance of getting these effects right—body language analysis is ill-suited for revealing the inner workings of a person's deeply held beliefs and attitudes, but it can help us understand why audiences react to candidates' style of delivery in their public communication. Considering the weight audiences give to post debate commentary, we believe it is a public disservice to make claims about what candidates "actually mean" or what they "actually believe" without any evidence to back such claims. As such, we hope our book inspires news media professionals to take more care in vetting experts on their programs and in scrutinizing the claims these experts make about candidates' nonverbal behavior. This sort of commentary can potentially damage the quality of public discourse rather than being helpful to voters in making decisions. In a democracy, understanding the role of verbal and nonverbal communication is critical in how we design events such as televised debates, how the media talks about candidates' performances in debates, and ultimately, how viewers weigh candidates' messages in deciding whom to support with their vote.

NOTES

1. James Comey was the head of the Federal Bureau of Investigation in 2016. As such, he was responsible for overseeing the investigation into Clinton's misuse of a private email server, and the mishandling of classified documents, during her tenure as secretary of state. In July of 2016, the investigation seemingly at an end, the FBI reported that although her behavior was extremely careless and likely violated the law in some cases, they recommended no charges be

filed against Clinton. The email investigation was used by Trump during the campaign, often leading crowds to chant "lock her up" at his rallies and inspiring the nickname "Crooked Hillary." Eleven days before the election, the "Comey Letter" informed Congress and employees of the FBI that a previously undiscovered trove of emails between Clinton and Huma Abedin (the vice chair of Clinton's campaign) had been found on Abedin's personal computer and that the emails may be relevant to the larger Clinton email investigation. The Trump campaign (e.g., Schreckinger, 2016, October 28), and news media (Perez & Brown, 2016, October 31), seized on the story speculating that a new round of investigations into Clinton's emails was in the works. Subsequently, the FBI announced two days before the election that the emails provided no new information regarding the overall investigation.

2. Trump also won a few other states carried by Obama in 2012 such as Ohio, Florida, and Iowa by larger margins. However, winning Michigan, Pennsylvania, and Wisconsin would have been enough for Clinton to have prevailed in 2016.

Appendix

History of Televised General Election U.S. Presidential and Vice Presidential Debates, 1960–2016

Note: The first candidate listed won the election that year.

1960

Four Presidential Debates (September 26, October 7, October 13, and October 21)
    John F. Kennedy (Democrat, U.S. Senator from Massachusetts)
    Richard Nixon (Republican, U.S. Vice President)

No Vice Presidential Debates

1964, 1968, AND 1972

No Presidential or Vice Presidential Debates

1976

Three Presidential Debates (September 23, October 6, October 22)
    Jimmy Carter (Democrat, former Governor of Georgia)
    Gerald Ford (Republican, U.S. President)

One Vice Presidential Debate (October 15)

Walter Mondale (Democrat, U.S. Senator from Minnesota)
Robert Dole (Republican, U.S. Senator from Kansas)

1980

First Presidential Debate (September 21)
 Ronald Reagan (Republican, former Governor of California)
 John Anderson (Independent, Representative from Illinois)

Second Presidential Debate (October 28)
 Ronald Reagan (Republican, former Governor of California)
 Jimmy Carter (Democrat, U.S. President)

No Vice Presidential Debates

1984

Two Presidential Debates (October 7 and October 21)
 Ronald Reagan (Republican, U.S. President)
 Walter Mondale (Democrat, former U.S. Vice President)

One Vice Presidential Debate (October 11)
 George H. W. Bush (Republican, U.S. Vice President)
 Geraldine Ferraro (Democrat, Representative from New York)

1988

Two Presidential Debates (September 25 and October 13)
 George H. W. Bush (Republican, U.S. Vice President)
 Michael Dukakis (Democrat, Governor of Massachusetts)

One Vice Presidential Debate (October 5)
 Dan Quayle (Republican, U.S. Senator from Indiana)
 Lloyd Bentsen (Democrat, U.S. Senator from Texas)

1992

Three Presidential Debates (October 11, October 15, and October 19)
 Bill Clinton (Democrat, Governor of Arkansas)
 George H. W. Bush (U.S. President)
 Ross Perot (Independent, Businessman)

One Vice Presidential Debate (October 13)
    Al Gore (Democrat, U.S. Senator from Tennessee)
    Dan Quayle (Republican, U.S. Vice President)
    James Stockdale (Independent, former Vice Admiral of Navy)

1996

Two Presidential Debates (October 6 and October 16)
    Bill Clinton (Democrat, U.S. President)
    Bob Dole (Republican, U.S. Senator from Kansas)

One Vice Presidential Debate (October 9)
    Al Gore (Democrat, U.S. Vice President)
    Jack Kemp (Republican, former Secretary of Housing and Urban Development)

2000

Three Presidential Debates (October 3, October 11, and October 17)
    George W. Bush (Republican, Texas Governor)
    Al Gore (Democrat, U.S. Vice President)

One Vice Presidential Debate (October 5)
    Dick Cheney (Republican, former Secretary of Defense)
    Joseph Lieberman (Democrat, U.S. Senator from Connecticut)

2004

Three Presidential Debates (September 30, October 8, and October 13)
    George W. Bush (Republican, U.S. President)
    John Kerry (Democrat, U.S. Senator from Massachusetts)

One Vice Presidential Debate (October 5)
    Dick Cheney (Republican, U.S. Vice President)
    John Edwards (Democrat, U.S. Senator from North Carolina)

2008

Three Presidential Debates (September 26, October 7, October 15)
    Barack Obama (Democrat, U.S. Senator from Illinois)
    John McCain (Republican, U.S. Senator from Arizona)

One Vice Presidential Debate (October 2)
    Joe Biden (Democrat, U.S. Senator from Delaware)
    Sarah Palin (Republican, Governor of Alaska)

2012

Three Presidential Debates (October 3, October 16, and October 22)
    Barack Obama (Democrat, U.S. President)
    Mitt Romney (Republican, former Governor of Massachusetts)

One Vice Presidential Debate (October 11)
    Joe Biden (Democrat, U.S. Vice President)
    Paul Ryan (Republican, Representative from Wisconsin)

2016

Three Presidential Debates (September 26, October 9, October 19)
    Donald Trump (Republican, Businessman)
    Hillary Clinton (Democrat, former Secretary of State)

One Vice Presidential Debate (October 4)
    Mike Pence (Republican, Governor of Indiana)
    Tim Kaine (Democrat, U.S. Senator from Virginia)

Bibliography

1992 Presidential Debates. (1996). *CNN.* http://www.cnn.com/ALLPOLITICS/1996/debates/history/1992/index.shtml

Abele, A. E., Cuddy, A. J. C., Judd, C. M., & Yzerbyt, V. Y. (2008). Fundamental dimensions of social judgment. *European Journal of Social Psychology, 38,* 1063–1065. doi:10.1037/0022-3514.89.6.899

Abramsky, S. (2016, February 12). Donald Trump, the most dangerous face in the Republican crowd. *The Nation.* https://www.thenation.com/article/donald-trump-the-most-dangerous-face-in-the-republican-crowd/

Adams, R. B., Gordon, H. L., Baird, A. A., Ambady, N., & Kleck, R. E. (2003). Effects of gaze on amygdala sensitivity to anger and fear faces. *Science, 300,* 1536. doi:10.1126/science.1082244

Adams, R. B., Jr., & Kleck, R. E. (2003). Perceived gaze direction and the processing of facial displays of emotion. *Psychological Science, 14,* 644–647. doi:10.1046/j.0956-7976.2003.psci1479.x

Adams, R. B., Jr., & Kleck, R. E. (2005). Effects of direct and averted gaze on the perception of facially communicated emotion. *Emotion, 5,* 3–11. doi:10.1037/1528-3542.5.1.3

Agiesta, J. (2016, September 27). Post-debate poll: Hillary Clinton takes round one. *CNN.* https://www.cnn.com/2016/09/27/politics/hillary-clinton-donald-trump-debate-poll/index.html

Agiesta, J. (2016, October 9). Clinton wins debate, but Trump exceeds expectations. *CNN.* https://www.cnn.com/2016/10/09/politics/clinton-wins-debate-but-trump-exceeds-expectations/

Aguinis, H., Simonsen, M. M., & Pierce, C. A. (1998). Effects of nonverbal behavior on perceptions of power bases. *The Journal of Social Psychology, 138*(4), 455–469. doi:10.1080/00224549809600400

Ahler, D. J., Citrin, J., Dougal, M. C., & Lenz, G. S. (2007). Face value? Experimental evidence that candidate appearance influences electoral choice. *Political Behavior, 39,* 77–102. doi:10.1007/s11109-016-9348-6

Alter, C. (2016, September 25). Why it's so hard for men to debate women. *Time.* https://time.com/4506394/presidential-debate-men-women/

Anderson, K. V. (1999). "Rhymes with rich": "Bitch" as a tool of containment in contemporary American politics. *Rhetoric & Public Affairs, 2,* 599–623. doi:10.1353/rap.2010.0082

Anderson, K. V. (2017). Presidential pioneer or campaign queen?: Hillary Clinton and the first-time/frontrunner double bind. *Rhetoric and Public Affairs, 20,* 525–538. doi:10.14321/rhetpublaffa.20.3.0525

Andersen, P. A. (2004). Influential actions: Nonverbal communication and persuasion. In J. S. Seiter & R. H. Gass (Eds.), *Readings in persuasion, social influence, and compliance gaining* (pp. 165–180). Boston, MA: Allyn & Bacon.

Andersen, P. A. (2008). *Nonverbal communication: Forms and functions* (2nd ed.). Long Grove, Ill: Waveland Press.

Andersen, P., & Andersen, J. (1982). Nonverbal immediacy and instruction. In L. Barker (Ed.), *Communication in the classroom* (pp. 98–120). Engelwood Cliffs, NJ: Prentice-Hall.

Andersen, P. A., & Bowman, L. L. (1999). Positions of power: Nonverbal influence in organizational communication. In L. K. Guerrero, J. A. DeVito, & M. L. Hecht (Eds.) *The nonverbal communication reader: Classic and contemporary readings* (pp. 317–334). Prospect Heights, IL: Waveland.

Andersen, S. M., Reznik, I., & Manzella, L. M. (1996). Eliciting facial affect, motivation, and expectancies in transference: Significant-other representations in social relations. *Journal of Personality and Social Psychology, 71*, 1108–1129.

Andric, M., Solodkin, A., Buccino, G., Goldin-Meadows, S., Rizzolatti, G., & Small, S. L. (2013). Brain function overlaps when people observe emblems, speech, and grasping. *Neuropsychologia, 51*, 1619–1629. doi:10.1016/j.neuropsychologia.2013.03.022

Antonakis, J., & Dalgas, O. (2009). Predicting elections: Child's play! *Science, 323*(5918), 1183. doi:10.1126/science.1167748.

Aristotle & Kennedy, G. A. (2007). *On Rhetoric : A Theory of Civic Discourse* (2nd ed). New York: Oxford University Press.

Associated Press. (2008, October 11). *McCain counters Obama 'Arab' question* [Video file]. https://www.youtube.com/watch?v=jrnRU3ocIH4

Atkinson, M. (1984). *Our masters' voices: The language and body language of politics.* New York: Methuen.

Atkinson, M. D., Enos, R., & Hill, S.J. (2009). Candidate faces and election outcomes: Is the face–vote correlation caused by candidate selection? *Quarterly Journal of Political Science, 4*, 229–249. doi:10.1561/100.00008062

Auer, J. J. (1962). The counterfeit debates. In S. Kraus (Ed.), *The great debates: Background-perspective-effects* (pp. 146–147). Bloomington, IN: Indiana University Press.

Axsome, D., Yates, S., & Chaiken, S. (1987). Audience response as a heuristic cue in persuasion. *Journal of Personality and Social Psychology, 53*, 30–40. doi:10.1037//0022-3514.53.1.30

Babad, E. (1999). Preferential treatment in television interviewing: Evidence from nonverbal behavior. *Political Communication, 16*, 337–358. doi.org/10.1080/105846099198668

Baggaley, J. (1980). *Psychology of the TV image.* Westmead, UK: Gower Publishing Company Limited.

Baggaley, J., & Duck, S. W. (1975). Experiments in ETV: Further effects of camera angle. *Educational Broadcasting International, 8*, 183–184. https://eric.ed.gov/?id=EJ133006

Bailenson, J. N., Iyengar, S., Yee, N., & Collins, N. A. (2008). Facial similarity between voters and candidates causes influence. *Public Opinion Quarterly, 72*, 935–961. doi:10/1093/poq/nfn064

Baird, J. (2008, September 13). From Seneca Falls to…Sarah Palin? *News Week.* http://www.cawp.rutgers.edu/sites/default/files/resources/08–09–13_newsweek.pdf

Banning, S., & Coleman, R. (2009). Louder than words: A content analysis of presidential candidates' televised nonverbal communication. *Visual Communication Quarterly, 16*, 4–17. doi.org/10.1080/15551390802620464

Barak, A., Patkin, J., & Dell, D. M. (1982). Effects of certain counselor behaviors on perceived expertness and attractiveness. *Journal of Counseling Psychology, 29*, 261–267. doi:10.1037/0022-0167.29.3.261

Barbara Lee Family Foundation (2016, April 26). Politics is personal: Keys to likeability and electability for women: A Barbara Lee Family Foundation Research Memo. *Barbara Lee Family Foundation.* https://www.barbaraleefoundation.org/wp-content/uploads/BLFF-Likeability-Memo-FINAL.pdf

Baril, G. L., & Stone, W. F. (1984). Mixed messages: Verbal-vocal discrepancy in freshmen legislators. *Political Psychology, 5*, 83–98. doi:10.2307/3790833

Baron-Cohen, S. (1995). *Mindblindness: An essay on autism and theory of mind*. Boston, MA: MIT Press/Bradford Books.

Bateson, G. (1963). Exchange of information about patterns of human behavior. In W. S. Fields & W. Abbott (Eds.), *Information storage and neural control* (pp. 173–186). Springfield, IL: Thomas Books.

Bauer, N. M. (2015). Emotional, sensitive, and unfit for office: Gender stereotype activation and support for female candidates. *Political Psychology, 36*, 691–708. doi:10.1111/pops.12186

Bauer, N. M. (2018) Untangling the relationship between partisanship, gender stereotypes, and support for female candidates. *Journal of Women, Politics & Policy, 39*, 1–25, doi:10.1080/1554477X.2016.1268875

Bauer, N. M., & Carpinella (2017). Visual information and candidate evaluations: The influence of feminine and masculine images on support for female candidates. *Political Research Quarterly, 71*, 395–407. doi:10.1177/1065912917738579

Beattie, G. (2016). How Trump bullies with his body language. In D. Lilleker, D. Jackson, E. Thorsen, & A. Veneti (Eds.), *US election analysis 2016: Media, voters, and the campaign* (p. 30). Poole, England: The Centre for the Study of Journalism, Culture and Community.

Beatty, M. J., & Kruger, M. W. (1978). The effects of heckling on speaker credibility and attitude change. *Communication Quarterly, 26*(2), 46–50. doi:10.1080/01463377809369293

Beebe, S. A. (1974). Eye contact: A nonverbal determinant of speaker credibility. *Communication Education, 23*, 21–25. doi:10.1080/03634527409378052

Benedictus, L. (2016, January 9). The crying game: How political tears became routine. *The Guardian*. https://www.theguardian.com/us-news/2016/jan/09/the-crying-game-obama-tears-politicians

Benetiz-Quiroz, C. F., Wilbur, R. B., & Martinez, A. M. (2016). The not face: A grammaticalization of facial expressions of emotion. *Cognition, 150*, 77–84. doi:10.1016/j.cognition.2016.02.004.

Benjamin, D. J., & Shapiro, J. M. (2009). Thin-slice forecasts of gubernatorial elections. *Review of Economics and Statistics, 91*, 523–536. doi:10.1162/rest.91.3.523

Benoit, W. L. (2007). *Communication in political campaigns*. New York: Peter Lang.

Benoit, W., & Brazeal, L. M. (2002). A functional analysis of the 1988 Bush-Dukakis presidential debates. *Argumentation and Advocacy, 38*, 219–233. doi:10.1080/00028533.2002.11821569.

Benoit, W., Hanson, G. J., & Verser, R. M. (2003). A meta-analysis of the effects of viewing U.S. presidential debates. *Communication Monographs, 70*, 335–350. doi:10.1080/0363775032000179133

Benoit, W., & Harthcock, A. (1999). Functions of the great debates: Acclaims, attacks, and defenses in the 1960 presidential debates. *Communication Monographs, 66*, 341–357. doi:10.1080/03637759909376484.

Benoit, W. L., McKinney, M. S., & Holbert, R. L. (2001). Beyond learning and persona: Extending the scope of presidential debate effects. *Communication Monographs, 68*, 259–273. doi:10.1080/03637750128060

Benoit, W. L., & Strathman, A. (2004). Source credibility and the elaboration likelihood model. In J. S. Seiter & Robert H. Gass (Eds.), *Perspectives on persuasion, social influence, and compliance gaining* (pp. 95–111). Boston, MA: Pearson/Allyn & Bacon.

Benoit, W. L., Webber, D. J., & Berman, J. (1998). Effects of presidential debate watching and ideology on attitudes and knowledge. *Argumentation and Advocacy, 34*, 163–172. doi: 10.1111/j.1460–2466.2002.tb02547.x

Benoit, W. L., & Wells, W. T. (1996). *Candidates in conflict: Persuasive attack and defense in the 1992 presidential debates*. Tuscaloosa, AL: University of Alabama Press.

Berenson, T. (2016, March 1). Here are Trump and Rubio's best schoolyard insults. *Time*. http://time.com/4242827/donald-trump-marco-rubio-insults/

Berger, J., Rosenholtz, S., & Zelditch, M., Jr. (1980) Status organizing processes. In A. Inkeles (Ed.), *Annual Review of Sociology* (pp. 479–747). Palo Alto, CA: Annual Reviews.

Berlo, D. K., Lemert, J. B., & Mertz, R. J. (1969). Dimensions for evaluating the acceptability of message sources. *Public Opinion Quarterly, 33*, 563–576. https://www.jstor.org/stable/2747566

Berquist, G. (1994). The 1976 Carter-Ford Presidential Debates. In R. V. Friedenberg (Ed.), *Rhetorical studies of national political debates 1960–1992*. Westport, CT: Praeger.

Berquist, G. F., & Golden, J. L. (1981). Media rhetoric, criticism and the public perception of the 1980 presidential debates. *Quarterly Journal of Speech, 67*, 125–137. doi:10.1080/00335638109383559

Berry, D. S., & McArthur, L. Z. (1985). Some components and consequences of a babyface. *Journal of Personality and Social Psychology, 48*, 312–323. doi:10.1037/0022-3514.48.2.312

Bickman, L. (1971). The effect of different uniforms on obedience in field situations. *Proceedings of the Annual Convention of the American Psychological Association, 6* (Pt. 1), 359–360.

Bitzer, L. F. (1959). Aristotle's enthymeme revisited. *Quarterly Journal of Speech, 45*, 339–408. doi:10.1080/00335635909382374

Bitzer, L. (1968). The rhetorical situation. *Philosophy and Rhetoric, 5*, 1–14. http://www.jstor.org/stable/40236733

Bitzer, L., & Rueter, T. (1980). *Carter vs Ford: The counterfeit debates of 1976*. Madison: WI: University of Wisconsin Press.

Blake, A. (2012, October 4). Six reasons Mitt Romney won the first debate. *The Washington Post*. https://www.washingtonpost.com/news/the-fix/wp/2012/10/04/six-reasons-mitt-romney-won-the-first-debate/

Blake, J. (2016, January 8). Why Obama's tears are so revolutionary. *CNN*. https://www.cnn.com/2016/01/08/politics/obama-gun-control-tears/index.html

Blair, H. (2005). *Lectures on rhetoric and Belles Lettres*. Linda Ferreira-Buckley & S. Michael Halloran (Eds.). Carbondale, IL: Southern Illinois University. (Original work published in 1783).

Blanc, J. M., & Dominey, P. F. (2003). Identification of prosodic attitudes by a temporal recurrent network. *Cognitive Brain Research, 17*, 693–699. doi:10.1016/S0926-6410(03)00195-2

Bond, C. F., Omar, A., Mahmoud, A., & Bonser, R. N. (1990). Lie detection across cultures. *Journal of Nonverbal Behavior, 14*, 189–204. doi:10.1007/BF00996226

Bono, J. E., & Ilies, R. (2006). Charisma, positive emotions and mood contagion. *The Leadership Quarterly, 17*, 317–334. doi:10.1016/j.leaqua.2006.04.008

Bordone, B. (2019, June 25). What would a better format for a presidential debate look like? *NBC*. https://www.nbcnews.com/think/opinion/democratic-debates-are-essentially-competitive-press-conferences-voters-deserve-more-ncna1021281

Bosker, H. R. (2017). The role of temporal amplitude modulations in the political arena: Hillary Clinton vs. Donald Trump. *Proceedings of Interspeech 2017* (pp. 2228–2232). doi:10.21437/Interspeech.2017–142.

Botelho, G. (2016, March 14). The day politics and TV changed forever. *CNN*. https://www.cnn.com/2016/02/29/politics/jfk-nixon-debate/index.html

Bowden, E. (2020, February 25). Democratic debate: Chaos reigns as shouting match breaks out in South Carolina. *New York Post*. https://nypost.com/2020/02/25/democratic-debate-chaos-reigns-as-shouting-match-breaks-out-in-south-carolina/

Brambilla, M., Rusconi, P., Sacchi, S., & Cherubini, P. (2001). Looking for honesty: The primary role of morality (vs. sociability and competence) in information gathering. *European Journal of Social Psychology, 41*, 135–143. doi:10.1002/ejsp.744

Briñol, P., & Petty, R.E. (2008). Embodied persuasion: Fundamental processes by which bodily responses can impact attitudes. In G. R. Semin, & E. R. Smith (Eds.), *Embodied grounding: Social, cognitive, affective, and neuroscientific approaches* (pp. 184–207). New York, NY: Cambridge University Press.

Briñol, P., Petty, R. E., & Tormala Z. L. (2004). Self-validation of cognitive responses to advertisements. *Journal of Consumer Research, 30*, 559–573.doi:10.1086/380289

Brockriede, W. E. (1975). Where is argument? *Journal of the American Forensics Association, 11*, 179–182. doi:10.1080/00028533.1975.11951059

Brooke, M. E., & Ng, S. H. (1986). Language and social influence in small conversational groups. *Journal of Language and Social Psychology, 5*, 201–210. doi:10.1177/0261927X8600500303

Brown, B. L. (1980). Effects of speech rate on personality attributions and competency ratings. In H. Giles, P. W. Robinson, & P. M. Smith (Eds.), *Language: Social psychological perspectives* (pp. 293–300). Oxford, England: Pergamon.

Brown, P., & Levinson, S. C. (1987). *Politeness: Some universals in language use.* New York: Cambridge University Press.

Brownlow, S. (1992). Seeing is believing: Facial appearance, credibility, and attitude change. *Journal of Nonverbal Behavior, 16*, 101–115. doi.org/10.1007/BF00990325

Brubaker, J., & Hanson, G. (2009). The effect of Fox News and CNN's postdebate commentator analysis on viewers' perceptions of presidential candidate performance. *Southern Communication Journal, 74*, 339–351. doi.org/10.1080/10417940902721763

Bucy, E. P. (2000). Emotional and evaluative consequences of inappropriate leader displays. *Communication Research, 27*, 194–226. doi:10.1177/009365000027002004

Bucy, E. P. (2016a). The look of losing, then and now: Nixon, Obama, and nonverbal indicators of opportunity lost. *American Behavioral Scientist, 60*, 1772–1798. doi:10.1177/0002764216678279

Bucy, E. P. (2016b). Image bites, voter enthusiasm, and the 2016 presidential election. In D. Lilleker, D. Jackson, E. Thorsen, & A. Veneti (Eds.), *US election analysis 2016: Media, voters, and the campaign* (p. 32–33). Poole, England: The Centre for the Study of Journalism, Culture and Community.

Bucy, E. P., & Gong, Z. H. (2018). In/appropriate aggression in presidential debate: How Trump's nonverbal displays intensified verbal norm violations in 2016. In C. Senior (Ed.), *The facial displays of leaders* (pp. 73–95). London: Palgrave MacMillan.

Bucy, E. P., & Grabe, M. E. (2007). Taking television seriously: A sound and image bite analysis of presidential campaign coverage, 1992–2004. *Journal of Communication, 57*, 652–675. doi:10.1111/j.1460-2466.2007.00362.x

Bucy, E. P., & Newhagen, J. E. (1999). The emotional appropriateness heuristic: Processing televised presidential reactions to the news. *Journal of Communication, 49*, 59–79.

Bucy, E. P., & Stewart, P. (2018). The personalization of campaigns: Nonverbal cues in presidential debates. W. R. Thompson (Ed.), *Oxford Research Encyclopedia of Politics.* New York, NY: Oxford University Press.

Bugental, D. B., Henker, B., & Whalen, C. K. (1976). Attributional antecedents of verbal and vocal assertiveness. *Journal of Personality and Social Psychology, 34*, 405–411. doi:10.1037/0022-3514.34.3.405

Bull, P. (1986). The use of hand gesture in political speeches: Some case studies. *Journal of Language and Social Psychology, 5*, 103–118. doi:10.1177/0261927X8652002

Burgoon, J. K. (1978). A communication model of personal space violations: Explication and an initial test. *Human Communication Research, 4*, 129–142. doi.org/10.1111/j.1468-2958.1978.tb00603.x

Burgoon, J. K. (1985). The relationship of verbal and nonverbal codes. In B. Dervin & M. J. Voight (Eds.), *Progress in communication sciences* (Vol. 6, pp. 263–298). Norwood, NJ: Ablex.

Burgoon, J. K. (1994). Nonverbal signals. In M. L. Knapp & G. R. Miller (Eds.), *Handbook of interpersonal communication* (pp. 229–285). Thousand Oaks, CA: Sage.

Burgoon, J. K. (2009). Expectancy violations theory. In S. W. Littlejohn & K. A. Foss (Eds.), *Encyclopedia of communication theory* (pp. 367–369). Los Angeles, CA: Sage.

Burgoon, J. K., & Aho, L. (1982). Three field experiments on the effects of violations of conversational distance. *Communication Monographs, 49*, 71–88. doi:10.1080/03637758209376073

Burgoon, J. K., Birk, T., & Pfau, M. (1990). Nonverbal behaviors, persuasion, and credibility. *Human Communication Research, 17*, 140–169. doi:10.1111/j.1468-2958.1990.tb00229.x

Burgoon, J. K., & Buller, D. B. (2004). Interpersonal deception theory. In J. S. Seiter & R. H. Gass (Eds.), *Readings in persuasion, social influence, and compliance gaining* (pp. 239–264). Boston, MA: Allyn & Bacon.

Burgoon, J. K., & Buller, D. B. (2008). Interpersonal deception theory: Purposive and independent behavior during deception. In L. A. Baxter & D. O. Braithwaite (Eds.), *Engaging theories in interpersonal communication: Multiple perspectives* (pp. 227–239). Los Angeles: Sage.

Burgoon, J. K., Buller, D. B., & Woodall, W. G. (1996). *Nonverbal communication: The unspoken dialogue* (2nd ed.). New York, NY: McGraw Hill.

Burgoon, J. K., Coker, D. A., & Coker, R. A. (1986). Nonverbal behaviors, persuasion, and credibility. *Human Communication Research, 12,* 495–524. doi:10.1111/j.1468-2958.1990.tb00229.x

Burgoon, J. K., Dunbar, N. E., Segrin, C. (2002). Nonverbal influence. In M., Pfau, J. P. Dillard, (Eds.), *The persuasion handbook: Theory and practice* (pp. 445–473). Thousand Oaks, CA: Sage.

Burgoon, J. K., Guerrero, L. K., & Floyd, K. (2010). *Nonverbal communication.* Boston, MA: Allyn & Bacon.

Burgoon, J. K., & Hale, J. L. (1988). Nonverbal expectancy violations: Model elaboration and application. *Communication Monographs, 55, 58–79.* doi:10.1080/03637758809376158

Burgoon, J. K., & Jones, S. B. (1976). Toward a theory of personal space expectations and their violations. *Human Communication Research, 2,* 131–146. doi:10.1111/j.1468-2958.1976.tb00706.x

Burgoon, J. K., Manusov, V., Mineo, P., & Hale, J. L. (1985). Effects of gaze on hiring, credibility, attraction and relational message interpretation. *Journal of Nonverbal Behavior, 9,* 133–146. doi.org/10.1007/BF01000735

Burgoon, J. K., & Walther, J. B. (1990). Nonverbal expectancies and the evaluative consequences of violations. *Human Communication Research, 17,* 232–265. doi:10.1111/j.1498-2958.1990.tb00232.x

Burnett, A., & Badzinski, D. M. (2005). Judge nonverbal communication on trial: Do mock trial jurors notice? *Journal of Communication, 55,* 209–224. doi.org/101111/j.1460-2466.2005.tb.02668.x

Burns, J. (2008, July 7). Gore blames TV camera operators for debate performance. *Cnsnews.com.* htttp://cnsnews.com/news/article/gore-blames-tv-camera-operators-debate-performance

Cacioppo, J. T., & Petty, R. E. (1982). The need for cognition. *Journal of Personality and Social Psychology, 42,* 116–131. doi:10.1037/0022–3514.42.1.116

Canary, D. J., Cody, M. J., & Manusov, V. L. (2008). *Interpersonal communication: A goals-based approach* (4th ed.). Boston, MA: Bedford St. Martin.

Cannon, L. (1984, August 24). Reagan accepts nomination to second term. *The Washington Post.* https://www.washingtonpost.com/archive/politics/1984/08/24/reagan-accepts-nomination-to-second-term/eb4fa322–ac2b-47e0–b14d-3abd62ae5d34/

Carli, L. L. (2004). Gender effects on social influence. In J. S. Seiter & R. H. Gass (Eds.), *Perspectives on persuasion, social influence, and compliance gaining* (pp. 133–148). Boston, MA: Allyn & Bacon.

Carlin, D. P. (1994). A rationale for a focus group study. In D. B. Carlin & M. S. McKinney (Eds.), *The 1992 presidential debates in focus* (pp. 3–19). Westport, CT: Praeger.

Carlin, D. B., Vigil, T., Buehler, S., & McDonald, K. (2007). *The third agenda in U.S. presidential debates: DebateWatch and viewer reactions 1996–2004.* Westport, CT: Praeger.

Carney, D. R., Cuddy, A. J. C., & Yap, A. J. (2010). Power posing: Brief nonverbal displays affect neuroendocrine levels and risk tolerance. *Psychological Science, 21,* 1363–1368. doi:10.1177/0956797610383437

Carpenter, C. J. (2012). A meta-analysis and an experiment investigating the effects of speaker disfluency on persuasion. *Western Journal of Communication, 76,* 552–569. doi:10.1080/10570314.2012.662307

Carter, J. S. (2019). Debating memes: Networked democracy and the politics of cynical laughter. In E. A. Hinck (Ed.), *Presidential debates in a changing media environment* (Vol. 2, pp. 243–262). Santa Barbara, CA: Praeger Publishers.
Carrier D. R. (2001). The advantage of standing up to fight and the evolution of habitual bipedalism in hominins. *PLoS One, 6*, e19630. doi:10.1371/journal.pone.0019630
Castelli, L., Carraro, L., Ghitti, C., & Pastore, M. (2009). The effects of perceived competence and sociability on electoral outcomes. *Journal of Experimental Social Psychology, 45*, 1152–1155. doi:10.1016/j.jesp.2009.06.018
Cesario, J., Jonas, K. J., & Carney, D. A. (2017) CRSP special issue on power poses: What was the point and what did we learn? *Comprehensive Results in Social Psychology, 2* , 1–5. doi: 10.1080/23743603.2017.1309876
Chaiken, S. (1987). The heuristic model of persuasion. In M. P. Zanna, J. M. Olson, & C. P. Herman (Eds.), *Social influence: The Ontario symposium* (Vol. 5, pp. 3–39). Hillsdale, NJ: Erlbaum.
Chaiken, S., Liberman, A., & Eagly, A. H. (1989). Heuristic and systematic information processing within and beyond the persuasion context. In J. S. Uleman & J. A. Bargh (Eds.), *Unintended thought* (pp. 212–252). New York: Guilford Press.
Chaiken, S., & Trope, Y. (Eds.). (1999). *Dual-process theories in social psychology.* New York, NY: Guilford Press.
Chaplin, W. F., Phillips, J. B., Brown, J. D., Clanton, N. R., & Stein, J. L. (2000). Handshaking, gender, personality, and first impressions. *Journal of Personality and Social Psychology, 79*, 110–117. doi:10.1037/0022–3514.79.1.110.
Chen, F. F., Jing, Y. & Lee, J. M. (2014). The looks of a leader: competent and trustworthy, but not dominant. *Journal of Experimental Social Psychology, 51*, 27–33. doi:10.1016/j.jesp.2013.10.008
Chen, F. S., Minson, J. A., Schöne, M., & Heinrichs, M. (2013). In the eye of the beholder: Eye contact increases resistance to persuasion. *Psychological Science, 24*, 2254–2261. doi:10.1177/0956797613491968
Cheng, J. T., Tracy, J. L., Foulsham, T., Kingstone, A., & Henrich, J. (2013). Two ways to the top: Evidence that dominance and prestige are distinct yet viable avenues to social rank and influence. *Journal of Personality and Social Psychology, 104*, 103–125. doi:10.1037/a0030398
Chiao, J. Y., Bowman, N. E., & Gill, H. (2008). The political gender gap: Gender bias in facial inferences that predict voting behaviour. *PLoS ONE, 3*(10), 1–7.
Cho, J. (2009). Disentangling media effects from debate effects: The presentation mode of televised debates and viewer decision making. *Journalism & Mass Communication Quarterly, 86*, 383–400. doi.org/10.1177/107769900908600208
Cho, J., Shah, D. V., Nah, S., & Brossard, D. (2009). "Split screens" and "spin rooms": Debate modality, post-debate coverage, and the new videomalaise. *Journal of Broadcasting and Electronic Media, 53*, 242–261. doi.org/10.1080/08838150902907827
Chong, D., & Druckman, J. N. (2007). Framing theory. *Annual Review of Political Science, 10*, 103–126. doi:10.1146/annurev.polisci.10.072805.103054
Chinni, D. (2016, September 25). Do presidential debates impact election outcomes? *NBC News.* https://www.nbcnews.com/storyline/2016–presidential-debates/do-presidential-debates-impact-election-outcomes-n653801
Cialdini, R. B. (1993). *Influence: The psychology of persuasion* (Rev. ed.). New York, NY: Morrow.
Cialdini, R. (2016). *Pre-suasion: A revolutionary way to influence and persuade.* New York: Simon & Schuster.
Cicero (1885). *The Orator.* Translated by J. E. Sandys. London, UK: Cambridge. (Original work published ca. 55 B.C.)
Cillizza, C. (2012, October, 3). Winners and losers from the first presidential debate. *The Washington Post.* https://www.washingtonpost.com/news/the-fix/wp/2012/10/03/winners-and-losers-from-the-first-presidential-debate/

Cillizza, C. (2016, January 5). President Obama cried in public today. That's a good thing. *The Washington Post*. https://www.washingtonpost.com/news/the-fix/wp/2016/01/05/why-men-should-cry-more-in-public/

Cillizza, C. (2016, May 16). Hillary Clinton has a likeability problem. Donald Trump has a likability epidemic. *Washington Post*. https://www.washingtonpost.com/news/the-fix/wp/2016/05/16/hillary-clintons-long-lingering-likable-enough-problem/

Cillizza, C. [@cillizzaCNN] (2019, October 19). *Andrew Yang "MATH" pin deserves more attention.* [Twitter Post]. https://twitter.com/CillizzaCNN/status/1184280099891351553.

Cillizza, C. (2020, January 15). The Warren-Sanders feud just got way uglier. *CNN*. https://www.cnn.com/2020/01/15/politics/bernie-sanders-elizabeth-warren-debate-2020/index.html on January 18, 2020.

Clayman, S. E. (1995). Defining moments, presidential debates, and the dynamics of quotability. *Journal of Communication, 45*, 118–146. doi:10.1111/j.1460-2466.1995.tb00746.x

Clinton, H. R. (2017). *What happened?* New York, NY: Simon & Schuster.

CNN Poll: Most watchers say Romney debate winner. (2012, October 3). *Politicalticker.* http://politicalticker.blogs.cnn.com/2012/10/03/cnn-poll-romney-wins-debate-by-big-margin/

Cohen, H. (1994). *History of speech communication: The emergence of a discipline, 1914–1945.* Washington, DC: National Communication Association.

Cohen, J., & Holbert, R. L. (2018). Assessing the predictive value of parasocial relationship intensity in a political context. *Communication Research, 48*, 1–26. doi:10.1177/0093650218759446

Colvin, J. (2020, February 2). Trump bashes Democratic rivals during pre-Super Bowl show. *Chicago Tribune*. https://www.chicagotribune.com/election-2020/ct-nw-trump-bloomberg-hannity-interview-20200202–hrtkx36kmbc6bovdnfsf3dis5e-story.html

Coman, J. (2004, September 26). Bush to turn on the charm in TV debates with "unlikeable" Kerry. *The Telegraph*. https://www.telegraph.co.uk/news/worldnews/northamerica/usa/1472693/Bush-to-turn-on-the-charm-in-TV-debates-with-unlikeable-Kerry.html

Conners, J. L. (2017). Presidential debate coverage and conflict bias in the 2016 campaign. In R. E. Denton (Ed.), *Political campaign* communication (pp. 125–139). New York, NY: Lexington Books.

Conscientious Objector to Fashion (1991, August 20). *The Telegraph.* https://news.google.com/newspapers?nid=2209&dat=19910820&id=PRJgAAAAIBAJ&sjid=MZQMAAAAIBAJ&pg=5739,3997624

Consenza, G. (2014). Grill's communication style: From sear words to body language. *Contemporary Italian Politics, 6*, 89–101. doi:10.1080/23248823.2014.886417

Consigny, S. (1974). Rhetoric and its situations. *Philosophy & Rhetoric, 7*(3), 175–186. Stable URL: https://www.jstor.org/stable/40237197

Corbett, E. P. J. (1971). *Classical rhetoric for the modern student* (2nd ed.). New York: Oxford University Press.

Cornfield, M. (2017) Empowering the party-crasher: Donald J. Trump, the first 2016 GOP presidential debate, and the Twitter marketplace for political campaigns. *Journal of Political Marketing, 16*, 212–243. doi:10.1080/15377857.2017.1345836

Cornwell, R. (2016, February 27). Ralph Nader: Ascetic, zealot-like, bordering on self-righteous. *The Independent.* https://www.independent.co.uk/news/people/profiles/ralph-nader-ascetic-zealot-like-bordering-on-self-righteous-a6893481.html

Costello, C. (2016, March 4). Transcript. *CNN.* http://www.cnn.com/TRANSCRIPTS/1603/04/cnr.01.html

Cuddy, A. J. C., Fiske, S. T., & Glick, P. (2008). Warmth and competence as universal dimensions of social perception: The Stereotype content model and the BIAS map. In M. P. Zanna (Ed.), *Advances in experimental social psychology* (pp. 61–149). San Diego, CA: Academic Press.

Cuddy, A. J. C., Wilmuth, C. A., Yap, A. J., & Carney, D. R. (2015). Preparatory power posing affects nonverbal presence and job interview performance. *Journal of Applied Psychology, 100*, 1286–1295. doi:10.1037/a0038543

Cummings, L., & Terrion, J. L. (2020). A "nasty woman": Assessing the gendered mediation of Hillary Clinton's nonverbal immediacy cues during the 2016 U.S. presidential campaign.

Feminist Media Studies. Advanced online publication. https://doi.org/10.1080/14680777.2019.1706604

Dailey, W. O., Hinck, E. A., & Hinck, S. S. (2005). Audience perceptions of politeness and advocacy skills in the 2000 and 2004 presidential debates. *Argumentation and Advocacy, 41*, 196–210. doi:10.1080/00028533.2005.11821630

Dailey, W. O., Hinck, E. A., & Hinck, S. S. (2008). *Politeness in presidential debates: Shaping political face in campaign debates from 1960 to 2004.* Lanham, MD: Rowman and Littlefield.

Dailey, W. O., Hinck, S. S., Hinck, R. S., & Hinck, E. A. (2017). Intensity of face threats in the 2008, 2012, and 2016 U.S. presidential debates. In R. E. Denton, Jr. (Ed.), *Political campaign communication* (pp. 77–102). Lanham, MA: Lexington Books.

Davis, L. (1978). Camera eye-contact by the candidates in the presidential debates of 1976. *Journalism Quarterly, 55*, 431–437. https://journals.sagepub.com/doi/pdf/10.1177/107769907805500302

Davis, S. (1999). The effects of audience reaction shots on attitudes toward controversial issues. *Journal of Broadcasting & Electronic Media, 43*, 476–491. doi.org/10.1080/08838159909364505

Debate Transcript (1988, October 13). October 13, 1988 Debate Transcript. *Commission on Presidential Debates.* https://www.debates.org/voter-education/debate-transcripts/october-13-1988-debate-transcript/

Decker, W. D. (1994). The 1988 Quayle-Bentsen vice presidential debate. In R. V. Friedenberg, *Rhetorical studies of national political debates, 1960–1992* (2nd ed) (pp. 167–186). Westport, CT: Praeger.

De Landtsheer, C., De Vries, P., & Vertessen, D. (2008). Political impression management: How metaphors, sound bites, appearance effectiveness, and personality traits can win elections. *Journal of Political Marketing, 7*, 217–218. doi:10.1080/15377850802005083

Deloitte & Touche, LLP. (2000, January 13). Women in elected office survey identifies obstacles for women as political leaders [On-line], 1–5. http://www.us.deloitte.com.

De Meo, A., Vitale, M., Pettorino, M., & Martin, P. (2011) Acoustic-perceptual credibility correlates of news reading by native and Chinese speakers of Italian. In W. S. Lee and E. Zee (Eds.), *Proceeding of the XVII CPhS* (pp. 1366–1369). Hong Kong: Department of Chinese, Translation and Linguistics, City University of Hong Kong.

Dennis, J., Chaffee, S., & Choe, S. (1979). Impact upon partisan: Image and issue voting. In S. Kraus (Ed.), *The great debates: Carter vs. Ford, 1976* (pp. 314–330). Bloomington, IN: Indiana University.

Denton, R. E. (2017). *The 2016 presidential campaign: Political communication and practice.* Cham, Switzerland: Palgrave Macmillan

DePaulo, B. M. (1992). Nonverbal behavior and self-presentation. *Psychological Bulletin, 111*, 203–243. doi:10.1037/0033-2909.111.2.203

DePaulo, B. M., Lanier, K., & Davis, T. (1983). Detecting the deceit of the motivated liar. *Journal of Personality and Social Psychology, 45*, 1096–1103. doi:10.1037/0022-3514.45.5.1096

DePaulo, B. M., Zuckerman, M., & Rosenthal, R. (1980). Humans as lie detectors. *Journal of Communication, 30*, 129–139. doi:10.1111/j.1460–2466.1980.tb01975.x

D'Errico, F., & Poggi, I. (2012). Blame the opponent! Effects of multimodal discrediting moves in public debates. *Cognitive Computation, 4*, 460–476. doi:10.1007/s12559-012-9175-y

D'Errico, F., Poggi, I., & Vincze, L. (2012). Discrediting signals. A model of social evaluation to study discrediting moves in political debates. *Journal of Multimodal User Interfaces, 6*, 163–178. doi:10.1007/s12193-012-0098-4

Devlin, L. P. (1994). The 1992 Gore-Quayle-Stockdale vice-presidential debate. In R. V. Friedenberg (Ed.), *Rhetorical studies of national political debates 1960–1992* (pp. 211–233). Westport, CT: Praeger.

Dewberry, D. R. (2019). Memes, political rhetoric, and discursive agency in the 2012 vice presidential debate. In E. A. Hinck (Ed.), *Presidential debates in a changing media environment* (vol. 2, pp. 203–220). Santa Barbara, CA: Praeger Publishers.

Diamond, J. (2016, January 24). Trump: I could 'shoot somebody and I wouldn't lose voters.' *CNN*. https://www.cnn.com/2016/01/23/politics/donald-trump-shoot-somebody-support/index.html

Dimberg, U., & Thunberg, M. (1998). Rapid facial reactions to emotion facial expressions. *Scandinavian Journal of Psychology, 39*, 39–46. doi:10.1111/1467–9450.00054

Dimberg, U., Thunberg, M., & Elmehed, K. (2000). Unconscious facial reactions to emotional facial expressions. *Psychological Science, 11*, 86–89. doi:10.1111/1467–9280.00221

Dion, K., Berscheid, E., & Walster, E. (1972). What is beautiful is good. *Journal of Personality and Social Psychology, 24*, 285–290. doi:10.1037/h0033731

Diaz, D. (2016, October 15). Trump: I "wasn't impressed" when Clinton walked in front of me at debate. *CNN*. https://www.cnn.com/2016/10/14/politics/donald-trump-hillary-clinton-appearance-debate/index.html

Docherty, G., & Foulkes, P. (2001). Variability in (r) production-instrumental perspectives. In H. Van de Velde & R. Van Hout (Eds.), *'r-atics: sociolinguistic, phonetic an diphonological characteristics of/r/* (pp. 173–184). Brussels, BE: ILVP.

Dolan, K. (2010). The impact of gender stereotypes evaluations on support for women candidates. *Political Behavior, 32*, 69–88. doi:10.1007/sl1109–009–9090–4

Dolcos, S., Sung, K., Argo, J. J., Flor-Henry, S., & Dolcos, F. (2012). The power of a handshake: Neural correlates of evaluative judgments in observed social interactions. *Journal of Cognitive Neuroscience, 24*, 2292–2305. doi:10.1162/jocn_a_00295

Dovidio, J. F., & Ellyson, S. L. (1985). Patterns of visual dominance behavior in humans. In S. L. Ellyson & J. F. Dovidio (Eds.), *Power, dominance, and nonverbal communication* (pp. 129–140). New York, NY: Springer-Verlad.

Dowd, M. (1992, October 16). The 1992 campaign: News analysis; a no-nonsense sort of talk show. *The New York Times*. http://www.nytimes.com/1992/10/16/us/the-1992–campaign-news-analysis-a-no-nonsense-sort-of-talk-show.html

Druckman, J. N. (2003). The power of television images: The first Kennedy-Nixon debate revisited. *The Journal of Politics, 65*, 559–571. doi:10.1111/1468–2508.t01–1–00015

Drum, K. (2015, August 4). If you don't get Donald Trump's appeal, you really need to catch up on your "celebrity apprentice" viewing. *Mother Jones*. http://www.motherjones.com/kevin-drum/2015/08/if-you-dont-get-donald-trumps-appeal-you-really-needcatch-your-celebrity-apprent

Dumitrescu, D. (2016). Nonverbal communication in politics: A review of research developments, 2005–2015. *American Behavioral Scientist, 60*, 1656–1675. doi:10.1177/0002764216678280

Dumitrescu, D., Gidengil, E., & Stolle, D. (2015). Candidate confidence and electoral appeal: An experimental study of the effect of nonverbal communication on voter evaluations. *Political Science Research and Methods, 3*, 43–52. doi:10.1017/psrm.2014.16

Dunyon, J., Gossling, V., Willden, S., & Seiter, J. S. (2010). Compliments and purchasing behavior in telephone sales interactions. *Psychological Reports, 106*, 27–30. doi:10.2466/PRO.106.1.27–30

Eagly, A. H., & Karau, S. J. (2002). Role incongruity theory of prejudice toward female leaders. *Psychological Review, 109*, 573–98. doi:10.1037//0033–295X.109.3.573

Eaves, M. H., & Leathers, D. (2018). *Successful nonverbal communication* (5th ed.). New York, NY: Routledge.

Eckstein, J. (2016). Sound arguments. *Argumentation and Advocacy, 53*, 163–180. doi:10.1080/00028533.2017.1337328

Edmonds, G. (1904). *Facts and falsehoods concerning the war on the south 1861–1865*. Memphis, TN: A. R Taylor & Company.

Edwards, J. L. (2012). Visual literacy and visual politics: Photojournalism and the 2004 presidential debates. *Communication Quarterly, 60*, 681–697. doi:10.1080/01463373.2012.725000

Ehninger, D. (1954). The logic of argument. In D. Potter (Ed.), *Argumentation and debate: Principles and practices* (pp. 101–123). New York, NY: Henry Holt.

Ekman, P. (1972). Universals and cultural differences in facial expressions of emotions. In Cole, J. (Ed.), *Nebraska Symposium on Motivation* (pp. 207–282). Lincoln, NE: University of Nebraska Press.

Ekman, P. (1985). *Telling lies*. New York: Norton.

Ekman, P., & Cordaro, D. (2011). What is meant by calling emotions basic. *Emotion Review, 3*, 364–370. doi:10.1177/1754073911410740

Ekman, P., & Friesen, W. V. (1982). Felt, false, and miserable smiles. *Journal of Nonverbal Behavior, 6*, 238–252. doi:10.1007/BF00987191

Endres, D., Senda-Cook, S., & Cozen, B. (2014). Not just a place to park your car: Park(ing) as spatial argument. *Argumentation and Advocacy, 50*, 121–140. doi:10.1080/00028533.2014.11821814

Erickson, K. V. (2000). Presidential rhetoric's visual turn: Performance fragments and the politics of illusionism. *Communication Monographs, 67*, 138–157. doi:10.1080/03637750009376501

Exline, R. V. (1985). Multichannel transmission of nonverbal behavior and the perception of powerful men: The presidential debates of 1976. In S. L. Ellyson & J. F. Dovidio (Eds.), *Power, dominance, and nonverbal behavior* (pp. 183–206). New York: Springer-Verlag.

Fang, X., van Kleef, G. A., & Sauter, D. A. (2018). Person perception from changing emotional expressions: Primacy, recency, or averaging effect? *Cognition & Emotion, 32*, 1597–1610. doi:10.1080/02699931.2018.1432476

Fallows, J. (2004, July/August). When George meets John. *The Atlantic*. https://www.theatlantic.com/magazine/archive/2004/07/when-george-meets-john/303443/

Fein, S., Goethals, G. R., & Kugler, M. B. (2007). Social influence on political judgments: The case of presidential debates. *Political Psychology, 28*, 165–192. https://www.jstor.org/stable/20447032

Felknor, B. L. (1992). *Political mischief: Smear, sabotage, and reform in U.S. elections*. New York: Praeger.

Festinger, L. (1954). A theory of social comparison processes. *Human Relations, 7*, 117–140. doi:10.1177/001872675400700202

Fish, S. (2008, February 3). All you need is hate. *New York Times*. https://opinionator.blogs.nytimes.com//2008/02/03/all-you-need-is-hate/

Fisher, B. A. (1978). *Perspectives on human communication*. New York, NY: Macmillan.

Fiske, S. T., Xu, J., Cuddy, A. J. C., & Glick, P. (1999). (Dis)respecting versus (dis)liking: Status and interdependence predict ambivalent stereotypes of competence and warmth. *Journal of Social Issues, 55*, 473–489. doi:10.1111/0022-4537.00128

Fitzgerald, J. (1966). *Peirce's Theory of Signs as a Foundation for Pragmatism*. The Hague, NL: Mouton.

Fix Team (2019, December 19). Transcript: The December Democratic debate. *Washington Post*. https://www.washingtonpost.com/politics/2019/12/20/transcript-december-democratic-debate/ on January 13, 2020.

Flock, E. (2012, Oct. 12). Body language experts disagree on Biden's aggressive debate performance, say Ryan was nervous. *US News and World Report*. http://www.usnews.com/news/blogs/washington-whispers/2012/10/12/body-language-experts-disagree-on-bidens-aggressive-debate-performance-say-ryan-was-nervous on October 25, 2015.

Forsyth, A. (2019). *Common law and natural law in America: From the Puritans to the Legal Realists*. Cambridge, UK. Cambridge University Press.

Foss, K. A., Foss, S. K., & Griffin, C. L. (2006). *Feminist rhetorical theories*. Long Grove, IL: Waveland.

Franken, A. (2016, October 22). Al Franken: My 10 favorite "Saturday Night Live" political sketches. *The Washington Post*. https://www.washingtonpost.com/lifestyle/al-franken-my-10-favorite-saturday-night-live-political-sketches/2016/10/17/56e9d5be-8739-11e6-92c2-14b64f3d453f_story.html?utm_term=.401a0f7688d5

Frazin, R. (2019, July 25). Biden: "I'm not going to be as polite" at next debate. *The Hill*. https://thehill.com/homenews/campaign/454659-biden-im-not-going-to-be-as-polite-at-next-debate on February 10, 2020

Fredal, J. (2018). Is the enthymeme a syllogism? *Philosophy & Rhetoric, 51,* 24–49. doi:10.5325/philrhet.51.1.0024

French, D. (2016, September 27). Donald Trump just kept getting worse. *National Review.* https://www.nationalreview.com/corner/donald-trump-just-kept-getting-worse/

French, J. P. R., Jr., & Raven, B. (1960). The bases of social power: In D. Cartwright & Z. Zander (Eds.), *Group dynamics* (pp. 607–623). New York: Harper and Row.

Friedman, H. S., Mertz, T. J., & DiMatteo, M. R. (1980). Perceived bias in facial expressions of television news broadcasters. *Journal of Communication, 30,* 103–111. doi:10.1111/j.1460-2466.1980.tb02022.x

Frizell, S., & Elliott, P. (2016, April 15). How the Brooklyn debate showed Democratic dysfunction. *Time.* http://time.com/4295555/democratic-debate-hillary-clinton-bernie-sanders-brooklyn/

Frye, J. K., & Bryski, B. G. (1978, March 16–18). *Accident and design: Implications of technical and functional factors of network television coverage of the Ford/Carter presidential debates.* Paper presented at the annual meeting of the Eastern Communication Association, Boston, MA.

Full tape with lewd Donald Trump remarks (*Access Hollywood*) (2016, October 21). *Youtube.* https://www.youtube.com/watch?v=NcZcTnykYbw

Funk, M. E., & Coker, C. R. (2016) She's hot, for a politician: The impact of objectifying commentary on perceived credibility of female candidates. *Communication Studies, 67,* 455–473, doi:10.1080/10510974.2016.1196380

Gabriel, S., Paravati, E., Green, M. C., & Flomsbee, J. (2018). From *Apprentice* to president: The role of parasocial connection in the election of Donald Trump. *Social Psychological and Personality Science, 9,* 299–307. doi:10.1177/1948550617722835

Galgano, T. (2019, August 8). CNN criticized for conflict-heavy framing of democratic debates. *CNN.* http://www.mediafiledc.com/cnn-criticized-for-conflict-heavy-framing-of-democratic-debates/

Garber, D. A. (1984). *Processing the news: How people tame the information tide.* New York, NY: Longman.

Gass, R. H., & Seiter, J. S. (2014). *Persuasion, social influence, and compliance gaining* (5th ed.). Boston, MA: Pearson.

Gay, V. (2004, January 21). Dean's theatrics draw mixed reviews. *Seattle Times.* http://old.seattletimes.com/html/nationworld/2001840708_deantv21.html

Gearan, A., & Balz, D. (2016, May 15). Even supporters agree: Clinton has weaknesses as a candidate. What can she do? *Washington Post.* https://www.washingtonpost.com/politics/even-supporters-agree-clinton-has-weaknesses-as-a-candidate-what-can-she-do/2016/05/15/132f4d7e-1874-11e6-924d-838753295f9a_story.html

Geer, J. G. (1988). The effects of presidential debates on the electorate's preferences for candidates. *American Politics Research, 16,* 486–501. doi:10.1177/004478088016004005

Geer, J. G. (2006). *In defense of negativity: Attack ads in presidential campaigns.* Chicago, IL: University of Chicago Press.

Gelang, M. (2013). Towards a political action. In I. Poggi, F. D'Errico, L. Vincze, & A. Vinciarelli (Eds.), *Multimodal Communication in Political Speech. Shaping Minds and Social Action: International Workshop, Political Speech 2010, Rome, Italy, November 10–12, 2010, Revised Selected Papers* (pp. 30–38). New York, NY: Springer.

Gelang, M., & Kjeldsen, J. (2011). Nonverbal communication as argumentation. In F. H. van Eemeren, B. Garssen, D. Godden, & G. Mitchell (Eds.), *Proceedings of the 7th Conference of the International Society for the Study of Argumentation* (pp. 567–576). Amsterdam: Rozenberg Publishers.

Gendron, M., Roberson, D., van der Vyver, J. M., & Barrett, L. F. (2014). Perceptions of emotion from facial expressions are not culturally universal: Evidence from a remote culture. *Emotion, 14,* 251–262. doi:10.1037/a0036052

Gentry, W. A., & Duke, M. P. (2009). A historical perspective on nonverbal communication in debates. *Journal of Leadership Studies, 2,* 36–47. doi:10.1002/jls.20079.

Giles, H., & Wiemann, J. M. (1987). Language, social comparison, and power. In C. R. Berger & S. H. Chaffee (Eds.), *The handbook of communication science* (pp. 350–384). Newbury Park, CA: Sage.

Gill, M. J. (2004). When information does not deter stereotyping: Prescriptive stereotyping can foster bias under conditions that deter descriptive stereotyping. *Journal of Experimental Social Psychology, 40*, 619–632. doi:10.1016/j.jesp.2003.12.001

Godfrey, D. K., Jones, E. E., & Lord, C. G. (1986). Self-promotion is not ingratiating. *Journal of Personality and Social Psychology, 50*, 106–115. doi:10.1037/0022-3514.50.1.106

Goethals, G. R. (2005). Nonverbal behavior and political leadership. In R. Riggio & R. Feldman (Eds.), *Applications of nonverbal communication* (pp. 95–115). Mahwah, NJ: Erlbaum.

Goffman, E. (1959). *The presentation of self in everyday life.* Garden City, NY: Anchor/Doubleday.

Goffman, E. (1974). *Frame analysis: An essay on the organization of experience.* New York: Harper & Row.

Goldberg, M. (2016, October 10). Hillary Clinton was a model of grace and poise throughout a disgusting ordeal. *Slate.* https://slate.com/human-interest/2016/10/hillary-clinton-shows-grace-and-poise-in-debate-with-donald-trump.html

Goldmacher, S., & Herndon, A. W. (2020, February 20). Will Warren's dominant debate performance boost her chances in Nevada and beyond? *New York Times.* https://www.nytimes.com/2020/02/20/us/politics/elizabeth-warren-debate.html

Goodwin, D. K. (2005). *Team of rivals.* New York, NY: Simon & Schuster.

Gong, Z. H. & Bucy, E. K. (2016). When style obscures substance: Visual attention to display appropriateness in the 2012 presidential debates. *Communication Monographs, 83*, 349–372, doi:10.1080/03637751.2015.1119868

Goring, P. (2017). The Elocutionary movement in Britain. In M. J. Macdonald (Ed.), *The Oxford handbook of rhetorical studies* (pp. 559–570). New York, NY: Oxford University Press.

Gourevitch, P. (2004, Oct. 18). Reality check. *The New Yorker.* https://www.newyorker.com/magazine/2004/10/18/reality-check-2

Grab a seat loser! (2016, October 10). *New York Daily News.* http://nydn.us/2dYNO3n

Grabe, M. E., & Bucy, E. P. (2009). *Image bite politics: News and the visual framing of elections.* New York: Oxford University Press.

Graber, D. A. (1987). Kind pictures and harsh words: How television presents candidates. In K. L. Scholzman (Ed.), *Elections in America* (pp. 115–141). Boston: Allen & Unwin.

Granhag, P. A., Giolla, E. M., Sooniste, T., Stromwell, L., & Liu-Jonsson, M. (2016). Discriminating between statements of true and false intent: The impact of repeated interviews and strategic questioning. *Journal of Applied Security Research, 11*, 1–17. doi:10.1080/19361610.2016.1104230

Grebelsky-Lichtman, T. (2016). The role of verbal and nonverbal behavior in televised political debates. *Journal of Political Marketing, 15*, 362–387. 10.1080/15377857.2014.959688

Grebelsky-Lichtman, T. & Shamir, J. (2011, May). *Success and failure in televised political debates: The role of verbal and nonverbal behavior.* Paper presented at the annual meeting of the International Communication Association, Boston, MA.

Grice, H. P. (1989). *Studies in the ways of words.* London, UK: Cambridge.

Griffin, R., & Teixeira, R. (2017, June). The story of Trump's appeal: A portrait of Trump voters. *Voter Study Group.* https://www.voterstudygroup.org/publication/story-of-trumps-appeal

Groarke, L. A. (2003). Why do argumentation theorists find it so difficult to recognize visual arguments? *OSSA Conference Archive.* Paper 50. http://scholar.uwindsor.ca/ossaarchive/OSSAS/papersandcommentaries/50/

Groarke, L. (2015). Going multimodal: What is a mode of arguing and why does it matter? *Argumentation, 29*, 133–155. doi:10.1007/s10503–014–9336–0

Groarke, L. (2017). Editorial cartoons and ART: Arguing with Pinocchio. In A. Tseronis & C. Forceville (Eds.), *Multimodal argumentation and rhetoric in media genres* (pp. 82–100). Amsterdam, NL: John Benjamins.

Gronbeck, B. E. (1995). Unstated propositions: Relations among verbal, visual, and acoustic languages. In S. Jackson (Ed.), *Argumentation and values: Proceedings of the ninth SCA/ AFA conference on argumentation* (pp. 539–542). Annandale, VA: SCA.

Grover, D. H. (1965). Elocution at Harvard: The saga of Jonathan Barber. *Quarterly Journal of Speech, 51*, 62–68. doi:10.1080/00335636509382703.

Guelzo, A. C. (2008). *Lincoln and Douglas: The debates that defined America*. New York: Simon and Schuster.

Gudykunst, W. B., & Ting-Toomey, S. (1988). Culture and affective communication. *American Behavioral Scientist, 31*, 384–400. doi:10.1177/000276488031003009

Guerrero, L. K. (2005). Observer ratings of nonverbal involvement and immediacy. In V. Manusov (Ed.), *The sourcebook of nonverbal measures: Going beyond words* (p. 221–235). Lawrence Erlbaum.

Guerrero, L. K., & Hecht, M., & Devito, J. A. (2008). Perspectives on defining and understanding nonverbal communication. In L. K. Guerrero & M. Hecht (Eds.), *The nonverbal communication reader* (3rd ed.) (pp. 3–20). Long Grove, IL: Waveland.

Gutgold, N. D. (2017). *Still paving the way for madam president*. Lanham, MD: Lexington Books.

Guyer, J. J., Brinol, P., Petty, R. E., & Horcajo, J. (2019). Nonverbal behavior of persuasive sources: A multiple process analysis. *Journal of Nonverbal Behavior, 23*, 203–231. Advance online publication. doi:10.1007/s10919–018–00291–x

Haberman, M., & Karni, A. (2019, December 12). Will Trump debate a Democrat in 2020? He's not so sure. *New York Times.* https://www.nytimes.com/2019/12/12/us/politics/trump-presidential-debate-democrat.html

Hall, C. C., Goren, A., Chaiken, S., & Todorov, A. (2009). Shallow cues with deep effects: Trait judgments from faces and voting decisions. In E. Gorgida, J. L. Sullivan, & C. M. Federico (Eds.), *The political psychology of democratic citizenship* (pp. 73–99). New York: Oxford University Press.

Hall, J. A., Coats, E. J., & Smith Lebeau, L. (2005). Nonverbal behavior and the vertical dimension of social relations: A meta-analysis. *Psychological Bulletin, 131*, 898–924. doi:10.1037/0033–2909.131.6.898

Hall, K., Goldstein, D. M., & Ingram, M. B. (2016). The hands of Donald Trump: Entertainment, gesture, spectacle. *Hau: Journal of Ethnographic Theory, 6*(2), 71–100. doi:10.14318/hau6.2.009

Hanrahan, T. (2015, Oct. 14). Jim Webb's complaints about debate speaking time, in 150 words. *Wall Street Journal.* http://blogs.wsj.com/washwire/2015/10/14/jim-webbs-complaints-about-debate-speaking-time-in-154–words/

Hart, W., Ottati, V. C., & Krumdick, N. D. (2011). Physical attractiveness and candidate evaluation: A model of correction. *Political Psychology, 32*, 181–203. doi:10.1111/j.1467–9221.2010.00812.x

Hassin, R., & Trope, Y. (2000). Facing faces: Studies on the cognitive aspects of physiognomy. *Journal of Personality and Social Psychology, 78*, 837–852. doi:10.1037/0022–3514.78.5.837

Haumer, F., & Donsbach, W. (2009). The rivalry of nonverbal cues on perception of politicians by television viewers. *Journal of Broadcasting & Electronic Media, 53*, 262–279. doi:10.1080/08838150902907918

Hayes, D. (2005). Candidate qualities through a partisan lens: A theory of trait ownership. *American Journal of Political Science, 49*, 908–923. doi:10.2307/3647705

Hayes, P. S. (2019, June 25). The Democratic debates are essentially competitive press conferences. Voters deserve more. *NBC.* https://www.nbcnews.com/think/opinion/democratic-debates-are-essentially-competitive-press-conferences-voters-deserve-more-ncna1021281

Heflick, N. A., & Goldenberg, J. L. (2009). Objectifying Sarah Palin: Evidence that objectification causes women to be perceived as less competent and less fully human. *Journal of Experimental Social Psychology, 45*, 598–601. doi:10.1016/j.jesp.2009.02.008

Heflick, N. A., Goldenberg, J. L., Cooper, D. P., & Puvia, E. (2011). From women to objects: Appearance focus, target gender, and perceptions of warmth, morality and competence. *Journal of Experimental Social Psychology, 47*, 572–581. doi:10.1016/j.jesp.2010.12.020

Heider, F. (1958). *The psychology of interpersonal relations*. New York: John Wiley.
Heilemann, J., & Halperin, M. (2012, November 1). The intervention. *New York Magazine*. http://nymag.com/news/features/heilemann-halperin-double-down-excerpt-2013-11/
Heilman, M. E., Stopeck, M. H. (1985). Being attractive, advantage or disadvantage? Performance based evaluations and recommended personnel actions as a function of appearance, sex and job type. *Organizational Behavior and Human Decision Processes, 35*, 202–212. doi:10.1016/0749-5978(85)90035-4
Heilman, M. E., Wallen, A. S., Fuchs, D., & Tamkins, M. M. (2004). Penalties for success: Reactions to women who succeed at male tasks. *Journal of Applied Psychology, 89*, 416–427. doi:10.1037/0021-9010.89.3.416
Heineman, B. W., Jr. (2011, March 27). The inside story of Ferraro's 1984 debate prep. *The Atlantic*. https://www.theatlantic.com/politics/archive/2011/03/the-inside-story-of-ferraros-1984-debate-prep/73070/
Helfrich, H., & Wallbott, H. G. (1986) Contributions of the German expression of psychology to nonverbal behavior research. *Journal of Nonverbal Behavior, 10*, 187–204. doi:10.1007/BF00987615
Hellweg, S. A. (1984, November). *The relationship of imposed format structures and emergent candidate verbal behaviors: A comparison of the 1984 primary and general election debates*. Paper presented at the annual conference of the Speech Communication Association, Chicago, IL.
Hellweg, S. A. (2004). Campaigns and candidate images in American presidential elections. In K. L. Hacker (Ed.), *Presidential candidate images* (pp. 21–47). Oxford, UK: Rowman & Littlefield.
Hellweg, S. A., & Phillips, S. L. (1981). Form and substance: A comparative analysis of five formats used in the 1980 presidential debates. *Speaker and Gavel, 18*, 67–76.
Hellweg, S. A., Pfau, M., & Brydon, S. R. (1992). *Televised presidential debates: Advocacy in contemporary America*. New York: Praeger.
Henry G. Bohn, editor. (1889). The works of the right honourable Joseph Addison: *The spectator*. Volume III. London, UK: Bell & Sons.
Heritage, J., & Greatbatch, D. (1986). Generating applause: A study of rhetoric and response at party political conferences. *American Journal of Sociology, 92*, 110–157. doi:10.1086/228465
Hess, U., Beaupré, M., & Cheung, N. (2002). To whom and why—cultural differences and similarities in the function of smiles. In A. Millicent (Ed.), *The smile: Forms, functions, and consequences* (pp. 187–216). New York, NY: The Edwin Mellen Press.
Hess U., Fischer A. (2013). Emotional mimicry as social regulation. *Personality and Social Psychology Review, 17*, 142–157. doi:10.1177/1088868312472607
Hietanen, J., K., Leppanen, J. M., Peltola, M. J., Linna-aho, K., & Ruuhiala, H. J. (2008). Seeing direct and averted gaze activates the approach-avoidance motivational brain systems. *Neuropsychologia, 46*, 2423–2430. doi:10.1016/j.neuropsychologia.2008.02.029
Higham, P. A., & Carment, D. W. (1992). The rise and fall of politicians: The judged heights of Broadbent, Mulroney and Turner before and after the 1988 Canadian federal election. *Canadian Journal of Behavioural Science / Revue canadienne des sciences du comportement, 24*, 404–409. doi:10.1037/h0078723
Hinks, D. A. G. (1940). Tisias and Corax and the invention of rhetoric. *The Classical Quarterly, 34*, 61–69. doi:10.1017/S000983880009125
Hoffman, K. S. (2011). Visual persuasion in George W. Bush's presidency: Cowboy imagery in public discourse. *Congress & the Presidency, 38*, 322–342. doi:10.1080/07343469.2011.602039
Holmes, S. A. (July 6, 2005). James Stockdale, Perot's running mate in '92, dies at 81. *The New York Times*. https://www.nytimes.com/2005/07/06/politics/james-stockdale-perots-running-mate-in-92-dies-at-81.html
Holzer, H. (2009, Feb. 13). Abraham Lincoln: From homely to heroic. *U.S. News & World Report*. https://www.usnews.com/news/history/articles/2009/02/13/abraham-lincoln-from-homely-to-heroic

Horiuchi, Y., Komatsu, T., & Nakaya, F. (2012). Should candidates smile to win elections? An application of automated face recognition technology. *Political Psychology, 33*, 925–933. doi:10.1111/j.1467-9221.2012.00917.x

Horton, D., & Wohl, R. R. (1956). Mass communication and para-social interaction. *Psychiatry, 19*, 215–229. doi:10.1080/00332747.1956.11023049.

Hovland, C.I., Janis, I.L., & Kelley, H.H. (1953). *Communication and persuasion*. New Haven, CT: Yale University Press.

Hudak, J. (2016, September 25). Seven important things to look for in the first presidential debate. *Brookings*. https://www.brookings.edu/blog/fixgov/2016/09/25/seven-important-things-to-look-for-in-the-first-presidential-debate/

Huey-Burns, C. (2015, June 18). At Trump's N.H. rally, true believers and big fans. *Real Clear Politics*. https://www.realclearpolitics.com/articles/2015/06/18/at_trumps_nh_rally_true_believers_and_big_fans_127030.html

Infante, D. A., Hartley, K. C., Martin, M. M., Higgins, M. A., Bruning, S. D., & Hur, G. (1992). Initiating and reciprocating verbal aggression: Effects on credibility and credited valid arguments. *Communication Studies, 43*, 182–190. doi.org/10.1080/10510979209368370

Jack, R. E., Blais, C., Scheepers, C., Schyns, P. G., & Caldara, R. (2009). Cultural confusions show that facial expressions are not universal, *Current Biology, 19*, 1543–1548. doi:10.1016/j.cub.2009.07.051

Jacob, C., & Guéguen, N. (2014). The effect of compliments on customers' compliance with a food server's suggestion. *International Journal of Hospitality Management, 40*, 5 9–61. doi:10.1016/j.ijhm.2014.03.010

Jacobs, S. (2002). Language and interpersonal communication. In M. L. Knapp & J. A. Daly (Eds.), *Handbook of interpersonal communication* (3rd ed.), (pp. 213–239). Thousand Oaks, CA: Sage.

Jacobs, T. (2009, March 4). Sex appeal may have hurt Sarah Palin. *Miller-McCune*. www.millermccune.com/news/sex-appeal-may-have-hurt-sarah-palin-1041

Jamieson, A. (2016, Oct. 10). Presidential debate: Trump accused of "stalking" Clinton on stage. *NBC News*. http://www.nbcnews.com/storyline/2016-presidential-debates/presidential-debate-trump-accused-stalking-clinton-stage-n663516 on January 26, 2017.

Jamieson, K. H. (1988). *Eloquence in an electronic age: The transformation of political speechmaking*. New York: Routledge.

Jamieson, K. H. (1992). *Dirty politics: deception, distraction, and democracy*. New York: Oxford University Press.

Jamieson, K. H. (1995). *Beyond the double bind: Women and leadership*. Oxford: Oxford University Press.

Jamieson, K. H., & Birdsell, D. S. (1988). *Presidential debates: The challenge of creating an informed electorate*. New York, NY: Oxford University Press.

Jaworski, A., & Galasinski, D. (2002). The verbal construction of non-verbal behaviour: British press reports of President Clinton's grand jury testimony video. *Discourse & Society, 13*, 629–649. doi.org/10.1177/0957926502013005452

Johns, R., & Shephard, M. (2011). Facing the voters: The potential impact of ballot paper photographs in British elections. *Political Studies, 59*, 636–658. doi:10.1111/j.1467-9248.2010.00874.x

Johnson, J. (2016, September 2). Trump starts subdued, then his cool quickly melts. *The Washington Post*. https://www.washingtonpost.com/politics/trump-yells-and-sniffs-his-way-through-the-first-2016-presidential-debate/2016/09/26/c990f05e-8403-11e6-a3ef-f35afb41797f_story.html

Johnson, R. H. (2000). *Manifest rationality: A pragmatic theory of argument*. Mahwah, NJ: Lawrence Erlbaum.

Johnson-Cartee, K. S., & Copeland. G. A. (1997*). Inside political campaigns: Theory and Practice*. London, UK: Praeger.

Johnstone, C. L. (2009). *Listening to the logos: Speech and the coming of wisdom in ancient Greece*. Columbia, SC: South Carolina University

Jones, B. (2019, February 5). Republicans and Democrats have grown further apart on what the nation's top priorities should be. *Pew Research Center*. https://www.pewresearch.org/fact-tank/2019/02/05/republicans-and-democrats-have-grown-further-apart-on-what-the-nations-top-priorities-should-be/

Jones, E. E., & Pittman, T. S. (1982). Toward a general theory of strategic self-presentation. In J. Suls (Ed.), *Psychological perspectives on the self* (pp. 231–261). Hillsdale, NJ: Lawrence Erlbaum.

Jones, J. M. (2008, October 17). Obama viewed as winner of the third debate: Completes "sweep" of three debates for Obama. *Gallup.* https://news.gallup.com/poll/111256/obama-viewed-winner-third-debate.aspx

Jones, J. M. (2012, October 8). Romney narrows vote gap after historic debate win. *Gallup.* https://news.gallup.com/poll/157907/romney-narrows-vote-gap-historic-debate-win.aspx

Jones, J. M. (2012, October 19). Obama judged winner of second debate. *Gallup.* https://news.gallup.com/poll/158237/obama-judged-winner-second-debate.aspx

Jorgensen, C., Kock, C., & Rorbech, L. (1998). Rhetoric that shifts votes: An exploratory study of persuasion in issue-oriented public debates. *Political Communication, 15*, 283–299. doi:10.1080/105846098198902.

Judge, T. A., & Cable, D. M. (2004). The effect of physical height on workplace success and income: Preliminary test of a theoretical model. *The Journal of Applied Psychology, 89*, 428–441. doi:10.1037/0021–9010.89.3.428

Judis, J. B. (2012, September 13). Nobody likes Mitt. *The New Republic.* https://newrepublic.com/article/107257/nobody-likes-mitt-the-election-popularity-contest-and-thats-ok

Juvonen J., Graham S., Schuster M. A. (2003). Bullying among young adolescents: The strong, the weak, and the troubled. *Pediatrics, 112*, 1231–7. doi:10.1542/peds.112.6.1231

Kahn, C. (2016, September 28). Majority of Americans say Clinton won first debate against Trump: Reuters/Ipsos poll. *Reuters.* https://www.reuters.com/article/us-usa-election-poll/majority-of-americans-say-clinton-won-first-debate-against-trump-reuters-ipsos-poll-idUSKCN11Y2VB

Kakkar, H., & Sivanathan, N. (2017). When the appeal of a dominant leader is greater than a prestige leader. *Proceedings of the National Academy of Sciences of the United States of America, 114*, 6734–6739. doi:/10.1073/pnas.1617711114.

Kalkhoff, W., & Gregory, S. W. (2008). Beyond the issues: Nonverbal vocal communication, power rituals, and "Rope-a-dopes" in the 2008 presidential debates. *Current Research in Social Psychology, 14*, 39–51.

Kanwisher, N., & Yovel, G. (2006). The fusiform face area: A cortical region specialized for the perception of faces. *Philosophical Transactions of the Royal Society, 361*, 2109–2128. doi:10.1098/rstb.2006.1934

Kaufman, S. L. (2016, October 10). Why was Trump lurking behind Clinton? How body language dominated the debate. *The Washington Post.* https://www.washingtonpost.com/news/arts-and-entertainment/wp/2016/10/10/why-was-trump-lurking-behind-clinton-how-body-language-dominated-the-debate/

Keating, C. F. (2006). Why and how the silent self speaks volumes: Functional approaches to nonverbal impression management. In V. Manusov & M. L. Patterson (Eds.), *The Sage handbook of nonverbal communication* (pp. 321–339). Thousand Oaks, CA: Sage.

Keating, C. F., Randall, D., & Kendrick, T. (1999). Presidential physiognomies: Altered images, altered perceptions. *Political Psychology, 20*, 593–610. doi:10.1111/0162–895X.00158

Keating, C. F., Randall, D. W., Kendrick, T. & Gutshall, K. A. (2003). Do babyfaced adults receive more help? The (cross-cultural) case of the lost resume. *Journal of Nonverbal Behavior, 27*, 89–109. doi:10.1023/ A:1023962425692.

Kellerman, K. (1992). Communication: Inherently strategic and primarily automatic. *Communication Monographs, 59*, 288–300. doi:10.1080/03637759209376270

Kemmelmeir, M., & Winter, D. G. (2008). Sowing patriotism, but reaping nationalism? Consequences of exposure to the American flag. *Political Psychology, 29*, 859–879. doi:10.1111/j.1467–9221.2008.00670.x

Kennedy, D. (2008, September 27). McCain's style undermines substance. *The Guardian.* https://www.theguardian.com/commentisfree/cifamerica/2008/sep/27/uselections2008.barackobama1

Kenney, K., & Simpson, C. (1993). Was coverage of the 1988 presidential race by Washington's two major dailies biased? *Journalism Quarterly, 70,* 345–355. doi.org/10.1177/107769909307000210.

Kenski, K. (2006). *The gender gap in political knowledge: Do women know less than men about politics?.* Unpublished Dissertation, University of Pennsylvania. https://repository.upenn.edu/dissertations/AAI3211093.

Kepplinger, H. M. (1982). Visual biases in television campaign coverage. *Communication Research, 9,* 432–446. doi.org/10.1177/009365082009003005

Kinder, D. R., Peters, M. D., Abelson, R. P. & Fiske, S. T. (1980). Presidential prototypes. *Political Behavior, 2,* 315–337. doi:10.1007/BF00990172

Kitsch, S. R., & Hinck, R. S. (2019). Hillary Rodham Clinton negotiates gender in the debates of 2016. In E. A. Hinck (Ed.), *Presidential debates in a changing media environment* (Vol. 1, pp. 249–270). Santa Barbara, CA: Praeger Publishers.

Kjeldsen, J. E. (2017). The rhetorical and argumentative potentials of press photography. In A. Tseronis & C. Forceville (Eds.), *Multimodal argumentation and rhetoric in media genres* (pp.52–80). Amsterdam, NL: John Benjamins.

Klein, J. (2012, October 3). Obama's debate strategy: Unilateral disarmament? *Time.* http://swampland.time.com/2012/10/03/the-debate/

Kleinke, C. L. (1986). Gaze and eye contact: A research review. *Psychological Bulletin, 100,* 78–100. doi:10.1037/0033-2909.100.1.78

Klinkner, P. (2014). *The causes and consequences of "birtherism."* Paper presented at the 2014 annual meeting of the Western Political Science Association.

Koenig, A. M., Eagly, A. H., Mitchell, A. A., & Ristikan, T. (2011). Are leader stereotypes masculine? A meta-analysis of three research paradigms. *Psychological Bulletin, 137,* 616–642. doi:10.1037/a0023557.

Klofstad, C. A. (2016). Candidate voice pitch influences election outcomes. *Political Psychology, 37,* 725–738. doi:10.1111/pops.12280.

Klofstad, C. A., Anderson, R. C., & Peters, S. (2012). Sounds like a winner: Voice pitch influences perception of leadership capacity in both men and women. *Proceedings of the Royal Society of London B, 297,* 2698–2704.

Knapp, M., & Hall, J. (2002). *Nonverbal communication in human interaction* (5th ed.). Boston, MA: Wadsworth.

Koppensteiner, M., & Grammer, K. (2010). Motion patterns in political speech and their influence on personality ratings. *Journal of Research in Personality, 44,* 374–379. doi:10.1016/j.jrp.2010.04.002

Koppensteiner, M., & Grammar, K. (2011). Body movements of male and female speakers and their influence on perceptions of personality. *Personality and Individual Differences, 51,* 743–747. doi:10.1016/j.paid.2011.06.014

Koppensteiner, M., Stephan, P., & Jäschke, J. P. M. (2015). More than words: Judgments of politicians and the role of different communication channels. *Journal of Research in Personality, 58,* 21–30. doi:10.1016/j.jrp.2015.05.006

Koppensteiner, M., Stephan, P., & Jäschke, J. P. M. (2016). Moving speeches: Dominance, trustworthiness and competence in body motion. *Personality and Individual Differences, 94,* 101–106. doi:10.1016/j.paid.2016.01.013.

Kozlowski, L. T., & Cutting, J. E. (1977). Recognizing the sex of a walker from a dynamic point-light display. *Perception & Psychophysics, 21,* 575–580. doi:10.3758/BF03198740

Kraft, R. N. (1987). The influence of camera angle on comprehension and retention of pictorial events. *Memory and Cognition, 15,* 291–307.

Kramer, R. S. S., Arend, I., & Ward, R. (2010). Perceived health from biological motion predicts voting behavior. *Quarterly Journal of Experimental Psychology, 63,* 625–632. doi:10.1080/17470210903490977

Kraus, S. (2000). *Televised presidential debates and public policy* (2nd Ed.). New York: Routledge.

Krauss, R. M., Apple, W., Morency, N., Wenzel, C., & Winton, W. (1981). Verbal, vocal and visible factors in judgments of another's affect. *Journal of Personality and Social Psychology, 40,* 312–319. doi.org/10.1037/0022-3514.40.2.312

Kreysa, H., Kessler, L, Schweinberger, S. R. (2016). Direct speaker gaze promotes trust in truth-ambiguous statements. *PLoS ONE* *11*(9): e0162291. doi:10.1371/journal.pone.0162291
Krieg, G. (2016, March 4). Donald Trump defends size of his penis. *CNN*. https://www.cnn.com/2016/03/03/politics/donald-trump-small-hands-marco-rubio/index.html
Kruse, M. (2016, July 21). Trump and the dark art of bad publicity. *Politico*. https://www.politico.com/magazine/story/2016/07/donald-trump-2016-convention-melania-trump-speech-dark-art-of-pr-214083
Kugler, M. B., & Goethals, G. R. (2008). The unbearable lightness of debating: Performance ambiguity and social influence. In J. B. Ciulla, D. R. Forsyth, M. A. Genovese, G. R. Goethals, L. C. Han, & C. L. Hoyt (Eds.), *Leadership at the crossroads: Leadership and Psychology* (Vol. 1, pp. 149–164). Westport, CT, Praeger.
Kunda, Z. (1990). The case for motivated reasoning. *Psychological Bulletin, 108*, 480–498. doi:10.1037/0033-2909.108.3.480
Kwampe, K. K. W., Frith, C. D., Dolan, R. J., & Frith, U. (2001). Reward value of attractiveness and gaze. *Nature, 413*, 589–602. doi:10.1038/35098149
Lampl, P. (1979). The sponsor: The League of Women Voters Education Fund. In S. Kraus (Ed.), *The great debates: Kennedy vs. Nixon, 1960* (pp. 83–104). Bloomington, IN: Indiana University Press.
Lanoue, D. J., & Schrott, P. R. (1981). *The joint press conference: The history, impact, and prospects of American presidential debates*. New York: Greenwood Press.
Lanoue, D. J., & Schrott, P. R. (1989). The effects of primary season debates on public opinion. *Political Behavior, 11*, 289–306. https://www.jstor.org/stable/586156
Lanzetta, J. T., Sullivan, D. G., Masters, R. D., & McHugo, G. J. (1985). Emotional and cognitive responses to televised images of political leaders. In S. Kraus & R. M. Perloff (Eds.), *Mass media and political thought: An information-processing approach* (pp. 85–116). Beverly Hills, CA: Sage.
Lau, R. R., & Sigelman, L. (2000). Effectiveness of negative political advertising. In J. A. Thurber, C. J. Nelson, & D. A. Dulio (Eds.), *Crowded airwaves: Campaign advertising in elections* (pp. 10–43). Washington, D.C.: Brookings Institution Press.
Leathers, D. G. (1997). *Successful nonverbal communication: principles and applications*. Boston, MA: Allyn & Bacon.
LeBlanc, P. (2018, October 18). Carly Fiorina says Trump's "Horseface" insult has brought politics to "a new low." *CNN*. https://www.cnn.com/2018/10/18/politics/carly-fiorina-donald-trump-horse-face-cnntv/index.html
Lee, M. T., & Ofshe, R. (1981). The impact of behavioral style and status characteristics on social influence: A test of two competing theories. *Social Psychology Quarterly, 44*, 73–82. doi:10.2307/3033703
Lee, Y. (2013). Babyfacedness, sex of face stimulus, and social context in face perception and person evaluation. *Psychological Reports, 112*, 800–817. doi:10.2466/01.17.PRO.112.3.800–817
Lederer, R. (2013, June 25). Lincoln as jokester. *Saturday Evening Post*. https://www.saturdayeveningpost.com/2013/06/lincoln-jokes/
Leffler, A., Gillespie, D. L., & Conaty, J. C. (1982). The effects of status differentiation on nonverbal behavior. *Social Psychology Quarterly, 45*, 153–161. doi:10.2307/3033648
Lehrer, J. (2011). *Tension city: Inside the presidential debates*. New York: Random House.
Lemon, J. (2019, June 27). Andrew Yang draws Twitter wrath and praise for ditching neck tie during democratic presidential debate. *Newsweek*. ttps://www.newsweek.com/twitter-wrath-praise-andrew-yang-ditching-neck-tie-debate-1446415
Lempert, M. (2011). Barack Obama, being sharp: Indexical order in the pragmatics of precision-grip gesture. *Gesture, 11*, 241–270. doi:10.1075/gest.11.3.01lem
Lenz, G. S., & Lawson, C. (2011). Looking the part: Television leads less informed citizens to vote based on candidates' appearance. *American Journal of Political Science, 55*, 574–589. doi:10.1111/j.1540–5907.2011.00511.x

Lev-on, A., & Waismel-Manor, I. (2016). Looks that matter: The effect of physical attractiveness in low- and high-information elections. *American Behavioral Scientist, 60*, 1756–1771. doi:10.1177/0002764216676249

Lie to me (n.d.). Lie to Me: Dr. Ekman inspired the award-winning television series. *Paul Ekman Group*. https://www.paulekman.com/projects/lie-to-me/

Linshi, J. (2015, July 8). It's official: More people are running for presidential nomination than ever before. *Time*. https://time.com/3948922/jim-gilmore-virginia-2016/

Lipman, V. (2019, April 19). The president's "Under audit" tax excuse is, and always has been, bogus. *Forbes*. https://www.forbes.com/sites/victorlipman/2019/04/10/the-presidents-under-audit-tax-excuse-is-and-always-has-been-bogus/#4ab85d231818

Lips, H. M. (1991). *Women, men, and power*. Mountain View, CA: Mayfield.

Lipton, J. (n.d.). *How to act human: Advice for Mitt Romney from Inside the Actors Studio*. https://www.youtube.com/watch?v=ctTePwJVdcU

List of rallies for the 2016 Donald Trump presidential campaign. (n.d.). In *Wikipedia*. https://en.wikipedia.org/wiki/List_of_rallies_for_the_2016_Donald_Trump_presidential_campaign

Little, A. C., Burriss, R. P., Jones, B. C., & Roberts, S. C. (2007). Facial appearance affects voting decisions. *Evolution and Human Behavior, 28*, 18–27. doi:10.1016/j.evolhumbehav.2006.09.002

Lizotte, M., & Meggers-Wright, H. J. (2018). Negative effects of calling attention to female political candidates' attractiveness. *Journal of Political Marketing, 18*, 240–266. doi:10.1080/15377857.2017.1411859

Lombard, M. (1995). Direct responses to people on the screen: Television and personal space. *Communication Research, 22*, 288–324. doi:10.1177/009365095022003002

Lopez, G. (2019, July 15). Donald Trump's long history of racism, from the 1970's to 2019. *Vox*. https://www.vox.com/2016/7/25/12270880/donald-trump-racist-racism-history

Lord, R. G., de Vader, C. L., & Alliger, G. M. (1986). A meta-analysis of the relation between personality traits and leadership perceptions: An application of validity generalization procedures. *Journal of Applied Psychology, 71*, 402–410. doi:10.1037/0021–9010.71.3.402

Los Angeles Times (2019, December 20). Undecided voters react to Democratic presidential debates. *YouTube*. https://www.youtube.com/watch?v=QJ27LB1gzxI

Lubell, S. (1977). Personalities vs. issues. In S. Kraus (Ed.), *The great debates: Kennedy vs. Nixon, 1960* (pp. 151–162). Bloomington, IN: Indiana University Press.

Luntz, F. [@FrankLuntz] (2016, September 26). Text from a GOP friend of mine in Congress. I'm sorry, Congressman, but tonight Hillary is coming across as presidential. #DebateNight. https://twitter.com/FrankLuntz/status/780594882104598528

Mackay, S. (2000, October 2). Nixon-Kennedy debates changed everything. *The Journal Times*. https://journaltimes.com/news/national/nixon-kennedy-debates-changed-everything/article_e5477796–acea-51f2–bdf4–7b810ae4e4bc.html

MacKinnon, C. A. (1979). *Sexual harassment of working women: A case of sex discrimination*. New Haven, CT: Yale.

Main, J. C., Jones, B. C., DeBruine, L. M., & Little, A. C. (2009). Integrating gaze direction and sexual dimorphism of face shape when perceiving the dominance of others. *Perception, 38*, 1275–1283. doi:10.1068/p6347

Mandell, L. M., & Shaw, D. L. (1973). Judging people in the news—unconsciously: Effect of camera angle and bodily activity. *Journal of Broadcasting, 17*, 353–362. doi.org/10.1080/08838157309363698

Manusov, V., & Harvey, J. (2011). Bumps and tears on the road to the presidency: Media framing of key nonverbal events in the 2008 democratic election. *Western Journal of Communication, 75*, 282–303. doi.org/10.1080/10570314.2011.571650

Manusov, V., & Jaworski, A. (2006). Casting nonverbal behavior in the media: Representations and responses. In V. Manusov & M. L. Patterson (Eds.), *The Sage handbook of nonverbal communication* (pp. 237–259). Thousand Oaks, CA: Sage.

Maricchiolo, F., Gnisci, A. Bonaiuto, M., & Ficca, G. (2009). Effects of different types of hand gestures in persuasive speech on receivers' evaluations. *Language and Cognitive Processes, 24*, 239–266. doi:10.1080/01690960802159929

Mark, D. (2006). *Going dirty: The art of negative campaigning*. Lanham, MD: Rowman & Littlefield.

Markus, G. B. (1982). Political attitudes during an election year: A report on the 1980 NES panel study. *American Political Science Review, 76*, 558–560. doi:10.2307/1963730

Martin, M. M., Anderson, C. M., & Horvath, C. L. (1996). Feelings about verbal aggression: Justifications for sending hurt from receiving verbally aggressive messages. *Communication Research Reports, 13*, 19–26. doi.org/10.1080/08824099609362066

Martin, M. M., Dunleavy, K. N., & Kennedy-Lightsey, C. D. (2010). The instrumental use of verbally aggressive messages. In T. A. Avtgis & A. S. Rancer (Eds.), *Arguments, aggression, and conflict* (pp. 400–415). New York: Routledge/Taylor & Francis.

Marsh, A. A., & Ambady, N. (2007). The influence of the fear facial expression on prosocial responding. *Cognition and Emotion, 21*, 225–247. doi:10.1080/02699930600652234.

Maslow, C., Yoselson, K., & London, H. (1971). Persuasiveness of confidence expressed via language and body language. In T. Veness & J. Ingrahm (Eds), *British Journal of Social and Clinical Psychology [Special issue]*, 10, 234–240. doi:10.1111/j.2044-8260.1971.tb00742.x

Masters, R. D., Sullivan, D. G., Lanzetta, J. T., McHugo, G. J., & Englis, B. G. (1986). The facial displays of leaders: Toward an ethology of human politics. *Journal of Social and Biological Structures, 9*, 319–343. doi:10.1016/S0140-1750(86)90190-9

Matsumoto, D., & Hwang, H. S. C. (2019). Culture, emotion, and expression. In K. D. Keith (Ed.), *Cross-cultural psychology: Contemporary themes and perspectives* (2nd ed., pp. 501–515). Hoboken, NJ: Wiley

Matsumoto, D., & Kudoh, T. (1993). American–Japanese cultural differences in attributions of personality based on smiles. *Journal of Nonverbal Behavior, 17*, 231–243. doi:10.1007/BF00987239

Maurer, M. (2016). Nonverbal influence during televised debates: Integrating CRM in experimental channel studies. *American Behavioral Scientist, 60*, 1799–1815. doi:10.1177/00002764216676250

Mazzara, E. (2019, October 15). The surprise star of the Democratic debate was on stage, but never said a word. *Huffington Post*. https://www.huffpost.com/entry/andrew-yang-debate-math-pin_n_5da67e0fe4b02253a2fa32b4

McAuliff, M., Saltonstall, D., & Katz, C. (2008, September 2008). John McCain, Barack Obama debate economy, bailout and Iraq. *Daily News*. https://www.nydailynews.com/news/politics/john-mccain-barack-obama-debate-economy-bailout-iraq-article-1.326180

McCain, T. A., Chilberg, J., & Wakshlag, J. (1977). The effect of camera angle on source credibility and attraction. *Journal of Broadcasting, 21*, 35–46. doi.org/10.1080/08838157709363815

McCann, S. J. H. (2001). Height, societal threat, and victory margin in presidential elections (1824–1992). *Psychological Reports, 88*, 741–742.

McCroskey, J. C., Hamilton, P. R., & Weiner, A. M. (1974). The effect of interaction behavior on source credibility, homophily, and interpersonal attraction. *Human Communication Research, 1*, 42–52. doi.org/10.1111/j.1468-2958.1974.tb00252.x

McCroskey, J. C., & Teven, J. J. (1999). Goodwill: A reexamination of the construct and its measurement. *Communication Monographs, 66*, 90–103. doi.org/10.1080/03637759909376464

McCroskey, J. C., & Young, T. J. (1981). Ethos and credibility: The construct and its measurement after three decades. *Central States Journal, 32*, 24–34. doi:10.1080/10510978109368075

McGeough, R. E., Palczewski, C. H., & Lake, R. A. (2015). Oppositional memory practices: U.S. memorial spaces as arguments over public memory. *Argumentation and Advocacy, 51*, 231–254. doi:10.1080/00028533.2015.11821852

McGrory, M. (1999, October 24). It's not the money, honey. *The Washington Post*. https://www.washingtonpost.com/archive/opinions/1999/10/24/its-not-the-money-honey/fl1ba7cc-7cfa-43b7-83d0-193daf5b2e6f/

McGuire, W. J. (1989). A mediational theory of susceptibility to social influence. In V. Gheorghiu, P. Netter, H. J. Eysenck, & R. Rosenthal (Eds.), *Suggestibility: Theory and research* (pp. 305–322). Heidelberg: Srpinger-Verlag.

McGuire, W. J. (2001). Input and output variables currently promising for constructing persuasive communications. In R. E. Rice & C. K. Atkin (Eds.), *Public communication campaigns* (3rd ed., pp. 22–48). Thousand Oaks, CA: Sage.

McHugo, G. J., Lanzetta, J. T., & Bush, L. K. (1991). The effect of attitudes on emotional reactions to expressive displays of political leaders. *Journal of Nonverbal Behavior, 15*, 19–41. doi:10.1007/BF00997765

McKeon, R. (1942). Rhetoric in the Middle Ages, *Speculum, 17*, 1–32. doi:10.2307/2856603

McKinney, M. S. (2018). Political campaign debates in the 2016 elections: Advancing campaign debate scholarship. *Argumentation and Advocacy, 54*, 27–75. doi:10.1080/00028533.2018.1446818.

McKinney, M. S. & Carlin, D. B. (2004). Political campaign debates. In L. L. Kaid (Ed.), *Handbook of political communication research* (pp. 203–234). New York, NY: Lawrence Erlbaum.

McKinney, M. S., & Warner, B. R. (2013). Do presidential debates matter? Examining a decade of campaign debate effects. *Argumentation and Advocacy, 49*, 238–258. doi:10.1080/00028533.2013.11821800.

Meadow, R. G. (1987). A speech by any other name. *Critical Studies in Mass Communication, 4*, 207–210. doi.org/10.1080/15295038709360127

Mehrabian, A. (n.d.). http://www.kaaj.com/psych/smorder.html

Mehrabian, A. (1967). Orientation behaviors and nonverbal attitude communication. *Journal of Communication, 17*, 324–332. doi:10.1111/j.1460–2466.1967.tb01190.x

Mehrabian, A. (1968). Inference of attitudes from the posture, orientation, and distance of a communicator. *Journal of Consulting and Clinical Psychology, 32*, 296–308. doi:10.1037/h0025906

Mehrabian, A., & Ferris, S. R. (1967). Inference of attitudes from nonverbal communication in two channels. *Journal of Consulting Psychology, 31*, 248–252. doi:10.1037/h0024648.

Mehrabian, A., Wiener, M. (1967). Decoding of inconsistent communications. *Journal of Personality and Social Psychology, 6*, 109–114. *doi:10.1037/h0024532*.

Mehta, S. (2012, August 11). Romney declares Paul Ryan the "intellectual leader" of the GOP. *Los Angeles Times*. https://www.latimes.com/politics/la-xpm-2012-aug-11-la-pn-romney-declares-paul-ryan-the-intellectual-leader-of-the-gop-20120811-story.html

Messaris, P. (1994). *Visual literacy: Image, mind, and reality*. Boulder, CO: Westview Press.

Messaris, P. (1997). *Visual persuasion: The role of images in advertising*. Thousand Oaks, CA: Sage.

Messaris, P., Eckman, B., & Gumpert, G. (1979). Editing structure in the televised versions of the 1976 presidential debates. *Journal of Broadcasting, 23*, 359–369. doi.org/10.1080/08838157909363945

Meyrowitz, J. (1986). Television and interpersonal behavior: Codes of perception and response. In G. Gumpert & R. Cathcart (Eds.), *Inter/Media: Interpersonal communication in a media world* (3rd ed., pp. 253–272). New York: Oxford University Press.

Michigan State University. (2017, September 11). "Power poses" don't work, eleven new studies suggest. *ScienceDaily*. http://www.sciencedaily.com/releases/2017/09/170911095932.htm

Milavsky, J. R., & Zhu, J. (1996). Equal time within televised presidential debates. In M. E. Stuckey (Ed.), *The theory and practice of political communication research* (pp. 93–121). Albany, NY: State University of New York Press.

Milbank, D. (2016, April 29). Trump's calculated misogyny. *Washington Post*. https://www.washingtonpost.com/opinions/trumps-calculated-misogyny/2016/04/29/c063a984–0e03–11e6–bfa1–4efa856caf2a_story.html

Miles, L. (2009). Who is approachable? *Journal of Experimental Social Psychology, 45*, 262–266. doi:10.1016/j.jesp.2008.08.010

Miller, A., Wattenberg, M., & Malanchuk, O. (1986). Schematic assessments of presidential candidates. *The American Political Science Review, 80*, 521–540. doi:10.2307/1958272

Minow, N. N., & Lamay, C. L. (2008). *Inside the presidential debates: Their improbable past and promising future*. Chicago, IL: University of Chicago Press.

Mitchell, A., & Jamieson, A. (2016, October 10). Trump planned debate "stunt," invited Bill Clinton accusers to rattle Hillary. *NBC News*. https://www.nbcnews.com/storyline/2016-presidential-debates/trump-planned-debate-stunt-invited-bill-clinton-accusers-rattle-hillary-n663481

Mitchell, R. L., & Ross, E. D. (2013). Attitudinal prosody: What we know and directions for future study. *Neuroscience & Biobehavioral Reviews, 37*, 471–479. doi:10.1016/j.neubiorev.2013.01.027

Montepare, J. M., & Zebrowitz-McArthur, L. (1988). Impressions of people created by age-related qualities in their gaits. *Journal of Personality and Social Psychology, 55*, 547–556. doi:10.1037//0022-3514.55.4.547

Mooney, A. (2011, April 7). Trump sends investigators to Hawaii to look into Obama. *CNN Politics*. http://politicalticker.blogs.cnn.com/2011/04/07/trump-sends-investigators-to-hawaii-to-look-into-obama/

More, D. W. (2000, October 12). Instant reaction: Bush beats Gore in second debate. *Gallup*. https://news.gallup.com/poll/2443/instant-reaction-bush-beats-gore-second-debate.aspx

Morello, J. T. (1988a). Argument and visual structuring in the 1984 Mondale-Reagan debates: The medium's influence on the perception of clash. *Western Journal of Communication, 52*, 277–290. doi.org.10.1080/10570318809389642

Morello, J. T. (1988b). Visual structuring of the 1976 and 1984 nationally televised presidential debates: Implications. *Central States Speech Journal, 39*, 233–243. doi.org/10.1080/01510978809363252

Morello, J. T. (1992). The "look" and language of clash: Visual structuring of argument in the 1988 Bush-Dukakis debates. *Southern Communication Journal, 57, 205–218.* doi.org/10.1080/10417949209372866

Morello, J. T. (2019). The "people's debate": Has the town hall format delivered on its grand promise? In E. A. Hinck (Ed.), *Presidential debates in a changing media environment* (Vol. 1, pp. 321–341). Santa Barbara, CA: Praeger Publishers.

Moriarty, S., & Garramone, G. (1986). A study of newsmagazine photographs of the 1984 presidential campaign. *Journalism Quarterly, 63*, 728–734. doi.org/10.117769908606300408

Moriarty, S. E., & Popovich, M. N. (1991). Newsmagazine visuals and the 1988 presidential election. *Journalism Quarterly, 63*, 728–734. doi.org/10.1177/107769909106800307

Moser, B. (2012, October 17). Romney's momentum takes a hit. *CNN*. https://www.cnn.com/2012/10/17/opinion/opinion-second-debate-roundup/index.html

Muller, B., Futrell, D., Stairs, D., Tice, D. M., Baumeister, R. F., Dawson, K. E., Mutz, D. C., & Holbrook, R. A. (2003, April 3–6). Televised political conflict: Nemesis or necessity. *Paper presented at the Annual Meeting of the Midwest Political Science Association*. Chicago, IL.

Murray, G. R., & Schmitz, J., D. (2001). Caveman politics: Evolutionary leadership preferences and physical stature. *Social Science Quarterly, 92*,1215–35. doi:10.1111/j.1540–6237.2011.00815.x

Mutz, D. C. (2007). Political psychology and choice. In R. J. Dalton & H. D. Klingelmann (Eds.), *The Oxford handbook of political behavior* (pp. 80–99). New York, NY: Oxford University Press.

Nabi, R. L., & Hendricks, A. (2003). The persuasive effect of host and audience reaction shots in television talk shows. *Journal of Communication, 53*, 527–543. doi.org/10.1111/j.1460-2466.2003.tb02606.x

NAFTA at 20 (2014, March 27). AFL-CIO. https://aflcio.org/reports/nafta-20

Nagel, F., Maurer, M., & Reinemann, C. (2012). Is there a visual dominance in political communication? How verbal, visual, and vocal communication shapes viewers' impressions of political candidates. *Journal of Communication, 62*, 833–850. doi:10.1111/j.1460-2466.2012.01670.x

Nagourney, A. (1996, June 10). With a smile, Dole tries to fight a stern reputation. *The New York Times*. https://www.nytimes.com/1996/06/10/us/with-a-smile-dole-tries-to-fight-a-stern-reputation.html

Neuman, W. L. (1998). Negotiated meanings and state transformation: The trust issue in the progressive era. *Social Problems, 45*, 315–335. doi:10.2307/3097189

Nevitt, J. (2016, May). Bizarre photos of Adolf Hitler that he didn't want world to see are finally uncovered 90 years later. *Mirror.* https://www.mirror.co.uk/news/weird-news/bizarre-photos-adolf-hitler-didnt-8009804

Newman, H. M. (1982). The sounds of silence in communicative encounters. *Communication Quarterly, 30*, 142–149. doi:10.1080/01463378209369441

Newport, F. (2016, August 26). Obama still wins on likability; Romney, on the economy. *Gallup.* https://news.gallup.com/poll/156857/obama-wins-likability-romney-economy.aspx?

Newton-Small, J. (2008, September 1). Palin's "good looking." *Time.* http://swampland.time.com/2008/09/01/palins_good_looking/

Niedenthal, P. M., Barsalou, L. W., Winkielman, P., Krauth-Gruber, S., & Ric, F. (2005). Embodiment in attitudes, social perception and emotion. *Personality and Social Psychology Review, 9*, 184–211. doi:10.1207/s15327957pspr0903_1

Nitz, M., Koehn, A., & McCarron, H. (2017). Too early to be funny? An analysis of late night comedy during the 2016 U.S. presidential primaries. In R. E. Denton (Ed.), *Political campaign communication: Theory, method, and practice* (pp. 103–122). Lanham, MD.

Nixon, R. (1962). *Six crises.* Garden City, NY: Doubleday.

Nixon, R. (1990). *RN: The memoirs of Richard Nixon* (First Touchstone edition). New York: Simon & Schuster.

Obama ahead with stronger support. (2012, October 19). *Gallup.com.* https://www.people-press.org/2012/09/19/obama-ahead-with-stronger-support-better-image-and-lead-on-most-issues/

Ohr, D., & Oscarsson, H. E. (2005). *Leader traits, leader image and vote choice.* Paper presented at the 2003 Meeting of the European Consortium for Political Research, September 18–21, Marburg, Germany.

O'Keefe, E. (2015, July 16). In San Francisco, Jeb Bush says he admires President Obama's charisma. *The Washington Post.* https://www.washingtonpost.com/news/post-politics/wp/2015/07/16/in-san-francisco-jeb-bush-says-he-admires-president-obamas-charisma/

Olivola, C. Y., & Todorov, A. (2010). Elected in 100 milliseconds: Appearance-based trait inferences and voting. *Journal of Nonverbal Behavior, 34*, 83–110. doi:10.1007/s10919-009-00882-1

Olson, K. M. (2015). Unqualified support: Joe Biden's disturbing performance of leadership, loyalty, and laughter in the 2012 vice presidential debate. In (pp. 219–224). C. H. Palczewski (Ed.), *Disturbing argument.* New York: Routledge.

Oreskes, M. (1988, August 19). The Republicans in New Orleans: Convention message Is garbled by Quayle static. *New York Times.* https://www.nytimes.com/1988/08/19/us/the-republicans-in-new-orleans-convention-message-is-garbled-by-quayle-static.html

Ortega, M. (2019). Interruptions as rhetorical leverage in presidential debate: Twitter as an aid to understanding the rhetorical power of transgressive behaviors in presidential campaigns. In E. A. Hinck (Ed.), *Presidential debates in a changing media environment* (Vol. 2, pp. 40–58). Santa Barbara, CA: Praeger Publishers.

Osgood, C. E., & Tannenbaum, P. H. (1955). The principle of congruity in the prediction of attitude change. *Psychological Review, 62*, 42–55.

Ottati, V., Terkildsen, N., & Hubbard, C. (1997). Happy faces elicit heuristic processing in a Televised impression formation task: a cognitive tuning account. *Personality and Social Psychological Bulletin, 23*, 1144–1156. doi:10.1177/01461672972311003

Palmer, M., & Simmons, K. (1995). Communicating intentions through nonverbal behaviors. *Human Communication Research, 22*, 128–160. doi:10.1111/j.1468-2958.1995.tb00364.x

Pancer, L. M., Brown, S. D., & Barr, C. W. (1999). Forming impression of political leaders: A cross national comparison. *Political Psychology 20*, 345–368. doi:10.1111/0162-895X.00148

Parker, A. (2016, September 6). Donald Trump says Hillary Clinton doesn't have "a presidential look." *The New York Times.* https://www.nytimes.com/2016/09/07/us/politics/donald-trump-says-hillary-clinton-doesnt-have-a-presidential-look.html

Patterson, M. L., Churchill, M. E., Burger, G. K., & Powell, J. L. (1992). Verbal and nonverbal modality effects on impressions of political candidates: Analysis from the 1984 presidential debates. *Communication Monographs, 59*, 231–242. doi.org/10.1080/03637759209376267
Pearce W. B., & Brommel, B. J. (1972). Vocalic communication in persuasion. *Quarterly Journal of Speech, 58*, 298–306, doi:10.1080/00335637209383126
Peck, A. (2019). Beautiful human sweater memes: Internet memes as vernacular responses to presidential debates. In E. A. Hinck (Ed.), *Presidential debates in a changing media environment* (Vol. 2, pp. 179–202). Santa Barbara, CA: Praeger Publishers.
Peek, L. (2016, October 20). Calm, informed, reasonable: Trump scores at final debate. *Fox News.* https://www.foxnews.com/opinion/calm-informed-reasonable-trump-scores-at-final-debate
Perks, L. G. & Johnson, K. A. (2014). Electile dysfunction. *Feminist Media Studies, 14*, 775–790. doi:10.1080/14680777.2013.829860
Perloff, R. M. (2013). Political persuasion. In J. P. Dillard & L. Shen (Eds.), *The SAGE handbook of persuasion: Developments in theory and practice* (2nd ed., pp. 258–277). Thousand Oaks, CA: SAGE.
Perloff, R. M. (2016). The blue-collar billionaire: Explaining the Trump phenomenon. In D. Lilleker, D. Jackson, E. Thorsen, & A. Veneti (Eds.). *US election analysis 2016: media, voters, and the campaign* (p. 45). Poole, England: The Centre for the Study of Journalism, Culture and Community.
Perez, E., & Brown, P. (October 29, 2016). Comey notified Congress of email probe despite DOJ concerns. *CNN.* https://www.cnn.com/2016/10/30/politics/clinton-emails-fbi-abedin/index.html
Peters, J. W. (2012, Oct. 9). Networks like split-screens in debates, even if the candidates don't. *The New York Times.* www.nytimes.com/2012/10/10/us/politics/networks-like-split-screens-in-debates-even-if-candidates-don't.html?_r=0
Petty, R. E., & Cacioppo, J. T. (1986). *Communication and persuasion: Central and peripheral routes to attitude change.* New York: Springer-Verlag.
Petty, R. E., & Wegener, D. T. (1998). Attitude change: Multiple roles for persuasion variables, In D.T. Gilbert, S.T. Fiske, G. Lindzey (Eds.), *The handbook of social psychology* (pp. 323–390). New York, NY: McGraw-Hill.
Pfau, M. (1987). The influence of intraparty debates on candidate preference. *Communication Research, 14,* 687–697. doi:10.1177/009365087014006004
Pfau, M. (1988). Intra-party political debates and issue learning. *Journal of Applied Communication Research, 16*, 99–112. doi:10.1080/00909888809365276
Pfau, M. (2002). The subtle nature of presidential debate influence. *Argumentation and Advocacy, 38*, 251–262. doi.org/10.1080/00028533.2002.11821571
Pfau, M., & Kang, J. G. (1991). The impact of relational messages on candidate influence in televised political debates. *Communication Studies, 42*, 114–128. doi.org/10.1080/10510979109368327
Pfau, M., Diedrich, T., Larson, K. M., & Van Winkle, K. M. (1993). Relational and competence perceptions of presidential candidates during primary election campaigns. *Journal of Broadcasting & Electronic Media,* 37, 275–292. doi:10.1080/08838159309364222
Philpott, J. S. (1983). *The relative contribution to meaning of verbal and nonverbal channels of communication: A meta-analysis.* Master's thesis: University of Nebraska.
Platt, R. (2012, October 17). Critics: Crowley violated 'sacred' role of impartial moderator. *KSL News.* http://www.ksl.com/?sid=22593365 on Oct. 25, 2015.
Plato (1987). Gorgias (D. J. Zeyl, Trans.). Indianapolis, Hackett. (Original work published ca. 380 B.C.E.).
Poggi, I. (2001). The lexicon and the alphabet of gesture, gaze, and touch. In A. de Antonio, R. Aylett, & D. Ballin (Eds.) *Intelligent virtual agents. IVA 2001. Lecture notes in computer science* (Vol. 2190). Berlin, DE: Springer.
Poggi, I., and D'Errico, F. (2010). The mental ingredients of bitterness. *J. Multimodal User Interfaces, 3*, 79–86. doi: 10.1007/s12193–009–0021–9
Poggi, I., D'Errico, F., & Vincze, L. (2011). Discrediting moves in political debate. In: F. Ricci et al. (Eds). *Proceedings of second international workshop on user models for motivational*

systems: the affective and the rational routes to persuasion (UMMS 2011) Girona. LNCS. (pp. 84–99). Berlin, DE: Springer.
Poggi, I., & Vincze, L. (2009). Gesture, gaze and persuasive strategies in political discourse. In M. Kipp, J. C. Martin, P. Paggio, & D. Heylen, (Eds.) *Multimodal Corpora. LNCS* (Vol. 5509) (pp. 73–92). Berlin, DE: Springer.
Poll: Bush, Kerry Even in 2nd Debate. (2004, October 9). *CNN.* https://www.cnn.com/2004/ALLPOLITICS/10/09/snap.poll/
Poll: Kerry Tops Bush in Debate. (2004, October 1). *CNN.* https://www.cnn.com/2004/ALL-POLITICS/10/01/debate.poll/index.html
Pollick, F. E., Paterson, H. M., Bruderlin, A., & Sanford, A. J. (2001). Perceiving affect from arm movement. *Cognition, 82,* B51–B61. doi:10.1016/s0010-0277(01)00147-0
Poniewozik, J. (2015, September 17). Review: In Republican debate, CNN Throws candidates into ring. *The New York Times.* https://www.nytimes.com/2015/09/17/arts/television/review-in-republican-debate-cnn-throws-candidates-into-ring.html
Poniewozik, J., & Rutenberg, J. (2016, October 5). Vice-presidential debate: How do you fact-check a headshake? *The New York Times.* https://www.nytimes.com/2016/10/06/arts/television/vice-presidential-debate-how-do-you-fact-check-a-headshake.html
Pornpitakpan, C. (2004). The persuasiveness of source credibility: A critical review of five decades' evidence. *Journal of Applied Social Psychology, 34,* 243–281 doi:10.1111/j.1559-1816.2004.tb02547.x
Poutvaara, P., Jordahl, H., & Berggren, N. (2009). Faces of politicians: Babyfacedness predicts inferred competence but not electoral success. *Journal of Experimental Social Psychology, 45,* 1132–1135. doi:10.1016/j.jesp.2009.06.007
Prysby, C. (2008). Perceptions of candidate character traits and the presidential vote in 2004. *PS: Political Science & Politics, 41,* 115–122. doi:10.1017/S1049096508080189
Quintilian (1968). Institutio oratoria (H. E. Butler, Trans). Cambridge, MA: Harvard University Press. (Original work published ca. 95 C.E.)
Racine Group. (2002). White paper on televised political campaign debates. *Argumentation and Advocacy, 38,* 199–218. doi:10.1080/00028533.2002.11821568
Rancer, A. S., Lin, Y., Durbin, J. M., & Faulkner, E. C. (2010). Nonverbal "verbal" aggression: Its forms and its relation to trait verbal aggressiveness. In T. A. Avtgis & A. S. Rancer (Eds.), *Arguments, aggression, and conflict* (pp. 265–284). New York: Routledge/Taylor & Francis.
Real Clear Politics (n.d.). General Election: McCain vs. Obama. *Real Clear Politics.* https://www.realclearpolitics.com/epolls/2008/president/us/general_election_mccain_vs_obama-225.html
Redlawsk, D. P. (2002). Hot cognition or cool consideration? Testing the effects of motivated reasoning on political decision making. *The Journal of Politics, 64,* 1021–1044. doi:10.1111/1468-2508.00161
Reilly, K. (2016, September 26). Donald Trump is proud of raising questions about Obama's birthplace: "I did a good job." *Fortune.* https://fortune.com/2016/09/26/presidential-debate-donald-trump-birther-obama/
Remembering Ed Muskie (1996, March 26). *PBS NewsHour.* http://www.pbs.org/newshour/bb/remember-jan-june96–muskie_03–26/
Remland, M. (1982). The implicit ad hominem fallacy: Nonverbal displays of status in argumentative discourse. *Journal of the American Forensic Association, 19,* 79–86. doi.org/10.1080/00028533.1982.11951229
Reeves, B., Lombard, M., & Melwani, G. (1992, May). *Faces on the screen: Pictures or natural experience?* Paper presented to the Mass Communication division of the International Communication Association, Miami.
Reid, T. R. (1988, October 2). For Dukakis, a challenge to be likeable. *The Washington Post.* https://www.washingtonpost.com/archive/politics/1988/10/02/for-dukakis-a-challenge-to-be-likable/f521be5d-9427–4dc0–bd8d-76215a104285/
Richards, A. S., & Hample, D. (2016). Facial similarity mitigates the persuasive effects for source bias: An evolutionary explanation for kinship and susceptibility to influence. *Communication Monographs, 83,* 1–24. doi:10.1080/03637751.2015.1014822

Richmond, V. P., McCroskey, J. C., & Payne, S. (1987). *Nonverbal Behavior in Interpersonal Relations*. Englewood Cliffs, N.J.: Prentice-Hall.
Rick Perry downplays debate meltdown. (November 10, 2011). *BBC News*. https://www.bbc.com/news/world-us-canada-15677595
Riggio, H. R., & Riggio., R. E. (2010). Appearance-based trait inferences and voting: Evolutionary roots and implications for leadership. *Journal of Nonverbal Behavior, 34*, 119–125. doi:10.1007/s10919-009-0083-0.
Riggio, R. Riggio, H. R., Salinas, C., & Cole, E. J. (2003). The role of social and emotional communication skills in leader emergence and effectiveness. *Group Dynamics: Theory, Research, and Practice, 7*(2), 83–103. doi:10.1037/1089-2699.7.2.83
Riggio, R. E., Tucker, J., & Throckmorton, B. (1987). Social skills and deception ability. *Personality and Social Psychology Bulletin, 13*, 568–577. doi:10.1177/0146167287134013
Riordan, C. A., Radloff, C. E., Goethals, G. R., Kennedy, J. G., Rosenfeld, P. (1986). Newscasters' facial expressions and voting behavior of viewers: Can a smile elect a president? *Journal of Personality and Social Psychology, 51*, 291–295. doi.org/10.1037/0022-3514.51.2.291
Riotta, C. (2020, January 22). Pete Buttigieg suffers awkward "please clap" moment while pitching himself as the next Obama to voters. *Independent*. https://www.independent.co.uk/news/world/americas/us-election/pete-buttigieg-please-clap-video-iowa-come-on-jeb-bush-obama-a9297506.html on February 8, 2020.
Rocha, V., Merica, D., Krieg, G., Bradner, E., Wills, A., & Blaine, K. (2019, June 28). The first Democratic debate, night 2. *CNN*. https://www.cnn.com/politics/live-news/democratic-debate-june-27-2019/h_e6ee3ea000f2c2f29b8612437b32ecab
Rogan, T. (2020, February 7). How Joe Biden will win with "stand up for Vindman" moment. *Washington Examiner*. https://www.washingtonexaminer.com/opinion/how-joe-biden-will-win-with-stand-up-for-vindman-moment on February 8, 2020.
Ritter, K., & Henry, D. (1994). The 1980 Reagan-Carter presidential debate. In R. V. Friedenberg (Ed.), *Rhetorical studies of national political debates 1960–1992* (pp. 68–93). Westport, CT: Praeger.
Rognoni, L. (2012) The impact of prosody in foreign accent detection: A perception study of Italian accent in English. In M. Grazia Busà and A. Stella (Eds.) *Methodological perspectives on second language prosody: Papers from ML2P* (pp. 89–93). Padua, IT: CLEUP.
Romaniuk, T. (2016). On the relevance of gender in the analysis of discourse: A case study from Hillary Rodham Clinton's presidential bid in 2007–2009. *Discourse & Society, 27*, 533–553. doi:10.1177/0957926516651221
Rosenberg, S. W., Bohan, L., McCafferty, P., & Harris, K. (1986). The image and the vote: The effect of candidate presentation on voter preference. *American Journal of Political Science, 30*, 108–127. doi:10.2307/2111296
Rosenberg, S. W., & McCafferty, P. (1987). The image and the vote: Manipulating voters' preferences. *Public Opinion Quarterly, 51*, 31–47. http://www.jstor.org/stable/2749056
Ross, R. (2010). Barack Obama's body language. *The American Spectator*. http://spectator.org/39422_barack-obamas-body-language/
Rowland, R. C. (2019). The 2016 presidential debates as public argument. In E. A. Hinck (Ed.), *Presidential debates in a changing media environment* (Vol. 1, pp. 228–248). Santa Barbara, CA: Praeger Publishers.
Rowland, R. C., & Garcia, R. (1985). The 1984 Democratic debates: Does format make a difference? *Proceedings of the National Communication Association/American Forensic Association conference on argumentation* (pp. 219–225). Washington, DC: NCA.
Rowland, R. C. & Voss, G. R. W. (1987). A structural functional analysis of the assumptions behind presidential debates. In J. W. Wenzel (Ed.), *Argument and critical practices: Proceedings of the Fifth SCA/AFA Conference on Argumentation* (pp. 239–248). Annandale VA: Speech Communication Association.
Russel, C. (2019, December 16). Trump says he may not debate Dem nominee under "biased" commission. *Liberty Headlines*. https://www.libertyheadlines.com/trump-debate-commission-biased/

Rutenberg, J. (2007, October 25). McCain reflects on P.O.W. past, and goes after Clinton. *The New York Times*. https://www.nytimes.com/2007/10/25/us/politics/25adbox.html

Saad, L. (2016, October 13). Viewers say Clinton wins second debate. *Gallup.* https://news.gallup.com/poll/196304/viewers-say-clinton-wins-second-debate.aspx

Saad, L. (2016, October 24). Clinton wins third debate, gains ground as "presidential." *Gallup.* https://news.gallup.com/poll/196643/clinton-wins-third-debate-gains-ground-presidential.aspx

Saad, L. (2016, November 8). Trump and Clinton finish with historically poor images. *Gallup.* https://news.gallup.com/poll/197231/trump-clinton-finish-historically-poor-images.aspx

Salant, R. S. (1979). The good but not great nondebates: Some random personal notes. In S. Kraus (Ed.), *The great debates: Kennedy vs. Nixon, 1960* (pp. 175–186). Bloomington, IN: Indiana University Press.

Salter, F. K., Grammer, K., & Rikowski, A. (2005). Sex differences in negotiating with powerful males: An ethological analysis of approaches to nightclub doormen. *Human nature: An Interdisciplinary Biosocial Perspective, 16*, 306–321. doi:10.1007/s12110–005–1013–4

Sandler, R. (2020, February 2). When they go low: Trump calls Bloomberg "little": Bloomberg calls him a fat liar with a "spray-on tan." *Forbes*. https://www.forbes.com/sites/rachelsandler/2020/02/02/when-they-go-low-trump-calls-bloomberg-little-bloomberg-calls-him-a-fat-liar-with-a-spray-on-tan/#addda125d176 on February 6, 2020.

Sanghvi, M., & Hodges, N. (2015). Marketing the female politician: An exploration of gender and appearance. *Journal of Marketing Management, 31*, 1676–1694. doi:10.1080/0267257X.2015.1074093.

Santucci, J. (2020, February 8). Nancy Pelosi: Trump impeachment witness Vindman's "shameful" firing a "brazen act of retaliation." *USA Today*. https://www.usatoday.com/story/news/politics/2020/02/08/trump-firing-impeachment-witness-alexander-vindman-brazen-act-retaliation-pelosi/4700103002/

Sauter, K. (1994). The 1976 Mondale-Dole vice-presidential debate. In R. V. Friedenberg (Ed.), *Rhetorical studies of national political debates 1960–1992* (pp. 45–68). Westport, CT: Praeger.

Scharp, K., Seiter, J. S., & Maughan, M. (in press). "My mom always tells that story to friends and relatives": Exploring the phenomenon of other-presentation. *Journal of Family Communication.*

Scheufele, D. A., Eunkyung, K., & Brossard, D. (2007). My friend's enemy: How split-screen debate coverage influences evaluation of presidential debates. *Communication Research, 34*, 3–24. doi:10.1177/0093650206296079

Schieffer, B. (2006, December 31). Ford's clumsiness. *CBS News*. www.cbsnews.com/news/fords-clumsiness/

Schiffrin, D. (1981). Handwork as ceremony: The case of the handshake. In A. Kendon (Ed.) *Nonverbal communication, interaction and gesture* (pp. 237—250). The Hague, NL: Mouton.

Schlenker, B. R. (1980). *Impression management*. Monterey, CA: Brooks/Cole.

Schlenker, B. R., & Leary, M. R. (1982). Audiences' reactions to self-enhancing, self-denigrating, and accurate self-presentations. *Journal of Experimental Social Psychology, 18*, 89–104. doi:10.1016/0022–1031(82)90083–X

Schmidt, M. S. (2014, November 22). G.O.P.-led Benghazi panel bolsters administration. *New York Times*. https://www.nytimes.com/2014/11/23/world/middleeast/republican-led-benghazi-inquiry-largely-backs-administration.html

Scholten, K., & McNabb, N. D. (2019). Don't misunderestimate the power debates: How the 2004 presidential debates reinforced George W. Bush as the moral choice. In E. A. Hinck (Ed.), *Presidential debates in a changing media environment* (Vol. 1, pp. 97–118). Santa Barbara, CA: Praeger Publishers

Schreckinger, B. (October 28, 2016). Trump hails new Clinton FBI review as "bigger than Watergate." *Politico*. https://www.politico.com/story/2016/10/fbi-clinton-new-probe-trump-hails-230460

Schroeder, A. (1996). Watching between the lines: Presidential debates as television. *The International Journal of Press/Politics, 1*, 57–75. doi:10.1177/1081180X96001004006

Schroeder, A. (2000). *Presidential debates: Forty years of high-risk TV*. New York: Columbia University Press.
Schroeder, A. (2016). *Presidential debates: Risky business on the campaign trail* (3rd ed). New York: Columbia University Press.
Schrott, P. R., & Lanoue, D. J. (1992). How to win a televised debate: Candidate strategies and voter response in Germany, 1972–87. *British Journal of Political Science, 22*(4), 445–467. doi.org/10.1017/S0007123400006487
Schwartz, L. (2015, May 14). The 8 dumbest presidential campaign blunders in modern political history. *Alternet*. http://www.alternet.org/election-2016/8-dumbest-presidential-campaign-blunders-modern-political-history
Segrin, C. (1993). The effects of nonverbal behavior on outcomes of compliance-gaining attempts. *Communication Studies, 44*, 169–187. doi:10.1080/10510979309368393
Seiter, J. S. (1999). Does communicating nonverbal disagreement during an opponent's speech affect the credibility of the debater in the background? *Psychological Reports, 84*, 855–861. doi.org/10.2466/pr0.1999.84.3.855
Seiter, J. S. (2001). Silent derogation and perceptions of deceptiveness: Does communicating nonverbal disbelief during an opponent's speech affect perceptions of debaters' veracity? *Communication Research Reports, 7*, 203–209. doi.org/10.1080/08824090109384814
Seiter, J. S. (2007). Ingratiation and gratuity: The effect of complimenting customers on tipping behavior in restaurants. *The Journal of Applied Social Psychology, 37*, 478–485. doi:10.1111/j.1559-1816.2007.00169.x
Seiter, J. S. (2017). Social Influence. In F. M. Moghaddam (Ed.), *The Sage encyclopedia of political behavior* (pp. 770–773). Thousand Oaks, CA: Sage Publications. doi:10.4135/9781483391144.n352
Seiter, J. S., Abraham, J. A., & Nakagama, B. T. (1998). Split-screen versus single-screen formats in televised debates: Does access to an opponent's nonverbal behaviors affect viewers' perceptions of a speaker's credibility? *Perceptual and Motor Skills, 86*, 491–497. doi.org/10.2466/pms.1998.86.2.491
Seiter, J. S., & Dutson, E. (2007). The effect of compliments on tipping behavior in hair styling salons. *The Journal of Applied Social Psychology, 37*, 1999–2007. doi:10.1111/j.1559-1816.2007.00247.x
Seiter, J. S., & Gass, R. H. (2010). Aggressive communication in political contexts. In T. A. Avtgis & A. S. Rancer (Eds.), *Arguments, aggression, and conflict: New directions in theory and research* (pp. 217–240). New York: Routledge.
Seiter, J. S., Givens, K. D., & Weger, H. (2016). The effect of mutual introductions and addressing customers by name on tipping behavior in restaurants. *Journal of Hospitality Marketing & Management, 25*, 640–651. doi:10.1080/19368623.2015.1040140
Seiter, J. S., Kinzer, H. J., Weger, H., Jr. (2006). Background behavior in live debates: The effects of the implicit *ad hominem* fallacy. *Communication Reports, 19*, 57–69. doi.org/10.1080/08934210600626856
Seiter, J. S., & Weger, H., Jr. (2005). Audience perceptions of candidates' appropriateness as a function of nonverbal behaviors displayed during televised political debates. *The Journal of Social Psychology, 145*, 225–235. doi:10.3200/SOCP.145.2.225-236
Seiter, J. S., & Weger, H. (2010). The effect of generalized compliments, sex of server, and size of dining party on tipping behavior in restaurants. *Journal of Applied Social Psychology, 40*, 1–12. doi:10.1111/j.1559-1816.2009.00560.x
Seiter, J. S., & Weger, H. (2013). Does a customer by any other name tip the same?: The effect of forms of address and customers' age on gratuities given to food servers in the United States. *Journal of Applied Social Psychology, 43*, 1592–1598. doi:10.1111/jasp.12110
Seiter, J. S., Weger, H., Jr., Kinzer, H. J., & Jensen, A. S. (2009). Impression management in televised debates: The effect of background nonverbal behavior on audience perceptions of debaters' likeability. *Communication Research Reports, 26*, 1–11. doi:10.1090/08824090802636959
Seiter, J. S., Weger, H., Jr., Kinzer, H. J., & Jensen, A. S. (2010). The role of background behavior in televised debates: Does displaying agreement and/or disagreement benefit either

debater? *Journal of Social Psychology, 150,* 278–300. doi.org/10.1080/ 002245409035110811

Self, J. W. (2017). *Presidential debate negotiation from 1960 to 1988.* Lanham, MD: Lexington Books.

Senior, C. (2018). The facial displays of leadership: A systematic review of the literature. In C. Senior (Ed.), *The facial displays of leaders* (pp. 1–26). London: Palgrave MacMillan.

Senior, C., Barnes, J., Jenkins, R., Landau, S., Phillips, M. S., & David, A. S. (1999). Attribution of social dominance and maleness to schematic faces. *Social Behavior & Personality, 27,* 331–338. doi:10.2224/sbp.1999.27.4.331

Seltz, H. A., & Yoakam, R. D. (1979). Production diary of debates. In S. Kraus (Ed.), *The great debates: Kennedy vs. Nixon, 1960* (pp. 73– 126). Bloomington, IN: Indiana University Press.

Shah, D. V., Hanna, A., Bucy, E. P., Lassen, D. S., Van Thomme, J., Bialik, K., Yang, J., & Pevehouse, J. C. W. (2016). Dual screening during presidential debates: Political nonverbals and the volume and valence of online expression. *American Behavioral Scientist, 60,* 1816–1843. doi:10.1177/0002764216676245

Shahid, A. (2011, March 3). Tucker Carlson ripped for tweeting Sarah Palin could "become surpreme commander of Milfistan." *NY Daily News.* https://www.nydailynews.com/news/politics/tucker-carlson-ripped-tweeting-sarah-palin-supreme-commander-milfistan-article-1.117016

Shogan, R. (1988, October 14). Analysis: Bush called dominant in debate: Dukakis seen as unable to make necessary gains. *Los Angeles Times.* https://www.latimes.com/archives/la-xpm-1988-10-14-mn-4030-story.html

Shrum, B. (2006). Debate strategy and effects. In K. H. Jamieson (Ed.), *Electing the president 2004: The insider's view* (pp. 114–139). Philadelphia, PA: University of Pennsylvania Press.

Silver, N. (2016, September 28). Election update: Early polls suggest a post-debate bounce for Clinton. *FiveThirtyeight.* https://fivethirtyeight.com/features/election-update-early-polls-suggest-a-post-debate-bounce-for-clinton/

Silver, N. (2017, May 3). The Comey letter probably cost Clinton the election: So why won't the media admit as much? *FiveThirtyEight.* https://fivethirtyeight.com/features/the-comey-letter-probably-cost-clinton-the-election/

Skipper J. I., Goldin-Meadow S., Nusbaum H. C., Small, S. L. (2009). Gestures orchestrate brain networks for language understanding. *Current Biology, 19,* 661–667. doi:10.1016/j.cub.2009.02.051

Smith, J. K. (2012). *Bad blood: Lyndon B. Johnson, Robert F. Kennedy and the tumultuous 1960s.* North Charleston, SC: CreateSpace.

Sofer, C., Dotsch, R., Wigboldus, D. H. J., & Todorov, A. (2015). What is typical is good: The influence of face typicality on perceived trustworthiness. *Psychological science, 26,* 39–47. doi:10.1177/0956797614554955

Sorokowski, P. (2010). Politicians' estimated height as an indicator of their popularity. *European Journal of Social Psychology, 40,* 1302–1309, doi:10.1002/ejsp.710

Spezio, M. L., Loesch, L., Gosselin, F., Mattes, K., & Alvarez, M. (2012). Thin-slice decisions do not need faces to be predictive of election outcomes. *Political Psychology, 33,* 331–341. doi:10.1111/j.1467-9221.2012.00897.x

Spillius, A. (2008, October 16). John McCain fails to land the big blows in final presidential debate. *The Telegraph.* https://www.telegraph.co.uk/news/politics/local-elections/3212595/John-McCain-fails-to-land-the-big-blows-in-final-presidential-debate.html

Stanford, G. W., Jr., & Gallagher, T. J. (2002). Spectral analysis of candidates' nonverbal vocal communication: Predicting U.S. presidential election outcomes. *Social Psychology Quarterly, 65,* 298–308. doi:10.2307/3090125

Stanford, G. W., Jr., & Webster, S. (1996). A nonverbal signal in voices of interview partners effectively predicts communication accommodation and social status perceptions. *Journal of Personality and Social Psychology, 70,* 1231–40. doi:10.1037//0022-3514.70.6.1231

Stanley, T. (2012, October 17). An Obama win to fire up the Democratic base. *CNN.* https://www.cnn.com/2012/10/17/opinion/opinion-second-debate-roundup/index.html

Stanton, Z. (2016, September 24). How to win a debate with mind games and tricks. *Politico*. https://www.politico.com/magazine/story/2016/09/presidential-debate-dirty-tricks-tips-mind-games-214282

Steinhorn, L. (2015, October 19). Likability shouldn't matter when electing a president. *The Hill*. https://thehill.com/blogs/pundits-blog/presidential-campaign/257274–likability-shouldnt-matter-when-electing-a-president

Stewart, G. L., Dustin, S. L., Barrick, M. R., & Darnold, T. C. (2008). Exploring the handshake in employment interviews. *Journal of Applied Psychology, 93*, 1139–1146. doi:10.1037/0021–9010.93.5.1139.

Stewart, P. A. (2012). *Debatable humor: Laughing matters on the 2008 presidential primary campaign*. Lanham, MD: Lexington Books.

Stewart, P. A. (2015a). Do the presidential primary debates matter? Measuring candidate speaking time and audience response during the 2012 primaries. *Presidential Studies Quarterly, 45*, 361–381. doi.org/10.1111/psq.12191

Stewart, P. A. (2015b). Polls and elections: Do the presidential primary debates matter? Measuring candidate speaking time and audience response during the 2012 primaries. *Presidential Studies Quarterly, 45*, 361–381. doi:10.1111/psq.12191

Stewart, P. A., Eubanks, A. D., Dye, R. G., Eidelman, S., & Wicks, R. H. (2017). Visual presentation style 2: Influences of perceptions of Donald Trump and Hillary Clinton based on visual presentation style during the third 2016 presidential debate. *American Behavioral Scientist, 61*, 545–557. doi:10.1177/0002764217707621

Stewart, P. A., Eubanks, A. D., & Miller, J. (2019). Visual priming and framing of the 2016 GOP and Democratic Party presidential primary debates. *Politics and the Life Sciences, 38*, 14–31. doi:10.1017/pls.2018.16

Stewart, P. A., & Ford Dowe, P. K. (2013). Interpreting Obama's facial displays of emotion. *Political Psychology, 34*: 369–385. doi:10.1111/pops.12004

Stewart, P. A., & Mosely, J. (2009). Politicians under the microscope: Eye blink rates during the first Bush-Kerry debate. *White House Studies, 9*, 373–388.

Stewart, P. A., Salter, F. K., & Mehu, M. (2013). The face as a focus of political communication: Evolutionary perspectives and the ethological method. In E. P. Bucy & R. L. Holbert (Eds.), *The sourcebook of political communication research: Methods, measures, and analytical techniques* (pp. 165–193). New York, NY: Routledge.

Stewart, P. A., & Senior, C. (2018). Politics, lies and video tapes: Nonverbal cues and signals in the age of "fake news." *PsyArXiv*. doi:10.31234/osf.io/v8krq

Stewart, P. A., Svetieva, E., Eubanks, A. D., & Miller, J. M. (2018). Facing your competition: Findings from the 2016 presidential election. In C. Senior (Ed.), *The facial displays of leaders* (pp. 51–72). Cham, Switzerland: Palgrave Macmillan.

Stewart, P. A., Waller, B. M., & Schubert, J. N. (2009). Presidential speechmaking style: Emotional response to micro-expressions of facial affect. *Motivation and Emotion, 33*, 125–135. doi:10.1007/s11031–009–9129–1

Stockemer, D., & Praino, R. (2015). Blinded by beauty? Physical attractiveness and candidate selection in the U.S. House of Representatives. *Social Science Quarterly, 96*, 430–443. doi:10.1111/ssqu.12155

Strack, F., Martin, L. L., & Stepper, S. (1988). Inhibiting and facilitating conditions of the human smile: A non-obtrusive test of the facial feedback hypothesis. *Journal of Personality and Social Psychology, 54*, 768–777. doi:10.1037//0022–3514.54.5.768

Strauss, D. (2016, October 9). Trump: Bill Clinton has been "so abusive to women." *Politico*. https://www.politico.com/story/2016/10/2016–presidential-debate-donald-trump-bill-clinton-229454

Streeck, J. (2008). Gesture in political communication: A case study of the Democratic presidential candidates during the 2004 primary campaign. *Research on Language and Social Interaction, 41*, 154–186. doi:10.1080/08351810802028662

Street, R. L., Jr., & Giles, H. (1982). Speech accommodation theory: A social cognitive approach to language and speech behavior. In M. Roloff & C. R. Berger (Eds.), *Social cognition and communication* (pp. 193–226). Beverly Hills, CA: Sage.

Stroud, N. J., Stephens, M., & Pye, P. (2011). The influence of debate viewing context on political cynicism and strategic interpretations. *American Behavioral Scientist, 55*, 270–283. doi:10.1177/0002764210392163

Stulp, G., Buunk, A. P., Verhulst, S., & Pollet, T. V. (2013). Tall claims? Sense and nonsense about the importance of height of US presidents. *Leadership Quarterly, 24*, 159–71. doi:10.1016/j.leaqua.2012.09.002

Sussman, A. B., Petkova, K., & Todorov, A. (2013). Competence ratings in US predict presidential election outcomes in Bulgaria. *Journal of Experimental Social Psychology, 49*, 771–775. doi:10.1016/j.jesp.2013.02.003.

Swanson, E. (2016, October 26). AP-GfK poll: Clinton a big winner over Trump in the debates. *Associated Press News.* https://apnews.com/02053bd99de048a1a83aa5b9682c5c2d

Swerdlow, J. L. (1984). *Beyond debate: A paper on televised presidential debates.* New York: Twentieth Century Fund.

Swint, K. (2008). *Mudslingers: The twenty-five dirtiest political campaigns of all time.* New York: Union Square Press.

Taber, C. S., & Lodge, M. (2016). The illusion of choice in democratic politics: The unconscious impact of motivated political reasoning. *Advances in Political Psychology, 37*, 61–85. doi:10.1111/pops.12321

Taber, C. S., Lodge, M., & Glathar, J. (2001). The motivated construction of political judgments. In J. H. Kuklinski (Ed.), *Cambridge studies in political psychology and public opinion. Citizens and politics: Perspectives from political psychology* (pp. 198–226). New York, NY: Cambridge University Press.

Talbert, B. (2012, January 7). Election 2012: Don't forget the 'Bubba' factor. *Orange County Register.* https://www.ocregister.com/2012/01/07/election-2012–dont-forget-the-bubba-factor/

Talley, L., & Temple, S. (2015). How leaders influence followers through the use of nonverbal communication. *Leadership & Organization Development Journal, 36*, 69–80. doi:10.1108/LODJ-07-2013–0107

Team fix (2016, February 13). The CBS News Republican debate transcript, annotated. *CBS News.* https://www.washingtonpost.com/news/the-fix/wp/2016/02/13/the-cbs-republican-debate-transcript-annotated/

Tedeschi, J. T., & Norman, N. (1985). Social power, self-presentation, and the self. In B. R. Schlenker (Ed.), *The self and social life* (pp. 293–322). New York: McGraw Hill.

Tedeschi, J. T., & Reiss, M. (1981). Identities, the phenomenal self, and laboratory research. In J. T. Tedeschi (Ed.), *Impression management theory and social psychological research* (pp. 3–22). New York: Academic Press.

Tenney, E. R., Meikle, N. L., Hunsaker, D., Moore, D. A., & Anderson, C. (2019). Is overconfidence a social liability? The effect of verbal versus nonverbal expressions of confidence. *Journal of Personality and Social Psychology, 116*, 396–415. doi:10.1037/pspi0000150

The 2008 candidate of hope and change? (2012, October 10). *Chicago Tribune.* https://www.chicagotribune.com/news/opinion/editorials/ct-edit-president-1004-20121004,0,1490034.story

Thompson, D. (2016, March 1). Who are Donald Trump's supporters, really? Four theories to explain the front-runner's rise to the top of the polls. *The Atlantic.* https://www.theatlantic.com/politics/archive/2016/03/who-are-donald-trumps-supporters-really/471714/

Thoresen, J. C., Vuong, Q. C., & Atkinson, A. P. (2012). First impressions: Gait cues drive reliable trait judgement. *Cognition, 124*, 261–71. doi:10.1016/j.cognition.

Thorndike, E. L. (1920). A constant error in psychological ratings. *Journal of Applied Psychology, 4*, 25–29. doi:10.1037/h0071663

Thornhill, R., & Gangestad, S.W. (1999). Facial attractiveness. *Trends in Cognitive Sciences, 3*, 452–460. doi:10.1016/S1364–6613(99)01403–5

Tian, Y. (2017). Disfluencies in Trump and Clinton first presidential debate. In L. Meurant & A. C. Simon (Eds.), *Proceedings of the conference fluency and disfluency across languages and language varieties* (pp. 106–109). Louvainla-Neuve, Belgium: Universitaires de Louvain.

Tiemens, R. K. (1970). Some relationships of camera angle to communicator credibility. *Journal of Broadcasting, 14*, 483–490. doi:10.1080/08838157009363614

Tiemens, R. K. (1978). Television's portrayal of the 1976 presidential debates: An analysis of visual content. *Communication Monographs, 45*, 362–370. doi.org/10.1080/03637757809375981

Tiemens, R. K., Hellweg, S. A., Kipper, P., & Phillips, S. L. (1985). An integrative verbal and visual analysis of the Carter-Reagan debate. *Communication Quarterly, 33*, 34–42. doi.org/10.1080/01463378509369576

Today Show (2016, February 19). Expert reads body language of Donald Trump and other candidates. *Today.* https://www.youtube.com/watch?v=jrVeIKH14PQ

Todorov, A. (2008), Evaluating faces on trustworthiness. *Annals of the New York Academy of Sciences, 1124*, 208–224. doi:10.1196/annals.1440.012

Todorov, A., Mandisodza, A. N., Goren, A., & Hall, C. C. (2005). Inferences of competence from faces predict election outcomes. *Science, 308*, 1623–1626. doi:10.1126/science.1110589

Todorov, A., Said, C. P., Engell, A. D., and Oosterhof, N. N. (2008). Understanding evaluation of faces on social dimensions. *Trends in Cognitive Sciences, 12*, 455 – 460. doi:10.1016/j.tics.2008.10.001

Todorov, A., Said, C. P., & Verosky, S. C. (2011). Personality impressions from facial appearance. In A. Calder, J. V. Haxby, M. Johnson, & G. Rhodes (Eds.), *Handbook of face perception* (pp. 631–652). New York, NY: Oxford University Press.

Tonn, M. B. (2019). The year of the alpha male writ large: The gender dynamics of the 2016 election and presidential debates. In E. A. Hinck (Ed.), *Presidential debates in a changing media environment* (Vol. 1, pp. 271–291). Santa Barbara, CA: Praeger Publishers.

Toon, M. B. (1994). Flirting with Perot: Voter ambivalence about the third candidate. In D. Carlin & M. S. McKinney (Eds.), *The 1992 presidential debates in focus* (pp. 109–123). Westport, CT: Praeger.

Trent, J. (1994). The 1984 Bush-Ferraro vice presidential debate. In R. V. Friednberg (Ed.) *Rhetorical studies of national political debates 1960–1992* (2nd ed.) (pp. 121–144). West Port, CT: Praeger.

Trent, J. S., Mongeau, P. A. Trent, J. D., Kendall, K. E., & Cushing, R. D. (1993). The ideal candidate: A study of the desired attributes of the public and media across two presidential campaigns. *American Behavior Scientist, 37*, 225–239. doi:10.1177/0002764293037002010

Tschorn, A. (2019, June 28). The 2020 Democratic debates: A pop of red, a naked neck and a sea of navy blue. *Los Angeles Times.* https://www.latimes.com/fashion/la-ig-democratic-candidates-debate-fashion-20190628–htmlstory.html

Tucker Carlson exposes his own sexism on Twitter (n/d). *Conservatives 4 Palin.* http://conservatives4palin.com/2011/03/tucker-carlson-exposes-his-own-sexism-on-twitter.html

Tumulty, K. (2007, April 26). The April 26 Democratic debate. *Time.* http://content.time.com/time/nation/article/0,8599,1615356,00.html

Ubel, S. (2008). Credibility lessening tactics utilized in the courtroom by male and female attorneys. *Communication Law Review, 42*, 42–51. https://pdfs.semanticscholar.org/6e13/5ad96556d01f4afe84a2405c20182aceb19d.pdf

Usher, S. (1999). *Greek oratory: Tradition and originality.* New York, NY: Oxford.

Van Hagen, I. (2019, July 31). "Throw your hands up": Bernie Sanders' debate exchange turns into an instant meme. *Newsweek.* https://www.newsweek.com/throw-your-hands-bernie-sanders-debate-exchange-turns-instant-meme-1451922

Vancil, D. L., & Pendell, S. D. (1987). The myth of viewer-listener disagreement in the first Kennedy-Nixon debate. *Central States Speech Journal, 38*, 16–27. doi.org/10.1080/10510978709368226

Vatz, R. E. (1973). The myth of the rhetorical situation. *Philosophy and Rhetoric, 6*(3), 154–161.

Ventre, M. (2008, October 1). Style often trumps substance in debates. *Today.* https://www.today.com/popculture/style-often-trumps-substance-debates-wbna26978473

Verhulst, B., Lodge, M., & Lavine, H. (2010). *Journal of Nonverbal Behavior, 34*, 111–117. doi:10.1007/s10919–009–0084–z

Verser, R. M. (2007). *The 2004 presidential election between George W. Bush and John F. Kerry: An analysis of visually comparative televised advertisements* (Doctoral dissertation). https://mospace.umsystem.edu/xmlui/bitstream/handle/10355/4696/research.pdf

Voth, B. (2017). The presidential debates 2016. In R. E. Denton (Ed.), *The 2016 US presidential campaign: Political communication and practice* (pp. 77–98). Cham, Switzerland: Palgrave Macmillan.

Viser, M., & Linskey, A. (2019, Nov. 6). Is Elizabeth Warren "angry" and antagonistic? Or are rivals dabbling in gendered criticism? *The Washington Post*. https://www.washingtonpost.com/politics/elizabeth-warren-faces-a-new-line-of-attack-shes-angry-and-antagonistic/2019/11/06/dd27b4fa-00af-11ea-8bab-0fc209e065a8_story.html

Wagenmakers, E. J., Beek, T., Dijkhoff, L., Gronau, Q. F., Acosta, A., Adams, R. B., Jr., Albohn, D. N., Allard, E. S., Benning, S. D., Blouin-Hudon, E. M., Bulnes, L. C., Caldwell, T. L., Calin-Jageman, R. J., Capaldi, C. A., Carfagno, N. S., Chasten, K. T., Cleeremans, A., Connell, L., DeCicco, J. M., ... Zwaan, R. A. (2016). Registered replication report: Strack, Martin, & Stepper (1988). *Perspectives on Psychological Science, 11*, 917–928. doi:10.1177/1745691616674458

Waldman, P., & Devitt, J. (1998). Newspaper photographs and the 1996 presidential election: The question of bias. *Journalism & Mass Communication Quarterly, 75*, 302–311. doi.org/10.1177/107769909807500206

Wallbott, H. G. (1991). Recognition of emotion from facial expression via imitation? Some indirect evidence for an old theory. *British Journal of Social Psychology, 30*, 207–219. doi:10.1111/j.2044-8309.1991.tb00939.x

Wanta, W. (1986). The effects of dominant photographs. An agenda setting experiment. *Journalism Quarterly, 63*, 728–734. doi:10.1177/107769908806500114

Wanzenried, J.W., Powell, F. C., & Franks, L. J. (1989) Perceptions of political competency and the impact of a televised debate. *Psychological Reports, 64*, 825–826. doi:10.2466/pr0.1989.64.3.825

Ware, P. D., & Tucker, R. K. (1974). Heckling as distraction: An experimental study of its effect on source credibility. *Speech Monographs, 41*, 185–188. doi:10.1080/03637757409375834

Warner, B. R., Carlin, D. B., Winfrey, K., Schnoebelen, J., & Trosanovski, M. (2011). "Will the 'real' candidates for president and vice president please stand up?" *American Behavioral Scientist, 55*, 232–252. doi:10.1177/0002764210392160.

Wasike, B. (2018). Gender, parasocial interaction, and nonverbal communication: Testing visual the effect of sports magazine cover models. *International Journal of Communication, 12*, 173–199. https://ijoc.org/index.php/ijoc/article/view/7577

Wasike, B. (2019). Gender, nonverbal communication, and televised debates: A case study analysis of Clinton and Trump's nonverbal language during the 2016 town hall debate. *International Journal of Communication, 13*, 251–276. https://ijoc.org/index.php/ijoc/article/view/9844

Watzlawick, P., Bavelas, J., Jackson, D. (1967). *Pragmatics of human communication*. New York, NY: W. Norton.

Waxman, O. B. (2016, October 20). A brief history of handshakes at presidential debates. *Time*. http://time.com/4538640/handshake-presidential-debates/

Weaver, J. [@jwgop] (2016, September 26). I have never seen a more unprepared candidate in a major moment. #Malpractice. *Twitter*. https://twitter.com/jwgop/status/780607591848091648

Weger, H., Hinck, E. A., & Seiter, J. S. (2019). Joe Biden's nonverbal ridicule as a case of strategic maneuvering in the 2012 American vice-presidential debate. In E. A. Hinck (Ed.), *Presidential debates in a changing media environment* (Vol. 1, pp. 143–162). Santa Barbara, CA: Praeger Publishers.

Weger, H., Jr., & Canary, D. J. (2010). Conversational argument in close relationships: A case for studying argument sequences. *Communication Methods and Measures, 4*, 65–87. doi:10.1080/19312451003680541

Weger, H., Jr., & Mohammed, D. (2017, June). *Strategic Maneuvering in the Background: How candidates encourage audience inference making through silent derogation in the*

background. Paper presented at the 2nd European Conference on Argumentation, Fribourg, Switzerland.
Weger, H., Jr., Seiter, J. S., Jacobs, K. A., & Akbulut, V. (2010). Perceptions of debater effectiveness and appropriateness as a function of decreasingly polite strategies for responding to nonverbal disparagement in televised debates. *Argumentation and Advocacy, 47*, 39–54. doi.org/10.1080/00028533.2010.11821736
Weger, H., Jr., Seiter, J. S., Jacobs, K. A., & Akbulut, V. (2013). Responses to an opponent's nonverbal behavior in a televised debate: Audience perceptions of credibility and likeability. *Journal of Argumentation in Context, 2*, 179–203. doi:10.1075/jaic.2.201weg
Weil, G. L. (2012, October 19). Presidential debates style over substance. *Times Record*. https://www.timesrecord.com/articles/commentary/presidential-debates-style-over-substance/
Weissman, J. (2014). *In the line of fire: How to handle tough questions—when it counts* (2nd ed.). Upper Saddle River, NJ: Pearson Education.
Weprin, A. (2016, Sept. 27). First Trump-Clinton debate is the most-watched debate of all time. *Politico*. www.politico.com/blogs/on-media/2016/09/first-trum-clinton-debate-smashes-ratings-records-228788
Westen, D., Blagov, P. S., Harenski, K., Kilts, C., & Hamann, S. (2006). Neural bases of motivated reasoning: An fMRI study of emotional constraints on partisan political judgment in the 2004 U.S. presidential election. *Journal of Neuroscience, 18*, 1947–1958. doi:10.1162/jocn.2006.18.11.1947
White, D. (2016, Sept. 27). Here's why the audience at the presidential debate clapped. *Time*. http://time.com/4508926/presidential-debate-clapping-trump-clinton/
Whitesides, J. (2012, October 15). Pressure on Obama to put bid back on track. *Real Clear Politics*. https://www.realclearpolitics.com/2012/10/15/pressure_on_obama_to_put_bid_back_on_track_293067.html
Wicks, R. H. (2007). Does presentation style of presidential debates influence young voters' perceptions of candidates? *American Behavioral Scientist, 50*, 1247–1254. doi:10.1177/00027642-7300054
Wiegman, O. (1987). Attitude change in a realistic experiment: The effect of party membership and audience reaction during an interview with a Dutch politician. *Journal of Applied Social Psychology, 17*, 37–49. doi.org/10.1111/j.1559–1816.1987.tb00291.x
Williard, C. (1988). *A theory of argumentation*. Tuscaloosa, AL: University of Alabama.
Winberg, O. (2019). Insult politics: Donald Trump, right-wing populism, and incendiary language. *European Journal of American Studies* [Online]. doi:10.4000/ ejas.12132
Windt, T. O. Jr. (1994). The 1960 Kennedy Nixon presidential debates. In R. V. Friedenberg (Ed.), *Rhetorical studies of national political debates 1960–1992* (pp. 1–27). Westport, CT: Praeger.
Winneg, K., & Jamieson, K. H. (2017). Learning from the 2016 U.S. general election presidential debate. *American Behavioral Scientist, 61*, 362–378. doi.org/10.1177/0002764217702770
Winship, M. (2015, October 28). The night the candidates were speechless. *Moyers*. https://billmoyers.com/2015/10/28/the-night-the-candidates-were-speechless/
Winter, N. J. G. (2010). Masculine Republicans and feminine Democrats: Gender and Americans' explicit and implicit images of the political parties. *Political Behavior, 32*, 587–618. doi:10.1007/s11109–010–9131–z
Witkower, Z., Tracy, J. L., Cheng, J. T., & Henrich, J. (2020). Two signals of social rank: Prestige and dominance are associated with distinct nonverbal displays. *Journal of Personality and Social Psychology, 118*, 89–120. https://psycnet.apa.org/doi/10.1037/pspi0000181
Woodall, W. G., & Folger, J. P. (1981). Encoding specificity and nonverbal cue context: An expansion of episodic memory research. *Journal of Nonverbal Behavior, 5*, 49–55. doi.org/10.1080/03637758109376046
Wooten, J. T. (1976, September 24). Sound of debate is off air for 27 minutes. *The New York Times*. https://www.nytimes.com/1976/09/24/archives/sound-of-debate-is-off-air-for-27-minutes-debates-sound-goes-off.html
Young, T. J., & French, L. A. (1996). Height and perceived competence of U.S. presidents. *Perceptual and Motor Skills, 82*, 1002. doi:10.1177/003151259608200301

Zajonc, R. B. (1968). Attitudinal effects of mere exposure. *Journal of Personality and Social Psychology Monographs, 9*(2, part 2), 1–27. doi:10.1037/h0025848

Zajonc, R. B., & Markus, H. (1984). Affect and cognition: The hard interface. In C. Izard, J. Kagan & R. B. Zajonc (Eds.), *Emotion, cognition, and behavior* (pp. 73–102). Cambridge: Cambridge University Press.

Zakahi, W. (2004). Presidential debates and candidate image formation: 1992, 1996, 2000. In K. L. Hacker (Ed.), *Presidential candidate images* (pp. 151–175). Lanham, MD: Rowman & Littlefield.

Zakahi, W. R., & Hacker, K. L. (1995). Televised presidential debates and candidate images. In K. L. Hacker (Ed.), *Candidate images in presidential elections* (pp. 99–122). Westport, CT: Praeger.

Zawadzki, M. J., Warner, L. R., & Shields, S. A. (2013). Sadness is believed to signal competence when displayed with passionate restraint. *Social Psychology, 44*, 219–230. doi:10.1027/1864-9335/a000106

Zelizer, J. E. (2016, September 24). The 8 biggest unforced errors in debate history. *Politico*. https://www.politico.com/magazine/story/2016/09/presidential-debates-errors-mistakes-gaffes-biggest-history-214279

Zuckerman, M., DePaulo, B. M., & Rosenthal, R. (1981). Verbal and nonverbal communication of deception. In L. Berkowitz (Ed.), *Advances in experimental social psychology* (pp. 2–59). New York: Academic Press.

Zurcher, A. (2016, November 6). Hillary Clinton emails—what's it all about? *BBC News*. https://www.bbc.com/news/world-us-canada-31806907

Index

Access Hollywood, 159, 167, 168
accountability for nonverbal behavior. *See* "off-the-record" nature of nonverbal behavior
actio. *See* delivery
affiliation, political, 91, 168
affiliative behaviors, 33, 47–48, 109–110
aggression, 36, 92, 109, 132, 157, 161, 165, 170; nonverbal, 44, 67–68, 73, 87, 101, 142, 158, 162, 163–165, 169, 171, 172; political, 15, 70–71, 80; reciprocating, 80, 140. *See also* other-presentation; insults; disparagement, nonverbal; politeness theory
agreement, nonverbal, 15, 53, 71, 78, 81n6, 111
Alexander the Great, 126
anger, expressions of, 18, 26, 31, 44, 46, 50, 56, 101, 110, 116, 140, 158, 161, 162, 165, 168, 169, 171, 172
anxious behavior. *See* nervous behavior; blinking; composure
appearance. *See* physical appearance
The Apprentice, 166–168
appropriateness of debaters' behavior, 27, 32, 162; and attentiveness/distraction, 6, 116; criteria for judging, 70–71; perceptions of, 9, 10, 18, 68, 77–79, 109–110, 165. *See also* expectancy violations theory

argumentation, ix, 3, 4, 16, 41, 105, 117, 126, 127, 129, 134, 141; design approach, 126, 146, 148–150; nonverbal communication as, 16–17, 44, 66, 72, 129, 142, 145, 146, 151, 153, 171–172. *See also* multimodal argumentation; strategic maneuvering
Aristotle, 74, 105, 126–129, 149, 171; *On Rhetoric*, book, 105, 126–127. *See also* rhetoric
artifacts, 37, 51, 84, 116, 141
Asman, Bob, 64
Atkinson, Max, 128
attacking other's image. *See* appropriateness of debaters' behavior; other-presentation
attention paid to nonverbal cues, 6, 32, 37, 39, 73, 107, 108, 115–116, 137, 138, 141, 170. *See also* distraction
attractiveness, 1, 7, 28, 32–33, 44, 48, 52, 55, 56, 70, 107, 111, 113, 115–116, 119, 139. *See also* halo effect; physical appearance
attributions, 8–9, 13, 56, 57, 121, 158
audience: complexity of, 12; composition of, 29, 130, 134, 147, 154–155, 166, 168; reactions (laughter, applause, heckling), 13, 17, 20, 21, 63, 86, 95–99, 112–113, 128, 142. *See also* reaction shots-controversy surrounding; rhetorical situation

221

authenticity. *See* sincerity
authority, principle of. *See* credibility

background behavior of non-speaking opponent. *See* reaction shots; reactions of non-speaking opponent; split-screens
balance theory. *See* consistency theories
Begala, Paul, 67
Benoit, William, 18, 21n1, 81n1
Bentsen, Lloyd, 96–97, 144
bias. *See* media bias
Biden, Joe, 13, 14, 19, 21, 66, 71–72, 98–99, 101, 102, 103, 108, 131–133, 140, 147, 154. *See also* Democratic primary debates of 2020 election cycle; vice presidential debate of 2012
Bitzer, Lloyd, 126, 129, 130–133
blinking. *See* eye behavior
Bloomberg, Michael, 20, 155
body language, 15, 19, 25, 42, 65, 144, 178
body movements, 34–35, 51–52, 59, 70, 115–116, 143
body orientation, 35, 59, 108
Booker, Cory, 45
Boxer, Barbara, 137
Buchanan, Pat, 156–157
Bush, Barbara, 139
Bush, George H. W., 8, 26, 38, 84, 88, 95, 107, 144; checking his watch, 65, 69, 87–88. *See also* presidential debates of 1988; presidential debates of 1992; vice presidential debates of 1984
Bush, George W., 26, 46, 63, 65, 67–68, 80, 85, 87–88, 108. *See also* presidential debates of 2000; presidential debates of 2004
Bush, Jeb, 26, 93, 98, 100, 167
Buttigieg, Pete, 54, 98–99, 140

camera angles. *See* visual presentation of debates
camera techniques. *See* visual presentation of debates
Carson, Ben, 93, 100
Carlson, Tucker, 138
Carter, Jimmy, 3, 9–10, 67, 68–69, 71, 76, 83, 90, 93, 97, 101. *See also* presidential debates of 1976
Carville, James, 87

channel discrepancy, 37, 53
character, perceptions of. *See* credibility
charisma, 8, 26, 128, 134, 160
cheating, accused of, 88
Christie, Chris, 100, 167
chronemics. *See* time
Cialdini, Robert, 111–113, 122, 122n1–123n3
Cicero, 105
Cillizza, Chris, 27, 41
civility, 91
Clinton, Bill, 49, 87–88, 98, 101, 112. *See also* presidential debates of 1992; presidential debates of 1996
Clinton, Hillary Rodham, 2, 13, 18, 20, 39, 72, 73–74, 79, 91, 94, 96, 97, 98, 101, 102, 103–104, 108, 110–111, 120–121, 143, 153, 156, 171, 172; double bind and, 132, 138, 140, 156–157; investigations of,, 158, 177, 178n1; shimmy and, 103, 163; shrill. *See* vocalics. *See also* presidential debates of 2016
close elections, 3–4, 7, 175
close-ups. *See* visual presentation of debates
clothing, 2, 45, 112, 116, 161, 167
coaches, political. *See* image experts
cognitive dissonance theory. *See* consistency theories
cognitive processing of nonverbal cues, 7, 11, 17–18, 25, 28–29, 58, 73, 98, 114–115, 122. *See also* elaboration likelihood model
Comey, James, 176, 178n1
Commager, Henry Steele, 149
Commission on Presidential Debates, 85, 86, 96, 98, 177
communication accommodation theory, 120
competence, perceptions of. *See* credibility
composure, perceptions of. *See* credibility
confidence, perceptions of, 37, 53, 57, 174
confirmation bias, 25
congruity theory. *See* consistency theories
consistency theories, 120
consultants,. *See* image experts
contempt, expressions of, 26, 31, 60, 63, 162, 163

Corax, 125
coverage. *See* equal coverage
credibility, 9, 18, 26, 32, 35, 52, 72, 74–76, 78, 80, 89–90, 101, 106, 107, 111, 114, 115, 137, 171; character, 33, 44, 46, 50, 52, 65, 72, 74–76, 79, 81n3, 91, 111, 127, 129, 132, 134, 143, 146, 147, 151, 169, 171, 175; competence/expertise, 9, 10, 12–13, 14, 18, 27, 32–33, 37, 39, 45, 46, 53, 54–59, 68–69, 71, 74–75, 79, 81n3, 90, 110, 111, 118, 137, 138–139, 140, 147, 154, 161, 165, 171, 173, 175; composure, 4, 10, 13, 15, 35, 53, 61, 67, 68, 74–76, 81n3, 111, 127, 132, 135, 150, 161, 172; dynamism, 35, 52, 72, 74, 111, 143; ethos, 16, 72, 127, 129, 143, 151, 171, 177; extroversion, 35, 74–75, 78–79, 81n4, 111; goodwill, 74, 111; honesty, 9, 37, 45, 46, 50–51, 52, 107; sociability, 32, 33, 50, 55, 74, 75, 78–79, 81n3, 111, 122; trustworthiness, 9, 32, 32–33, 35, 37, 39, 46, 50–53, 56, 59, 62, 74, 111, 158, 159, 160, 166, 177
cut-away shots. *See* reaction shots; reactions of non-speaking opponent; split screens
crying, 27, 101

Daley, Richard, 20
debates. *See* France, debates in; Gubernatorial debates; Italy, debates in; live (non-televised) debates; Switzerland, debates in; Lincoln-Douglas debates (1858); political debates; presidential debates; primary debates; vice presidential debates
deception/deceptiveness, 28, 37, 51, 53, 62, 68
decorum, 70, 158, 161, 165
defending images of self and other. *See* other-presentation; self-presentation
"defining moments" in political debates, 9–10, 75, 96–97
delivery, 8, 42, 51, 78, 105, 125, 126–127, 128, 129, 143, 144, 149, 154, 158, 168, 170, 171, 178; actio, 143, 144, 149
demeanor, 15, 42, 55, 68, 83, 135, 140, 159, 162, 165, 171, 172, 175

Demosthenes, 125
direct effects model of immediacy. *See* immediacy
derision. *See* disparagement, nonverbal
disagreement, nonverbal, 13, 15, 26, 28, 73, 74–77, 78–79, 80, 81n3, 81n4, 81n5, 81n6, 95, 109, 146, 169, 171
disgust, expression of, 26, 29, 31, 63, 73
disparagement, nonverbal, 13, 17, 66, 71, 73, 77, 80, 109, 112, 148, 156, 166
distraction, 17, 66, 73, 98, 116, 117, 118, 119. *See also* elaboration likelihood model
Dole, Bob, 6, 76, 97, 111. *See also* Presidential debates of 1996
dominance/status, nonverbal cues of, 26, 30, 33, 35, 36, 37, 38, 44, 45, 46, 54, 55–59, 60, 71, 89, 109–110, 158, 161, 167, 168, 171, 172
double bind, 101, 110–111, 122, 126, 138–140, 158, 177; Hillary Clinton and, 156–157, 161, 162
Douglas, Stephen, 1, 63
Drum, Kevin, 167
dual-screen debates. *See* split-screens
Dukakis, Kitty, 95–96, 135
Dukakis, Michael, 2, 8, 39, 75, 84, 95–96, 107, 135, 173
dysfluencies/dysfunctions, speech, 57. *See also* Presidential debates of 1988

Eagleton, Thomas, 70
Edwards, John, 2
Eisenhower, Dwight, 44
Ekman, Paul, 25, 31, 50
elaboration likelihood model, 7, 17, 116–120, 123n2
emotional bonds with television personalities. *See* parasocial relationships
emotions, 8, 9, 27, 29, 31, 32, 33, 36, 47, 56, 95, 109–110, 127, 135, 171, 172; anxiety, 26, 37, 68; appeals to. *See* pathos. *See also* facial expression
enthymeme, 126, 128–129, 143, 167, 171
equal coverage, 91–94
Erickson, Erick, 138
ethological and evolutionary perspectives, 109–110

ethos. *See* credibility
evolutionary perspectives. *See* ethological and evolutionary perspectives
eye behavior, 68, 69, 73, 77–78; blinking, 14, 68, 116; eye contact, 31, 33, 44, 48, 49, 51, 87, 106, 108, 111, 128, 143, 161, 165; eye-tracking, 6; gaze, 31, 33, 45, 55, 56, 68, 69, 106; pupil dilation,; rolling eyes, 14, 65, 73, 79, 86, 109; shifty eyes, 68, 69, 111; simulated eye contact (by looking at camera), 90
expectancy violations theory, 77, 80, 107–108, 116
expertise, perceptions of. *See* credibility
extroversion, perceptions of. *See* credibility

facial expressions, 6, 9, 11, 17, 18, 26, 28, 29, 31–33, 39, 41, 43, 45, 46, 47, 48, 51, 52, 56, 60, 67, 70, 73, 75, 76, 77–78, 87, 89, 99, 101, 103, 105, 106–107, 113, 116, 127, 128, 132, 143, 144, 158, 160, 162, 166, 167, 171. *See also* frowning; smiling; fear; surprise
facial features/structure, 11, 32, 33, 52, 54, 55, 56, 57
facial feedback hypothesis, 30
fact-checking, 99
fallacy: *ad hominem*, 95, 146, 147–148, 170; implicit *ad hominem*, 73
fear, expression of, 26, 27, 31, 36, 45, 46, 50, 56–57, 110, 161
feminine, 56, 101, 136, 137, 138–139, 140, 156, 157, 161, 165
Ferraro, Geraldine, 76, 87, 138, 139. *See also* vice presidential debate of 1984
Fiorina, Carly, 70, 100
Fisher, Walter, 126, 133–135
flustering debaters, 18, 60, 66, 68, 73–74, 98
Ford, Gerald, 3, 9–10, 68, 83, 84, 86, 90, 92, 93, 94, 101. *See also* presidential debates of 1976
format of televised debates, 35, 41, 42, 59, 74, 77, 85, 91, 149, 150; criticism of flawed formats, 4, 149–150. *See also* argumentation, design approach
framing effects, 121, 137
France, debates in, 71

frontrunner, 93, 97
frowning, 30, 56, 68–69, 73, 74
functional theory (Benoit), 21n1–22n2, 81n1

gaffes, 10, 13–14, 65, 69, 80, 84–85, 103, 149
gaze. *See* eye behavior
gait, 35. *See also* body motion
gender stereotypes. *See* double bind
gestures, 6, 25, 26, 28, 34, 35, 38, 48, 59, 71, 89, 103, 105, 106–107, 111, 115–116, 125, 127–128, 129, 132, 161, 165, 167, 169, 172; adapters, 51; affinity, 59; co-speech gestures, 34; discrediting, 60, 61, 171; defiance, 59, 169; emblems, 17–18, 34; pistol grip, 167; precision grip gesture, 129–130, 144, 172
Goffman, Erving, 12, 121
good will, perceptions of. *See* credibility
Gore, Al, 63, 65, 67–68, 71, 80, 84–85, 87, 95, 108, 114. *See also* presidential debates of 2000
Golden, Soma, 149
Grillo, Beppe, 127
Groarke, Leo, 142
Gubernatorial debates, 116

hair, 2, 3, 56, 57, 88, 161
halo effect, 32, 113, 139
handshakes. *See* touch
haptics. *See* touch
Hart, Gary, 33
hard interface theory, 29
head movement. *See* agreement, nonverbal; disagreement, nonverbal
height : camera angles and, 93; candidate, 24, 28, 38, 54–55, 57; Ross Perot on too tall stools, 87–88; podium manipulation to appear taller, 2, 54, 84, 86
heuristics, 7, 32, 98, 112, 113, 119. *See also* elaboration likelihood model; framing effects
Hewitt, Don, 64, 83, 86
Hickenlooper, John, 61
Hitler, Adolph, 89
honesty, perceptions of. *See credibility*
Hovland, Carl, 50, 105

humanism v. social science, 151n1
humor, 1, 6, 12, 15, 19, 20, 21, 44, 67, 76, 84, 91–92, 96–98, 127. *See also* insults, memes

image experts, 87–88
image management. *See* other-presentation; self-presentation
immediacy, 31, 38, 46, 48–49, 101, 106–107, 122
importance of political debates, 3–4, 104, 175
impression management. *See* other-presentation; self-presentation
inappropriateness. *See* appropriateness, perceptions of input-output framework (of persuasion), 115
insults, 2, 20, 70, 95, 96–97. *See also* discrediting; humor
integrity. *See* trustworthiness
intentional behavior, 11, 13, 24, 25, 66–74, 77, 101
interpersonal deception theory, 68
interruptions, 19, 71, 73, 79, 97, 103, 109, 162, 165, 169; visual, 170
involvement, nonverbal, 24, 26, 35, 46, 48, 106, 107
involvement, with issue, 119
Italy, debates in, 60, 71, 127

Jamieson, Kathleen Hall, 136, 137, 170, 175
jewelry. *See* artifacts
joy/happiness, expressions of, 18, 26, 29, 31, 33, 36, 46, 50, 55, 56, 110, 166

Kaine, Tim, 15
Kasich, John, 167
Kennedy, John F., 3, 4, 5, 14, 15, 23, 81n2, 83, 86, 90, 96–97, 104. *See also* presidential debates of 1960
Kerry, John, 63, 91, 104n2. *See also* presidential debates of 2004
kinesics. *See* body motion
Klein, Joe, 41
Klobuchar, Amy, 20, 154
Kohl, Helmut, 93

laughter, 13, 14, 20, 21, 66, 71–72, 73, 96–98, 101, 103, 110–111, 112, 156
leadership ability, perceptions of, 4, 9, 12, 46, 48, 54, 55, 56, 90, 93, 109, 110, 136–137, 139, 165, 175. *See also* credibility
"leaked" behavior. *See* deception; unintentional behavior
lectern. *See* height
likeability, 2, 12, 13, 26, 32, 44, 46, 47–50, 67, 76–77, 91, 97, 106, 107–108, 110, 111, 113, 150, 157–158, 160, 166, 175
Lincoln, Abraham, 1, 63
Lincoln-Douglas debates (1858), 1, 63
Lippmann, Walter, 105
Lipton, James, 50
live (non-televised) debates, 78–79, 81n7
logos, 127, 128, 129, 171
Lovitz, Jon, 84–85
Luntz, Frank, 87, 154

MacKinnon, Catherine, 136
masculine, 56, 101, 110, 136, 137, 139, 140, 157, 161, 165
McCain, John, 14, 15–16, 18, 68–69, 78, 96, 131, 138. *See also* presidential debates of 2008
McFarlane, Seth, 91–92
McGuire, William, 115
media bias, 5, 86, 99, 101, 104. *See also* visual presentation of debates
Mehrabian, Albert, 28
memes, 103–104
memorandum of understanding, 65, 85, 86–87
mere exposure effect, 114, 122
micro-expressions, 15, 32
mimic, mimicry, mimicking, 29, 33
mirror. *See mimic.*
mode of presentation (visual vs. auditory), effects of, 83, 86, 104n2
moderators and panelists, 13, 19, 21, 90, 99–100, 103, 112; Crowley, Candy, 99; Diaz-Balart, Jose, 54; Holt, Lester, 97; Lehrer, Jim, 41, 65, 67, 96; Shaw, Bernard, 95–96; Tapper, Jake, 100; Trewitt, Henry, 71–72, 96–97; Warner, Margaret, 135; Woodruff, Judy, 96–97

Mondale, Walter, 51, 71–72, 76, 83–84, 94, 96–97, 98. *See also* presidential debates of 1985; vice presidential debate of 1976
motivated reasoning, 114–115
multimodal argumentation, 126, 141–144, 171, 177
Muskie, Edmund, 27

Nader, Ralph, 45
narrative paradigm, 133–135
need for cognition, 119
negativity in politics, 70–71, 77, 80
negotiation, pre-debate, 55, 64, 84–87. *See also* memorandum of understanding
Nervous behavior, 10, 11, 14, 51, 68, 69, 88, 113, 168. *See also* composure; unintentional behavior
newspersons, 20, 25, 27, 100–102, 155
Nixon, Richard, 3, 5, 8, 14, 15, 20, 23, 65, 68, 69, 71, 77, 81n2, 83–84, 85, 86. *See also* presidential debates of 1960
Nodding. *See* agreement, nonverbal
nonverbal communication: ambiguous nature of, 25, 69, 70, 77, 107, 142; characteristics of, 25–30; cultural nature of, 25, 26–27, 31, 130, 137, 151n1; definition of, 23; embodied nature of, 28–30, 33, 58; intentional v. unintentional, 13, 14, 24, 25, 68, 77; lack of scholarly focus on, 4, 141–142; strategic,, 3, 11, 44, 46, 66, 68, 71, 90; as a talking point/topic in and of itself, 20, 61, 66, 100–102, 138, 156; universal nature of, 26–27, 31; and verbal communication, 6–8, 9, 21, 23, 25, 28, 34, 42, 43, 44, 53, 60, 72, 125, 141, 142
non-speaking debater. *See* reaction shots; reactions of non-speaking debater; split screens

Obama, Barack, 6, 8, 14, 15, 18, 19, 25–26, 27, 35, 41, 68, 69, 71, 72, 77, 78, 87, 92, 95, 99, 103, 108, 116, 131, 133, 143, 144, 179n2. *See also* Presidential debates of 2008; Presidential debates of 2012
Obama, Michelle, 114

On Rhetoric, 105, 126. *See also* Aristotle
"off-the-record" nature of nonverbal behavior, 70–71, 148
other-presentation: defending images of others, 15–16, 71–72; enhancing images of others, 15, 71–72; undermining images of others, 14–15, 60, 66, 70–71, 74–75, 76, 81n1, 87–88, 163–165, 166, 169–170, 171

Palin, Sarah, 2, 49–50, 102, 131–132, 138. *See also* vice presidential debates of 2008
panelists. *See* moderators and panelists
paralinguistics. *See* vocalics
parasocial relationships, 16, 43, 47, 50, 114–115, 153, 166–168
pathos, 127, 129, 151, 171, 172, 177
Perot, Ross, 69, 87–88, 96–97. *See also* presidential debates of 1992
Perry, Rick, 10
personality, nonverbal cues of, 35, 37, 118, 154
persuasion, 7, 9, 17, 18, 21, 33, 98, 105–122, 125, 126, 128, 129, 171
Pfau, Michael, 46, 107
photographs, 7, 89, 102, 141, 142
physical appearance, 11, 24, 37, 52, 55, 61, 116, 138, 156, 161
pitch, vocal. *See* vocalics
Plato, 126
podiums. *See* height
politeness theory, 79, 108–109
political debates: importance of, 3–4; viewers, number of, 3
pollsters. *See* image experts
post-debate coverage, 100–102
posture, 28, 34, 35, 44, 45, 59, 87, 106–107, 143
power, bases of (French and Raven), 113
power posing, 30
pragma-dialectics. *See* strategic maneuvering pre-debate negotiation. *See* negotiation, pre-debate
preparation for debate, candidates', 42, 50, 67, 69, 78, 84, 90, 131–132. *See also* memorandum of understanding; negotiation, predebate; image experts

Index 227

presidential debates: presidential debates of 1960 (Kennedy-Nixon), 3, 4, 5, 14, 15, 20, 23, 54, 64, 68, 69, 71, 77, 81n2, 83–84, 85, 104, 117, 118, 119; presidential debates of 1976 (Carter-Ford), 3, 9–10, 38, 54, 68, 71, 83–87, 90, 92, 93, 94, 95, 99–100; presidential debates of 1980 (Carter-Reagan), 3, 38, 60, 67, 68, 69, 85, 94–95, 149; presidential debates of 1984 (Mondale-Reagan), 71–72, 83–84, 95, 96–97, 98, 99–100; presidential debates of 1988 (Bush-Dukakis), 2–3, 38, 65, 75, 84, 95–96, 99, 107, 135; presidential debates of 1992 (Bush-Clinton-Perot), 49, 65, 69, 86–88, 92, 95, 96–97, 110; presidential debates of 1996 (Clinton-Dole), 64–65, 68, 110, 111; presidential debates of 2000 (Bush-Gore), 63, 65, 67–68, 80, 93, 108, 110; presidential debates of 2004 (Bush-Kerry), 46, 57, 63, 65, 75, 80, 85, 86, 87, 88, 91, 95, 104n2, 110, 115; presidential debates of 2008 (McCain-Obama), 14, 18, 35, 58, 61, 68–69, 78, 95, 97, 130; presidential debates of 2012 (Obama-Romney), 6, 19, 41–43, 68, 77, 87, 88, 92, 95, 99, 103, 108, 116; presidential debates of 2016 (Clinton-Trump), 2, 3, 18, 38, 48, 73–74, 91, 92, 94, 97, 98, 99, 100, 101, 102, 103–104, 108, 120, 140, 153–154, 157, 159, 160–166, 168–170, 172, 174–177
presidential, candidate image of, 20, 110, 127, 130, 157, 158–159, 161, 162, 165, 166, 172, 173, 174, 175
press assistants. *See* image experts
prestige, 161. *See also* dominance/status
primary debates, 59, 112, 150; audience reactions in, 97, 155; influence of, 3; Democratic primary debates of 1984 election cycle, 97; Democratic primary debates of 2008 election cycle, 21, 72, 143–144; Democratic primary debates of 2016 election cycle, 13, 37, 72, 91, 93, 156; Democratic primary debates of 2020 election cycle, 13, 19, 20, 54, 61, 98–99, 108, 112, 120, 140, 150, 154, 155; Republican primary debates of 1980 election cycle, 93; Republican primary debates of 2008 election cycle, 96; Republican primary debates of 2012 election cycle, 10, 50, 150; Republican primary debates of 2016 election cycle, 2, 54, 92–94, 100, 153, 167; screen time for candidates in, 92, 114
production techniques. *See* visual presentation of debates
props. *See* artifacts; vocalics
proxemics, 18, 38, 67–68, 73, 74, 87, 88; personal space, 9, 39, 42, 44, 73, 74, 107, 108, 140, 170, 171; para-proxemics, 88–89. *See also* expectancy violations theory
pundits. *See* post-debate coverage

Quayle, Dan, 84–85. *See also* vice presidential debate of 1992
Quintilian, 105, 125

radio versus television, exposure to debates via. *See* mode of presentation
rate of speech. *See vocalics*
rattling debate opponents. *See* flustering debaters
reaction shots, 68, 72, 80, 84, 91; controversy surrounding, 64–66, 85–87, 118; and biased portrayal of debates, 94–95, 99. *See also* audience; memorandum of understanding; reactions of non-speaking opponent; split-screens
reactions of non-speaking opponent, 7, 64, 65, 66, 67–68, 74–79. *See also* reaction shots; split screens
Reagan, Ronald, 3, 8, 12, 33, 45, 61, 67, 68, 69, 71–72, 93, 94, 95, 98, 101, 128, 135. *See also* presidential debates of 1980; presidential debates of 1984; Republican primary debates of 1980 election cycle
regulating flow of debates, 19, 42, 62, 66, 109
relational messages, 9, 38, 43, 107
relationships between candidates, 19–20, 66, 120–121
relationship between candidate and audience. *See* parasocial relationships

relationships with television personalities. *See* parasocial relationships
relevancy, as criterion for judging appropriateness of political aggression, 70
responding to debate opponents' nonverbal behavior, 79, 140, 165
rhetoric, 4, 5, 16, 125–126, 129, 130, 131, 136, 138, 141, 146; canons of, 105; rhetor, 130, 131; rhetorical situation, 127, 130–133, 154–160; rhetorical use of nonverbal behavior, 140, 153, 158, 170, 171–173. *See also* Aristotle; ethos; logos; *On Rhetoric*; pathos
ridicule, 28, 79, 132. *See also* disparagement, nonverbal
Rogers, Ted, 118
Romney, Mitt, 6, 19, 41, 68, 71, 77–78, 87, 88, 92, 95, 99, 103, 108, 116, 132. *See also* presidential debates of 2012
Ross, Ron, 25
Rove, Karl, 87
Royal, Ségolène, 71
Rubio, Marco, 2, 167
Ryan, Paul, 14, 66, 92, 131, 132. *See also* vice presidential debate of 2012

sabotage, 87–88. *See also* flustering debaters
Sanders, Bernie, 13, 19–20, 22n2, 61, 100, 120–121, 154, 156, 158. *See also* Democratic primary debates of 2020 election cycle
sarcasm, 163, 166
Sarkozy, Nicholas, 71
Saturday Night Live , 6, 84
Schroeder, Alan, 5, 49, 50, 77, 83, 132
Schmidt, Helmut, 93
screen time. *See* time
self-presentation, 44–46, 66–67, 76, 111; defending one's own image, 13, 61, 67, 81n1; enhancing one's own image, 12–13, 44–46, 81n1, 159, 160–161, 165–168; undermining one's own image, 13–14, 41, 50, 66, 67–70, 75–76, 135, 144, 162–163, 168–169. *See also* image experts
self-presentation, strategies of. *See* self-presentation

sighing, 73
Silver, Nate, 174, 176
similarity, 46, 107, 112, 175
sincerity, 29, 46, 47, 50, 50–51, 72, 129
smiles, 6, 13, 15, 29, 30, 31, 32, 43, 44, 45, 47–48, 50, 52, 56, 66, 68–69, 73, 76, 106, 110–111, 140, 143, 158, 161, 162, 166; Duchene, 47, 165, 166
sociability, perceptions of. *See* credibility
social comparison theory, 112–113
social meaning model. *See* immediacy
social media, 6, 37–38, 88, 103–104, 167; Twitter, 19, 37, 103, 138, 167; YouTube, 103. *See also* memes
social proof, 98, 112
sophists, 105, 149
sparring partners, 50, 87
spin doctors. *See* image experts
split-screens, 13, 42, 55, 64, 65, 67, 74–79, 80, 91. *See also* reaction shots; reactions of non-speaking opponent
Steyer, Tom, 19
Stockdale, Admiral James, 10, 95, 114. *See also* vice presidential debate of 1992
strategic behavior. *See* intentional behavior
strategic maneuvering, 126, 145–148, 170
strategy. *See* preparation for debate; image experts
surprise, 26, 28, 31
Switzerland, debates in, 71

television: role in amplifying nonverbal behaviors, 9, 10, 28, 51, 55, 107, 143, 149. *See also* television production techniques
television production techniques. *See* visual presentation of debates
television versus radio, exposure to debates via. *See* mode of presentation
time: equal screen time for candidates, 91–93
Tisias, 125
touch, 38, 106, 111; and expectancy violations, 108; handshakes, 20, 38–39, 101
town hall debates, 35, 42, 49, 59, 69, 73, 85, 95, 147, 149, 170. *See also* format of televised debates

Trump, Donald, 2, 3, 15, 18, 20, 25, 37, 39, 54, 61, 70, 73, 91, 92–94, 96–99, 100, 101, 102, 103–104, 108, 110, 114, 115, 120, 153, 158–160, 167–168. *See also* presidential debates of 2016; Republican primary debates of 2016 election cycle
Trump, Melania, 114
trustworthiness, perceptions of. *See* credibility; deception
Twitter. *See* social media

unintentional behavior, 11, 13–14, 24, 53, 66–74, 68, 72, 77, 101. *See also* gaffes
unity, principle of. *See* similarity

van Eemeren, Frans, 145, 147. *See also* strategic maneuvering
veracity: as criterion for judging appropriateness of political attacks, 70; perceptions of, 33, 76, 142. *See also* deception; honesty
vice presidential debates, 92; vice presidential debate of 1976 (Dole-Mondale), 51, 76, 104n1; vice presidential debate of 1984 (Bush-Ferraro), 76, 87, 139–140; vice presidential debate of 1988 (Bentsen-Quayle), 96–97, 144; vice presidential debate of 1992 (Gore-Quayle-Stockdale), 10, 84–85, 95, 114; vice presidential debate of 2008 (Biden-Palin), 49, 50, 102, 131–133, 147, 148; vice presidential debate of 2012 (Biden-Ryan), 14–15, 66, 71, 92, 101, 103, 132–133, 142, 148; vice presidential debate of 2016 (Kaine-Pence), 15, 71–72
Vindman, Alexander, 98–99
visual presentation of debates: biased presentation of debates, 5, 94–95, 99, 102; camera angles and techniques, 80, 88–91, 93–94; color, 20; lighting, 20, 69; makeup, 20, 69
visual versus auditory presentation. *See* mode of presentation
vocalics, 28, 36–37, 49, 52, 54, 60, 61, 70, 96, 106, 115–116, 125–126, 128, 143, 157, 160, 165, 172; enunciation, 36; pitch, 23, 36, 39n1, 44, 51, 52, 57–58, 127; pronunciation, 36; rate of speech, 23, 36, 37, 51, 52, 87, 120; shrill, 156, 157, 158, 162, 173; vocal variety, 36, 37, 57; vocal quality, 36, 45, 48, 173; volume, 23, 36, 44, 52, 116, 127. *See also* laughter
volume. *See* vocalics.
voting behavior, 35, 43, 48, 55, 76, 101, 134, 137, 138, 155, 168

Walker, Scott, 93
Warren, Elizabeth, 19–20, 22n2, 120, 140, 155. *See also* Democratic primary debates of 2020 election cycle
Webb, Jim, 91–92
Willard, Charles, 142
Wood, Julie, 20

Yang, Andrew, 38, 112
YouTube. *See* social media

About the Authors

John S. Seiter (PhD, University of Southern California) is a Distinguished Professor of Communication Studies in the Department of Languages, Philosophy, and Communication Studies at Utah State University. His research focuses broadly on persuasion and specifically on topics such as political aggression, effective approaches to compliance gaining, deception detection, nonverbal influence, and persuasion in hospitality contexts. His work has been recognized by multiple "Top Paper" awards at both regional and national conferences. His coauthored book, *Persuasion, Social Influence, and Compliance Gaining*, is in preparation for its seventh edition. He is coauthor of another book, *Arguing, Reasoning, and Thinking Well*, and co-editor of the books *Communication in the Classroom: A Collection of G.I.F.T.S.* and *Perspectives on Persuasion, Social Influence, and Compliance Gaining*. Previously, he was recognized as his university's "Professor of the Year," and his college's "Researcher of the Year." He sits on the editorial boards of several journals.

Harry Weger Jr. (PhD, University of Arizona), is Professor of Communication at University of Central Florida in Orlando. His research interests include argumentation in political debates, arguments between close relationship partners, persuasion in hospitality contexts, and the ways in which communication designs influence argumentation practices. Harry has served as editor of the journal *Argumentation and Advocacy* and currently sits on the editorial boards of four other journals. His research appears in journals such as *Argumentation, Argumentation in Context, Argumentation and Advocacy, Communication Monographs, Communication Methods and Measures*, and the *Journal of Social and Personal Relationships* among others.